Sharing Fencelines

Sharing Fencelines | | |

THREE FRIENDS WRITE FROM NEVADA'S SAGEBRUSH CORNER

Carolyn Dufurrena

Linda Hussa

Sophie Sheppard

The University of Utah Press
Salt Lake City

Drawings for "The Flying Heart Museum," "Shared Fencelines," and "Firehall" by Sophie Sheppard.

LIBRARY OF CONGRESS CATALOGING IN PUBLICATION DATA
Dufurrena, Carolyn, 1953–
    Sharing Fencelines : Three friends write from Nevada's sagebrush
corner / Carolyn Dufurrena, Linda Hussa, Sophie Sheppard.
        p. cm.
    ISBN 0-87480-712-3 (pbk. : alk. paper)
1. Ranch life—Nevada. 2. Country life—Nevada. 3. Nevada—Social
life and customs. 4. Nevada—Environmental conditions. 5. Dufurrena,
Carolyn, 1953– 6. Hussa, Linda. 7. Sheppard, Sophie. 8. Women
ranchers—Nevada—Biography. 9. Nevada—Biography. 10. Female
friendship—Nevada. I. Hussa, Linda. II. Sheppard, Sophie. III. Title.
    F845 .D84 2002
    978.1'0082'091734—dc21   2001006519

Printed on acid-free paper

06 05 04 03 02 01
5 4 3 2 1

❧ Once the realization is accepted that even between the closest human beings infinite distances continue to exist, a wonderful living side by side can grow up, if they succeed in loving distance between them which makes it possible for each to see the other whole against the sky.

—Rainer Maria Rilke

CONTENTS

Sharing Fencelines

✎ Introduction

Linda Hussa

THE FIELD IS CLOSED BY A GATE WE MADE IN THE SHOP ONE WINTER day. A simple iron pipe gate to connect a fence to a fence. No old buggy wheels welded on to spruce it up, no iron wrought in leaf or scroll. Just a gate, and as it happens, my favorite on the whole place.

The scrap pile out behind the corrals is our hardware store, our personal shopping mall. We stroll through the wrecked, obsolete machinery and vehicles that have been collecting out by the creek for some fifty years, thinking, imagining a part or something resembling a part. Useful things out here have several lives. A tire becomes a tow chain, becomes a hay tub, becomes a retaining wall to stop creek-bank erosion, becomes a nesting box for a Canadian goose. We improvise, take material from one context, one design, to another. It's what makes working in the shop in January bearable.

In the case of my favorite gate, we measured the distance between the gateposts and started hunting pipe and pipelike things. A tine bar off the harvester reel stepped off the right length for the main upright. It had holes drilled in it, but that didn't matter; it was pipe and it didn't have to hold water. We trimmed off the bent and tweaked ends of pipe, measured off the lengths we needed for the standard pipe gate design, welded them in place. It was nearly chore time before we finished, carried it out to the pasture fence, and hung it on the post. With dark coming on we stood there admiring our day's work. It swung with a push of a finger, straight, true, every bit as good as a store-bought one.

One windy day we happened to be in the vicinity of the new gate when we heard a sort of moaning sound. John drove onto the stackyard, but I hopped off the feed truck and followed the sound to the gate. The north wind was playing along the holes in the tine bar like a kid blowing across the top of a pop bottle, but better, more notes and some played like chords. When all we needed was a gate in the fenceline, it turns out we made a large, rusty flute that sings the wind. Sometimes the unintended consequences are the true art.

I knew Linda Dufurrena and admired her photographs of ranching life and the Nevada landscape years before I met her daughter-in-law, Carolyn. The Dufurrenas are neighbors—150 miles to the east, as we have neighbors in Lakeview and Adel, Oregon. State boundaries don't define us, but our geography does, and our work, and our love of the stillness, and our feeling that we belong to a community without boundaries.

Linda invited me to bring Sophie Sheppard and come to their sheep camp in Lovely Valley for an overnight with some of her friends. Sophie and I drove east from Cedarville past the sign that warns travelers there are No Services for 100 dirt-road miles. We know how to change a tire, we know the country, and this wasn't our first camp out. We crossed the Sheldon Refuge without meeting another car, hit pavement east of Gooch Camp, turned right at Denio, and went 30 miles farther on to the Dufurrena Ranch at the top of the east arm of the Black Rock Desert. From there we went by caravan 45 minutes north into the mountains, corrals and cabin built within aspen grove and granite. At the top of a pass with a view of the Black Rock Desert, it is lovely in its seclusion.

While we ate dinner at tables beneath the aspens we watched their sheep trail across a hillside five miles distant. The herder and his dogs took the band to water in a draw and then bedded them—in the round—on the open ridge. The full summer moon rose orange, and just below, the sheep lay down for the night as another moon taking its repose. It is not unusual to experience such things when in the company of the Dufurrenas.

After that weekend, Sophie and I were invited to join Dufurrena and Dufurrena Adventures, a company Carolyn and Linda built on the premise that people should experience Nevada by rolling a bed on the ground, and waking to a wash of dawn across the desert. Carolyn teaches geology and Linda, of course, photography. By "giving their country" to others for more than a decade, D&D Adventures has become a gathering of friends. Those friends are ours now, too. Sophie instructs guests in painting the country; I talk about writing.

On one of our trips we took the D&D Adventure guests west, toward Virgin Valley. Following Carolyn, they pulled their cars off on the road cut on Highway 140 just opposite Thousand Creek Gorge, halfway up Thousand Creek Grade, overlooking the valley to the east. With car doors slamming, they got out and gathered to hear her talk about the events that formed the valley behind her.

I looked out on that landscape, my mind already working on poetry, maybe of my great-grandfather, a boy of eight, walking beside the wagons from faraway Ohio, across a dry valley such as this one, across many valleys on the Oregon Trail, or of the young girl who died on the crossing and was buried under valley-floor sediment. Her mother cut a pink rosebud from a beaded purse and nailed it to her daughter's wooden marker. It's the people that come to me when I look into that valley.

Sophie interprets the scene in paint with a palette made of earth elements, color and form. She would say, "All that vast space spread out. Distance pales and blues the colors. Up close, the values are clearer, distinct. See how the shadows under that sagebrush at our feet are darker than the whole side of that mountain that is shaded, but 50 miles away? And the salmony, creamy-colored rocks next to us look pale violet in that canyon across the way, and pale blue in that mountain out there, even though they are the same kind and color of rock. It is the distance that interests me, and how all that space transforms things."

Carolyn was seeing it as layers of time. "The road cut is Miocene, uplifted by faulting," she said. "The Canyon Rhyolite, which forms the base of the section there, is uplifted too, on the south. The pink sandstones are eroded from the Canyon rhyolite, and the tuffaceous sediments on top of them are products of its eruption. The valley floor is younger, Pliocene, and the basalt flow younger still, 1 to 5 million years, although the crease, perhaps a fault, perhaps widened by a river flowing south, did hold the lava flow and then the Pliocene sediment around it eroded."

"That long lava ridge . . . ," I begin.

"Railroad Point?"

"Yes, Railroad Point. It formed in a crevice of some kind?"

"Right. Then the sediments eroded around it and left the lava lying there like a welt on the earth's skin."

"So, what we're seeing is a like a lost wax cast of a valley that no longer exists?"

"You could say that."

Thinking aloud I say, "Things are not always what they seem."

"Not hardly," she laughed.

             ↬

If I had to pinpoint a moment our friendship became defined from the outside it would have been at the 1998 North American Interdisciplinary Conference on Environment and Community in Reno, in a lecture room, winter light coming in from the east and the south.

Carolyn led a panel titled, "Shared Fencelines: Rural Environmentalists and Ranchers Discuss the Realities of Environment and Community." The panelists included Sophie, me, and a rancher from Adel, Oregon, who did not show up. We were to discuss grassroots activism to protect place. The tension of presentation was immediately reduced when we (unintentionally) all arrived wearing the same outfit: jeans, white turtleneck, black wool blazer. The audience responded to our embarrassment good-heartedly. We all joined in joking that it was the country-folks-going-to-town outfit, that at the outskirts of every ranch town there was a sort of Superman telephone booth–closet where the unisex town outfit hung for anyone venturing forth. You had only to run it through the washer, iron it up, and put it back for the next person. Not so far from the truth. We were prepared to talk about the projects we had taken on as beneficial to the communities and the land where we lived, and that's where we began. Then a woman asked how it was that we were friends. "I mean," she said to Carolyn, "Sophie is an environmentalist, and you and Linda are ranchers."

"What exactly is an environmentalist?" Carolyn asked, moving to her mental dictionary. "Let's see, shall we?" She pretends to open a large, heavy book and staggers under its imaginary weight. "Unabridged," she says. She opens the book, "Says here in the Book of Webster, '*environmentalist: noun, 1. A person who seeks to protect the natural environment, as from air and water pollution, wasteful use of resources, and excessive human encroachments.*' Well, I'm for that, especially that last part. Wait, there's another part of the definition. '*2. A person who believes that environment is more important than heredity in influencing intellectual growth and cultural development.*'" She looked over the open book. "Oh, that's me. That's us," she laughed, "and judging from your presence here today, it's probably all of you, too." She clapped her hands together as if closing the dictionary and then opened them. "I rest my case."

The discussion continued. Sophie and I told them about how environmentalism impacted our community as a by-product of a social gathering of women. Years before in Surprise Valley several of us started meeting on winter Saturdays to learn to spin wool from a rancher and friend, Bettie Parman. Among us were a few women who worked for the government, a few who worked at home, vegetarians, carnivores, ranchers, former hippies, and some too old to have been. Bettie taught us, as she had taught herself, by trial and error, and practice. The group was without design or restriction, which is probably why it endured. The rules were: show up with your spinning wheel or drop spindle, wool if you have it, and spend part of the day together trying to make something. The gathering moved up and down the valley to different ones' houses. Sometimes there were wire gates we had to muscle open to reach the sweetness of gathering together. We liked each other without credential or prejudice, and we liked working with the colored wool of sheep and llama, the cloud-soft hair of angora goat and rabbit. Our hands that fed and birthed and cared for the gentle animals were now working their sweet-smelling wool and hair we had carried in baskets to the meeting place. Conversations just happened. To the calming musical swish and whir of the spinning wheels, talk would begin. Children or grandchildren rank as safe topics to find your footing in a group. In time other topics of community concern arose. If they developed with potential to polarize a group as diverse as ours we worked at them like working a burr out of wool, one strand at a time. If agreement wasn't possible, there was at least an opportunity to hear a different point of view, and identify what created those tangles. We decided that if the UN required members to bring spinning wheels to assembly there would be fewer disagreements, maybe, no wars, and, certainly, warmer children.

This book came out of conversations on the trails and back roads of Nevada, around campfires on D&D Adventures, and at conferences and readings when a hand would go up in the audience and the question would be, "How did you come to live out there?"

Which answer do we give? How much of the story do we tell, yet protect our privacy and that of those dear to us? Artists struggle to explore tensions and depth of emotion without revealing a self-portrait in paint or ink or stone. The short version is: "my job" or "to visit." The long version is as complicated as mapping DNA. A fantastic set of circumstances had to occur to turn each of us in the path of life's wind. In the process we found the way of balance to tell the story of what brought us here and what keeps us here, to find the music that is sometimes a single note and sometimes a chord.

We come from different places. Carolyn is a geologist sent to explore the desert and find uranium. Instead she found Tim Dufurrena. She was a midwestern woman who knew a lot of stuff that didn't particularly have a Nevada ranch-life application. But that didn't stop her. She became a rancher. When their son, Sam, was old enough to go to school, she went too, as a teacher. She was French Ford Middle School Teacher of the Year, and then she chose to move nearer home to teach in a one-room schoolhouse on the edge of the Black Rock Desert. She still teaches in a one-room schoolhouse on the desert, to five students whose favorite thing about a field trip to Winnemucca was going through the car wash.

Sophie is a painter, from a family of artists. Her parents brought her to Surprise Valley on camping trips, and it stuck in her memories. Many years later, she and her husband, Lynn Nardella, and her son, Jason, came for a barn dance and never left. She joined the Lake City Ladies Club in the early '70s (where they wore nylons and the secretary wrote the minutes in verse), and was presented with a dance shawl at the Paiute Pow-Wow in Fort Bidwell.

Horses have always been the center of my work and my life. I came to Surprise Valley to gather cattle off the summer grazing land and got gathered up myself by John Hussa. Here I found the things I needed: community, friends, neighbors, a killdeer, a wasp, and a little girl named Katie.

I think we all began writing to make sense of our daily lives and to somehow anchor the elders who are leaving us behind. The three of us have lived in the Great Basin long enough to know the joy of creating with the things we have at hand: a gate in a fenceline to open to ideas and friendships. The battles we have engaged in require no special education or expertise; what we need finds us. The battles require what all art—including the art of life—requires: show up, pay attention, and allow the magic: "Let's see what grows out of this rusty pipe mess." It's Neighborhood Watch. It's getting involved in your community and holding as precious and fragile the things that make it home to you. There are no real answers, but sometimes we pretend there are. The bottom line is we believe that each of us—if we are lucky enough to find our home country and community, the place where we belong—must do what we can to return the gift.

The Flying Heart Museum

Carolyn Dufurrena | | |

✎ At Cody's Wedding

THE AIR SHIMMERS IN THE PARKING LOT OUTSIDE HEAVY GLASS DOORS, but in here it is cool and relatively quiet. The racket of tinkling slot machines in the Reno airport lobby fades behind me, muffled by green carpet. I walk with the crowd toward the baggage carousels.

My husband Tim stands waiting with our son and his cousins who have flown in from San Francisco. He is six feet tall, black-Irish handsome, clean-shaven, forty. He hides his curly hair under a baseball cap, wears faded Wranglers and tennis shoes. The clean-pressed long-sleeved shirt, even though it's the middle of July, is the best clue to his occupation. The teenager has the same Wranglers and tennis shoes, but the two-sizes-too-large T-shirt of his generation. Tim's cousin Tom is a lankier, twitchier version of him, but with the same green eyes and slow, crooked smile. Tom points with his chin at something above them, says something that makes them both chuckle.

My eyes follow his gesture to the two images hanging side by side on the wall, huge transparencies that the local convention and visitors bureau has selected to amuse the tourists. One of the images is a swarthy young man, maybe twenty, in a white lab coat. His dark eyes smile confidently from behind a forest of test tubes filled with colored water. The image is an advertisement for the University of Nevada. Next to him, across the conveyor belt that brings the luggage out from behind the scenes, is a cowboy on a sorrel horse. He's roping a calf in a mountain corral. His face is mostly hidden beneath a big black hat and beard; he's wearing a red plaid shirt. He faces you, but he's watching the calf.

Both men in the pictures are Basque, although you wouldn't necessarily recognize that unless you knew them. That their images should appear side by side in this bustling, impersonal place is a good example of Nevada irony.

Nevada is a very large, empty place. Many of us live in isolation here. Yet even though our communities lie hundreds of miles apart, people who have been here for a long time tend to know each other. So, in a peculiar way, Nevada is also an intimate place. The two very different men in these photographs have known one another all their lives; their families have neighbored for three generations, just across a mountain. Today, both families will gather out in the desert, in tangential celebrations.

My husband looks at the image of himself, a bearded roper, a younger man when that image was captured, and at the scientist in the lab coat, the young bridegroom we'll join later today. The suitcases slide out onto the clanking aluminum carousel. Tim turns, sees me, smiles a little. He nods to our son, Sam, and they pick up the bags. We fall into step, walking into the heat of desert summer.

Highway 395 rises north from the Reno airport, a smooth expanse of recently widened concrete elevated above the sadness of the seedier neighborhoods: fleabag motels, transmission repair shops, tattoo parlors. Today the skyline is dominated by a fantasy landscape of new casinos, lit like Popsicles at night, green, pink, yellow, their mirrored facades too bright in day.

Traffic backs up at the I-80 interchange, where the highway east, still elevated above the town, slides across residential neighborhoods and the railroad yard by the Truckee River. More casinos dripping Victorian fake greenery from high-rise window boxes have sprouted here, another kind of memory-less sadness. Time is frozen, welcoming back the Platters, Paul Revere and the Raiders, the Diamonds to the Celebrity Showroom. The real Nevada doesn't emerge until I reach the canyon.

It's a thirty-mile stretch, watered by the Truckee River, fringed by cottonwoods. The walls are steep; brooding volcanic flows overhang the highway. Soon the mood of the drive is lightened by the wide, shallow river flowing over cobblestones, and by the clear sky.

Beyond the canyon lies an empty quarter; empty is always better than false. It is all white playa, bleached foothill, silhouette of mountains graying into distance beyond wide valleys. Interstate 80 slingshots north and then east across this expanse of colorless terrain. It's five hours from Reno to Elko, and another six to Salt Lake City from there. Most people let it go at that, hunker down and drive.

The journey takes us across the floor of ancient Lake Lahontan. Long, perfectly horizontal benches hundreds of feet above the highway mark high stands of the lake: climb up to them, and you will find tufa-encrusted boulders, smoothed cobbles of beach where Pleistocene waves rolled. From a small plane above them, you would see giant ripples in sand, covered with sagebrush now, that record the massive energy of wind and water.

Instead of heat waves and burning white playa, imagine eight thousand square miles of sparkling blue water, island mountain ranges marching off north in rows, fringed with serviceberry, oak trees, the kind of plant community you find now in the Sierra foothills of California. Mammoths, camels, saber-toothed cats: it's not so long ago, but it was another world.

The highway climbs slowly across this ancient lake bed, through a thousand feet of altitude. In a couple of hours we are driving across foothills, looking down at the remnants of the lake, a river draining gravelly alluvial fans. Empty country teaches patience: the open landscape of distance will not change soon. Curving east around more mountains on the way to Winnemucca, we are high enough to see that northward is yet another country, emptier still, with more rugged mountains, wide blue valleys. It looks inaccessible, this terrain across the ancient lake bed. There is a way to get there, of course, if that's your destination. If you stopped someone on a gravel road out there, he would be happy to direct you, down a road that may not be on your map. This is ranching country; the Basques settled here a hundred years ago.

Five of them, brothers, arrived just after the turn of the last century. Of the five, two returned to the green mountains of their homeland; another was murdered in sheep camp. Two brothers stayed to herd sheep. They took their wages in sheep instead of money; they made a place for themselves and the families that were to come in this austere landscape.

The older brother, Alex, bought a little ranch called Wilder Creek on the Oregon border. It had some solid rock-walled buildings, an apple orchard, some hay meadow, good mountain grazing. He raised horses, a lot of horses:

work horses for haying, saddle horses, brood mares, mules even. He planted cherry trees, plum trees, pears. Later he bought another place for winter pasture a few miles west; it was lower country, protected from the worst of winter's weather. He married late, as Basque men tend to do, a woman from Wyoming named Julia with a daughter and a son. Together they had another boy, and the three children grew up on the little ranch together.

When the Second World War came, John, the elder son, went to fight. From Italy, he wrote his father, "I don't think I'll make it home." That same year a crippling fall in the orchard, picking cherries, mangled Alex's arm. Buster, the younger son, was eleven. There were no men around to work, so the ranch was sold, the horses too. The family moved a hundred miles to town. That was all right with Julia.

John survived the war. He came home and went to cowboying in Battle Mountain over east of Winnemucca. Buster worked on the ranches near Wilder in summers and on weekends. He visited his father, who had gone back to the sheep camps. The shattered elbow had been pinned, but would never again be steady. Alex still worked his forge, shaping steel shoes, but he could not keep the broken arm from shaking. His hand bore a constant mass of scarring, knuckles torn and bleeding from his own chisel. He was not a person who could survive in town.

Quinn River Ranch, thirty miles down the valley, swallowed the Wilder homestead; it had been a big corporate outfit since the 1880s. John and Buster both married and returned to work for the company that now owned their home. They spent their summers at Wilder with the cowboys, winters at the headquarters, in the steep-pitched, tin-roofed white ranch houses with heavy wooden doors and Byzantine plumbing. First John, then Buster, lived with their families in the main house, reserved for the ranch manager. They raised seven sons between them there at Quinn River and at Wilder, at their father's place, no longer theirs.

Tim and I live in this house now. We sleep in the same high-ceilinged bedroom that he shared with his brothers as a boy. Seven ancient windows, nine panes apiece, wrap the northeast corner of the room, looking out on ancient elms where owls hoot in winter. My old New England painted trunks, shoved up against the wall, make shelves for piles of jeans and leather strips, boots and magazines. Coils of rawhide laces and sweaty neckerchiefs surround a Chinese porcelain figure and a rose-colored, carved jade bowl. Pieces of arrowheads and silver earrings are tossed in cardboard box lids; photographs of horses, grandparents. The relics of our lives entwine, signposts on the path we've taken.

⌁

It was the summer of Watergate. I was an archaeology student with a summer job from the Peabody Museum in Cambridge, Massachusetts, part of a graduate student's survey crew. For twelve weeks that summer, we combed the valley floors and the rugged spines of the Ruby Mountains in Elko County for artifacts; we went skinny-dipping in the hot springs, got drunk at the Basque festival in Elko. We read the news in a weekly news magazine, and then we started the campfire with it. It was the antithesis of my safe, intellectual, urban life. When I went home at the end of that summer my mother says I told her I'd never really leave Nevada again.

The next year I was back, this time at a geology field camp in Eureka. I scratched rocks, identified fossils, measured, mapped, hiked. I learned to understand the processes that shaped the place, the tiny structures that pointed to larger patterns in the earth. What I remember now, though, is the coolness of a limestone rock shelter on a blistering afternoon, the way it felt to let my eyes relax as their focus stretched to meet the shimmering horizon; sheltered in the earth, yet able to see forever.

I left the desert again, to finish my degree and get another one, but I took the silence with me when I left. I missed the isolation, the time and space for thought and reflection. That need had taken me into field geology, and it was to lead me past it. Along the way, as if by accident, I met a bearded man with that shelter and the far horizon in his eyes.

⌁

Grown-ups gather in the hot shade under the ancient apple tree, as the cousins arrive from their various directions. Tim is the eldest of Buster's three sons. He and his brothers, Dan and Hank, have stayed on the land; his uncle John's four boys have ventured out. Today John's eldest is a doctor, driving down from Idaho for this gathering; Quinn, a dentist, comes back from Elko; Joe, hurt in a wreck with a horse years ago, works close to home in Winnemucca; Tom, the architect from San Francisco, is the closest in age and sensibility, perhaps, to Tim. Side by side, they could be brothers, Tom the urban version of his cousin. They point with their chins, curl their desert-dry sense of humor around every phrase. His small, blonde wife, Hilda, is a commodities trader from New York.

Most of the year we follow our own paths. But it is time to come back together, to see where we have been, to watch our children become friends. John and Joan will not live on this place too many more years: it has been her plan to gather us all, while the opportunity exists. There are several birthdays and anniversaries clustered around this time; Tom has been made a partner in his architectural firm, but we won't find that out till later. The clan gathering is more important than any individual landmark.

A grassy hill slopes down two sides of the back lawn from the alfalfa field behind the house to the place where the apple tree spreads its shade. Kids roll down, over and over, from sunlight into shadow. Mothers sit nearby on the hillside; knees drawn up over bare feet, toes buried in green grass, they exchange details of school and doctor, day care, travel, ear infections, braces. Three sets of tennis-shod boy-feet hang down out of the tree. This age group is flicking bark projectiles. They practice looking innocent at the warning glances their near misses draw. The men fill lawn chairs around the barbecue, curly dark heads alternating with suntanned bald ones. Ice-cold beers are held first to foreheads before drinking. Quiet laughter rolls back and forth across the yard.

Three generations of this family have produced eighteen males and only two females. The kids' ages range from Jason, now twenty-one, to the cluster nearly ready for kindergarten. The little boys are armed with hose and water balloons: there is danger brewing at the four-foot level. This year, a divorce and remarriage have brought three lanky, green-eyed, blonde girls into the circle of mostly boy cousins. They are softball players. They can all handle a hose, and they consign themselves to battle.

The teenagers retreat to Grandma's basement sewing room, a dark cave draped with quilts and piles of fabric. We hear their newly deep voices behind closed doors: a surfer, two cowboys, two skaters, talking about something they all have in common. They don't see each other often, but the clan bonds are still strong. Disgusting music, we moms comment, coming through. "No, not ours," the boys disclaim. "It belongs to Seamus," the eighth grader with the hennaed braids out there in the water balloon fight.

They are swarthy people, the Basques, not particularly tall. There are a lot of green eyes, the rest darkest brown. They are proud, tenacious beyond words, deeply private. They carry their family name like a banner, three or four or five generations after leaving the old country. Even now, there are aspects of their stories I will never understand. Shadings of voice, pauses implying events not appropriate for lighthearted conversation, nuances of expression that don't fully translate.

Yet it's a thoroughly American barbecue. Long tables set up in the shade have gradually filled with bowls of salad, plates of hard-boiled eggs and raw vegetables. A watermelon rides a sea of ice cubes in a big aluminum washtub. The little boys take turns daring each other to ride its slipperiness, in ankle-deep, freezing water. Along with the chicken and ribs and barbecued beans are grilled chorizo, crusty French bread, and Great-grandmother Julia's garbanzo-and-chorizo side dish. In the seasons when Tim came home from college to help with fall riding, Julia would send a pot of this spicy stew back out into the world with him. It is still the birthday choice for some of the teenagers, who never knew the woman.

The adults will tell stories in the shade all afternoon, until some of us slip away later for the wedding reception in town.

"Twenty thousand acres are burning near Midas, fifty thousand down south; there's a fire near Lakeview," someone says. No clouds in the hazy sky, not a sign of lightning. The fires have all been caused, inadvertently, by man: a cigarette, a catalytic converter on the shoulder of the road, fireworks in the dry grass. "Anything burning out your way?" Fire is part of life here, like dust, like stars.

Children drift through, the water fight finally over, grazing the tables for cookies and leftover chorizo, absorbed in their world. They take turns on the trampoline around the other side of the house, the older ones making sure a four year old isn't catapulted over the fence. Adults are welcome, they promise, but only if they jump too.

Uncle Johnny tells the story about running mustangs on the Black Rock again, when it was still something people did. Buster looks out across the alfalfa field from under the apple trees on the bluff, across the river to the meadows where his father's horses wintered one year, half a century past. Either one of them might tell part of this story: how they'd brought the horses in after they sold the ranch, drove them together, a hundred-odd head, Buster and his older brother John. It was a three-day drive across the desert from Wilder to these meadows, stopping at ranches along the way. Buster might even tell how he, in his fourteenth winter, swam the river horseback after school to gather the horses when buyers came, his parents gone for two months to Mexico to bury Alex's brother, his own brother working a ranch job far away. Buster the only one around to keep a tally in a little book of where the teams went, who would pay for them after his father returned.

Some tales are for entertainment, lighthearted recollections of family history. Others—stories of tenderness, courage, sorrow—are held for a particular moment, when today's events touch the surface of the past, and we reach beneath their reflection, for strength or solace, into the clear pool of memory.

⇜

Down the dirt road a few miles, the wedding reception is in full swing. Hundreds of people stand at the bar, trying to make themselves heard. They laugh, dance, drink, and yell stories in each other's ears. The round, white-draped tables are surrounded by grandmothers holding babies, talking about trips to Spain and Ireland, children at university. People who haven't seen each other for months, or years, people with a common history, renew that history on the threshold of the next chapter.

Sam has gone over ahead of us from the family gathering to the reception. "At the beginning," he said, "almost everyone I saw was some kind of Bengoa." He means the extended family, and almost-family, cousins, men who had cowboyed for Quinn River Ranch when they were young, married one of the daughters, sold or bought sheep or cows or horses, traded dogs. They are all here.

Frankie Bengoa leans on the bar next to my husband, one foot on the rail. "How are those dogs working out?"

Frankie, older and taller, gone for years to California, has moved back to town. He has given Tim two border collies, working dogs; in fact, they made the deal at the last wedding, two years ago. Teddy, the pup, and Jack, the old dog, were both languishing in town, nervous, getting into trouble. Border collies are worse than teenagers without work. The pup is still excitable, but the old dog is teaching him, slowly. Sometimes they fight with Cookie, the young Australian shepherd female Sam got when Tim took the job at Quinn River. They are carving a place in the territory for themselves.

In a lull between dances, our neighbor Gary says, "I saw a little mare bunch come off the mountain yesterday, mustangs, hell bent for election; didn't see anything chasing them, but something must have got 'em started. They hit the drift fence and come on down to the flat, through that dry grass."

In the wake of their hooves, a wisp of smoke rose, became a tendril, then a flame. "That fire burned along the fence a ways, then the wind took it north." Shod horses throw sparks from steel shoes on stone; sparks fly from rock to rock with the passing of unshod hoofs. "You can only see them in the dark, but you know those sparks are there in the daytime when these horses get to runnin'."

Perhaps because so much time is spent in solitude here, people learn to pay a closer kind of attention to the artifacts of daily life. It's recognition of levels of cause and effect, acknowledgment that at the smallest scale, all things in this world are intimately connected. A passing hoof throws a spark, starts a fire. A clump of delicate ferns under a boulder's lee by a sandy trail suggests more water than would first be assumed. Subtle evidence implies conditions that a person will appreciate only if he is truly awake.

❦

The disc jockey follows the Rolling Stones with Basque *jotas:* wedding circle dances with cowboy stomp. The combination keeps the dance floor full, the partners varied. In the very back of the big, high-ceilinged room, I watch the five bridesmaids line up in a shadowed alcove facing a big office window. They kick off their pumps and watch their reflections, practicing a formalized dance, jumping and twirling. Then the groom and his groomsmen take the space in turn, leaping, kicking, spinning in the impromptu rehearsal space. They have all been friends at college; they dance in competition for the University of Nevada Basque Club.

Wedding dances, part of the mass, have twined through the arching, butter-yellow space of the packed white-stucco church. The flute and drum have sounded, signaling the union, the same flute and drum that called Basque men to war. In the club they learn dances for both occasions. Cody's mom, Sandra, stands next to me, watching the young men practice.

"Where are you teaching next year?" she asks. She is a small, beautiful woman, smooth dark hair, razor-cut above her shoulders. She looks younger than she is, dressed in a simple black sheath with a string of pearls, the summer wedding choice these days.

"Back to the ranch," I reply. Back to the remote rurals, a sprinkling of far-flung one-room schools, where I started ten years ago; now that Sam has graduated I don't have to be in town; it's the logical choice, and the choice of my heart, too.

"What will you do with your place here—sell it?"

"Haven't decided."

"It'll be good to get back home after all this time," she says.

I nod.

"How many students?"

"Four or five, maybe; can't ever tell till the doors open."

"It'll be different," she says, "getting used to being home."

I nod toward the newlyweds. "So, what's next for these two?" I ask lightly.

She answers back, just as lightly, "A semester in Spain at the university there, then back to try for medical school, both of them."

We are sharing our last summer with children at home. Sam and her daughter, Sandy, will both go off to college in the fall. It's an end to our pattern, one that a lot of ranch families follow: when the kids are old enough for high school, the family divides. Mom moves to town, away from Dad, and the family lives a double life for the duration: two households, two can openers, two sets of laundry, two phone numbers. Two sets of expectations. Drive home with a load of groceries to the ranch after the football game on Friday night, back to town at dawn on Monday morning. Partition your lives, your energy, and your dreams.

And because we are creatures of habit, we become accustomed to it. Find a privacy, a peacefulness in the town place, a space that isn't shared with the extended family, with the community, the way the ranch house is. Plant a few irises, gifts from Amparo, my neighbor on the ranch. Invest some energy in this temporary home. Settle in.

Now, at the end of this summer, that pattern ends, and a new one begins. Move out of the place in town, have it painted; find a responsible renter. Have a garage sale for that extra vacuum cleaner, can opener, pile of towels. Dig up the irises in August, when they're through for the season. Withdraw my heart from that house in town that is no longer my home. Learn to share space again.

It will be just Tim and me, the two of us, like it was in the beginning, I tell myself. Only I can't remember what I was like then, and we're neither of us the same.

✧

The Bengoas came from Idaho, another Basque-rich country, unsettled in the early years of the twentieth century, with miles of open rangeland for the sheep to graze. Three brothers, their wives and children, shared the ranch and, for a long time, a single, enormous red house. The men had their territories: Chris was the cowman, Cleto the farm chief, Frank the mechanic and everyone's right-hand man. The women's territories were delineated in other ways.

The two Basque families, the Dufurrenas and the Bengoas, shared the mountain range between their valleys before there were fences, and after. King's River Ranch, the Bengoa place, is the farthest north in that box-shaped valley next to the Oregon border. A jumbled wall of granite mountains shelters it from the north wind; ramparts of red rhyolite guard the east. A lower, softer range of mixed topography lies to the west, the mountains where our family summered sheep, and later cattle too. Its ridgeline is the boundary, more or less, between the two ranches. Windswept or cloaked in high aspen basin, it stretches the better part of thirty miles. The country is mostly BLM-administered public land with scattered forty-acre deeded parcels.

Not so long ago, there was only the land, and these people, and their livelihoods. When the country was still empty, the two families worked both sides of the mountain together in that tradition known as neighboring.

The riding would start in spring, Bengoas from the east side, coming up from their winter grazing in the valleys to the south, Dufurrenas from the west, driving the herds north from meadow pastures at the headquarters on the Quinn River. When the cattle had reached the summer country, some thirty miles away, branding would start.

Back and forth across the top of the mountain, crews of thirty men and women would gather the bunches, doing the work of spring and summer. After they branded at Wilder, they moved over the mountain to the Bengoas' and rode out of the home ranch in the valley there. The two families would ride to the top of the mountain from the east side this time, gathering down through the canyons, mothering up, branding, their work defined only by the length of the summer days and the mountain geography.

By the Fourth of July, they finished the southern canyons at Ugalde's Nine-Mile, another small Basque outfit. Then there would be a break, time enough for a trip to town, time enough for a wedding.

The drift fences on the ridgeline went in first, in the fifties, dividing BLM grazing land into two parcels. Sometimes calves jumped through the fences; snow brought the fences down in winter. The cattle mixed, and so the neighboring went on, cowboys guiding the animals back over the ridge to their home country in the fall.

The Bengoa boys, a little older, went away to high school and then to college. By the time they had kids, there was another kind of fence, the allotment fence, dividing the government land (nobody called it public land then), concentrating the cattle into mountain pastures. While part of the mountain, a third, was rested, another two-thirds was used a little harder.

That started to change the neighboring. The Bengoas kept their cattle in the desert longer. We branded our calves a little earlier; they branded theirs later, at home. The allotment fences turned the mountain into a patchwork of spring and summer pasture, divided and divided again, separating us from our old neighbors, dividing the present from the past.

Frankie and Tim were kids before the allotment fence: though separated by several years, the work they shared made them close. Cody and Sam came along just after the allotment fences went in. They are separated by the same number of years, but they don't know each other well.

Sandra looks around the crowded room, at the bridesmaids slipping on their shoes. "Time for the next dance," she says.

⌐ɔ

In my first year in the country, as they say here, I was working in the red rhyolite above the Bengoas' place, looking for minerals for a Colorado exploration company. Tim was working for another ranch down the valley. I guess you'd say we were courting, when courting involves only the work that each of you does, black sky above the steam of hot springs at night, a campfire in the wilderness. No dining, no dancing, no movies. He helped me take water samples, crack rocks looking for mineralization. I showed him country he hadn't seen before. Turnabout is only fair.

"Want to come with me tomorrow?" he asked, when I overheard the conversation he was having with someone on the telephone. "I'm going to help the Bengoas."

I could ride, sort of. A seventh-grade summer at camp, a few trail rides in Colorado on family vacations. Old Chris, Cody's grandfather, had smiled at me, the city girl one of his cowboys had snagged in passing. They put me on a gentle, ugly horse.

We waited horseback in the yard. I took off my jean jacket, deciding I wouldn't need it, and dropped it across my saddle horn, unsure what to do with it. The horse, startled, huffed, humped up, took a crow hop. I had no idea what to do. I looked straight ahead, and found Tim's eyes looking straight back at me. He wasn't laughing at me, or condescending. "Drop the jacket," he suggested quietly. So I did. The old horse settled under me. Somebody got down, took the jacket, hung it on a post. Nobody laughed at me, at least right then. They gave me the benefit of the doubt; I saved face by not falling off. Then—nothing. No teasing, no bullshit, nothing. We just turned and left the yard, weaving through willow-fringed meadows behind a mass of cattle.

Tim rode a runaway brown colt that kept bolting; he'd bring him back, get him settled. Then a rabbit would jump up from the brush, the colt would panic again, and off they'd go, Tim's pressed white shirt barely visible in a cloud of dust. The horse I was passenger on knew what he was supposed to do: he just followed the cows. I admired the scenery.

We could barely see the desert windmill that was our destination when a storm blew through, driving a cold, late-fall rain into our faces. Chris gave me his old hat; a pair of ancient leather gloves, stiff as wood. It felt good to pull them on over my frozen red hands. Later his wife, Mary, brought us lunch, thick sandwiches and hot coffee. In the back of her pickup he found a square of green irrigating canvas and a bit of twine. He slit the canvas part way up the middle, and poked holes for the twine with the point of his branding knife, fashioning a pair of chaps. Tied the whole awkward arrangement around me. It wasn't pretty, but it was a lot warmer out of the wind.

"Do you want to go back to the house? You can ride back in the truck, and we'll bring the horse," Chris offered.

Not me, not for a second. Tim wasn't saying anything. He was driving cows.

They brought the trailer finally, at the end of the drive, and we bumped back up the long valley in the cold rain of darkening afternoon. Shivering, wet to the bone, I followed the men through the living room into the big, high-ceilinged kitchen. Yellow light warmed dark wood walls and over-stuffed leather armchairs polished by years of use. An impossibly long, linoleum-topped table was set with heavy ceramic plates, thick white mugs, great bowls of food. Glass-paned cabinets held stacks of white dishes, heavy glass tumblers. The aroma of freshly made coffee, chile rellenos, and stew was intoxicating. Standing in the kitchen, the men passed a half-gallon bottle of Early Times, one slug apiece, to warm up. Chris jokingly offered it to me. Shaking from the cold, my plaid shirt still damp, I took it. He laughed like hell, but it was fine with him if I were one of the boys; we all needed to get warm. Tim stood off to one side, watching me, smiling a little behind his big black beard.

I can't say, even now, if that day wasn't bait. Willingly taken, to be sure. I loved the cold in the morning, the smell of horses and leather, wet jeans and dust, the meadow-hay sweetness of cattle kept in outside country, their quiet energy as they moved along, the low, rolling clouds bringing rain—all of it. I loved all of it, that day.

They let me be who I was, and go along, and if I learned something or liked it, that was okay. There was a space held there for me; I could just be.

The day was an invitation, like putting a salt lick in a clearing and backing off to see what the deer will do. Here's the life, what do you think? Quiet, focused, waiting for me to make the choice. Nobody had ever put me in that place before.

My childhood world had been tight, disciplined. There were specific rules for dress, for behavior, for achievement. Expectations were clear, and none of them had anything to do with guys that chewed tobacco and said "ain't." I'd never been totally comfortable in the white-gloves-and-pearls life, as cozy and protected as it was intended to be, although I had no idea what an acceptable alternative might be. Now here I was, in country as rough and remote as any I'd ever know. And I felt comfort, a closeness with strangers that was all about work done together, cold and dust and rain shared.

There was a deep privacy acknowledged. In this kitchen, there were things going on that weren't spoken conversation, subtext that was all eyebrow and smile, but that communicated acceptance nonetheless.

One clamped hand loosened that day on the desert around my idea of who I was and what I would become. But only one. Back in Denver on the way to the office, weaving through the Mousetrap in the morning rush of traffic, I argued with myself: career, friends, status, money, all the trappings of success I would lose if I left.

I could feel this thing tugging at me. Yet what could I be in Tim's world? The cook? Still, something in that quiet, focused waiting, the accepting silence, recognized what I knew needed acknowledgment: he saw through the cleverness and urban polish into something I barely recognized about myself, something that surfaced that stormy November afternoon.

I valued independence above all things; yet the loneliness that is freedom's partner was eating away inside me. I needed the huge, empty spaces to range through, and the warm, yellow hearth at its center, too.

Still, trust is not something you lose twice. It would be easy to panic, bolt just like Tim's brown colt, to leave him, or make him leave this hard life that he loved. And if I did take him away, would I destroy what it was I was coming to love?

The culture was a loose net thrown lightly over a whole mountain range: "our mountain," our territory, our way of life, but not in a proprietary sense. In a simpler sense, these people were like bands of mustangs I had seen roaming the foothills. Like the horses, they had their favorite haunts in summer, knew the sheltered spots in winter, too. They knew the best place to trail sheep through this stretch of country, the aspen groves with the deepest shade in summer. Their lives were woven together with those of the animals they tended, and the landscape they all shared.

The Basque families were like groves of aspen trees: individuals to the naked eye but connected at the roots, all one organism. If you try to move an aspen tree, even in winter, it will likely die. I knew I couldn't do that to him, even then.

I didn't choose this life that day in Denver, or even that winter. It would be three years before I could trust the harbor in those hazel eyes, the balance of freedom and shelter they would promise—and deliver.

This life is not easy, but it is rich in a way I am still coming to know. No matter how wide the circle I take, then, now, whenever, for me it always closes here.

‹›

Late in the evening, Tom and Hilda slip into the reception, more long-lost brothers home again. Tom's high-rise San Francisco office is a world away, but he still has friends here. We sit together with those friends at one of the white tables, sip ice water, and catch up. Tim is leaning on the bar, deep in conversation with one of the Bengoa sisters, moved away to Washington and back now only for occasions like this.

Old Chris is not here at his grandson Cody's wedding. He and his two brothers are dead of cancer; their wives have moved to town, or remarried. The kids are around, working here and there on other places. King's River Ranch, across the fenceline, has been sold to a wealthy veterinarian who lives in California. It wasn't so long ago, but that world has ended. We are still here, on our side of the fence, but it's not the same.

The party has consolidated in the other room; I can see Sam's long-sleeved tan shirt now and then, moving across the dance floor. We sit for a long time, laugh and talk, remember. I watch my son, circling, restless for flight. He will be leaving soon.

⇥ Learning How to Fall

OLD SILVER POPLARS AND OLDER LILACS SHADE THE WHITEWASHED
rock walls of the bunkhouse at the Wilder buckaroo camp; they keep the
place cool in summer. The boys don't mind the bull snake that lives in the
walls' secret cavities: he helps with the mice, and I suppose gives them
somebody to talk to. Bare concrete floors are easy to sweep.

It's a spare accommodation, just a place for cowboys to lay a bedroll while
they're working up on this end of the ranch. Sam will spend much of the
summer after graduation here, thirty miles from home, with the one or two
other young men who cowboy for the ranch.

The cowboys are up the canyon somewhere when I pull up, ostensibly to
bring cat food for the kittens, who are still learning to catch mice. But really
I am here to mop the bunkhouse floor. Sam thinks that's silly, that the floor's
just fine. Nonetheless, I swish Clorox into corners, chasing out the evidence
of last winter's furry inhabitants. The spare mattress will go to the dump,
cobwebs will be swept away. I stack the mops and buckets by the front door
and breathe in the sweet smell of meadow hay and apple trees. Beyond the
orchard, I see cattle and their spring calves grazing away across the foothills
that stretch as far as I can see, and farther.

⇥

"That blue roan heifer in the horse barn needs water," Tim says, putting on
his hat as I carry breakfast dishes to the sink. The heifer was late to come to

term. All the others had calved out and been moved to outside pasture, so she had no companions to watch for example, commiserate when things went wrong. And things had gone wrong.

Farming had started. Everyone was busy doing something else, and she must have calved during the night. The calf had hung up on her too narrow hips. Half mad with pain and fear, she had dragged the partially delivered fetus around for hours before Tim found her.

We've been back a month at the ranch Tim and his brothers have leased, after living the first three years of our married lives in a West Texas oilfield town. I am still a city girl, green as an August apple. Sam is barely three.

"Just slide the bucket into the stall," Tim instructs. "Don't mess with her. I'm trying to graft a leppie calf on her, and she's pretty mad." He drives out of the yard as Sam and I make ready to play milkmaid, tying our shoes and chattering.

A cold spring wind blows through tall Lombardy poplars leafing out around the house as Sam follows me across the yard to the little six-stall horse barn. The creek roars by on the other side, so I have to holler at him a little. "Just stay right behind me, next to the fence."

Three paneled stalls with big new wooden gates face each other across a central alley in the brown metal building. At each end of the alley is a gate. One leads into a larger space for training colts, the other to the outside network of passages used for working animals into one paddock or another, a maze of slender lodgepole-bordered pathways.

There is no string or handle on the bucket, and I am not strong enough, or tall enough to reach over and drop it into the heifer's stall. There is not enough space to slide it under. She stands, glaring at me from the corner of her cell, the tiny red orphan calf cowering away from her. I speak soothingly as I fill the bucket. "Stand back, sweetie," I caution, leaving my boy halfway down the alley. "I'm just going to open this gate and slide her water in." Slip the latch like so, and crack the gate, just this little bit. It is too far.

She drops her head and paws the earth, exactly the same way the cartoon bulls did that we all watched on Saturday morning. I still don't get it. I think I will have more time, but I don't. She comes across that roomy stall like a freight train. She flattens me and the bucket too. I roll over and jump up to see the wide brown eyes of the only son I'll ever have staring at eleven hundred pounds of enraged bovine maternity bearing down on him, far enough away to get a full head of steam before she hits him.

She scoops my little boy up with her big blue nose, and launches him. He arcs through the air in his little rainbow sweater, mouth open, too surprised and out of breath to scream. His small body clangs against the shiny Powder River gate and falls beneath it. I have carefully latched it, just in case. She clangs into the gate, lowers her gigantic head, snuffs him once. She decides not to stomp him, turns for me. I step aside and she runs by to slam into the locked wooden gate at the other end of the short alleyway. I race for the still form quiet in the soft dirt of the barn floor, turn him over, pick him up. His eyes are open, his mouth full of blood and dirt, face pale.

I gather him to me, turn to wrestle the big metal latch on the new gate. My shoulders are angled into the corner where the gate meets the wall, and when the heifer slams into my back, my boy is protected from the blow by my body. I manage to free the gate just as she's readying for another shot, and climb up on it. It swings open. The heifer charges by, snorting down the alley. I reach over the pole fence and gently drop Sam into the big paddock. Surely she will settle down there in the lower corrals. Surely there's one gate shut down there that will keep her. I climb over, pick him up, clean his mouth of dirt. He's crying a little, but he is still in shock, I think. His eyes are so dark I can't see the pupils to tell if they are the same size.

I hurry across the big corral to the main gate, fight with the chain that hooks it shut. Sam is still tight against my chest. Then I hear the snort behind me. Incredibly, the heifer has found her way through the maze of pens, and she is charging full steam again. She hits me just as I figure out the hook, and her momentum carries all three of us through the big gate. Sobbing, I run for the house, cursing myself for my stupidity and my clumsiness and my ignorance. Out of the corner of my eye, I glimpse her, free at last, heading for the open desert.

I call Grandpa's place, where Tim has headed. They are back in minutes. There is no concussion, just the shock and the bloody mouth. We keep Sam on the couch for a while. "Don't let him go to sleep," says Buster, "just in case."

We have been lucky. It's just a thing that happened, and mostly these things that happen are recoverable, but not always. It's a long way to the doctor if there's real trouble, and it's important to be more careful than you think you need to be. There's no way to protect yourself from your own ignorance. You just have to get lucky.

They don't shoot that blue roan heifer, though some people might have.

She runs with the rest of the herd all summer on the mountain. But she goes on the truck to market that fall.

⌇

We baptized him late, in the Episcopal Church, back when I still went to church, and he went with me. The traveling clergy would be in town Saturday night of Easter weekend: they had to be back in Nixon, on the Pyramid Lake Paiute Reservation, for Sunday-morning services, so the Easter Vigil service was our best choice. Tim was out of the negotiations from the beginning: "It's your thing. Do whatever," he said with his I-don't-do-organized-religion shrug.

The Easter Vigil is ancient ritual: traditionally it began at sundown on the Saturday night before Easter morning; baptism was a traditional part of this service. The people prayed all night in darkness.

The Paschal candle will be the only light at the beginning of this baptism, but a cold breeze keeps blowing it out. It's a new candle, and the wick won't stay lit. The woman holding it—a priestess? I think—won't begin the ceremony until she can get the flame to stay. Finally it does, and she moves into the dark space where we all wait.

We have each been given a small, yellow candle at the door. We light them one by one from the sputtering big candle, and gradually the smaller lights seem to give strength to the larger. Their yellow warmth fills the space. Sam, apparently fearless at eight years old, steps up on the little hand-painted stool one of the deacons has made him to receive his blessing. The bishop hands him a blue pocket mirror.

"Always look in this mirror so you can see behind you, remind yourself of the way that you have come."

Ah, the way we have come. One of our neighbors had teased us the other day: "Aren't you guys short a house up there at your place?" We have moved again, back into Tim's parents' house while I return to school, so I can get a teaching contract, so we can buy a house of our own. There has been another leased ranch and a farm between this decision and the blue roan heifer of five years ago. It will take about two and a half years for me to become an elementary school teacher, but we have learned the economic reality of starting a new ranch is more than hard work and frugality.

For a semester and a summer, I live in Reno during the week, three hundred miles away. I drive back to the ranch Thursday nights, where Tim and Sam stay. He's the only kid for miles around, playing baseball by himself.

The three of us sleep on couches and, later, in Tim's brother's bedroom, which he graciously moves out of.

When Sam comes to visit me in Reno, my friend Betsy and I take him and her two kids to the park to swim one day. All day, sitting in the shade, she and I mull over my situation. My advisor at the university has informed me it will take another two and a half years, instead of the summer term I had anticipated, plus another year of student teaching, to finish this teaching degree, master's in geology notwithstanding. My son will grow up on the ranch, but without me.

Betsy looks off across the rolling green grass, watching our children play and fool around. She's from a farming family too, in Georgia. She knows the complications and the difficulties. She hasn't gone back home, but she's not going to encourage me to leave, either.

We spend all day in shade and sun, and then stop for ice cream and at the grocery store. We load up the car, almost dark, haul the kids in, dump them in her small, redwood-fenced yard, carefully groomed, birch trees, brick paths. We drink wine and watch the sun throw last light through thunderheads over the Sierras. Finally it's too dark to see, and we come in to sort through the bags of peaches and green onions. She passes me food; I stash it in the fridge.

"Oh, my God," I say. The diamond is gone from my wedding ring. "Shit." It's too prophetic.

We look and look, and think about all the places we have been that day. Search the car, the carpet, creep around with a flashlight in the backyard. I give up.

We feed the kids spaghetti, finish the wine. Sam comes to us, eyes just above tabletop level. "Can we have strawberries for dessert?"

"Sure, go get 'em," I say, ruffling his dark hair. I watch him open the refrigerator door and come to me, holding the green plastic pint of berries in both hands. As he crosses onto the living room carpet, the diamond falls, like a promise, out of the strawberries.

⟿

I stay in school. Sam starts second grade at the ranch. The day he gets on the bus to ride the thirty miles across the flat and over the mountain pass to the one-room school in Denio, I have already left for Reno. He picks a fight with an eighth grader the first week.

The school district hires me to teach the upper-grade students in Denio before I finish my certification: I'll be able to teach and complete the requirements in the summer, and by correspondence. Sam is in the other classroom, but at least I'm within range now.

No teacher's child is ever in quite the same category as the other children, in anyone's eyes. That's the way it is, in every isolated rural community where you are the teacher, and you teach your family and your in-laws' children and their best friends' children. It is an impossible situation. When Sam eventually ends up in my class, I am twice as hard on him as the other children. But he does have basketball.

In that desert rural basketball league, everyone in school plays. We have enough kids for two teams, Big Kids and Little Kids. Like the other children's bedrooms, Sam's is lined with small, and then larger, trophies, for Most Inspirational Player, Most Hustle, Most Valuable. The coaches are ranchers from across the road. They take the kids from the first bounce of the ball to their high school teams. All winter, they practice twice a week in the community hall. The green metal building across the road from the bar, the only other going concern in town, has a regulation-size basketball floor, glass backboards at regulation height; the community sees to it that the floor is stripped and waxed every November after the barbecue-and-buckaroo dance season is over. It takes a week, but then the hall is ready for basketball season, gleaming wood in the middle of nowhere.

At first I think it is outrageous, ninety minutes of practice twice a week in the afternoons, games all day Friday. The little ones, kindergarten through second grade, scrimmage before the other teams arrive in steamed-up, lumbering yellow buses. It's seventy miles to the nearest school in Orovada. Paradise Valley is farther, and McDermitt, on the reservation, farther still, two hours and fifteen minutes at fifty-five miles an hour.

"Do you want me to come over and help?" I offer, the new teacher unsure of the rules. "No, really," Bill, the coach, said. "We'd just as soon you didn't." So I stay at my desk in the silent little school building, correcting papers in the darkening afternoon. They will ask me to run the clock on game days, or keep score.

On game days the gym will be packed. The whole community will show, grandmas lining the single row of wooden benches crammed up against the wall, uncles leaning on the doorjamb, hats in hand. Mothers will work concessions until their children's turn to play, fishing dripping hot dogs out of kettles, Cokes out of coolers in the noise and echoing banter of the community hall.

Sam will get better each year, an army of little statues lining his dresser and shelves by sixth grade. But that year he won't get the trophy at the end-of-season banquet. His coaches retire. Boys his age move away; the team at school dwindles from twenty students to thirteen.

Tim has begun easing him away from me, as gently as he can, into the world of men: cowboying, football, baseball. Sometimes I think we're teaching him the opposite lessons; sometimes I think it's just our sensibilities that are so different. Sam will say later, "There's really no way I could have had parents who were more different than you and Dad." But at least he smiles when he says it.

Our parenting is not a power struggle, but Sam must feel the pull between his parents, back and forth, like the tides between the sun and the moon. Through the toughest times, he is the force that holds us together.

"It's almost like custody," my friend Kate tells me at the time. "Either Sam's with you, or he's with Tim." For the next few years, I get Sam during school time, in the winters; Tim gets him in the summers. I get Sam's help around the house we've built on Buster's place; he does the lawn mowing and rototilling and moving of big pieces of furniture. Tim gets his time on the mountain. We take off only one or two days a summer from work, and all our vacation pictures have fish in them.

Then comes high school. Sam and I move again, into the house in town. For a few years, it's almost like I get him back. This is when he finally tells me about the dream he has had, over and over, all this time.

It always starts the same way, on an endless plateau, pockmarked with bottomless holes; the cliff's edge is visible but not near. An unseen destination, a careful walking between. He is careful to avoid them, but in spite of his care, something happens to trip him up. He falls; the hole becomes a chute that launches him out the side of the plateau into space, into free fall.

"I always land," he says. "It always hurts. No one else is around. I lie there a long time, while one at a time every broken bone heals itself. Then I climb to the top and start across the plateau again."

There are variations to the dream. Sometimes colonies of angry badgers come all at once out of the holes to attack. Sometimes he lies flat on the cliff edge, needing to reach something over the edge, taking every precaution. Hangs on tight, and still, something happens.

"The wind blows me over the cliff, even though I'm flat on my stomach. I always land, every time."

Some say dreams grow up out of the days of your life; others say they bring you lessons from a place we cannot know. Perhaps they are metaphors for experiences we can't consciously recall. Perhaps all these things are true.

~⊘~

Overnight, Sam goes from being the only kid in his one-room, eighth-grade class to one of three hundred high school freshmen. Winnemucca is still a small town, but it seems huge to him that first year. And it's a basketball town. The town kids have played basketball together for years, parents and coaches alike envisioning their teams from the time their children were in second grade. Sam cuts his losses. "I'm going to wrestle," he says.

In high school wrestling, a win is achieved by accumulating points; the most points are garnered through pinning your opponent's shoulders to the mat for three seconds. Literally, it's called a fall. The first year, even though he knows nothing, Sam somehow avoids the fall; through sheer force of will, he refuses to cost the team the points they would lose if he gave up.

They practice two and a half hours every night after school; all through the winter mornings they run, a loop that starts in the dark and stretches with each week of the wrestling season. We live at the bottom of the last hill, three blocks below the high school. They come pounding silently up the frozen street past our little gray house at 6:30 A.M., like clockwork. Bundled in sweats and beanies, clouds of steam trailing their lithe bodies, watching the pavement one step in front of their feet. Sam is always first or second in; those years of running up and down the basketball court make this part easy for him. Like his father, he minimizes his achievement.

"I'm only fast for a wrestler, Mom," he tells me. "Wrestlers can't run."

The tournaments are brutal, and long, soaked with a powerful mix of emotion, mental toughness, and the full range of adolescent male hormones: adrenalin for speed and moves, testosterone for strength and bravado—and what is the hormone associated with courage? All in a matrix of waiting, hours of waiting. Boys swathed in nylon warm-ups and sweatshirts bounce softly on their toes, eyes shut, Walkmans on heads, isolating themselves at the eye of an invisible storm.

Rows of dads sit up high, far away from the contest, or stand around outside in the freezing air, smoking to settle their nerves while their sons are inside waiting for a match. Others are kneeling supplicants at the edge of the mat, video cameras in hand, shouting advice to kids who can't afford to shift their focus away from the business at hand. I am one of the ones at the edge of the mat. I tape all of Sam's matches, and when I get to know the mothers of the other wrestlers, we trade off; you can't really let yourself become involved when you're behind the camera.

During the season, dual meets are every Friday night and all day Saturday, sometimes Wednesday nights, too. At the Winnemucca tournament, five matches run continuously on five wrestling mats, five rounds of double elimination over two days. Masses of boys, nearly men, roll acrobatically around on their shoulders, warming up. Like strong, young bears, they are ferocious in their play. Then the whistle blows that signals the end of the pretournament warm-up. They pile into color-coordinated heaps around their coaches, who crouch, back muscles taut in gray shirts, whistles dangling. They are built like their students, dense, tight, each muscle carved. They lean forward, shoulders broad, giving advice, focusing their kids' energy on the battles to come.

It is as fair as fair can be made, this formalized, ancient warfare, hand-to-hand combat. Hands will be shaken. Weights must near equal; there will be no cussing.

And then the whistles. Matches start, flashbulbs pop. Agonizing pain, broken elbows, blood dripping from noses and eyebrows. How can my son put himself in this arena? I wonder. But he goes, willingly enough, and alone. It is brutal, but some brutality, I find, has its elegance.

On Sunday morning, back at the ranch, Tim's dad and the uncles come for coffee and to watch the tapes I've made. Tim and his brothers all wrestled in high school, teammates with the man who coaches Sam now: Jim Billingsley. A three-time state champ himself, he is tougher than Patton, ruthless, excellent.

They watch Sam's matches and sometimes those of kids he'll wrestle on his way to the Zone tournament. Every throw, every move, is dissected. He lives each victory, each defeat, over again the day after. They watch the contest once, then, "Rewind that, let's look at this again," and Hank is down on the floor, rolling over his shoulder, or showing how to shift his weight. "Don't they teach you to do a sit-out anymore?" Hank asks, and then he shows him that. This move works here; it leads into the head-and-arm, Sam's best pinning combination.

They sit around the living room with their coffee, snow outside, windows steamed from breakfast, giving advice, listening, and telling stories. The sessions surely help Sam's wrestling technique, but by the time they are over, he is confident of more than that.

The rest of the week, he and his father talk on the phone almost every night. By the end of his junior year, he wins some awards, makes it to the Zone tournament. Billingsley, the local legend, retires at the end of the season, but his assistant is a great guy. He'll take over; the kids already know him and the program. Things are looking good.

It's January. Crunch time, Sam's senior year. He's not talking; he's still losing weight. It's dark in the morning when he leaves to run, dark at night when he gets home after practice. He works on his bench presses, on the head-and-arm. When Metallica is on really loud when I come home, I know it's been a tough day.

There are five of them fighting for that spot at 145 pounds. It's too light for him this year, but that's where he wants to wrestle.

I make a lot of soup that winter in town. It's what we both eat, even though he can eat whatever it is he wants to eat now. There is so much energy roaring out of him, I want to stuff him with pies and steak and mashed potatoes. But it's cabbage soup or a chicken thigh most nights. Not much water. Even as he grows into the man he will become, I watch his body dwindling before my eyes; he has lost twenty-five pounds since the end of football season. A lot of the time, he seems to be thinking about something else.

The last tournament I have on tape is at South Tahoe High School. Sam wrestles four matches, the last one against a junior-varsity kid from his school. He's a sharp-faced, lanky kid whose face has not appeared since Sam's first tournament three years ago. He's been in trouble, out of school, out of wrestling. I hear a rumor he's been living in a car with his girlfriend. But now he's back, and he's at least a foot taller than Sam. "He's a head-hunter," the coach mutters under his breath. Sam wrestles him, and he pins him. But not easily.

He is as alone as I have ever seen him, and now I see that he has two opponents: he is not just wrestling the sharp-faced headhunter boy. He is wrestling something within himself, some darkness inside his heart, a thing that divides his focus, dilutes his determination. He is walking between the badger holes, anticipating the fall.

On the way home from that tournament, we stop at Macy's to buy the suit that Sam needs for a trip to Washington, D.C., another plan that sounded like nothing more than a great senior-year opportunity last summer, and now casts a dark shadow over the end of the season. He weighs 142 pounds. The pants hang on him. The symposium is the week between the end of regular wrestling season and the Zone tournament.

He looks like a million bucks in that suit. But there's a price for everything, and the price for this trip is his seat on that bus to Zone. It goes to the sharp-faced headhunter boy instead.

In the end, I think with a mother's ubiquitous appetite for guilt, it's me that put him back on the plateau with the badger holes. I forced him to divide his focus, put too much pressure on him. My intentions were all good, but I set him up, just as surely as I did in the barn with that heifer fifteen years before.

Then I catch myself; it's his choice, too. If the dream is the journey, maybe that's been part of my job, to keep putting him up there, showing him again, so that he explores another path, another possibility. Move carefully through the obstacles, but know that you must move. Know that things will happen to put you in free fall, but you will land. In the dream, he heals every time. He gets up. He starts his journey again.

⊖

At the Wilder bunkhouse, there is a little, faded holy card tacked with a horseshoe nail to the bookshelf, left by some Mexican buckaroo. San Martin Caballero, the patron saint of cowboys. He is young and dashing for a saint, riding a big white horse. I think at first to pull it off, but the paper is stronger than it looks. It won't tear, and so I leave it there in the dusky coolness of the rock-walled bunkhouse, guarding the romance novels and the Louis L'Amours.

I remember a conversation I've had with Tim, that Tim has no doubt had with Sam, about learning how to fall.

"You have to pick your spot," he explained to me. "If a horse blows up with you, and you know you're going to go off, you focus on a spot on the ground. You may feel like you're completely out of control, but that spot is always where you'll land. Pick a spot that's smooth, with no rocks in it; you may be bruised, but you won't break anything. If you just learn how to fall, you won't get hurt," he said, staring at something in the past. "If you don't, you won't get up." Then, after you learn how to fall, you can learn how not to.

There was a day that came for Tim, just cowboying, as it does for most young men who buckaroo, when the decision became his to make. A snake, a rock, however it happened, the horse blew up. "That horse had me bucked off, and I just decided, no. It's so much a mental battle. Choose when, choose where, learn that you can choose whether or not to fall."

⊖

Sam doesn't have that dream anymore. "Once, in the middle of it, I just realized it was a dream," he tells me. That was the last time. The message, finally, had made the journey from the place where dreams come from to the place where, lessons learned at last, they can be put to rest.

We push our kids, we show them things, we hope they learn to love what we do; we delight with them when they find their passion. We try to teach them, in our own individual ways, how to cushion the falls life has in store, how to get up again, and head back up the mountain. Fathers, mothers, we have our different perspectives, but the desire of our hearts is still the same. Light a candle to San Martin Caballero, for all loosely rooted cowboys, for all boys learning to be men.

⇦ The Flying Heart Museum

THE SCHOOL DAY BEGINS, ALL FLUORESCENT LIGHTING AND LOUD cheerful announcement, all lines and regimentation. It is three hours before we even look up from our forced march through the curriculum. At eleven-thirty, we break for lunch; off the children go, more or less in a line when they leave the room, although I become increasingly apathetic about the linearity of it all as the year progresses. Then it's my turn.

The building is enormous, two stories, modern, built on sand from the old lakeshore up above the town. We have no playground equipment: as is true at many schools these days, swings and slides and monkey bars are considered a liability. One child will surely fall, and his parents just as surely sue. They need so badly to use their bodies: some kind of hard, physical work, something that will make them tired and happy. That leaves the big green playground, where mass games of football and soccer still move like waves, fifty kids to a game. They will play all winter, through the snow. A couple will break legs and ankles, even though no tackling is allowed.

Carved out of sagebrush hillside, an island of desert is caught, a block of school property between the building and the backs of the subdivision's last row of houses.

Of course, the children aren't allowed to play out there. Sometimes their footballs go awry, the wind catches a Frisbee or lofts a baseball, and someone goes out to retrieve it. But they get in trouble for exploring between the big sagebrush, playing those kid games of hide-and-seek, looking for lizards under the brush. I find pathways twisting down the slope, bike trails, sometimes blocked with big caliche-crusted cobbles: No Trespassing! Our Territory!

The slope from the bike rack is steep, and makes a great jump-off point for the legions racing home at three. A star of bike trails radiates from the asphalt margin, and many days at lunchtime, I slip out my classroom door and walk unnoticed, to the bike racks, buttoning my black overcoat, to pedal home for lunch.

The year our school was built, they planted wildflowers along the sidewalks by the street: cosmos, bachelor buttons, rudbeckia, those tough red-and-yellow daisies that take over everything. Flax. Desert winds and rain that first year brought some of the seed into the empty lot, down the gullies at the edge of the asphalt, into the sage and rabbitbrush. The next year the children hunted the lot like it was Easter, peering between clumps of brush, racing back to the playground with a limp fistful of color for me to put in my hair.

Now it's three years later. The steep hill off the edge of the asphalt is eroding badly. A gully cuts through the sand, revealing gravel underneath. It's still navigable. My long, black Macy's coat flies out behind me—Miss Gulch, incognito, humming the witch's theme from *The Wizard of Oz*— and in seconds I am down the bike trail, surrounded by sagebrush, blond dry grasses, blue-belly lizards.

The trip home takes the better part of a minute, maybe. The steep start gives me good momentum on the sandy path twisting through the tall brush. I am invisible from any distance, and the path is clear, open, fast once I'm on it. The sparkle of the gravel, the sharp desert smell, the mineral crunch under the wheels, reminds me of my other home, the faraway one where I am free. Then a little berm to climb, and I roll out between the houses, over the curb, onto a paved street; back into suburbia.

Even with my hands in my pockets against the chill wind, I can make the downhill turn onto my street without touching the handlebars, if there's no traffic.

My house is just down the hill. I've planted hollyhocks, irises, and brought silver poplars from the buckaroo camp at Wilder, even though Tim says I'll regret it when their rhizomes start to take over my well-groomed postage stamp of lawn.

It's too small to live in all the time, but I don't need much in Winnemucca, just a place to sleep during the week, till Sam gets out of high school. There's a wind chime out front, a wood-burning stove behind the red-painted door. A broken brand on the brick mantelpiece; a brick holds an old rope coiled over somebody's chaps, just to remind me what it smells like at home. An old black-and-white cat too poor to make it through the winter at the ranch claims the big upholstered chair in front of the stove. We tried bringing Sam's dog, Cookie, in, but she couldn't take it, and neither could we. Cow dogs need to work even more than they need their boys.

I play with pieces of arrowhead on the counter while I heat a pot of soup. I eat under the trees, listen to the dry leaves rattle. I have to get away from them, just for a while.

&

The girl is a wiry thing, pixie blonde with ancient brown eyes, black corduroy overalls, and those big, clunky shoes they all wear now. She catches me just outside the building with my arms full of books one afternoon. I am on my way to a teachers' meeting when she tags me from behind. "I can't go to creative thinking today." There's always something with this one; I am ready to be annoyed. She has her tough face on, but I can see she's been crying. "I have to go to court."

Ten years old, she reads as fluently as I do. She knows how to kick her brother where it hurts the worst. She's learned the hard way how to protect herself, and I think, *God, this kid needs a break from her life.*

I want to gather her in, but of course my arms are full, and she's on the trot anyway. I settle for slowing her down. "Be brave," I say. "Tell the truth." Her chin comes up, her eyes full of all the sadness and cynicism in the world.

I gaze across the frozen sagebrush, snow melting into alkali mud. I haul my load to the meeting, where we try to map diversion, engage these sad children with something that will make them interested in a larger history, a bigger world.

I dream, idly, of transporting them to the one-room school I used to teach in, with no intercom, no harassment policy, no head lice, no interruptions. I would read them some wonderful stories, put out the hay bales for hurdles, give them some time to think. There would be lizards under the swing set, real deer on the lawn, and the expanse of the desert outside the playground fence to feed their spirits while their hearts healed.

Jose

They pin dots on the map to show me where they're from. Michoacan, Col-
ima, Guanajuato, Tamazula. "Angel doesn't talk English," they tell me. As
far as I know, he doesn't talk at all, or read, even in Spanish. One afternoon
early in the year, we discuss these places they are from. I raise my eyebrows
at Angel. He makes his eyes big and round, the expression he will use all
year when he is trying to distract me from my question, and chirps,
"Paranganacutirimicuaro." It is three weeks into the term, the first word I
have heard him speak.

"Paranganacutirimicuaro." Jose, across the table from Angel, laughs at
the look on my face. "It's a volcano," he explains to me. "In Mexico, where
he lived." Angel's face breaks like sun after snow. He says it again. "Paranganacutirimicuaro. Paranganacutirimicuaro."

I start looking for it immediately, on our shiny new technology-grant I-
Mac computer. Everything, after all, is on the Internet, once the filter is dis-
abled. I find a gorgeous, false-color composite satellite photo of a volcano in
Mexico; it takes five minutes to fill the screen. When the image is complete,
Angel shakes his head. It's not the right volcano (or maybe he's just shaking
his head). He and Jose and Ismael stand around the computer in a tight
semicircle, hands deep in pockets, hips cocked. Jose translates for Angel.

"It's not your volcano, but it's in Mexico," I say. They shrug, and go to recess to play soccer.

One day when it rains too hard to go out to recess, the kids have break
time in the hallway: jump rope, games of catch. I watch Jose build a loop
out of a length of jump rope in the hall, spin the lariat over his head, drop it
down, and almost jump through it. The fibers are too limp. The loop won't
stiffen. "Where did you learn that trick?" I ask him.

"My father was a trick roper in Mexico," he tells me. "He taught me."

It's a common rope trick, common for a person from a certain background. We both know that cowboy stuff doesn't cut it here in Winnemucca,
in Jose's crowd.

Jose, my Indio boy from Michoacan, was held back last year; for most of
these children, it's too hard to learn the language and the curriculum at the
same time. He is still small, quick, sharp. He's got the Raiders jacket, the
long belt and baggy jeans; fifth grade is a little young in this neighborhood
for the *vato* look. In the town park with his family one weekend in the fall,

something happened. He won't say what. For a week, he wandered the playground alone at recess, not playing soccer, no football either. It was after that the Raiders jacket showed up. Armor.

Deep in the heart of winter, we study the thirteen colonies of New England. I read out loud to them from *Witch of Blackbird Pond*, about a beautiful girl from Barbados trying to fit in to the cold Puritan colony of her dead mother's sister. Jose is trying, for my sake, but it really doesn't matter much to him. It's not his history, after all. (He doodles rosebuds on his multiplication tests, elaborate crosses on his reading papers.)

The assignment today is a picture of a New England village, the town common with small bands of sheep and cattle on it, the church with the steeple, the cooper, and the schoolhouse. You know, you studied it too. It makes them squirm in their seats, reading about it, and so we draw pictures. "Draw this picture," I say. "See the village green, where people shared the common pasture. See the community well, the blacksmith, the church, the school."

Jose does a lovely job, and writes his caption describing what's going on in his picture. "Two gooses are fighting on the grass." I collect the posters to hang on the wall. The stapler chunks rhythmically in my hand: Clarissa, Jennifer, Tyler, Jose . . . there, off to the side between the rows of shops along the common, stands a big square building. It is bigger than the church, which we all know is supposed to be the biggest building in town. A gigantic pink heart, with golden wings, labels a brown log building. It has a name: The Flying Heart Museum.

You know how your spirit betrays you when you're not thinking to protect yourself. Jose has been dreaming, doodling away, and his pencil has discovered this flying heart, as big as the Puritan meetinghouse, right in the middle of this repressed, bundle-boarding New England community. Jose knows how to jacket things for respectability, so they'll be acceptable to me, to his new peer group, to the white community. He has drawn the log cabin around the heart, and labeled it. At recess I ask him, gently, "So, Jose, what's in there, in your Flying Heart Museum? Who would go in to visit? If you lived in that place, what would you keep there?"

It's too hard, too many questions, much too intimate. "I dunno." He scuffs the asphalt of the playground with his tennis shoe, looks longingly at the soccer game forming up on the grass.

"Yes, go," I say.

They long so for their home, these kids. They draw the Mexican flag over and over, make quilts of its repeated image in art class. Their *abuelas*, their grandmothers, are down there; their mothers work making beds at the casinos.

In February, we build models of colonial homesteads hacked out of the dark woods along the Saint Lawrence River by the French. Construction paper, scissors, glue. "You are all neighbors," I say. "You have to figure out how to make it through the winter."

They argue about whether watermelons would grow there or sunflowers. They cut out little 3-D fences and fence in their milk cows. Carrots sprout from their vegetable grid paper. They argue about their woodlots. "If you leave your trees on the north side of your farm, they will shade my corn. Put them behind the house, away from the river. Come on, give us a break." Making a home in an imaginary world: they are old for this, some of them almost twelve. But they submerge themselves in the project.

They come from farming, most of them; no matter that this is fantasy farming. How many horses? (The girls always have too many horses.) How many milk cows? Should we plant a garden? Will we have enough food for our animals? Will we survive the winter? Jose meticulously builds three-dimensional loose-hay stacks. One cow, some geese. Pole fences. He gets too involved in the construction of the little boat that he will tie up to his dock and doesn't get his project finished. But he is happier than I've seen him since the Flying Heart Museum opened.

Jose's uncle Martin has worked for us on the ranch for several years. One day early in spring, the telephone in the classroom rings. It is my father-in-law, trying to find out if Martin is coming back, or staying in Mexico with his family. I say, "Jose, the phone's for you." The children gasp. (These kids don't get phone calls.) A rapid-fire conversation in Spanish takes place, in which Jose is the conveyor of information, having to do with how we might find Martin and whether he's bringing his wife and kids back from Mexico. Jose knows the answers; when he hangs up the phone, he knows no one in that class will ever look at him quite the same way again.

Arturo

Arturo did not know me last night. I saw him at the pizza place as I pulled up, at least I thought it was he, but the floppy hat, the big baggy coat, I couldn't be sure. He was incognito.

I ordered, sat, waited, not wanting to embarrass a young man already forced into public with his mother and his baby sister. The little girl ran right over, of course; we were the only others in the restaurant. She waved a complimentary mint at me.

Arturo, with your ancient Mayan face, your golden-bronze skin, your artist's vision, why are you hiding? What has happened to you in the last two years? Are you locked in the Flying Heart Museum too? (On his last day, as he left school, he hugged me, a no-holds-barred, big-boy bear hug). The gangbanger thing, does that keep you safe now, right-hand man?

Reading was always a problem. It was hard to find a place at home, sleeping on the couch. *I guess,* you said, *I could go in my mom's room to read.* Too many brothers and sisters, no quiet place. No place of your own.

"Senora," I ask as she gathers up the younger one, as he takes their pizza and heads for the door, *"como se llama su hijo?"* (She has other children, she can't tell which son I ask about.) *"Por favor dise hi* from me, *Senora* Dufurrena. I was his teacher . . . ," my Spanish failing me, again.

"Ah," she smiles. "Si. Okay. I will tell." In her crinkled eyes I can see, he knew me, too. We watch his back out the door.

Quinceanera

Lola Martinez is tiny, Costa Rican, blonde, sharp. She teaches English as a Second Language at the grammar school, only now we call it English as a Learned Language. She has been here for twenty-five years, and she takes care of the Hispanic people in our town, although for her there is always the private issue of being Costa Rican, and not Mexican. For some years there was the *tienda* in the alley between the main street and the neighborhood, a tiny, pink-trimmed white house with blue-painted iron bars across the windows. From the shelves lining the one-room store, she sold groceries and christening dresses and Mexican honey, and if you had a bad toothache, or a child with a fever that wouldn't break, and you had no money for a doctor and couldn't take off work to see one anyway, you might find some penicillin or tetracycline with a label in English that you couldn't read, but that said, "For Veterinary Use Only." These things you can buy in any feed store for a sick rabbit or a chicken, if you can speak English, and no one will be the wiser, or care, if you choose to use them on your family. For these things Lola got in big trouble. "Dealing drugs" isn't always what a person thinks.

Lola came from a good family in Costa Rica, the only daughter of a wealthy man's second marriage. Separated by more than years from her older siblings, she came to America, made her own way, and became a teacher of English to Spanish-speaking people. She bought a single-wide trailer, then a rental house or two, the store. She adopted a Mexican girl from one of her classes, the kind of child that breaks your heart, makes you want to take her in, and, then when you do, breaks your heart a million times again. She raised the adopted daughter and sent her to college, where she became pregnant by her Iranian boyfriend. The result was Little Lola, Lolita, who now lives, off and on, with her grandmother.

Now Little Lola is fourteen, and soon it will be time for her *quinceanera*, the fifteenth-birthday celebration. Pre-Columbian in origin, it was the festival that marked the day a girl became too old to sacrifice to the insatiable Mayan gods. These days that celebration looks like a wedding, a debutante ball, or, if you are cynical, a meat market for adolescent female children. A *quinceanera* is expensive, and elaborate, and Big Lola wants to take the girls to Italy to see the pope instead, but Lolita has begged and pleaded. Her friends have given her their baby-sitting money, two hundred dollars. With it, she bought the invitations and the dress in Mexico on a Christmas church trip, and so she will have her way.

To Big Lola's dismay, Little Lola has been dating a twenty-two-year-old dishwasher at the casino. Big Lola thinks it's "a bunch of shiT" (she emphasizes the expletive, biting off the end of the word and spitting it out between her white teeth). She has forbidden her granddaughter to see the older man. The dishwasher has called Big Lola and said, "I just want you to know I have always treated Little Lola with nothing but respect, and I would not desecrate your granddaughter before her *quinceanera*." Big Lola's response was to hold up her right hand in a shape like a cup, and then to tightly squeeze her hand and say, "I wanted to take his balls and do thiS!"

There will be a High Mass with the giving of symbolic gifts. There will be two hundred and fifty prime rib dinners. (Lola does not like Mexican food, and nobody knows how to cook Costa Rican.) After that, a formal dance with fourteen attendants: seven boys in tuxedos, seven girls in long pink-satin gowns with bolero-style white-satin jackets. (The boys are all Mexican, but two of the girls are white.)

Little Lola and her friends have made impossibly complicated, intricate centerpieces for the tables: twenty-five plastic champagne glasses filled with white aquarium pebbles, pearls around the rim, inverted and glued to Styrofoam plates. Twenty-five plates rimmed with peach-colored lace, with silk bows and roses and greenery, tall white candles growing from the upturned champagne glasses, three white helium balloons tethered to each stem. "Marta" Stewart gone mad.

The night of the party, people stand around for a long time waiting for the meal, which Little Lola's aunt has had catered from Battle Mountain. Instead of prime rib, it turns out to be iridescent roast beef, baked potatoes, macaroni and mixed vegetables, and macaroni salad in Rubbermaid salad bowls, which, when the last servings are ladled out, show the plastic labels still clinging to the bottoms of the bowls. There are pink and yellow, banana and strawberry puddings in Styrofoam bowls. There is not enough food, quite, for the crowd that shows up. But it doesn't really matter, people are excited, there are balloons all over the dance floor and glitter and two bottles of champagne on each table. The Hispanic Youth Group from the church runs the bar, and serves beer and ungodly sweet strawberry daiquiris for four dollars (they're raising money for another trip to Mexico).

The principals in the ritual have their head table along one side of the dance floor, opposite the band, with their own bottles of champagne. (It never comes up, but aren't all these kids underage?) They are ready to cut loose, you can see, but they're bound by the steps, as are we all. We stand in line for cake: seven individual layers are connected by two tiered plastic stairways. Little plastic figurines represent the attendants; a bridelike figure at the summit represents Little Lola. An orange fountain bubbles under the apex of the structure. The cake, predictably, tastes like cardboard. (It must, after all, have taken days to assemble this structure.)

On the cake table, a sixteen-inch-tall, porcelain-headed collectible doll reposes, dressed to the nines in peach-colored lace and satin. We ask one of the attendants in line for cake ahead of us about the significance of the doll. She explains that there is a symbolic dance done in the course of the evening. The honoree begins in the center of the floor, dancing alone with the doll. After a bit, her parents come out onto the dance floor, and dance with her a while, and then they take the doll away from her, and give her a pair of high-heeled pumps. My feminist streak must be showing. The girl giggles at my look of horror. "She doesn't have to dance in those shoes. She just dances around with them." She adds that Little Lola isn't going to do that dance tonight (her grandmother's influence, perhaps); the doll is there just for the symbol.

Finally it is time for Little Lola's formal presentation. She stands in the middle of the floor with all her attendants, a princess surrounded by her court. A slow, grapevinelike dance begins to a Mexican love song. The tuxedos and satin gowns swish in a graceful double chain. The dancers twirl like figures on a music box (braces flashing, gum snapping all around). The bandleader makes a speech that ends, *"Feliz Compleanos a su quinceanera, Lolita,"* and then it is time to party.

During the first couple of numbers after the Happy Birthday song, it becomes obvious that the crowd is changing. The families are still here; women and girls at the tables, boys cruising. But the bar at the back of the dance floor is filling up, and soon it is lined two deep with dark-skinned men. They are not here with their families. They are watching the proceedings with interest, like lions, waiting.

I overhear two women talking at the next table that some white girl wants to have a *quinceanera* now. Well, you can't blame her; all her friends are doing it.

Hunting Magic

William's landscape was a refuge, holes he hid in from his father, when his father was unhappy. "My stuff is all in my caves," he bragged one day, meaning homework, toys, crackers, canteen. "It's where I go when I have to."

He is an undersized child who could be described by the phrase "failure to thrive"; he is named for Kaiser Wilhelm, he says. His father seems to beat him because he is small, because he wants him to be tough, because he is a disappointment, a tiny failure instead of the giant Aryan he envisioned. So William goes to his caves. They are not really caves, just some holes tunneled out of the side of the hill in hard-packed sand, roots of sagebrush holding the sand tight, like arthritic fingers. Alkali-cemented, caliche-capped, tight enough for the children who hide there, not quite homeless, sheltering there as our kind has done for millennia. In the earth, we are invisible to predators.

He is one of a string of children moving through the distance up the morning hillside, around red outcrops of volcanic rock, through the rice grass, along the pathway into their past. They rush headlong from the yellow bus, the better part of a mile ahead of me. They disappear, before my eyes, into the earth.

I follow, herding the stragglers and the ones who have forgotten their inhalers, stopping at the points of interest designated on the interpretive sign at the base of the hill, which everyone else has, of course, ignored. We clamber into a big rock shelter. The shelter faces east in a north-facing reentrant of the slope. From where we stand, I can see several other caves at the same elevation, carved out by waves pounding an ancient, curving volcanic wall. Like a strong, half-closed hand it holds us, and we look out across a windy valley, sheltered from the wind. "Imagine the lake," I say, "stretching to the horizon. Squint." It's the sparkling distance of forever out there; ten thousand years back is just a heartbeat really.

The children run on. I permit myself to stand just for a minute longer, in that silent space, watch that blue distance. I cannot tell, in that moment, whether I am looking into our past, or our future.

By the time I catch up, Annie has found a tiny, hand-size cavelet in the tufa crusting the volcanic rock. She crawls around, her blonde ponytail exactly matching the color of the rice grass between the sagebrush, looking for other tiny spaces, elves' houses she could slip into. She is sure someone lives in there—and she's probably right.

We snake around the hillside on the contour, reach the entrance to the cave we will tour, and sit on benches overlooking the Carson Sink, waiting our turn. The children are like dogs let off a chain after too long. They twitch, giggle, cannot sit still. We watch the group ahead of us file out at last and stand to take their place, then crouch and duckwalk into the cave. The first sensation is cool humidity, then the stench of bat guano—overwhelming. Perhaps because the season has been a wet one, maybe because the metal door that seals the cave has been locked for a long time. A government agency now guards the flakes and shards that remain in the shelter from the excavation. Our guide is a docent from the museum in Fallon; BLM staff used to run this tour, but now focus their energy closer to home in Carson City. A nice man in the BLM office tells me on the phone, "The woman on staff is just burned out on doing cave tours."

We talk about the skeletons that were taken from here. "They were not Paiute," the docent says, "but people from before." Though the tribe has petitioned to have the bones buried on the reservation, she says they will stay in the basement of the university, in case someone wants to study them. I wonder whose people they were, where they came from.

I spend most of the tour settling the squirmers. The rest of the children seem to be listening. They walk from the entrance down the staircase to the wall left partially excavated, look at the artifacts protruding from the silt, dangling little white tags; they've pushed the buttons on the panel that lights up and tells you, in sequence, what the periods of occupation were. When we are back outside, I stop them. "What did you like the best?" I ask.

"What will you remember?" The thing they will take with them from their journey to the past? Of course, it is the stench from the bat shit the children will remember best about the day.

We move on, to the next lesson.

Above us, jets leave contrails in sweeping arcs through the autumn sky above Fallon. The planes glint silver in the afternoon; they seem from a distance to be sparkling birds, poised to dive on something in the marshes. Their thunder overwhelms the empty desert.

The children race in little knots between piles of basalt boulders at the margin of the Pleistocene lake, a mile around the shoreline from the cave. Ten thousand years ago another hunter broke the silence of this place, chipping a talisman across the black rock, a snake-shape slithering, a circle and an arrow, a sign that might be a map to water. Was he waiting for antelope? Waiting for mammoths? Surely the water stood high against the outline of the valley. Was it hunting magic he made?

Or children's art: "Your fathers are going hunting. We'll be gone a few hours. You kids better be right here when we get back."

One of my students, Michael, a slender Paiute boy, runs his small brown hand over a huge boulder, the surface covered with thumb-size depressions: a medicine rock, used for grinding plants into powders to heal, to cure. His quick, dark eyes ask me, *What?* I begin to explain, but before my words are out I see his gaze shift, torn between the knowledge he wants and the disappearing backs of his pack of friends, who have already found another treasure up the trail. His eyes shift back to mine: another question. "Yes, go." He disappears.

They cannot soak up enough, of rocks and obsidian chips, of lizards twisted up in the protection of stickery tumbleweed. They run, and run, and run, and the assignment, to make a rubbing of one of the petroglyphs, save a bit of ancient history, ends up as fragments of crumpled newsprint and grocery sack, brightly colored chalk powdering the boulders. It doesn't work. The chalk picks up every irregularity in the rock. The designs are too subtle. Or maybe it's that the hunting magic works only in this one spot, can't be taken away. I walk along, picking up pieces of paper bag and chalk fragments, watching my lesson evaporate, replaced by another one, the one I should have anticipated, the one I can't teach. The one about the space; about the lizards and the way you feel hiding behind those big black boulders and your friends come by, just as those antelope did in the distant past.

The roar of the jet engines is constant, deafening. I look across the valley toward the Naval Air Station, trying to see the giant predator that must be crouching there, belching that sound. But all I see are wisps of smoke—farmers burning ditches—and the flashes of windshields crossing the valley. There is nothing to focus my vision on the crushing sound that completely overwhelms my experience, until mercifully it stops.

This is the hunting magic of our people, the demonstration of military might—louder, faster, more deadly than any God-made thing. All this power, all this deadly force, at someone's beck and call: thank God we're on our side.

I turn back to look for my students. The last of them are disappearing over a hill, like a herd of small antelope, laughing. They do not seem to have heard.

Now it is late afternoon. The bus driver grumbles about the washboard gravel as we creep into the lake-margin dunes, our last stop before ice cream and the trip home. The sun is low now, near the ridge, and the air is cooling off.

A towering sand dune has gathered itself into a black, volcanic, boomerang-shaped embayment in the mountains east of Fallon. The Pony Express boys built a remount station here near the foot of this shifting mound of sand, heaping black basalt boulders into a crude, roofless shelter from the wind. It is little more than a horse trap with walls high enough to crouch behind. Signs and pamphlets tell us the layout of the station, the history. We find a little fireplace in a corner of one room; stand in another spot where a man died of his wounds. We walk through the room that was the stable, the tack room. The boys, for that is all they were, used the stop to shelter from the wind, to rest, change mounts, drink water, before the ride off west toward San Francisco. Gaps in the wall face the head of the canyon to the east, the direction the riders would come from, pelting out of the desert with lathered horses, pursued by bands of Paiutes incensed over the invasion of their territory.

I watch Michael while the kids get the lecture about the stop. He betrays no sign of knowing that it was his people shooting the arrows at the mail carriers.

The subject of fifth-grade social studies is American history, and in the classroom we have done Indian reports. "Pick a tribe," I said. "Discover how they lived. Find a story. Tell it."

Michael picks the Paiute. He already knows where they live. "In a double-wide over the mountain. My mom drives the bus."

"No, no, I mean before."

"Oh, sure," he says. "Okay."

His poster shows white teepees on the prairie, big white headdresses. It's an honest mistake for a kid that can't read very well. That's what the picture shows, after all, for Indians in the social studies book.

He doesn't have a story, either. "My mom doesn't know any stories," he says. There are no picture books of Paiute stories in the school library, although there are many from the larger tribes now.

Later, in the back room of the county library, I will find a booklet of yellow construction paper, stapled, put together by some students at the reservation school. Michael doesn't like to read, but he will learn every one of the stories in this collection and tell them to his mother.

The children swarm around the remount structure, clamber over the roofless walls, play chase and cavalry as though they have never been outside in their entire lives. A kid picks up a rusted horseshoe, crusted with sand, an unidentifiable iron lump that must have had something to do with shoeing or wagons or something. We aren't supposed to take this stuff, it's part of the site, but I see kids trying to worm pieces of the find into their pockets, the pieces crumbling into unrecognizable flakes of rust. I wait. They lose interest, toss the chunks in corners.

It's just as well they learn it now: you can't take it with you. Maybe it's better that way.

Perhaps we are always hunting magic. Hunting refuge in our dreams, in our refugee hearts; hunting in the landscape, in each other. Hunting in the past, in the desert, in the silence of caves and the great windswept space of the playa, wishing for the invisible hand on the shoulder, the voice in the ear murmuring, yes, this is the place. You are home. It's all right.

⊸ Desert River

THE HILLS ARE ALL WHITE AGAIN. IT'S APRIL, BUT STILL SNOW SPITS
sideways off and on all day. Nothing is really sticking; it's just winter blowing itself out. Inside the quiet of the morning ranch house, seventeen baby
chickens scrabble in a cardboard box on the burgundy carpet of my office. I
have discovered a set of weathered deer antlers somebody brought home
last fall, and it is in the box too, for the balls of fluff to practice roosting. A
heat lamp clamps the edge of my old drafting table, shining down on them,
maintaining a constant temperature. It is important that they not get too
cold, or too hot, in this fragile state of their chicken lives.

The chicks are starting to feather out, white, red, yellow, black. I have
several different breeds this time, to entertain my little niece from Virginia
who will be coming to visit in the summer. There will be the dependable
egg layers, Barred Rocks and Rhode Island Reds, but this year I have
splurged on Silkies, red and blue, with goofy-looking feathers on their
heads like Louella Parsons hats. There are Auracanas, which lay pastel-col-
ored eggs, Speckled Wyandottes, and the ones with feathers on their feet. It
will be the multicultural chicken menagerie of the neighborhood. The
chicks have cost me nearly fifty dollars. My neighbors would find this an
outrageous expenditure: the common breeds are a dollar and twenty-five
cents apiece. These have averaged close to three dollars. I am disproportion-
ately excited.

Of course, the chicks travel with me, back and forth to town. From Monday through Friday they live on the washing machine in my tiny galley kitchen in Winnemucca. My two cats are fascinated by the peeping and scratching that comes from the cardboard box under the heat lamp. I have had serious talks with both of them, and they know it is unacceptable to reach in, even once, with talons stretched.

The fledglings make the weekend pilgrimage to the ranch in the backseat of the old silver Caddy. Sleek, gray-leather seats cushion their traveling home, towel-draped against the cold. The sack of chick starter, heat lamp, and watering dish are lumped on the floor with bills to be paid, Sam's boots and calculus homework.

The dryer hums and thumps, its low cadence companion to the humid silence. The bigger chicks stretch their long, prehistoric necks, always looking up and out of their cardboard prison, conscious of the larger world outside. *It's too cold to let them out,* I think, watching. They eat. They deposit little wet blobs behind them, tilt water droplets down their throats. They nap under the light, learn to climb the antlers. They hop to the highest tines to fluff out near their artificial sun.

They don't have the roosting thing down yet, though. As they fall asleep, their knobby heads drop slowly forward, like old men snoozing on their chins (except, of course, they have no chins). Their beaks sink, slow and slower, until they touch the newspaper. They sleep like that, balanced on the pinpoint of their noses. Breathing makes them sway gently back and forth. If they are perching in the antlers, their beaks drop until they lose their equilibrium and fall off on their little heads. Indignant, they fluff up, look around to see who saw, and settle back into their chicken dreams.

The baby birds are my promise to myself that spring will come. Mornings, the weak sun crawls up into the sky, but it's ten-thirty before it really feels like daylight. The nights are supposed to be getting shorter, but it seems to happen more slowly each year. I can't escape the feeling that a long, celestial finger is reaching toward Earth, slowing our planet's progress through the heavens, the season of death and dreaming dragging on us like an invisible hand. Just when you think you might give up, the planet shifts a bit, the sun stays high a moment longer. Snow in the high country sags, a trickle of moisture starts out. By the first of April, the chicks come into the feed store.

It still feels like winter when we begin the work of spring, just as everything we do in summer calls the autumn, and autumn in turn prepares for winter. These chickens will not begin to lay till August, and their eggs will supply next winter's Sunday breakfasts. Amparo has tried to teach me how to butcher them, but it is a messy procedure, and I am not good at it, in any sense.

Only Jesus and Amparo have stayed the winter this year, and Miguel across the road. Jesus is working on his citizenship papers, practicing every night for the Constitution test. Juan Chavez returns from Mexico with his wife, Marta, in time to drag the fields and clean the ditches for the water that will bring the lush growth of summer. And soon the river will come, weaving its way through the feather edge of cold and hunkered-down hopelessness that hides at the end of this gray season. We are all waiting for the water.

❧

April, and still the snows come; winter's ebb tide laps at our feet. Lambs conceived last November are being born. Last night ten of them froze solid to the birthing ground; coyotes took seven more. Chavez tells us his father in Mexico, who is eighty-five, is very ill. Chavez is not a young man himself, although he still does a young man's work each day, especially in the spring. I close my eyes, imagine it is only a couple weeks till full green, warm spring days, gentle rain.

"Who is God?" Tim asked his mother, years ago.

"He is the one who brings the baby calves in spring," she answered, a ranch mother's measured response to a child, a more complicated answer than first appears.

Our sons and daughters learn early that there is as much death in spring as life. It is a promise of renewal given, but sometimes taken back, creation tithing to winter.

Like spring, the river has not reached the ranch yet, but it is coming. The creek that flows into the reservoir a few miles above the alfalfa fields is running fresh. The reservoir is rising, and the ditches that feed the alfalfa a few miles below it run full. Dan turns the overflow water away from the fields into Great Basin wild rye, five hundred acres of head-high wild meadow that once fed Pleistocene deer and horses, perhaps the mammoths that grazed through here.

It is a blond expanse, bordered on the east by rolling sagebrush, on the west by the fields of alfalfa, an unexpected savannah outside the neat rows and fences of the farm. Once you are within its borders, the ryegrass seems endless.

Cattle spend the winter in this outside country. The rye shelters them from the cutting winds of winter, and provides sustenance through the coldest months. We will gather them today along with others that have wintered on the ranch meadows. Today is turnout, the beginning of the season's journey. It takes us first to the low foothills, then into the canyons, and finally to the high meadows of summer.

Tim has hired a new cowboy, and we take the truck and trailer to the upper end of the lane; he unloads his horse on the shoulder of the highway. He will gather the floodplain of the river and meet us a little later. "Watch out for the river," Tim cautions. "I don't think it's here yet, but it could come today."

We climb back into the truck and drive up the highway slowly, Tim watching for cows and calves in the lane. A white-faced black cow—we call them black baldies—has birthed a little brown calf near this two-mile stretch of highway easement through the alfalfa fields. We see her, up the highway. The calf is dead, lying half on the pavement, probably hit on the road last night. Tim mutters to the cow under his breath, "Yes, and if you're not careful, you'll end up just like he is, dead on the road."

It's a constant problem in the spring, cows coming out of the ryegrass after dark to lie near the relative warmth of the pavement. The dogs herd them back into the protection of the tall grass, but often they return during the night, and some of them end up like this young cow, standing on the shoulder of the road.

Tim drives around the north side of the fields, to a narrow wooden bridge over the creek. We unload the horses, tighten cinches, look around for a moment to see where the animals are before we start off along the border of the ryegrass. The cattle stash their calves like Easter eggs under bushes here and there, sometimes a mile away from where they are feeding. It's no use to drive a cow along the trail without her calf. She'll come right back for him. So if an animal isn't paired, we let her go. The cows are nearly unstoppable anyway, galloping across the flat ahead of us to gather up their young ones. We hang back, watching them pick up their calves, and set off after the rest of the herd at a trot.

Riding slowly along the edge of the rye, we spy three red backs moving inside its waving perimeter. Tim points at an insignificant-looking stream of water, four inches across. It meanders along the well-defined margin of the tall grass. "Be careful in here, it's a mess when it's wet." This is where the overflow from the fields spreads out, softening the hard ground, darkening it. The ground is hard as concrete till it's wet, and then in a horse's stride length becomes a bottomless alkali bog. The cattle can negotiate it, their secret trails through the plain hidden. Tim sends the dogs in to bring them out.

"Gather down the fence toward the highway," he tells me. "Come along the highway into the ryegrass from the other side. It's drier over there. I'll go back up the creek and start this other stuff over." He waves his hand at the vast sagebrush flat that he knows conceals twenty or thirty head in invisible swales. I nod, acting more sure of myself than I feel; he starts off.

The cows move ahead of me, in and out of the tall, yellow grass. After a while I see the new cowboy cross the highway. No cows are ahead of him; he must not have found any. He charges right into the rye after a little bunch. I look around for Tim; sure enough, there he is, watching from the far side, ready to help us if we need him. When he sees we are okay, he turns his horse back north into the sagebrush.

Between the waters, the river and the creek, is this other treacherous channel: the highway. Between the fields, the stretch of two-lane is empty most of the time, except when sleepy travelers or long-haul truck drivers blast through. We call it the lane. It makes it sound cozy, but it isn't. The new hand and I take the bunch up the lane, watching both ways for traffic. The cowboy has gone on ahead to turn the leaders when I see the black baldy cow, still standing there as the herd moves by her. Some of the other cows stop to snuff the still, brown body at her feet. She stands over him like a statue, her white face turned toward me.

"Bring everything," Tim had said.

I scream at her, I wave my hat. I send the dogs. Eventually she turns and follows the bunch, but she fights me every step. A mile or more up the road, I see her make a decision. I gather my reins a little tighter. She turns to charge my horse. We sidestep, let her go by.

She will stand there on the shoulder of the road for two more days, snuffing her dead calf, unable to abandon the small body, as though the force of her wanting it might bring life back. On the third morning, she will be gone. After that, one of the men will take the calf's body away, too.

‿

We turn the herd onto a trail, parallel to the big road but far enough away that we don't have to worry about traffic. The drive north takes the better part of a week, moving the cattle thirty miles toward the summer country near the Oregon border.

It is slow going with cows and young calves. The cows turn and fight the dogs if you push too hard with them, so you just have to dawdle along, letting them make their way. It's like taking a bunch of kindergartners on a walking field trip through town: there's a lot to look at, and the ultimate destination cannot even be imagined. The adults know where they're going, but for the kids, it's walking recess. They'll take your word for it that this is the path that we are on, but they have to play and sniff and taste everything out there too.

The morning has been chilly, and the sun is just starting to feel warm between my shoulder blades when we jump a little bunch of antelope. Seven of them dance along ahead of the herd of seventy cows and calves. The antelope trot, circle, stop, stare. Afraid, but too curious, they can't stand not getting just a little bit closer.

Cookie, the Australian shepherd, hides well back from the herd behind a sagebrush, waiting for me to call her up. Sam and I share this dog. If Sam is riding, Cookie is his dog. This morning, she will stay with me.

Cookie entrances the antelope. They circle back, surround her. They approach to ten yards away, stretch their necks toward her. She waits, her eyes on me. "Stay there, Cookie," I call, wanting to see what they will do. Step, step. They draw nearer, freeze, bolt away.

"Okay," I laugh, and she scampers closer. The little antelope herd follows our horses for several miles like this, jump and start, dashing boldly between the two riders, flanking the rear of the bunch of cows and calves, circling to the front, dashing away. Their feet barely touch the ground.

The leader cows have reached the windmill where we will drop them for today. They will have a chance to water, rest their calves, and feed away until tomorrow morning, spreading out across the wide flat. We push a little harder, seeing that Buster has brought up the truck and horse trailer. Tim leans on the truck, his horse beside him, cow boss waiting for his crew. They are talking, but they are watching us too. Tim's father was the ranch manager here for years, and cow boss before that. They have both made this ride a hundred times, in their turn.

As we holler the last pairs into the grassy area around the windmill, I see a cow that stubbornly refuses to move on through. I am ready to give the dog permission, but something holds me back. As I get closer, I can see. The big red cow stands, head down, just on the edge of the grass. She is cleaning off a slick heifer calf, born just moments ago after a morning's worth of walking labor.

I hold Cookie back with a look. She crouches, several yards behind. The rest of the cattle drink water at the well, slowly spread out for an afternoon's grazing.

I watch the cow, licking her wobbly-headed calf, and I think, *Whales calve. So do glaciers.* A life that did not exist five minutes ago suddenly appears at your feet, bloody and slimy, independent of the body that nurtured it through its creation. The bright light, the first desperate breath, the sudden cold breeze in the space that surrounds—it never gets old for me, the spring tide of this moment.

I leave the cow and her calf a wide berth, catch up to the rest of the herd. A quarter mile on, I reach the trailer where Tim waits.

"Why'd you leave that cow back?" Tim asks from under his hat. I explain; he nods with a little smile. I am still learning, but this is the right choice to have made this time. We load up the trailer and drive home, in the warmth of companionable silence.

Juan Chavez calls that night to Mexico, to find out about his father. Marta stands next to him. The exchange in Spanish is too rapid for me to understand, but the body language when he hangs up is clear.

How can old people die in April? They've made it through the worst of the winter. It's only a few weeks now—isn't it?—till the full, green warm days, when it will be worth it to make it another year. Hang on, Juan Chavez's father in Mexico; Juan is dragging fields. Soon he will plant those amazing gardens he always plants, the big one behind his white house that he disks with the tractor, that is always two weeks ahead of everyone else's garden. He will plant all the little gardens too, at the pumps and in the corners of the fields where there is a little extra water, wherever it looks like things will grow. I understand only this phrase: *"Carreterra in la manana."* I am driving the tractor in the morning.

He sits slumped over, looking at the phone for just a minute. Then he stands up, says the same thing he always says after we come feeling our way across the road in the dark to tell him he has a phone call, or when he comes over in the evenings, like this evening, to receive a message from the familiar voices of his faraway home. *"Gracias, Tim. Bueno noch'."* Weddings, babies, family illness, christenings. The death of his father. *"Gracias, Tim. Bueno noch'."*

❧

Weekends in spring I walk the river channel. Chavez's tractor growls patiently along out in the field, dragging last year's sticks and lumps of earth into a smoother plane, imperceptibly sloping toward this channel.

I follow the channel upstream beyond the field, into the wild-rye river meadow. Crossing the crust of last year's green moss, I backtrack the trail of a raccoon indented in the softening muck. His feet are the size of half-dollars; he is coming to investigate the chickens, no doubt. A rabbit's tracks are overlaid by a coyote's; they end in a gray fluff of fur and guard hairs. A small pile of feathers shows me the winter meeting between hawk and pheasant. Not a bone is left.

Wild roses are still dormant, dark thickets. The willows along this channel are a red stick forest, buds swelling, waiting for the right combination of light and temperature, and waiting, like the rest of us, for the water.

The Quinn heads in the volcanic tablelands of the Owyhee plateau, desert country that straddles the borders of Oregon, Idaho, and Nevada and defines the structural edge of the Great Basin, part of the Continental Divide. It is open, empty, wild country. In some years storms drop heavy loads of snow on the Owyhee. In others the low, gray clouds skim over it, hoarding their moisture for some less-subtle geography. In the springs that follow those seasons, the riverbed stays dry.

From the headwaters, the Quinn snakes west into the valley, tilting south into the Great Basin, then west again through the swale between two mountain ranges. The topographical bends and angles of this country caught homesteaders, like hoofprints catch seeds, the way leaves gather in corners. Sod House is such a place, a widening of the river meadow around the tip of a mountain range. The river turns abruptly here, almost ninety degrees, tracing the imperceptible tilt of the land. Across the wide flat it slides, to make another nearly right-angle turn in the middle of the valley, southwest this time, at Hog John, where another homesteader once hunkered between earth and sky. The riverbanks are steep and slippery with alkali mud; once you're in the channel, the only scenery is heaven.

From Hog John the river channel zigzags across the flat and winds along thirty miles of nameless valley, under the bridge at the Bottle Creek crossing, down to us at Quinn River Ranch. The only place a traveler sees the channel is at the bridge, and until the river makes it there, you wouldn't even notice it.

Some springs, the river roars brown foam across the flat. Like a mad housewife returning to long-neglected duties, the water rolls debris of dry years before it, piling sticks in corners, cleaning its own channel as it floods. It spreads out across the meadows, three hundred feet across, six feet deep. In July it's back within its banks; by mid-August only isolated pools of stagnant water remain. Alkali mud, sticky and gray, records the footprints of all who pass. By November the channel may look as though water hadn't run there for a thousand years. The trails of deer, beavers, birds, and children harden through the winter.

Sam and I have seen its passage into our valley only once. The river slithered its greasy, gray way through the first loop at the Bottle Creek crossing, about four one Friday afternoon, pushing a roll of cocoa-powdered foam before it. The water meandered through the meadows, then swelled, soaking the pastures of the ranch that is our nearest upstream neighbor. A week passed before the river had softened and saturated the twenty miles of concrete channel mud enough to finally reach our bridge.

When the river does appear, it happens in an afternoon. In an hour it overruns dormant grass and greasewood, transforming desert into wetlands and wetlands into the rich ryegrass that will be stirrup-high two months later. The wetlands bring the birds, a few at first, then more—ducks and coots and mud hens. Black-crowned night herons nest in the willows; their gawky, tall blue cousins stab morsels in the shallow water. A flock of white egrets fills a single cottonwood tree, flopping awkwardly in the branches, looking tropical and somehow misplaced. The lookout stretches his neck, opens his wings; the mob follows him, lifting into the air, graceful as sailplanes once airborne. Twenty-eight white gliders, planing off down the river, out of sight.

This spring day, I take Tim's two border collies for a run in the afternoon. The river has just gotten to the bridge, and I want to feel that brilliance of light on water in my eyes.

I ride the bike slowly, letting the old dog pace himself down the gravel road east from the ranch. Teddy, barely out of puppyhood, is off in a cloud of dust. Jack trots the center of the road, straight as an arrow. He is always working.

The flooded meadow is sparkling, beautiful; its beauty masks the danger there on days like this. Grasses growing fast now up through the shallow water make the place look like a rice paddy. The dogs wade in for a drink and a cooling off.

I see the whirlpool at the culvert before they get there, and hop off my bike to call them back. As usual, the old dog turns right around. Teddy, exuberant, clueless, swims right into it.

The water here may look still, but it isn't. The entire meadow's worth of river funnels into a five-foot pipe between half-drowned clumps of willows that mark the low-water channel. Today the culvert is several inches underwater, one corrugated aluminum lip just visible.

I think at first he is strong enough to swim through the vortex. It doesn't seem to catch him. But then his nose goes under once, and when he surfaces, he looks confused. He's swimming as hard as he can, and it's still pulling him under. I edge closer to the culvert and think maybe I can grab him, but only if I stand in the water at the top of the culvert myself.

I holler at him, and I realize I'm not going in after him. A voice in my head is saying, *He's a dog.* I can see him struggling, his head a couple inches under water, a foot from my hand. Then he disappears.

I run to the other side of the road. My stomach aches, sour with fear. I imagine him, directly under my feet. Is he struggling? Unconscious? Does he see the light at the downstream end of the culvert? How long can a dog hold his breath? I watch for him. I talk to him. *Come on, Teddy, hold on; come on, Teddy.*

A big stick floats out; debris collects in culverts, sometimes blocking them completely. Yellow, muddy water. Avocets. Blackbirds. Cool spring breeze. I look around. *Come on, Teddy.* I imagine his limp black body emerging from the culvert, and wonder which way I will jump in to retrieve it. I wonder what I will say to Tim if he doesn't appear at all. *"I took your dogs for a run. I lost Teddy. He's in the culvert at the bridge. I guess we'll get him later."*

And then I see his head, just under the water, as he drifts out. His nose pokes up. Still conscious, barely. He gets a breath, coughs. He sees me, and weakly tries to swim, but I'm standing right over the downstream mouth of the pipe, and he's helpless against the current. Stupid woman. I dash down the gravel embankment, calling to him, working my way through the willows to a gravel bar he can see. Slowly, he seems to realize that I've moved. He turns, drifting and swimming, toward me. He crawls out. His legs give under him. We both sit down, hard. Teddy lies still, coughs again. I hold his dripping head, my hands trembling. We wait.

Minutes pass before he stands up, coughs once more. Shakes the huge dog-shake that blesses me with the river's crystalline water.

Things change so fast here. Months of quiet go by; nothing happens, and then one day the water comes. Death stares you in the face, then seems to lose interest, turns away. It retreats into the margins of time and space, the transitions between spring and winter, field and desert. The margins are where the danger lies, and I missed this one.

༄

Not long ago I gave a talk to the state water-planning advisory board at a Basque restaurant in Winnemucca. I was the after-dinner entertainment at one of their field meetings. The board had come into the Nevada outback, looking for water to take to the cities. Diplomacy dictated that the little people that live in these desert communities be allowed to speak. People had testified all day.

I showed photographs of the river, of the birds that nest here, of the hay fields that the river helps sustain, of the willows hiding the culvert that almost captured Teddy. I tried to explain what the river meant to us as they had their dessert and coffee, their crème de menthe and sodas.

It was the wet spring of a wet year, and every river meadow was flooded; every creek ran full. The men from the advisory board, mostly urban, mostly from Las Vegas, smiled at me noncommittally when I told them that this spring was the exception, not the rule. They assured me that their water would come from someplace else.

"Probably the Virgin River or the Colorado," they said. "You have nothing to worry about from Las Vegas." The golf courses and endlessly propagating subdivisions with drip-irrigated trees and sprinklers on timers to water flawless green lawns would steal their water from some other state.

"Reno, on the other hand, could be a problem," they said. Development. Double-wides on the floodplain. More tourism. Recreation. Jethro Bodine wanted to build a *Beverly Hillbillies* theme park and casino in a mall in downtown Reno. He'd need a Cement Pond, I bet.

Interbasin transfer, they said quietly to themselves. *There's so much extra water in the West. Watersheds across the West, barely populated, just full of extra water.* The states own the water that rises within them, and the oldest water rights within those states belong to the ranches. Water can't be taken unless you can find someone willing to sell their water rights, or their ranch, or both. Or unless you can somehow prove that there is extra water that nobody needs for a long time, if ever. Then the water can be stripped from the land, and taken in a pipeline to some urban center across the mountains.

Dams hold the surface water back, particularly in country like this where the year's water may come all at once, in two weeks, if it comes at all. But now dams are a bad thing, and so are the farms and ranches that use the water, though they put most of it back into the ground. The farms and ranches are keeping it from the subdivisions and the casinos. They are the obstruction to growth.

On behalf of the Clinton administration, various agencies of the Department of Interior have filed suit to get title to the water from the western states it falls in, so that the federal government can control it. It is an expensive lawsuit. States know this. Some of them, like Idaho, have already conceded their water to the BLM or the Forest Service. And while the lawsuits are in progress, no water wells can be drilled on federal land.

The Carson River, the Truckee, and the Walker River drain the snowmelt from the Sierra Nevada into the Great Basin. Like a birdbath, it evaporates. Farms and ranches and the wildlife that shelter there still get a crack at it, but more and more people need a hot, thirty-minute shower, a swimming pool in their backyard, a hotel casino with a fountain, pumping water twenty-four hours a day into the heat of summer, to glorious Italian music.

It's a dangerous place to take water for granted, I told the board. And there is a story I remember that I don't tell them, a story from a spring when there was not enough water.

When Sam was eight, there was no Quinn River. No mountain streams fed its flow. Cattle hunkered in the brush, in the deepest shade they could find. Their water was drying up, and we had to move them higher, toward a spring that would surely still have water.

We started late from the home ranch, one of those mornings it's blistering by seven. By the time we gathered the cattle from the high meadow, parched in early June, they were cranky and hot, their calves stubborn and wobbly. Up through the tall sagebrush and the snowberries, we drove them hard, every inch of the way. Sam kept losing his hat in the dusty willow thickets. He was too young for a day like this. Tim promised a cool drink at the spring on top. There was nothing to do but keep going.

Dust-choked, we topped the high canyon, glimpsed cottonwoods in a notch on a north-facing slope. We followed Tim into the trees. He climbed down, and I saw him stop, turn, look up across the pass above us. The spring was just a darker blotch in the dusty soil, a few puddles.

"I'll take 'em over the top, try the spring in the next canyon," he said softly. "You'd better take him down." The boy was flushed, goofy with the heat. There was nothing else to do. We headed down the canyon, hotter now in midafternoon, toward the pathetic little trickle that remained of the main creek. We fought through the hot brush, sneezing. I knew it was a bad idea, but when we got there, we drank our fill of tepid, muddy water.

This year, I told the men, there was plenty of water, but most years, there isn't. Most years there is sand in our drinking glasses by the end of July. We run the drip lines to the garden at night to minimize evaporation. We haul water to the sheep, move the cattle farther into the high country. We wait. Dry years teach us to wait.

I remember a Spanish word, *esperanza*, the word for *hope*, the sound of softly running water. Inside it, *espera*, the word for *wait*. Tim's father tells me, "I remember seven years together when the water did not run." He understands the meanings of both of these words. *Espera, esperanza*. Wait for the water, wait and hope, and watch. Perhaps faith is the echo that is left when the memory of heaven fades.

⌐

I watch Amparo through my kitchen window. Pulling irises in June, it's a sure sign she's moving. She tends the garden, does laundry, maintains herself. She listens to Jesus moaning in the bedroom. Now it has been three days since she's watered her garden, the roses and hollyhocks, Shasta daisies in front, pansies in rings of quartz cobbles at the door, Michaelmas daisies, clouds of tiny lavender stars on the driveway side, carefully spaced zinnias in front of the fence of slender willow poles, woven side by side into the wire fence, giving the climbing roses something to hang onto. For years she has worked her magic on the vegetable garden in the back, tomatillos, squash, chiles, rhubarb. She has coaxed them all so beautifully to fruition. Now the lawn is not mowed. Her husband has still not left the bedroom, still drunk ten days after the barbecue. It is time for him to move on.

Perhaps he is afraid to sober up this time. He has passed his Constitution test, he is almost there, but there is something with the IRS, some papers. She doesn't understand; I don't either. And then there is this: once he is a citizen, she can be too. She will have some rights then that she doesn't have now.

She has no way to get to town, she says, but if I buy the ingredients, she will make mole, that Aztec mystery of chocolate and chile. Tim and Sam have left for Oregon, to be gone a week branding. Spaces in the house swirl with the memory of them. My parents who had come for a visit will be leaving too, in a day or so.

Amparo works all afternoon on the dinner in her hot kitchen, roasting the chicken, frying taquitos, stirring the sauce. We eat it up at my mother-in-law, Linda's, welcoming whoever was around. *Amparo, you come too,* we insist. The mole is rich and dark, little pieces of chicken and carrots and onions rolled up in the tortillas. It tastes just slightly of loneliness.

The next day, in twilight, she pulls a great black tub full of irises, but there is not room to pack them in the truck. When they leave, the irises sit there by the empty trailer, in the sun.

The cattle make the trek into the canyons and high meadows where they will stay a few weeks, depending on rain and what's left of winter's snowbanks. Teddy and the other dogs move to Wilder with the cowboys, to chase jackrabbits and get into other kinds of trouble.

Spring melts imperceptibly into summer. Alfalfa grows, the men change the water in the fields at night, drive tractors in the afternoon. The chickens feather out and grow. They pick bugs around the lawn, fenced away from tender shoots in the fast-growing garden.

I have dragged Amparo's tub of iris bulbs into the walk-in cooler, where they wait for autumn to be replanted. They might still survive, though their blooming cycle will take time to recover.

The river soaks the earth, slides back into its banks. It slows, feeding the meadows and fields through gravel bars underground now. *Espera. Esperanza.*

✎ You Are Learning to Drive Cows, He Said

I RECITE FRAGMENTS OF THE LESSON IN MY HEAD. *DON'T CROWD THAT* cow. *Follow too close and she'll turn around and fight you.* If she thinks she's getting away, she'll go right where you want her to go. Put yourself in a position that suggests a path to her. *Use common sense.*

The fragments are usually thrown at me over a shoulder, riding away down a canyon. *Pay attention.* The leaders will move right out; the rest will follow, just like people. Some have more energy; some have less. It depends on the individual, the weather, the heat, the age of their calves.

Sometimes it's over his shoulder at a trot, because three miles up the road, the leaders have decided they don't like the power-line road after all. *Keep the ass end going.* Keep pressure on the rear. They'll get there.

If you're riding flank, stay way away off to the side once they're lined out. They want to move away from me, so if I get too close I push them off their line. If I move right, they do too; if I push too hard to the left, they slide off the road and wander out into the brush.

Look. Think. Wait. Don't get in a hurry and leave something behind that one of the cowboys is kicking off the ridge in your direction.

It's really pretty simple. *See where you're going; figure out how to get there. Don't make it more complicated than it is.*

I remember my great-aunt Gertrude talking to me at an Indian Hill

Club luncheon in the same way. Crinoline bit the backs of my thighs. My chin cleared the spotless linen tablecloth by three inches. "This is your salad fork. Don't use it on the entrée. This is your finger bowl. Don't eat the lettuce leaf; it's the vehicle for the pears. Use the forks from the outside in, one for each course. The dessert fork is farthest from your hand, so of course you use it last. It's really quite simple. Just common sense." It was all there, just a lot to absorb in one lesson.

There's a choice you make, at some point. Either you're going to ride, or you're not. It's fine if you want to garden; gardens feed everyone. And the cooks work as hard or harder than the men, longer hours. Up at 2:15 A.M. for 3:00 breakfast, lugging fifty-pound sacks of beans and flour, making home-made doughnuts three and four dozen at a time, days in a row during branding, washing up late, great stacks of plates and coffee cups, after the rest of them are asleep. It's honorable work, and respectable work; but I need the space of outside country. I need to understand the work. I need to see the clump of trees that is home from a high rim in the breaking day. So I am learning to drive cows.

⇜

The season's journey takes the cattle north, away from the river into the high country where there are no roads; they follow the greening of the bunchgrass as they move steadily into the upper elevations.

This range of mountains is not wide, roughly fifteen miles. Thirty million years ago, low andesite-shield volcanoes spread their purplish flows across these miles; later more violent eruptions of viscous ash flow and thin layers of basalt buried them. The whole volcanic mass sliced and slid, so that now layers of basalt, tuff, and rhyolite parallel and repeat along the ridge-and-valley structure, like long snakes of white and red and black slithering along ridge and canyon, rising gradually to the north. It is steep, rocky, raw country.

Springs rise in the heads of these canyons. Water runs along the buried surfaces of the tilted flows, carried to the lower benches hidden from the sun's heat, to emerge and pool at the turning of a canyon. Cattle, horses, deer, chukar gather at the tiny oases. Coyotes den nearby, where they can take advantage. Sage grows taller in these crannies. Wild roses bloom. Above, golden sunflowers cape the dark ridges; paintbrush, lupine, phlox grow low.

The allotment fence keeps the lazy ones from coming back to the flat, from drifting back into their comfortable winter pasture. It won't be so pleasant in July down there. It also gives the lower country a full growing season to recover from their passage; the grass will have gone to seed and be dormant by the time these cattle pass through in the fall.

The fence crosses the mountain roughly east to west. Like a bracelet on a long arm it separates the elevations of winter and spring from the upper valleys of summer. We start the gathering in the farthest edges of the low country; like raking leaves in your yard, we push the cattle into the lower canyons, toward the fence. Every cow and calf passes through the gate into summer.

Here, at the ranch, there is little direct instruction. Cowboying is a largely unspoken art form, historically mostly the territory of men. Maybe, I think, this nonverbal thing isn't just a cowboy thing. Maybe it's just another guy thing. Maybe men hardly talked at all before the invention of professional football and car engines, before there were sports bars.

I pester Tim with questions. It drives him crazy. "Trailing cows just depends. If they want to go, if they're hungry for green grass, you can take a lot. If it's hot and they don't feel like it, you may take only fifty. You just have to open the gates, and keep pushing them."

The first day of the ride, we reach the corral at gray daylight, quietly saddle up. The cattle slip away into the canyon ahead of us like ghosts; we ride single file between steep, black walls. Two by two the riders peel off up side canyons, until only Louie, our adopted Basco grandfather, and I are left, each riding on opposite sides of the creek's main fork. The walls of the canyon are so steep that Louie can see the animals above me on my side, and I can see the ones above him. We talk softly back and forth.

Louie motions. "There's a few up there," he says, pointing with his chin. I start up the steep, loose-rocked slope, zigzag. The bay horse, Charlie, is young, energetic. He loves to chase cows. I don't know this yet, but I am about to find out.

I make a mistake: cut across the sidehill too soon, and I don't get high enough to come out above and behind the pairs on the hill. Two or three is what I see, but that may not be all of them. When they see me, we are eye to eye across the hill. They arrow off ahead of me, contouring the steep slope. Damn. I keep climbing, but there's not much choice in the way of trail.

The horse takes a few lunges straight up the hill, a little canter on a suggestion of trail between jagged rocks. There is nothing but the humid gray air on my right. The part of my brain in charge of my survival comments on my behavior, "Well, that's pretty *western*," using the private derogatory for outsiders who think they know how to operate here.

I overshoot the pairs; directly below me they split, two pair cutting back, two staying on the trail ahead. I circle back until I see Louie, watching from below, anticipating my screwup, backtracking, starting up the steep draw to cut them off. I leave then, take off through the rocks after the ones still ahead of me.

That's when I hear the hollering from across the gorge. Tim, off his horse, on the skyline, waving that big black hat. His words float to me across the misty distance. ". . . God dammit to hell, get down offa there . . . Go back . . . Dammit."

I rein in, chastised, and come at a walk in twenty yards to the ragged edge of a black precipice that makes the bottoms of my feet tingle. The cattle have found a way down off this thing, but I can't see how.

Sheepish, I pick my slow way back along the trail to the bottom. Louie's halfway up the other side, gathering a bunch, letting me settle my embarrassment by myself. A quarter mile up the main canyon I round a bend, and see what Tim saw, the fall I would have taken in just a few more moments. *My God*, I think.

I watch from the bottom of the canyon as Louie picks his slow, careful way through the basalt crags. The cattle clatter ahead of us on another invisible trail. He has worked his way just above them; they think they're getting away if they sneak down onto the trail. When he is back at the bottom of the canyon, another half mile or so up the way, I apologize. He says, more gently than he needs to, "Well, I picked 'em up." What about the others that had been ahead of me on the black cliff? "They're still ahead of you, on the trail." There was really no place else for them to go.

We follow backs and swishing tails, red, black, butterscotch, caramel, through groves of baby aspens, clumps of chokecherry, thistle. I look for Tim above us, but he has disappeared in the gray morning.

Later, his direct gaze shows me several different emotions, but all he says is, "You would never have made it down that slope, and neither would your horse. If I tell you to go back, it's because I can see something you can't."

Use common sense. Pay Attention. Look at everything, the whole picture, not just what's in front of you. Then just go again the next day.

The next day smells like rain; we clamber into the pickup at three in the morning. We catch horses in the dark at Texas Spring: Tim and Sam, Tim's brother Hank and his two teenage kids, Louie. The horses are eager to go in the predawn chill, stomping in anticipation.

Louie looks at Sam, who will ride Tim's big sorrel appaloosa. "You're mounted today, boy," he grins.

Sam grins back and grunts as he swings a leg over. "It's a ways up here, anyway."

A long fast trot up a dirt road, then a well-marked trail through tall sagebrush, then a not-so-obvious trail over rock and hardscrabble, then no trail at all. There are no sounds but the creak of saddle leather, the chink of spurs, the huffing of horses, occasional clink of steel on stone as a hoof strikes a spark. Riders peel off in pairs and threes up the forks of the creek, hooves thumping quietly.

Tim takes one group north; Louie takes the rest of us up the south trail. We part at the highest fork of the creek. He looks at me. "You rode this last year, didn't you?"

"Mmmm," I nod, noncommittal, looking around.

The light is pretty dim down here, and there are no landmarks. Louie shifts his attention. "Remember the little meadow up there on top?" he asks Sam. Sam remembers. "Well, you guys spread out in there. Kick everything over the top that wants to go this way, and gather the rest. We'll meet you up there in that meadow. You'll see us. And Tim'll see you."

Sam takes Chief up the west ridge. I stay in the bottom. I slow down this time, letting him get ahead of me in case cattle cut back behind him. Wait and listen for cows bellowing to each other, or until a rider shows himself ahead of you half a mile, trailing half a dozen red backs across the ridgeline. For a long time, I don't see anybody.

I've been called a quick study, but I'm wondering whether that's really true. I have a good visual memory, and a poor auditory one. I take notes. I make maps to understand where I am in my world. This is a new kind of perception, feeling with all my senses in the vast space around me for the people who are part of this day, this gathering of animals across hillside and canyon, all headed someplace they cannot see, but know.

Snaking up the draw, my horse picks his way through layers of basalt; I hear the cattle clacking stones ahead of me around a bend in the canyon, but I can't see them. I have to learn to trust that even when I can't see, they're there; not to rush, not to panic. The clues I hear, the birds that start up ahead of me, are proof enough of what's happening.

The line of light from the rising sun hits the ridge above. I see Sam and Chief, his big sorrel and white haunches glowing like fire in the sun.

I barely hear Tim's whistle; Sam turns and looks back. His father is on the highest rim a little way behind. Watching our progress. Sam reins in, backtracks along the skyline. They sit just a bit on that ridge in the sunlight, heads turned toward each other. Then Sam nods, points his sorrel north through the rimrock a thousand feet above me. Tim allows himself to watch his son a moment longer, turns off, and disappears from my view. In a moment, I am alone again, in this landscape that looks like no human has ever touched it.

We all converge somehow on the same meadow; cattle file through the gate, calves kicking and playing, cowboys appearing over the ridges and up from draws, pushing everything through into the basins of summer.

This day has gone well, but there are other days that don't. Soon I will find myself in another kind of space, trying to convince another bunch of mammals that I know what I'm doing. It won't be any easier.

⌁

I bring my briefcase into the meeting room of the Resource Advisory Council, another low-ceilinged, fluorescent-lit, Formica-surfaced government space. Half the fifteen seats at the U-shaped table are filled. I find my spot; lay my pile of papers and my purse in front of the chair.

She walks purposefully in behind me in her Birkenstocks, almost five feet of lavender calico and navy-blue cardigan and iron will and hostility. (I too wear Birkenstocks, but never to these meetings. I don't wear cowboy boots, either.) They have put us right next to each other again. I take a breath, turn, and smile.

She slaps her pile of papers down on the table.

"You're in my space," she snaps.

"Good morning, Daisy," I say. It's time to get started.

Daisy and I, and thirteen other citizens, find ourselves appointed to the Bureau of Land Management's Resource Advisory Council. Interior Secretary Babbitt had himself signed our letters. The RACs would replace a succession of previous citizen advisory councils, councils that have advised the BLM on the disposition of public lands since the Taylor Grazing Act. In 1934, this act of Congress created the concept of home ranch and attached federal range that became the framework within which we do business in the western United States. At one time these councils were locally elected, and they functioned in a local, practical way: where to build a fence, where to develop a spring. They spent the small monies generated by local ranchers' grazing fees, stored in the BLM's Range Betterment Fund.

The new councils are comprised mostly of urban citizens; just two of us live on the land. I am an unlikely choice to represent the cattlemen and the farmers, but that's what Interior wanted, something new and different. I am not involved in cattlemen politics; I am not much of a cowgirl, and I can't see how my voice will make a difference. Still, I can verbalize my ideas. And so I have made a place for myself in a society of minimal talkers, talking for them. They don't have to spend time at the conference table arguing when they could be out in the desert doing something else.

By Bruce Babbitt's mandate, the Resource Advisory Councils will write standards and guidelines for livestock grazing on public lands in the West. Standards are designed to raise everyone's level of concern. Remember standards for health care? Standards for education? We will establish standards for the natural world.

Ranchers who use the public lands must justify their very existence to Clinton's first administration. I like where I live. I want to be able to stay here. This is America, after all; the only way to have any influence in the making of public policy is to participate, to play the game.

So here I am, in this Formica labyrinth, breathing this stale air. Almost all the meetings take place in these low-ceilinged rooms, acoustic tiles, fake wood-grain molded plastic and metal chairs. There are no windows in these rooms. There are no colors.

We each have a little fake wood-grain name tag with a pin on the back, and a bigger one on a metal stand on the desk, so we know where we're supposed to sit. Someone always sets up the table ahead of time, nameplates arranged in some kind of neutralizing pattern to minimize conflict. They want us to look more like a group of concerned citizens than an armed camp, so they always seat me next to Daisy. I feel like somebody handed me a black hat when I walked in the door.

I have a seat on the "Resource Users" pod. This group includes four other seats, all filled by men. The representative of the Nevada Cattlemen's Association is a pretty traditional cattleman; there is a soft-spoken permitting agent from Sierra Pacific Power, who will turn out to be the voice of reason; two seats for the mining industry, filled by gold-mine geologists. One of them was so dedicated to the process that he came to meetings sick enough that he could hardly hold his head up. They will both be transferred in the first year.

The other two pods, five members each, are designated "Environmental Advocates" and "Members of Government or Academia." Four of the five seats on the "Environmental" pod are women: a recreationist, a Sierra Club activist, a woman from the Nevada Wildlife Federation, and a wild horse and burro advocate. Bob, an independent archaeologist, rounds out that group. The "Government" pod includes a county commissioner, a guy that works for the State of Nevada, a Native American seat, empty more than it is full, a biology professor from the university, and a Reno socialite who represents the Public at Large. We are a motley crew.

The Standards and Guidelines for Grazing Management incorporate every aspect of the great outdoors: soil, water, habitat, and wildlife, particularly species that might be threatened or endangered. For each Standard, there are Indicators; to achieve each, there are Guidelines, a list of Dos and Don'ts for ranchers to follow in the course of their animal husbandry. We will have eighteen months to learn everything there is to know about the ecosystem, and write the regulations to cover it.

Another stipulation of our charter states that we must reach consensus. Three of five members of each pod must concur in order to adopt any one statement, any one definition. No Majority will rule here. We must all agree on how we will manage the ecosystem. I'm thinking we'll be here the rest of our lives.

Ecosystem management. It's an arrogant term, really. Think of the complexity it erases. Think of the ecosystem that is your house. The piles of laundry clean and dirty, the flow of junk mail through the mail slot, packages piling up on the front doorstep. It's an old house I live in; every morning there is a new representative of the lower phyla in my bathtub.

How many of us really understand the way our plumbing works? What really brings the precious water in, where the waste really goes? Is it important to understand, as long as it works? Or the kitchen! Scary heart of the whole, food in all stages of storage, preparation, decay. Things are created and destroyed in your habitat every day, some little, some big. The ecosystem of your life may be small, but it is complicated. And it is, at least partially, private.

Now imagine that you own your house, but the lot on which it is built is owned by a large absentee landlord, as are all the other lots in your neighborhood. There are fences between your lot and the others on your block, which the landlord owns but you must maintain. Same with the sprinkler systems, the landscaping. Imagine that everyone in the neighborhood has equal access to your yard, because of course it is really everyone's yard.

Children on dirt bikes can ride through it, little old ladies can come and pick berries from the bushes that grow in the back, which you water and fertilize. Neighborhood packs of dogs can play there. The neighbor that bred rabbits fifty years ago and let them out in his yard is not responsible for the progenies that tunnel under the fence. They may take up residence and proliferate indiscriminately under your rosebushes. You may not kill them, or even move them to someone else's yard. They are now Mustang Bunnies, protected by the landlord.

In 1995, the new administrator for your landlord has appointed fifteen people that you will never meet to decide what your place should look like. The lawn is of particular importance, even though most of the fifteen people don't know much about lawns as a general rule. They do other things, not landscaping or plumbing or sprinkler systems. Some of them, though, are part of the neighborhood beautification society, and they have decided that there are people in the neighborhood not keeping things up to snuff. They have spent a few days in other people's backyards, and they are not impressed with what they have found. So they have complained to the administrator, who will never see your yard. He in turn has created this council to reinvent regulations he has already written, but that will sound better if they are in the neighborhood's vernacular.

Here is where this analogy fails: neighborhood lawns don't support families. Ranching families make their livings from their "neighborhood lawn" in the same way someone with a home-owned business does. What if, instead of the council regulating only the quality of your lawn, they included the quality of your house? The lawn is, of course, an extension of the activity in the house—isn't it? What if there was someone in your life who told you how often to take out the trash? Someone who maintained that what we need around here are some standards! Let's identify the indicators of a healthy system: the dishes are always done every night before you go to bed. There are never unpaid bills lying around.

Better write some guidelines. We will have no dirt on the white linoleum kitchen floor. Put down the seat, dammit! Tote that barge, lift that bale, drink decaf, quit smoking, get on that Stairmaster; yes, now. The neighborhood beautification society will be around to make sure you're following the regulations.

Ecosystems are dynamic, disturbance-driven. Do you have a dysfunctional brother-in-law coming for an extended visit, wandering around, lopping the heads off the roses? Maybe he needs Rogaine, Viagra; get him into therapy. Are there flocks of migratory, preadolescent girls clogging first the hot tub in the backyard, then the bathroom, tying up the phone? Add on a bathroom. Get another phone line.

It is your responsibility to make things flow smoothly, and always your place must look pretty and undisturbed. Emotional tempests that follow the El Nino of job layoffs, the swoop and glide of the markets, shifts in the jet stream, the slipping of the magnetic field, the precession of the planets must all be managed, including that damn butterfly, fluttering his wings in the rain forest in Brazil. Standards must be adhered to, and if you want to occupy this space, you must keep your corner of the universe up to the standards that we here at the Department of *House and Garden* expect from you.

If your personal ecosystem is complicated, imagine the interactions that take place out in the larger world. Now imagine being personally, fiscally, responsible for the health of a watershed, for the quality of the soils, the length of the grass, and the clarity of the streams, whether or not there are herds of elk or dirt bikers, flood, fire, or drought romping through the countryside. In the new West of 1995, this is where we were.

⊖

A great gray mass of paper begins to coalesce in the corners of my life. It gathers like a distant wave, meeting itself across the wall of the bedroom of my little house in town. It is like a tsunami of information on the horizon, waiting to be read, after the sixth-grade essays on the geography of Antarctica, after the math quizzes are corrected.

We are inundated by a sea of words, and we will simply disappear underneath. The sea will rise and rise until there is no way to deal with it all, because none of it is ever, ever thrown away, even when its relevance is exhausted. Nights after school, I wade into the drifts of pages and pages of soulless, boring paragraphs; it is like trying to swim in tapioca. I read and highlight and underline, and I breathe and I do not drown.

Council members start hauling the paper to the meetings in those wheely suitcases with leashes. Like square dead dogs they become our companions. We could not leave them home: they are the papers we have requested, and in this prodigious documentation might be something that will be essential to the argument, to the logic, to the document we are trying to write.

Each day there is another tiny piece of the puzzle to be turned over, identified, placed. We spend days of meetings defining the words *Standard* and

Goal. We argue about the idea that ranchers should be able to "make progress toward a goal" without being penalized. Think of having to score seven hundred on the SAT the first time around. You can take a test-preparation class to improve your score. Shouldn't there be an option to help a rancher learn new ways to operate without taking away his livelihood? If there is something wrong with a stream, it can't be magically fixed overnight, but it can often repair itself over time with changes in the manner of use, without livestock being removed from it.

There are days of explanation in the little low-ceilinged rooms, of how cattle and sheep used to be run, how they are run now. A forest of fences and regulations protects the environment now. We fax actual-use numbers to the BLM office every thirty days; they know exactly how many animals we have, and where they are on the range.

The meetings are an exercise in stamina, in perseverance. Bob, the archaeologist, practices Chinese characters in the margins of his government publications during discussions, and we talk at the breaks about the huge dunes he searches in the deserts of China for microblades. He believes there are no more wild-rye meadows in Nevada, although I promise him if he comes to my house I will show him. He will resign from the RAC soon after the second Native American representative vacates his seat.

Daisy leads the charge against the ranchers, drinking from a well of emotion so deep I am amazed at the conviction behind her hostility. It is absolutely critical, everyone tells me, not to be emotional, not to get excited. Explain. Do not rant. I start to wonder whether some guy in a big cowboy hat abused her horribly when she was little.

Yet for all her energy, she doesn't understand a lot of the basic processes. What happens to water when it leaves a rocky canyon and sinks into a porous alluvial fan has nothing to do with grass or cows, and everything to do with the porosity of poorly sorted rock layers. Still, there's a disjunction here. You can't fight emotion with logic, and that's what we're being asked to do.

We spend a lot of time talking about how much grass a cow can be allowed to eat before it does damage to the resource. We draw analogies: "your front lawn" is of course my favorite. "What will happen to your front lawn in Reno if you don't mow it all summer?" I ask her. It needs to be mowed to stay healthy. "That's different," she clips. "I put a hundred inches of moisture on my lawn in a summer." Even Sierra Pacific Power has shut off the fountain in front of their Reno offices that summer.

❧

Here's what Daisy doesn't appreciate: Tim worked with four different BLM range conservationists in the twelve or so years of the last weather cycle. Like the blind men and the elephant, each of them saw the land through only a portion of the drought cycle; their opinions of the quality of our care for the range varied accordingly. Bob was assigned to us in the late '70s and early '80s. These were wet years; Bob figured from the way the range looked that we were doing everything right, that we should maybe even get more cows. Tim decided to wait. The drought years that followed, from the mid-1980s through 1996, were progressively drier. Three more "range cons" passed through our lives. "I know Jack [one of the drought-era employees] thought we were lying to him when we told him what these meadows looked like in spring," Tim said. "But it was just that he hadn't been here in the wet years, and we couldn't convince him that two years earlier, and two or three years from now, these meadows would look that way again."

It takes time to learn the geography of place, and more time to watch the effect of climate and use changes on that geography. The best BLM people were the ones who spent enough time on a piece of the land to see for themselves what happens to it in different parts of the climate cycle. Those who had spent enough time to know the people living in that landscape, to learn how they work, anticipate what they would do under stress. The best had come to believe that people are a part of the landscape too. But government personnel policy is much like corporate personnel policy: three years, and it's time for the employee to move on. The result is more a product of the flow of bureaucracy than anything else.

More than half the animals that were on the range when the Taylor Grazing Act was passed have been removed through successive cuts. After a certain point in the reduction process, it makes little difference in the quality of the range. If anything, it leaves dry feed that builds up over years, fodder for fire.

More frustrating, since the 1960s, is the political fallout. When the range is in drought, cow numbers are cut, but when the range is in a wet part of the cycle, we can't put them back. In any case, when the rain starts to fall again, the mountain looks like there has never been a cow on it.

Most of the meetings are far away, Reno, or Carson City, or Gardnerville; most of the time it's two full days. I call home every night. I can tell the boys don't want to worry me; I never get the full story of their day.

While I'm sitting in the motel room trying not to miss them, I read an editorial in the *Economist* that says, "America has been searching since the end of the Cold War for a new enemy. Except today she is looking within her own borders." Cattle ranching has become one of the Evil Empires supplied by our national media's imagination, so that people who didn't realize they were in danger can be rescued. In common parlance, range is always overgrazed, and we are always either "millionaire cowboys" or "welfare ranchers." Neither is true, but how do you even begin to educate people into what's really true when they hire somebody else to mow their lawn?

⌘

I call home one night between meetings from Carson City, exhausted. I can tell, as I ramble on about my worries with the council and the lack of understanding of the issues that there is something I am missing at the other end of the line. "Your son has some news for you." Tim passes the phone to Sam.

"Hi, Mom? I, uh, jackknifed the truck and horse trailer."

I sit, scrunched up against the uncomfortable motel pillows, looking at myself in the generic mirror; I wait for what's coming. While I am off arguing about definitions in a windowless room, my son is nearly-maybe-killing himself, and his horse, backing up a trailer on the highway, going too fast. He's okay; the horse is okay, but the truck is, uh, not okay. I can't get the details out of him. Sam's never been one for overstatement, especially on the telephone. He is wry, humorous about it, but not very forthcoming. "I'll show you where it happened," he says, "when you get home." It's that what-could-have-been that makes you hold your breath.

⌘

I weave my way through heavy traffic after the RAC meeting: Gardnerville to Carson City to Reno, three urban areas connected by fifty-mile-an-hour two-lane highway through what used to be farms and ranches, now rapidly becoming strip malls and developments, rubber-tomahawk gift shops and gas stations. There are little acreages out there where people pretend they're still living in the country: a horse, a bunch of dogs, and some old trucks in the backyard. It is rush hour, and there will be four more hours of highway beyond the city.

Up ahead, the road is clogged with flashing lights and vehicles. Ambulance, highway patrol, something that looks like the dogcatcher's truck parked in the middle of the road. We crawl up on the accident: a pinto horse, sorrel and white, somebody's pet, or one of those animals someone gives a kid who doesn't have time to ride it. The animal has literally been caught in traffic. The horse sits unaccountably in the center lane, his long neck drenched in blood. I can't believe he is sitting up straight until I pull even in the creeping parade. Both his forelegs stretch out in front of him in a way no horse's legs are meant to go, broken at the shoulder. A highway patrolman in Oakleys waves me through, scowling. It takes most of the miles home to leave that scene behind me.

~

Some days, a few of the many, the council meets out in the meadows and the canyons and the hillsides. We look at grasses and woody debris and willows poking their heads up through the sandbars. It is beautiful and real, after the windowless cubicles. It is where we try to understand our business, where we feel the truth of our actions.

One trip took us to Soldier Meadows, an old ranch at the end of the west arm of the Black Rock Desert. Even for Nevada, this place is way out there. It had been a cavalry fort in the years after the Civil War. White-stucco buildings, a big barn, irrigated meadows at the end of a long desert valley. One hundred thirty years later, it's still the last outpost, the jumping-off point into the Empty Quarter. I had spent the better part of a year once near here, back in my geologist life; the land feels familiar to me.

Our destination is the Summit Lake exclosure, a big, steep-sided basin drained by rocky, shallow little creeks. Exclosure means "close out," and there has been recreation, but no livestock grazing here for twenty years. Our caravan of government Suburbans negotiates the twisting jeep trail up through sagebrush and little groves of aspen. We lunch at an old sheep camp; there is a cabin in the trees, an ancient stone beehive oven next to the creek. People feel more friendly, talk more freely in the open.

The Summit Lake Paiute Reservation is at the bottom of this canyon. This stream feeds Summit Lake, in which is a population of Lahontan cutthroat trout, a Threatened Species. Fish numbers counted through the trap by tribal fish biologists have dropped steadily since a high in 1975. This was the reason the basin was closed to grazing, to protect the riparian area near the creek banks for the threatened fish.

The riparian area, indeed, looks lush and beautiful. There are lots of trees, fallen and otherwise, lots of underbrush. Willows block most of the access to the creek. We see three or four groups of campers, tents set up right on the bank, trucks backed up next to their tents, in the few places where there is access to the water.

The creek itself seems perfect at first glance. But the uplands, the hillsides that feed sediment and water downhill to the creek, don't look so good. The last time I was here, in 1979, the bunchgrass was thick along the hillsides and over the top of the mountain. I remember a herd of twenty antelope bounding out in front of me as I crested the slope above us.

Old plants not renewed by the trimming of grazing have grown rank, weak; there has been less reseeding of new grasses. When hoofed animals walk the hillsides, their hoofprints form small catchment basins in which seeds and water collect. Without disturbance on the hillside, the grass seeds, the water, and the sediment wash down into the creek. These hillsides are gullied, the grass much sparser than two decades past.

Worse for the fish, silt has choked the crossing of the creek, traversed now only by four-wheelers and pickup trucks. Grass has grown up in the silty bottom and now pokes up thick above the crossing. Although shallow water still runs through it, the fish cannot negotiate it. Because of this, there are now two separate populations of cutthroats: those that migrate up from Summit Lake to the silted-in crossing, and those in the headwaters of the stream above.

I remember this basin full of grass instead of sagebrush, and the stream running clear and fresh across gravel in this shallow crossing. The people on this tour may well not trust my memory: I am defending my home and my way of life, the lives and homes of others like me. If there were BLM pictures of this place at that time, we could trust them, they say. And there probably were. But nobody knows where the pictures are now, because the employees who took them, who knew this place, are long gone. Photos that ranchers took from the same time period are suspect. They are fighting for their lives; therefore, their evidence is tainted.

On the way down the canyon we park all those Suburbans and stand in a meadow. It is matted with dead grass underneath like a teenager's head of hair that gets combed only on top. Baby sagebrush is sprouting everywhere. People remark that once this meadow had been bigger. That's what I remember too. A man with some credentials explains that with no big grazing animals to knock back the brush, the meadow is disappearing. In a few years it will all be sagebrush, like so much of the rest of this canyon. The group agrees that twenty years of no grazing at all might not be the best thing for the landscape in this particular case. The rancher who still holds the grazing permit for this now unusable parcel offers the suggestion that a herd of cattle grazed through here could knock back the brush, open up the meadows a bit. That seems like a good idea to everyone. People nod as Daisy comments that the cattle would have to be tended all the time: a quarter mile of fenceline requested by the ranchers on the ridgeline has not been built, cannot seem to be approved by the BLM. It would be possible for the animals to drift out of the exclosure into some other territory, and this would never do. So a cowboy would have to be found who could stay with them. The rancher winces.

"Well, where are all the cowboys?" Daisy demands. The rancher shakes his head.

"We can't find them. There just aren't many around anymore." Real cowboys, who know how to run cows, not the actors you see on TV driving minivans and pickup trucks to the rodeo, are a very scarce commodity. They can't live in the two-dimensional virtual reality in which the rest of America functions. They are solitary souls; many widowed or divorced, many on the high side of fifty. They live a lean life. They need only a space to throw their bedroll for the winter, a place to stay warm. But more than that, they need to be useful. After a half century of working their bodies, their hands, their hearts out, the things they know have no application in our society. And we are a society with no respect for its elders. With all our panic over endangered species, you'd think we'd notice we are driving them out of existence.

⌁

In the canyon above Summit Lake, the council is pleasantly surprised to find it has been *making progress toward* a goal. We are very close indeed to agreeing, all of us, on what needs to be done with this particular piece of country at this particular point in time. The rule is, in working groups, you stay till you have an agreement. No doctor appointments, no bailing out.

This isn't the mandate for this group, but it's working that way this day. We can all feel it, and it feels good. And then John, the district BLM guy from Carson City, says, "Well, I gotta plane to catch. Who's riding with me?" And just like that the day ends. No closure, no agreement, just some government guy's personal agenda. Nothing is resolved, on the fence, on the fish, on the exclosure.

Susie Stokke, resource manager for the BLM in Surprise Valley, where Sophie and Linda live, had been on the tour, too. Later, she will say to me, "You guys were really close to getting something done out there. What do you think happened?"

Bureaucracy is what happened that day. I looked back at the minutes of that meeting recently, to try to reconstruct what had been said. The unscheduled stop in the canyon above Summit Lake, at the ends of the earth beyond the Black Rock Desert, was not included. Today it's the moment that people remember on that tour. But officially, it has ceased to exist.

Ultimately, we finished our work on the Standards and Guidelines. We incorporated the words that gave the rancher some leeway, would give him a grace period of one year, if he could be shown to be *making progress toward* the goals he might have fallen short on, given the variables of climate and resources. We reached the consensus we had been mandated to reach. We submitted our guidelines. We felt pride of authorship. It had been nearly three long, difficult volunteer years.

That summer, in-house editors at the BLM changed the words. The language we had fought for so hard was eliminated by what one lobbyist involved in the process told me were "midlevel policy wonks." All that will-of-the-people blathering had been just that.

A friend of mine who works in a state regulatory office asked me, "Why are you surprised? That's the process. People start out all excited, ready to make a difference, really *get someplace.* Then after you build this thing, and everybody loves it, or can at least live with it, it goes away. When it comes back, it does what they wanted it to do after all, not what you decided on. And it moves you a quarter of an inch, in some direction. Then later you do it all again."

Sometimes you can do something about the way things are, and sometimes you can't. The powerful continue to manipulate the powerless. You can't let it poison you. Take what you can from your experience. Then just go again the next day. Never forget, and never give up either. When consensus fails, when the people on the ground are trumped by upper management, find another way.

&

In the meantime, summer ripens. Between meetings, away from all the talk, I am *making progress toward* another goal. I am still learning to drive cows.

Antelope Valley is not really a valley, but a piece of foothill country that flanks the mountain like the wide collar on a schoolgirl's dress. Under the fabric, her collarbone is the structural hinge of the Continental Divide. Down her back the rain slides north into the Columbia River watershed. Down her chest rain runs into the Great Basin. At the point of her left shoulder is the little buckaroo camp we call Wilder; her outstretched arm points into the high country of summer. About two hundred head of cattle spend the eight weeks of early turnout season in Antelope. In July we gather them and move them across the highway into their late-summer pasture.

Antelope is full of little nooks and crannies, green meadows rising through rosebushes to granite crags. Purples rust into yellow; old homesteads hide down in the draws near secret springs. Most of the ranges in Nevada break east and west: shadows in the canyons define a geography that becomes familiar. In Antelope, the land breaks north and south. The same light conceals what it defines in other places.

When we pull the trailer up to the wire gate, shapes of animals barely emerge from darkness. I expect Tim to drop Sam and me off at this lower fence, and we will gather cows and calves across Antelope. I imagine he and Steve, the hired man, will drive around, park the truck and trailer, and meet us at the opposite fence, eight miles away.

Plans for the day change. Or perhaps I have imagined things incorrectly. Steve unloads and cinches up. He and Sam wait politely while I get ready. There is, of course, no conversation. Steve goes around the few animals that hang by the fence, and they obediently set off down the road. I drop back a little and watch the cowboys trot out ahead.

Yesterday they left twenty head in the branding corral up ahead, a small wood-and-wire enclosure in the middle of the valley. There are no houses or barns or sheds anywhere near. It's just a halfway house, a place to keep cattle overnight before continuing the longer drive over the hill into the Harness Place, the old homestead with a fenced meadow, which is today's destination. Steve swings down at the corral, opens the gate, and these animals join the others on the trail.

Sam is confident now. The dynamic between us has changed in the last few years, since he's been riding with his dad. He passed me by several years ago in Tim's School of Cowboying. He knows the country, knows what to do. He's patient, methodical. He's also a cross between the two of us. He remembers what it's like not to know what's going on. And he knows how to tell me what he's thinking.

Steve peels off into the shadowed draws of the alluvial fan. Sam and I follow the bunch for a couple of hours across the foothills. The trail parallels a fault line, and we pass just above several steep draws, which drop away below the trail. At the top we hold the bunch to wait for the men. We can hear them, behind us somewhere, hollering at the bulls who would rather fight with each other than move. There aren't supposed to be any cattle left up here, except the ones we are bringing across. The first gather got most of them, Tim has said.

We dawdle on the top of the ridge, holding the cow-calf pairs in the bright, hot morning. I see movement out of the corner of my eye and trot ahead to investigate. Around the south side, the sunny, early-morning side of the hill, are at least fifty head, staring like kids caught smoking in the parking lot. To Tim this would imply a broken fence somewhere. I just see a bunch of cows someplace they're not supposed to be. I wave at Sam; he circles around behind, and we gather them into the main bunch, now close to eighty head. He spies another handful on the next parallel ridge and goes off to get them.

Meanwhile, the cattle I am holding are getting restless. I can still hear the bulls fighting behind us. I decide to nudge the bunch along the ridge. It's too soon.

Tim trots around from behind me somewhere, stops them. "Steve's going to need these cows to move those bulls along," he admonishes. I wait.

Finally the bulls crest the brow of the hillside, three of them. Two red, one white, all huge rolling shoulders, raw power and dust. It is mostly a shoving match, the older white bull and one of the red ones pushing the third, younger one out of their territory.

"Keep back," Tim hollers. "When they're fighting, they'll run right over the top of you."

At last they turn and line out. I contour the steep hillside below the herd. Steve is in the drag. Tim and Sam are both down in the draws. The last time I was here, I'm thinking, I got too far behind them, and they snuck off down into those canyons on me. So I ride right below them on the trail. Out of sight of Steve, I can hear him hollering.

"Get a line on it, you sonsabitches!"

Later that evening Tim will explain, "You had the herd too high on the hill. Steve was trying to ease them down to the saddle into the Harness Place, and you weren't letting him."

I go over my lessons in my head. *You have to watch everything.* Remember that you're part of a whole, a line of cowboys moving a lot of animals across a great deal of space, even if there are only two of you. Try to see what you do in relation to the others. *Everything you do affects everyone else.* We either benefit from your presence, or we have to compensate for you.

This day is different, I think. We're not driving cows down the flat, but along a steep hillside. I can't see the other riders; I'm too far ahead. Pressured from front and back, two pair squirt out behind me, and sure enough, go pounding down the draw. I curse, turn my horse, and crash after them through tall sagebrush.

Sam appears, on a faster horse, overtakes and turns them, gets them stopped. I ride back to the bunch, not looking at Steve. I can feel him up there, though, steaming. Tim is still down below; I see him every so often, outflanking runaways in and out of the draws ahead of us. I guess things aren't going too well.

Eventually the trail leads over the saddle into the Harness Place. Its triangular meadow slides down the canyon between steep rock walls; there are apple, plum, and cherry trees down below near a trough-size pond. I can see a stream of dust as cattle dribble through a hole in the fence, a half mile below us. We wait while Sam rides down to the break; he turns the beasts back into the meadow, plugs the leak. I see him turn his head, look at something I can't see. Steve opens the gate and the herd moves through into tall, green grass. I turn to ask him something, but he is gone. Sam reappears. "Leave the gate open, Mom. Dad'll be back over the top in a minute with some more." He disappears too.

Without saying anything, they all know what to do. Should I help? Should I stay here? Will the cows try to escape the meadow through this gate? It's as likely as anything else, I think; I stay. Somehow I feel as though there must have been a way for me to do better.

I climb down off the roan horse, tuck myself gratefully deep into the shade of a granite boulder veined with rusty red quartz. In the shade it's so much cooler. I lean my hot face against the rough rock. The bulls' bellowing echoes back and forth between gray granite walls. It anchors the sharp, high melody of a bird whose song I've never heard before.

At last Tim finally pushes six high-headed, wild-eyed cows and their feisty calves through the gate. The bulls are fighting, the cows are hot, Tim glares. He swings down at the spring, turns to his sopping wet horse, pulls the cinch, and drags the saddle off him in one sweaty motion. He leads him under the only tree and lets him cool off before watching him drop his head to the spring and drink huge horse gulps. Tim's blue chambray shirt is dripping too. He stands shaking his head, wipes his forehead with the back of the hand that holds his big black hat. It's ten-thirty in the morning.

That night, I sit in the cool shade of the house, scrunched up in my chair. Tim rattles ice into tall glasses in the kitchen, making highballs. I listen to him moving quietly through the routine of evening.

"It's not that I'm mad at you," he says, standing at the doorway between the kitchen and the living room. "Sometimes I'm just mad at the day, the way things are going. Sometimes I can't yell at the person I want to, so I yell at you. I know it's not right." He walks over, leans down to hand me my drink. Beads of condensation pick up the light. I turn the glass in my hand, watching the drops of moisture slide down, cooling the glass.

"It's the dailiness of it that's important," he says, settling into his chair. "How many stampedes are there, after all?" he says.

"Well, none."

"No. That shit never happens. It's just what people imagine, the excitement of life that appeals to them. It's the routine that gets you through the year, not the Hollywood stuff. It's easy to get people for branding. Lots of noise, smoke, horses going every which way. It's not nearly as easy to get anybody to help you drive cows. The romance of that disappears pretty quickly. No matter how smart you are you can't anticipate everything." He looks at me, cocks his head, quizzical. "You did a good job out there today."

⟜

I think of the best days of our life together; most of them have been wordless and on horseback. Cold, hot, rainy, snow blowing in my face: the day we brought the leppie calf back, snowing so hard we couldn't see a thing. I was frozen solid, but I never felt more alive. That calf made it too. Another day, folds of hills and canyons blushing red, we topped the highest ridge anywhere around just at daybreak. You turned without a word, and pointed. Three buck deer, antlers like tree branches, lounging on the highest basalt ledge.

Show me the things nobody sees but you. Keep showing me. Your silence, sometimes is more articulate than words.

⤳ Cherry Pie

I AM RUSHING TO PICK CHERRIES, ONE OF THOSE HOT MORNINGS WHEN I have been dreaming of not being able to open my eyes. It is eight o'clock before I can wake up, and I wander around the house, shaking off the heavy mask of sleep. The cowboys have been leaving around four in the morning; when the dogs settle down, I drop back to sleep.

Through my dreams I remember Tim reminding me that Sam would be waiting for me at Wilder, the summer buckaroo camp, at nine-thirty. I need to pick cherries before I pick him up. Now I'm awake. I throw my thermos and a cup on the seat, a ladder and an empty cooler in the back of the truck. Cookie comes along for company.

Gates are nothing but a hassle by yourself. Stop the truck, remember not to put it in park or it'll blow the fuse. If you do, then you have to shut off the truck. Then you'll have to find those needle-nose pliers, change the fuse, start it up, take it out of park, take out the fuse, and put it in the side pocket with the pliers. Put the truck in neutral, set the emergency brake. Open the gate, look for snakes, look for cows. Drive through the gate, put it in neutral, set the brake. Shut the gate. Drive to the next gate.

The cherry tree is in a lovely little pocket of meadow surrounded by granite canyon walls. Twenty miles north of headquarters, it is another homestead absorbed by the larger ranch in the years following World War I. The orchard here must be a century old. Apple trees, plum trees, the kinds of plums that turn just black with red hearts dripping sweetness, planted by some long-ago hand on an east-facing slope, high enough to escape the freezing air of spring mornings that hangs on the valley floors, nips the blossoms from fruit trees planted on the flat.

Big yellow rattlesnakes guard the orchard, but most of the tall grass has been grazed off. We'll have plenty of time to see each other, the snakes and I. Usually that's all that's necessary, a little warning, so a person can avoid a confrontation.

There is only one cherry tree, a small one. Old pieces of farm machinery, a cherry picker, and a meadow rake are parked close around it. Inside this rampart, steel posts draped with rusty hog wire—layers of defense raised at different times to keep marauders away. The tree is hard to get to, all right. One branch, loaded with handfuls of ripe fruit, has still been torn partway down. These are the last cherries this branch will bear. I balance my bowl on the rake, climb up and steady myself, and prepare to finish what that thief has started.

Pie cherries, sour and brilliant. They are so ripe the juice runs down my arm as I pick them off the high branches. Wasps cling to their scarlet ripeness in the sun. I pick and pick. At first I'm jumpy, feel the pressure to fill the bowl and get on with all the things lined up before me in the day. A smooth gray thrush yammers at me, thoroughly invaded by my huge presence. The birds have begun working on this tree, but haven't yet cleaned it out completely. It is slow work to fill the big bowl, one, two, three fruits at a time. Soon there is only the sound of the bees, lowing of cattle in the deep shade under nearby willows, the trickling of water down through the yellow orchard grass.

I know I should get Sam, so I start collecting my bowls and ladders for the trip to Wilder. He and Steve have probably gotten the cows pushed down to the well by now, and they're sitting in the hot sun at buckaroo camp waiting for me. I have Steve's pickup, fresh from the shop, after that little backing-up adventure Sam had with the trailer. The rear and side windows are sealed with duct tape and cardboard that says, "Daniel Smith, Artist Materials." Sam's uncle Hank has somehow unfolded the crumpled cab, with a backhoe and a log, he says, until it is nearly its old shape. The passenger side door now opens. Only a few shards of green glass sparkle in the bed of the truck, and that red roan horse just has a bad scratch on his nose. I think about that other horse, the one on the highway in Carson City, the one that didn't escape.

It is good for me to get back out into the desert, after the days of RAC meetings. I heal myself in the space and silence, away from the noise, the casual violence of commerce and industry that is the city. It takes about two days now, one for each day of meetings, for me to feel normal.

Make a pie with cherries that you pick yourself. Bring them home, wash them. Take an afternoon to pit them, one cherry at a time. All afternoon, five plastic quart bags maybe. Do it without the radio on, in the quiet of your kitchen, alone with your thoughts. Or no thoughts. Clean the sticky juice from your hands, your arms, and legs, unless you're more careful than I am. Pour the cherries in a pan, warm them up with sugar and some tapioca. These are really sour cherries, and red, red. Use more sugar, maybe.

Sam helps me pit the cherries for a while in the darkened kitchen of this summer afternoon. Blinds drawn, swamp cooler humming. Hot sunshine outside. We talk about college; we talk about the daily stuff. We talk about nothing in sweet, companionable silence. I say without thinking, "I'm toying with the idea of making a pie."

He's a supportive son. Encouraging. Leaves me to my musings for a two-hour siesta. He knows enough to leave a silent space for the potentiality of a pie to perhaps become reality.

I'm one of those people that really can't make a decent piecrust. The pie always tastes pretty good, but for looks, I believe the adjective would be *lame*. I'm usually okay with the dry ingredients, flour and sugar and a little salt; I'm even getting to be better about the Crisco, which I cut into the dry ingredients bravely. It's reassuring that the flour's cold. I've started keeping it in the freezer in summer because of the ants, but I can see now that piecrust is the real reason to do so. I can feel the panic rise into my throat as I start to dribble ice water over the flour and butter mixture. A calm and gentle voice echoes in my memory, "Just don't fuck with it too much."

Maybe I'm not fucking with it enough. It's not holding together. I am almost afraid to touch the mixture in my big steel bowl. Maybe the flour is too dry; after all, this is the desert.

"Well," the voice says, "just put in a little more water. It's okay, really. You just don't want it to get pasty, and if you handle it too much, of course, it will get tough." And of course, after you put in the water, it's Too Late. Putting in the water is the point of no return. "People," the voice says, "just get too worked up over it. It's just pie."

The voice belongs to my friend Kate. Kate is my pie counselor. She has taught me everything I know about fruit, the canning and cooking thereof, and especially she has made me brave enough to occasionally attempt a cherry pie.

Whenever Kate comes to visit with her family, she has a new piecrust recipe. "It's so easy, you'll want to make a pie every week," she says, encouraging me.

She walks me though it, step by step. Shows me with the first crust; I will manage the second. Her long, delicate fingers gently manipulate little blobs of Crisco into perfect, pea-size particles in oceans of flour and salt. This crust is half butter, half Crisco. We'll use the Cuisinart to mix the flour and the fat. "No, it's not cheating," she says. "It's just pie."

Then, "What's happening here?" she asks. A crack widens in the pale-yellow circle she is rolling into the first pie shell. It mirrors the furrow deepening in her tan forehead. "I've never made a pie like this before." Her long fingers are careful, confident. Still the crust has no body. "If this happened to me when I was first learning to make pie, I never would have done it!" she says, as the upper crust betrays her. She compromises on a lattice crust, but still the dough has no strength even to be woven. "Damn," she says. "I'm having pie anxiety, for the first time in my life." I feel relief.

The telephone rings. You know how mothers sense when their children are in trouble. It is Kate's mom, the matriarch of pie. She is tall and dark, like Kate. She has been gardening and weaving rugs in her stone house in Utah. Perhaps she has been imagining us making pie. She laughs when I explain our morning. Sweet woman that she is, she comforts me. "Oh, you know, once I made a pie in Seattle, and I just couldn't make it work, no matter what I did." Once, years ago, in that humid air, one pie crust out of ten thousand flawless pies. Well.

"God, I feel like a beer," Kate says after it's all over, pies in the oven. "Maybe your kitchen has bad pie karma," she says, looking around. "Maybe it's too dry. Tomorrow we'll just use butter."

❧

In my August kitchen, I do manage to get a crust rolled out, although it falls to pieces under my rolling pin. Am I pressing too hard? The crust seems thin, or maybe my pie plate is too big. It seems larger than nine inches. Of course, it's a handmade pie plate; these handmade things are never standard, but then that's part of their charm. I cheat and use a pastry cloth, given to me by another friend who is not afraid of pie. I have a pint of tapioca and cherry juice left over when I load the shell, which I'm afraid to add: sogginess. It will make good hotcake syrup.

The pie is not too bad, tart, but flaky. A still, hot afternoon, bees buzzing, calves swishing their tails under deep shade. A light crust, if not a visual masterpiece; a pie that will remind me of hot yellow grass and tiny green frogs clinging to the edge of the ditch where I washed the sticky juice from my arms. Someday I'll make another pie, maybe sometime in November. I still have four bags of frozen, pitted scarlet cherries, heavy with the juice of desert summer. I will remember where they came from.

⌐⊃

Between the cherries I picked this morning and the pie, there was a fire. It was not a big fire, I would discover later. But all fires are scary, and this was my first one.

The cherries had been sitting on the table in the kitchen in their cooler, unpitted, waiting. It was siesta time, the summer almost over. Men and animals alike draw the deepest rest from the afternoon they can; there are just these few days of summer left.

Miguel came in, in a rush. "*Una llamara por favor* . . ." It's always another phone call, to his wife in Mexico, with his Mexican calling card, directions in a language I need to get better at. . . . I resent the intrusion. No, he says, he needs to call Dan. Then I smell the smoke on him. He sees me smell it.

"*Fuego, Carolina, a la pompa,*" he urges me. I yell at Tim, run across the road to get Steve. Dan and somebody else come barreling through the yard, throwing a plume of dust behind them. They head for a column of smoke. I can see it from my kitchen window, rising from the willows.

Tim growls at me, "You don't have to run; it's okay." He makes some calls.

"Do we need shovels?" I ask.

"Not if it's in the willows," he replies. "Water."

How can he anticipate this? I wonder. We climb into Tim's truck, Steve in back, Sam and I in front, putting on our shoes. We drive to the top of the hill across the river and sit there, looking.

I'm biting my tongue, but he feels my question. "Shovels won't help this fire if it's in the willows. We're going to need water." The grass under the willows is dense, waist high. Fire travels too fast, shovels tangle in the brush. The river is on one side, the irrigation ditch on the other. There is no wind yet.

"Drive down the west side of the Barn Field. Check it out," Tim tells me, as we go back to the house, where he will get out and call the Denio fire truck. "Stay near the radio."

Steve and I bump across the pasture into thick willows that fringe the river. He has never been in these fields. The willows have grown so thick we can't see the fire, just the soft, green-gray fronds sliding across the hood.

I can hear Tim on the radio, talking to someone. Steve backs into a clearing, parks off the track. He trots off into the willows with a shovel. I can hear Antonio and Martin, hollering at each other. Hot smoke drifts with snatches of excited Spanish through the gracefully waving fronds. I stand there for a while, waiting, and then I can't stand it. I pull the truck closer to the crackling sound, still unable to see.

I nose the pickup through dense brush and tall, blond grass, right into the middle of the burn. Miguel, Antonio, Martin move methodically back and forth between the irrigation ditch buried in green willows and the blackened earth, smoking and smoldering under their feet. They hand me buckets. Sam emerges from the other side of the thicket. We take turns filling five-gallon containers, dumping them on smoking knots of willow roots, heaps of last year's dried manure hidden under burnt-black grass.

The little lime-green fire truck from Denio rumbles into the clearing. The community has bought it for six thousand dollars, depreciated, from the BLM. Men from Denio have spent time refurbishing pumps and hoses. It looks brand new, which I guess is how fire trucks are supposed to look. I climb on top, to get out of the way. We unroll red hoses. Tim drags one into the smoking brush.

Miguel and Antonio and Martin have put the flames mostly out with their bucket patrol. The ranch water truck rumbles up. Sam takes a hose as Denio Dan, the retired firefighter, shows him how to drape the hose around his neck, focusing the spray more easily. They look like snake handlers, striding through the brush with long, red pythons. I stay on top of the fire truck, coiling and uncoiling the red hose as Tim moves in and out of the willows, keeping the python from tangling his legs.

The fire is contained in a couple of hours. It has been all consuming, for that time, but as fires go, it was nothing.

꩜

Tuesday morning, August third, a year later. Hot and quiet, heavy summer. My boys are gathering cattle in the high basins at Maggie Creek and Holloway Mountain. They have most of the ranch horses in a corral on the mountain, and they've been driving up there at three o'clock and get saddled by daylight.

It is breathless, sultry, at the deserted headquarters. I gather a few pairs that have slipped into the alfalfa field from somewhere, put them away. I garden some, fold laundry. I look for cattle in the lane. Time holds its breath, waiting for something.

I take the dogs, chained up in the shade in August heat—they'll kill themselves, working in this weather, but it drives them crazy not to go. We ride through the field, alfalfa and red clover, splashing in the checks where the water has worked its way down from the crossing ditch.

I finish my circle, still restless. Ride home, make lunch. Tim and Sam come in, eat, fall onto the couches for a siesta. The south wind is picking up. I watch the elms waving away to the north.

At two-thirty, lightning strikes on the road to our summer sheep camp, and at Deep Creek, too high in the hills for us to do anything about it from the ground. Shovels, water, radios; cowboys shaken out of sleep.

The fire is a wicked red smile at the base of the half circle of volcanic hills we call the Horseshoe. The Denio fire truck is there when we arrive. Someone calls the BLM. *"We can't tell you not to fight it,"* the dispatch lady says, *"and we have no resources available right now."* There are thirty-two lightning strikes right around town.

We're on our own.

The fire, only a few acres across, moves east toward the canyon, then north. It swirls a small circle in a fickle wind. Denio Dan takes the fire truck, loads up cowboys and shovels, and drives to the other end of the fire; it is still several hundred yards north of the road, and burning parallel to it in the basalt boulders and sagebrush. Hard to get to in the little truck. Not big, not yet.

The road's ungraded shoulders are full of dry weeds, but the fire truck wets them down; it will probably stop the flames. The wind changes again, the fire backing south and west. Smoke rolls; dirty, opaque.

We move the vehicles. Sam and I find a pipe wrench and drive to the windmill a quarter mile away downwind. We lift the heavy iron pipe and screw it into the connection that will bring water to the two big, round troughs. The fire truck holds only 250 gallons of water. It can refill here.

The sheep camp road turns south below the windmill and runs for several miles before turning west at the hot springs and connecting to the highway that divides our valley. The pickups gather below the windmill, watching. Curious humans, fascinated by fire. A stinkbug crawls across the gravel. I watch him for a minute, then pick him up and toss him into the back of the truck. Cows and calves gather in the corner of the crested wheat field, nervous at the smell of smoke.

The fire eats a fence post, crosses into the seeding, into the main chute of the valley. Here, convection currents make invisible Ferris wheels, cycling hot summer air high up into the atmosphere, bringing cool air down; dust devils often dance along the meeting line of the convection cells. On any late-summer afternoon, this valley is a wind furnace. Tim has decided to open the gates, just in case. We won't see him again for a while.

We watch, fascinated: in the convection of valley air circulation, the fire grows into a flame-cored whirlwind, sixty feet tall. It sucks the smaller flames into itself, black smoke towering, turning in a slower column around it. It is a live thing, beautiful, terrible.

Antonio leans on his shovel at the bend in the road, one elbow on the old wooden sign that points the way to Lovely Valley. He is silhouetted by smoke—and then suddenly, by flame. The whirlwind roars, blowing the heat south. The tongue of fire that has run west across the fenceline into the seeding turns, full on us.

The pickups easily outdistance the flames, but the big vehicles, the water truck and the grader, are slower. I drive south with my thirteen-year-old niece, Magen. She came with her dad, now piloting the water truck. The red whirlwind paces us, cutting southwest across the flat. This is when I get nervous, and I tromp the accelerator of the quirky old truck that doesn't always start, and sometime dies on you. It will be good to be out of the way of this thing, I think.

Jackrabbits dash back and forth in front of the pickup. The dust is bad; we roll the windows up. The sky darkens. We cannot see the sun.

The gravel road turns west across the fire's path to reach the highway, and we beat the fire there, and turn north. It is then I see the cattle, close to the highway, running before a wall of flame, coming fast. We drive, against the wind. Two small parcels of land where horse people have moved in crouch in the fire's path: double-wides, new barns, corrals, trucks. One man is driving out with his horses loaded, two vans following, full of stuff.

We pass a woman on a three-wheeler with a shovel, looking at us over her shoulder. A man with a little Bobcat loader is making tiny circles around the power poles in the path of the wall of fire. Several carloads of tourists, looking startled. Cows and calves, running down the shoulder of the road, all backed by the red tower of smoke and flame. It reminds me of the Wizard of Oz. We are all displaced; the rules are all different inside a twister.

When it seems like we are behind the fire line, I pull over to the shoulder of the highway. As soon as I stop, Tim's brother Hank is at the door, grabbing the radio.

"Antonio, Antonio," he shouts into the mike.

"Antonio, did you get through?" No answer.

"Antonio, where is Dan?"

Nothing. Black smoke has rolled across the road. Some of the vehicles in the racing caravan must have turned the other way. We can't see them, and the fire has jumped the highway. It has split into four fires, and now burns in all directions, unstoppable, it seems, until the wind dies.

Another big cloud of smoke hangs to the north over Denio; someone says on the radio that there's a fire at Wilder. Get back to the headquarters, get some saddles. We may need to open some gates, get the animals out of there.

Then I am in another pickup, driving north, to find saddles at the neighbors', to catch horses. It is twenty miles over Denio Summit to the next valley, straddling the Oregon-Nevada state line. In that valley, another fire burns, started by the same dry lightning. It is a line of smoke drawn like a crooked seam in a nylon stocking along the base of a long rise of hills. The hills lead to Wilder, and all the summer country. The foothills are dotted with cattle, just starting the move down from the summer pasture, with antelope, with deer, sage hen. It is important to keep the fire low, out of the cheat grass.

Teri, our postmistress, lives nearby. She is just finishing disking around her house with a little blue tractor. She loans our hired man her tractor. He takes off up the road, to try to clean the weed-choked ditches before the fire meets the gravel. The wind is steady, from the north.

Teri grabs her shovel, and we follow. Mostly we sit in the pickup and wait, stand on the road, wait, lean on shovels, wait. There's no point getting in front of something you're not going to stop. Ranchers from the Oregon side of the line are building a firebreak along an old windmill road, parallel to the fire line, uphill. They will try to stop the fire there. The small tractor growls and clanks over rocks back and forth along the firebreak, silhouetted by a smoky sunset. Other pickups appear from the north, black shapes with headlights on in the smoke, dragging, spraying. Volunteer firemen from Denio light a line of backfire, a water tender following closely behind. The wind holds steady, and the backfire does what it's supposed to, growing toward the main fire, away from the firebreak. The fires seem attracted to each other; when the two fire lines meet, the flames roar up, hissing, waves of fire crashing on each other, and then die surrounded by their blackened landscape.

The community fights the Denio fire, and in a few hours, the community wins. One lone BLM fire engine from Burns, Oregon, lumbers up near the end. "Well, you guys got this one," the redheaded kid driving grins. We have a little chat about him being out of his jurisdiction, and we ask if he wouldn't mind slipping over the hill to look at our other fire, since he's in the neighborhood on this crazy night. Noncommittal, he drives on to check the perimeter of this burn.

The huge red glow of it lights the night sky over the summit, and we head back south. Tim says, "It looks bad, but I was more worried about what the Denio fire could do." But soon it would be different.

As we crest the summit, we are moving toward the gates of hell. Fire burns through 180 degrees of vision, all across the valley, up into the foothills on both mountainsides. The highway is clogged with stopped traffic at the Harness Place hill. Travelers stand on the darkened roadway in baggy shorts and Tevas, watching; they let their dogs out to pee; children sleep in backseats.

We sit on the shoulder of the road for a long time, watching the fire move north. It eats one power pole after another. Cows and calves are bawling for each other in the brush somewhere. There's not much we can do till daylight now.

Dan roars up in the grader. The north seeding fence runs five miles across draws and sagebrush hills; it's still north of the fire, but the flames are getting closer. Its eastern edge climbs the foothills into the high country where our two herders are, each with their band of sheep. I wonder if they are watching, from up there.

The fire is in the sagebrush draws, coming slower, then faster. Tim sends Denny and Sam in behind Dan to cut the fences so no animals will be trapped. We watch the grader lights get smaller and smaller, bobbing in and out of sight as he crawls across the valley. For a while there is only the sound of the fire crackling, cattle bellowing, the low growl of the grader disappearing, and the wind.

The kid in the Burns fire engine shows up at ten-thirty that night, and we listen to BLM dispatch traffic on his radio. The fire on the other end is burning all across the valley, west to Big Creek, east into our foothill lambing grounds. The kid calls in his location, and dispatch replies, "Thank you, but please don't call in any more fires now. We have nothing to send you. I'm sorry." Someone gives me a cold beer, and when I drink it, it makes me dizzy. I remember it's been a long time since I ate.

The pickup headlights flash as the cowboys turn around at the far fence corner. We watch the lights come slowly closer. Sam tells me later they cut the fence in four places, but there were still cattle running toward the flames, away into the dark, running everywhere.

Tim thinks we had better get the three horses that are still at Wilder; we'll need them at first light to gather the animals. It is eleven o'clock. When we pull into the yard a half hour later, we see the hired man's truck parked with headlights pointing into the moonless wrangle pasture. The dark is total, except for the fires. I see another glow in Long Hollow, twenty miles north of us. Steens Mountain is on fire. We've heard from panicked Oregon ranchers that Secretary Babbitt is fishing up in the Steens, politicking the local people for a national monument. Along with millions of other western acres, it's already planned to be part of this administration's environmental legacy. I hope it's a crappy day for him too.

Finally, I see a flashlight beam, shining on legs of men and horses. Quietly swishing through the grass, clacking a stone, the men bring them into the barn. One of the horses has gotten into a fence. The flashlight plays across darker stripes in his bay chest and front legs where the wire has ripped him. We load him up. Tim stays the night on the hill; the rest of us drive home to try to sleep.

The drive down through the valley is silent, tense. Flames burn to the pavement on both sides of the road. The red line of fire outlines our neighbors' houses; a big tractor growls along in the dark, churning firebreaks around dry pastures. The neighbors save each other, this first day and night. There are fires everywhere, and all we know is that the BLM will try to fly this fire tomorrow to assess the damage. Back in the house, too exhausted to sleep, I shower, wander around; get coffee ready for three-thirty breakfast. Even the house smells like burnt brush.

I wake well before the alarm, pull on my smoky jeans. Make coffee, bacon, sausage, eggs. Nobody really ate yesterday, and probably nobody will eat today.

Somehow men and horses converge at the hill where Tim is at first light. It is an endless iteration this day: drive here, get horses, come back, meet the trailer, catch more horses, drive out, drop off cowboys, come back. The morning ripens as we begin the gather that would normally take the best part of a month. The wind starts early.

This day the worst smoke is in the canyons and on the foothills below the west seeding. It's been little used, and there's a lot of dry feed in there. In the hour and a half that it takes to bring the cattle up across this field the fire has blown up. Long, red lines stretch south across the foothills on both sides of the valley, making a V that meets at the Harness Place hill.

The cowboys are our teenage children and our neighbors. They bring the cattle down the highway fenceline, to the seeding that burned yesterday, and trust that they'll head for home.

"Don't hurry," Tim tells the kids. "Keep 'em mothered up."

I hear Hank yelling to his kids, "If you're still okay when you get 'em through the lower fence, try to get 'em out of that side." He indicates the unburned fields on the east side of the highway that will probably go today. The kids nod, keep the bunch together.

Traffic is heavy; tourists, people with motor homes. The state highway people pilot them through the burning valley every so often. No fire help except the kid from Burns, and two engines from the Sheldon Refuge. The fire crews have no idea where anything is, structures or fences or water; there's no one to tell them.

I watch through binoculars in the wavery heat, men gathering the other seeding in front of the fire line, five miles long, sweeping the big field like a red broom. Fire whirlwinds are dancing again. Little bunches of cows keep boiling up out of the deep wash in the middle, where we can't see if a rider is driving them, or the fire, or both.

The fire jumps the highway behind the herd, even with two fire engines parked up there foaming and spraying water. It is midafternoon, and the wind blasts like a furnace over the summit. Some of the men have gone up the wash ahead of the fire, which has once more cut us off from each other. Tim and Sam are up there ahead of the smoke, moving cows back to the north. The highway is closed; a state trooper shakes his head, "No, you can't take that horse trailer up there, not now."

The men have changed horses on the side of the road, and Magen and her mom, Ginny, are holding four or five sweat-soaked mounts apiece on the highway shoulder, waiting for a ride to the headquarters. The horse guy who lives in the middle of the flat brings his trailer, and we load the two trailers, drive south. I look back at the pillars of smoke rising from the fire line, where my husband and my son have gone.

It is never a gentle country, and I am a bad churchgoer. Nothing in my safe childhood prepared me for this place. It is elemental: fire, flood, freezing cold, plagues of insects, young people and animals dying for no reason. I have prayed for things before, and it hasn't worked out. I make a picture of my boys in my head, and draw the circle of white light around my loved ones, and their horses. I call my mother on the cell phone after the horses are put away, and I tell her what is happening. She'll be praying too, she says; pass it around the prayer chain. "Let us know what happens." This is not jolt-of-adrenalin fear, but the heavy dread of watching the apocalypse unfold.

The road is choked with gawkers. Lots of people from outside are here, with video cameras, king-cab pickups full of kids, dogs, grandmas, beer coolers, all stopped on the highway, catching up on news, trading stories. It's not their fire now. Someone says there'll be four hundred firefighters here tomorrow. I wonder what will be left to burn by then. There's not a fence left in the entire valley. No one has heard from Buster, waiting up there at sheep camp for the canyons to clear; he has started out twice, and radioed to say, no, he can't make it out yet.

I stand for hours on the highway with everyone else, forever, all afternoon. And then, there they are, Tim and Sam and Bob and Clint and Josh, faces black with soot, horses wet, everything filthy. Safe. A north breeze lifts the hair plastered to my forehead. The smoke is clearing, a little. The state trooper lets a line of cars go through. The breeze holds steady in the flat light. Fires are still burning in the Steens and all around the country, but it's looking better here. I don't remember getting home.

By the next morning there are indeed four hundred firefighters on the scene, tankers of Jet A, hotshot crews from Utah and the Arizona Strip, New Mexico, Wyoming. Choppers, portapotties, a mobile kitchen that will serve Salisbury steak the first night, chicken-fried the next. A mushroom forest of little pop-up dome tents grows at the maintenance station, where they set up camp. The choppers fly, the hotshot crews head for the smoke, up high now, and we turn to mopping up.

Cattle are everywhere. Miraculously, and because Tim sent those boys in to cut fences that were in the fire's path, we didn't lose a single animal to the fire itself. Still, a black and white pair has been hit on the road in the night, and someone has had to shoot them. Five more calves will fall victim to traffic in the fenceless wasteland in the next few days.

For the next week we drop off crews of cowboys all over the blackened valley to gather the animals, bring them home, sort them out. They're easy to drive, attention not distracted by anything at all to eat for twenty-five miles down the valley. Some are resting still, in the burn, calves exhausted from the days before. Windmills and water troughs scorched, the power poles that drive the pumps are heaps of charcoal. Although the power company crew was out there in the burning night replacing poles even as they were still smoking, those weakened by the blaze, burned partway through, will tip over, cutting power to one part of the valley or another. The crane and its accompanying trailer full of long poles creep up and down the valley, metallic praying mantis weaving wires back together so the cell-phone repeaters can work and the pumps can pump water.

All the cattle will come to the home ranch, to the river meadows we usually save for fall. The pump has been on at the upper end for ten days, and I remember that I was going to tell Tim, before this all started, that there wasn't any water in the river channel that day; that seems like a month ago. Tim is spending time with the people at the fire camp. They will be there for a week after the blaze is out, assessing the damage and mapping the fire, planning the rehab. They will fly Tim around in the helicopter to look for animals that may have been trapped in the fire, and Tim will show the BLM's district manager places that have burned before, and how they burned in this fire. One patch of the crested wheat seeding had burned a few years ago, and so this time, there was less to burn. The fire went through more quickly, burned with a little less heat, and left some vegetation.

That evening, Sam and I drive the river meadow to see how far the channel has filled. In the low, flat light of a cloudy afternoon, the ryegrass is so tall it brushes the truck windows; the grill winnows seed heads and flings them across the hood in fistfuls. Taller, dark greasewood is scattered across the golden expanse, and I imagine Africa. We turn on the headlights in the lowering light, looking for an invisible jeep trail. The channel has been dry since June, and we creep along the edge of the meadow, watching for the shorter grass and willow thickets that trace the sinuous meander bends. They are all empty, miles up the river. Six-inch cockleburs grow in the channel bottom. There are troughs spaced along the meadow, and from the uppermost trough, half a mile below the pump, we see the channel is still just damp. Sam hikes back to the truck, and I walk the channel, looking for the water.

In a dense willow thicket just below the pump, a five-foot beaver dam has grown, ten days of water backed up behind it. It must have been there for a while, in some form: cockleburs are growing on it too. The boys will take the backhoe and clean it out, but it will take days for the water to make it down the eight or so miles of channel to the road. Thirsty cows, lots of them, all coming across the blackened wasteland, and no water when they get there.

Tim tosses and turns that night in bed. He worries that the cattle will crowd the one full trough and knock away the pipes that bring the water in. Finally, he gets up. "I have to go check the water."

I can't sleep either, so I get dressed too, and we drive out to the trough with the vault of summer stars bright in the clear night sky. The trough is full.

By Tuesday after the fire, the balers are running again, hay is being cut. The fires are out; the firefighter dome tents disappear. Maybe there will be some money for a seeding, maybe some more to buy pipe to replace the wooden fence corners. We sort cattle, put them away for now in fall and winter pastures. People are starting to call, looking to buy hay. I wash windows, mow the grass, get back into some kind of routine. For days, when the wind is from the north, it's full of soot. Every time I sit down, I fall asleep.

Within a week after the fire, lines of government trucks are driving down the highway, lights on like a funeral procession. After waffling for a few days, someone in power decides that the devastation is worthy of the disaster designation. This could be good, people say, or it could be bad. State agencies, federal agencies, committees, and advisory boards smell disaster money. Like cultural scar tissue, within days they cover the fire, ready to divvy up the money, coordinate efforts, come to consensus, get a piece of the action.

There is seed to be sought; there are fence posts to buy, seeders to find, priorities to establish, damage to assess. We know that there will be changes from this fire, changes to the way we run livestock, changes in the patterns of local wildlife. I ask Tim, "If you could have done anything about this fire, would you have stopped it?"

He looks over the blackened valley and says, "Not down here. I would have saved the canyons and the lambing grounds," where the ewes hide their lambs from the cold April wind. Those are all gone. "But down here on the flat? It's good this burned." Nature uses fire for renewal. The charred brush will melt into the soil; enrich it for coming generations of plants.

It's not the end of the fires this season. There's another fire Wednesday night, but this time there aren't a hundred other fires burning at the same time, and our local BLM fire boss makes the ninety miles from town to this fire in ninety minutes. He's good at what he does, and they keep it under control; it's out the next morning.

⊖

The kitchen is quiet. The boys are gone. I rummage through the big freezer in the walk-in for something for dinner, and come across a plastic bag of frozen cherries. Why not? I think. I have some butter, and a free morning.

It goes together smoothly: flour, salt, sugar. Butter, Crisco, whirled up in the food processor. The voices of anxiety that used to babble in my head when I got to the ice-water stage are silent. The crust rolls out obediently on a sheet of waxed paper. Tapioca, cherries, sugar, a little almond flavoring, stirred together for the filling. I sprinkle sugar, a pinch of cinnamon on the crust. The pie browns nicely as I wash the dishes. "No reason," the voice whispers in my ear, "you can't make a pie a week."

After all, it's just pie.

↤ Moving into Fall Pasture

"GOOD MORNING, LEONARD CREEK SCHOOL."

"May I speak to your librarian [or technology director, or fund-raising coordinator, or music department chair]?"

"This is she." I sigh, looking out the window into what passes for the schoolyard. Jose, Marisela, and Rosa are playing soccer in the gravel. A small, blond boy is scuffling in the dirt of a long, open equipment shed that forms the boundary of my territory. Another boy sits on the steps of the converted construction trailer, reading a book.

Beyond the schoolyard, across the pole fence, great white locust trees throw shade over the 150-year-old lawns of Leonard Creek Ranch. Peacocks and hound dogs, a pot-bellied pig, two milk cows, a flock of geese, and an old rodeo horse wander the lawns, including the postage stamp where the children play at recess. There is a spotted fawn curled on my doorstep, shedding.

The school is more than ninety miles from Winnemucca, at the end of a long stretch of gravel road, skirting rugged mountains. The vast expanse of the Black Rock Desert stretches away to the south, disappearing in a white haze.

This is my new job, my new school. Sam has gone away to college. My house in town has a new coat of paint, and a new person living in it. The garage is still full of my stuff, but I don't have the energy to go back there to get it now. Town seems a lot farther than ninety miles to me these days.

The children and I, except for the small, blond boy, have all driven nearly thirty miles from our widely scattered homes to school this morning. Jose, who is thirteen, brings his sisters in a rattling red-and-white car with Texas license plates and a door that ties shut. Sometimes, in the early-morning light, I can see their dust trail rising like a fat, white snake ahead of me. The sisters will sleep under quilts in the backseat until they get to the schoolyard. Rosa, nearly fifteen, will uncurl herself from her nest and stand under the locust trees, brushing glossy black hair as long as the blond boy is tall.

On school picture day, we drive fifty-four mostly gravel miles to Denio, neatly combed and dressed our best. We pass through the moonscape left by the fire; on our way home, we venture up the canyons. See, the wild roses have grown back six inches high through the blackened ground. A tuft of leaves pokes bravely from a soot-crusted sagebrush stump. Grasses make a green fuzz along the burnt shoulders of the trail. Crested wheat, they say, will start with the first rains. The desert will recover.

If the fires function as a reset button for the landscape, perhaps the departure of our children does the same for us, the initial devastation of loss gradually salved by something growing up to take its place. New children in this new place need me. The shifting patterns of life flow whether I fight the current or let it carry me. My last RAC meeting was the first Friday of the school year. I dropped my five new students off to register for cards at the library. Their moms would oversee the children and take them swimming later. I would spend a few hours with a part of the council, rewriting recreation guidelines for the Black Rock Desert, another exercise in futility.

The faces around the table are familiar; we have become almost a family. I would enjoy the morning, but the council members would go to a Basque hotel for lunch, and I would meet the schoolkids for pizza.

⟜

Now it is late October; we are all getting used to the new school routine, and we are ready for a celebration. *Dia de los Muertos* is an ancient festival, from long before the coming of the Catholic Church. We are having lunch at the school on the ranch, although we should be eating it in the cemetery, between the tombstones, I suppose.

Aida, one of the mothers, is making *posole* with pork and *limon* to squeeze on it, with red chile sauce and finely shredded lettuce and radishes.

The children make skeletons: *calacas,* a word that sounds to me like bones rattling in the wind. The skeletons have hats and gloves and strings of beads, because Death in Mexico is a woman: *La Flaca,* they say, the Skinny One, *La Dientona,* the One with Big Teeth, the Bald One, the One with Big Hair. She's our favorite, the One with Big Hair.

They put the skeletons together with little brass paper fasteners. They learn the names of the bones, sort of.

These days in Mexico, there are sometimes problems with *Dia de los Muertos,* they say. People getting roaring drunk in the cemeteries, staying up all night and being rowdy. Halloween is so much safer, a bland festival compared to this, just pumpkins and cute little witches. Here, Death stares you in the face, wearing a hat with feathers and your grandmother's pearl necklace.

The children draw tombstones and decorate them, and on the tombstones they put the names of people they want to have in their cemetery on the bulletin board, with the pumpkins and the skeletons in floppy hats. I explain that they can use anyone who lived before that they would like to remember. So far, there lie Christopher Columbus, Emiliano Zapata, Benito Juarez, and Pancho Villa. Jose is looking at the social studies book, at the chapter opener, which always has a photograph characteristic of the country that is the subject of that chapter. On this page, it is the photograph of *campesinos* with donkeys in a desert canyon.

"Ah, Mrs. Dufurrena, this is my grandfather!" Jose exclaims.

"What? Your grandfather? Really?"

"No no no, not really my grandfather, my great-great-grandfather." Language is failing us again.

"You mean your great-great-grandfather lived in this way?"

"Yes yes yes, my grandfather Agapito Bautista, who carried sticks on the backs of donkeys to Guadalajara. It was a week, two weeks, from the little village of Talpa, where there is an angel and a devil in the church, but the devil is more bigger."

He has been here only since last winter, but his English is getting much better, and now when I leave the school and drive across the desert valley to my home, I can hear myself talking in the rhythm and the cadence of his speech.

"My great-great-grandfather, my father's great-grandfather, he lived to be 125 years old. When he was taking the sticks to Guadalajara to make pencils and paper, he was 60, 70 years old."

We calculate that he must have been born in 1865. The map shows us that he must have crossed several deep canyons of the Sierra Madre to get to Guadalajara with his donkeys and his loads of sticks. Jose says he thinks he did this until he was 80. So Agapito's tombstone is added to our cemetery.

I look questioningly at Rosa, the quiet older sister with the ancient Indian face. Does she have a person for her tombstone? She almost never speaks unless I ask her a direct question. I cannot tell for a long time whether it is because she is slow, or because she is shy, or because my Spanish is simply inadequate to the situation.

"Ah," she says. "Sor Juana."

"Who?"

"Sor Juana Inez de la Cruz," she says with enthusiasm. "Ah, yes, yes," they all chorus. We have hit on something they can explain to me, and I imagine a teacher in Mexico, standing in front of the class, teaching it to them, and now to me.

"Sor Juana, she put on pants!"

"Yes, yes," pipes up the little sister. "In Mexico girls did not go to school. She put on pants, and go to school, so girls in Mexico could go to school and learn to read." They don't know anything about when she was born, or when she died, and none of our American encyclopedias have a reference to her, so Rosa and I head into the tiny office where the computer is, and move piles of papers and books and lunches from the desk. After a while we make the connection to the Internet, not a surefire thing out here where the modem connection is under the window that leaks and where wasps build nests in the telephone switch boxes and where the equipment has been purchased fourth-hand by the small independent telephone company.

But there she is, scrolling with interminable slowness down the screen from 1750, Sor Juana Maria Inez de la Cruz, nun and writer of poems, plays, and dialogues, apparently a passionate feminist. Rosa smiles. The website is in Spanish. She reads the poems, the plays, the letters I cannot. Later, when she finally gives me the tombstone she has made for Sor Juana, it is a disappointment. The richness of the Spanish website does not translate. Her tombstone says only, "She Did Many Different Things."

Enchiladas, posole, Coca-Cola, Fritos, cookies, popcorn, and a flowery plastic tablecloth to go with the big tissue-paper flowers we have made to decorate the table. Outside, the life of Leonard Creek Ranch goes on in the brittle sunshine. It is weaning time, and hundreds of cattle bellow in the lots below the schoolyard. Saddle horses, pickups, are parked against the fence. We have plenty of food, so everybody comes to eat. Frenchy and Ted; Frenchy's son Glenn; his wife, Susan; their hired man, Fidel; and Jesus Bautista and his wife, Aida. Diego and Savannah motor around under table level; our friend Dale has come too, from the ranch across the Black Rock. She rolls up silverware in napkins and spreads out the paper plates. The boys find metal chairs, and we squeeze sixteen of us around the table where we do our schoolwork. The food is good; everyone eats a lot. When they finish, the children get their picture taken with the school sign.

Later I drive home across the wide valley; Quinn River's lower fields are golden with ripe grass; cattle graze through miles of meadow, never plowed. Cows and their calves, big now, will spend the fall months here, through sorting, weaning, preg testing. The calves will go to Oregon, California, to be put on pasture to grow some more. The mother cows will work their way through these meadows and finally out into the low country for winter: the river meadows and protected warmth of the flats near the ranch.

Tim and I move a bunch after I get home from school, from one pasture into another.

"You start 'em up from the bottom, I'll go get this calf from outside the fence."

I take Sam's dog, make the long, slow trot down to the far corner. The animals move easily in front of me, gathering together at the bottom of the field, moving up lazily as we weave back and forth behind them. A few pairs hang in the drag, big calves getting a last bite to eat before they move. And, I think, it is the signal, between the cow and calf: if we lose each other, I'll meet you right here, later.

The late-afternoon sun is still hot on my back as Cookie and I work through the tall ryegrass on the far side of the meadow. Calves jump out ahead of us, kicking and playing; Tim works the tules in the dry sloughs to the east. The black-and-red sea of moving backs flows ahead of us, our paths gradually converging. When they are all through the fence, heading north, Tim swings down. He closes the gate, remounts, and together we turn toward home.

Shared Fencelines

Linda Hussa | | |

✎ Shared Fencelines

Scientists have established all water everywhere, including that inside the tiniest living organism, moves in tides like the sea.

—*Old Wives Tales of Gardening*

I OPEN THE GROUND. I TURN THE EARTH. I CLIMB INTO THE CAB OF A 150-horsepower tractor as I would a ladder to a tree house. Pulling a sixteen-foot disk, I cut the field on the bias through oat stubble and wads of Russian thistle into dirt faded by sun, pitted and packed by wind, settled by winter. The first line is a pen drawn across paper—freehand. The second is proving the theory of the straight line. Later it will be mathematics: the properties, measurement, and relationships of points, lines, angles, surfaces, and solids as I meet corners and jogs in the fenceline.

People on the road wave. As my work moves away from the road I am out of their line of vision. Intent on what is ahead, I don't look their way; they don't look mine.

(I drive my 150 horses in one harness of wire and steel, RPM's, and diesel smoke, pulling together. At the end-row they collect in both my hands. Force, compulsion, struggle against my guidance. They want to move. Their long, brilliant bodies compress and swing to make the turn. By midfield I have them named for the desert's stones, storms, snakes, rivers, and colors subtle as a minor key.

Owyhee pulls out from his mates. I whistle him up and he steps back in. But he rolls an inside eye at me to let me know he made the decision on his own. (He takes orders from no one.)

The earth parts, crumbles as well-mixed pastry dough does before water is dribbled in, falling away from the disks in an action that puts me on my knees in the garden soil, tipping the seed packet to the sun; *sow after any danger of frost is past.* If I waited for weather's guarantee I would not drill this field until the Fourth of July. Besides, most grains are hardy and can take a nipping. The sprout may brown and wither at the tip, but if there is moisture for the root to chase it will recover and make hay.

We are late getting on this ground, delayed by spring rains, unusual in Surprise Valley. Native people recognize a duality of the element: the male rain, violent thunderstorms driving the seeds into the soil; the female rain, gently nurturing to bring forth crops. The storms of 1998, called El Nino, little-boy rains, full of mischief and destruction on the Pacific Coast, have been generous and beneficial to us on the east side of the Warner Mountains, bringing a heavy snowpack to irrigate our fields into summer by gravity flow. The temperatures never fell below zero. Nitrogen-laced rains have fallen steady through the spring, fed the soil, and closed the gap between surface moisture and groundwater. The water table has risen within inches of the surface. Postholes fill and dirt tamps like peanut butter. But we don't care if fences need propping and the schedule has gone awry. Eight years of drought have branded our memories with the consequence of doing without.

I realize I have not looked up at the mountains all morning. There is fresh snow on the peaks, black sky behind. Clouds bounce spotlights of sun, splashing here and there. A flight of desert pelicans wheels against the dark curtain of the hills, then bursts bright like fireworks.

This is not our ground but the neighbor's just across the fenceline and has been since the '30s. We leased the ranch from the family after the neighbor died. He was an industrious man despite an injured back. Pitched forward at forty-five degrees like a broken board he scurried over his land afoot, or awobble on his Super M FarmAll tractor, exhaust puffing smoke rings into the air as he planted rye in this corner. Hardy, willing rye.

His ranch is dry. He sank no well to irrigate and expand. Cattle numbers were evenly matched to the amount of feed his fields produced. He refused to take a seat in the banker's chair to mouth promises and know the clammy fear of not meeting the payment. His ledger was large, leather bound with every detail of hay baled, grain sacked, beef birthed, cut, and shipped, even the cellar shelves and bins recorded. Still, the long pages were sparsely filled.

Bigger operators looked down on ranchers such as he, berated as small potatoes if they didn't have full-time men and modern haying equipment and stock trucks. None took note if he had a meager gain. He was nothing to them; they never looked his way.

While big ranchers used chemical fertilizers to boost the feed when spring rains came, he believed in the natural way and cleaned his lots into the manure spreader to refresh the soil across the upper bench, the hay fields, the pond field. He lashed truck tires to a beam, dragged in squirrel mounds and busted up the manure so the goodness would carry down and the feed rise even. He burned out his ditches so the smallest forked twig or fallen feather would not pause or turn the water flowing from his neighbors' land. Come it did, when creeks ran high, down ditch and swale bleeding through his black earth, soaking up his meadowland, and he was thankful for the providence of water not owed him by decree, but a gift of his neighbors' diligent irrigation.

I would see his dust from our place and know he went twice with the disk east-west, then crosshatch, twice with the harrow and then in the drill box seeds of summer's crop slid past each other, whispering gossip to the dirt. The packers dragging behind would be his long fingers patting the surface to seal the moisture in.

Rye is not the most palatable hay. Give cows good wild hay or oats, not to mention hard wheat or sweet beardless barley, and they will trod the rye or bed on it. But if rye is their only choice, they will maul it and ruminate and stay fat through the coldest winter. If the neighbor caught the storms just right, Bull's-eye! He could get a crop of rye they would talk about in town.

The neighbor was a frugal man. His family lived by work without extravagance. He taught his boys to work beside him. He fired no stove in the shop while they made winter repairs. No Watkins man or Fullerbrush man turned down his lane. Timid charity ladies with empty envelopes tapped at the side door. When his wife said they must ask him they did not bother.

She fed the family of seven from the land's produce, never shirking work. But hers were not the ideas that selected the seed or culled the cow herd. Her kingdom was small: beets and kale in the garden rows, spuds and winter squash in the dank cellar, the damp-mopped linoleum, the woodpile she split and stacked and packed to the cookstove in the kitchen, to the wash stove in the shed, to the tall, black stove in the parlor. His was defined by the old fences that, as he aged and his health worsened, fell into disrepair. Posts leaned from the weight of snow drifted on west-blowing winds, sagging wires leaked his cattle like milkweed blown around, the meadows choked with chicory and bull thistle, his uncut bull calves thrust thickened seed into sister cows, and bored holes through the fence to terrorize the neighbors' herds once his cows bred up.

Their two milk cows fed along the roadsides, in open gates where they were not welcome and well known for their nuisance. Boys from the neighboring ranches shoved them up a chute, pulled the flank strap tight, bucked them out, their sharp spurs digging, then sent them galloping down the lane with feed sacks tied to their tails, milk turned to butter in their bags. I don't suppose anyone cared about them lying on the road ruminating; there isn't much traffic on the county road going into the desert. But ladies riled at a Guernsey lapping up their sweet peas, and when ladies riled, men spurred into action. One hauled the old spotted cows across the lake and dumped them out. It was a week before they wandered home off the alkali flats caked with white mud, all cockleburred, bags as tight as ticks.

True to his upbringing the neighbor knelt on unpadded rails at first mass every Sunday morning to give his reply. Alone he pondered before the alter of the lost Son. Then, bothersome, wholly inventive, the slumped-shouldered old badger would crawl through the fence wire after dark and set our irrigation headgates his way.

We used to fight him and his needy ways, cussing when we found the water changed from a dry corner to the swift run down a cutting swale toward his place, cussing when we saw a dust in our replacement heifers that was his bulls fighting with ours to service our handpicked cows, cussing when he cobbled up holes in the fence instead of fixing it proper. We couldn't keep him honest, so we denied him friendship for a roll of barbed wire and a share of water.

On a summer day John and I were riding through our cattle in a field next to the neighbor's place. We could see his green truck kneeled down in the soft mud along a string of willows. Sod had been flung across the meadow by his tires spinning across the mire. Muttering to each other we rode through the corner gate to give him a hand. He was nowhere around. It was the best part of a mile to his house. We figured he'd gone walking home. Suddenly we were confronted, not with a man we could berate under our breath, but an empty pickup, a sultry, hot afternoon, and a long walk across the fields for a crippled old man.

I got off my horse and into the lumpy, out-at-the-knees driver's seat. I had a different view through his window screen. John tied his lass rope to the bumper, and I started the engine. A little pressure on the rope by his horse pulled the truck out, easy. John led the horses and I drove the truck toward his house.

We hadn't gone far when we came on the old man sitting under an overhang of gooseberry in the fencerow. I got out. I could feel the damp breath of the meadow rising. He mopped at his face with a bandanna. Thick mud had slipped into his house shoes and dried into casts from ankles down. "Just resting," he said and bobbed his head, embarrassed to be caught sitting in the shade while the sun was still up. He walked his hands up the hog wire fence, pulling, steadying, as he got to his feet. As usual, he had on the foot-wide leather belt that supported his back. He snugged it up a few holes, thanked us, said we were right neighborly.

Holding his weight heavily against the half-open door and the back of the seat, his face changed, and he said, "When I was a boy, eight or ten, I lived with my stepfather on the Stain Ranch on the back road to Alturas. I had gone riding along the road, and I tried to cross a downed piece of fence. A wire got stuck between my horse's hoof and the shoe. It was wedged tight and I couldn't free him. I struggled a good long while.

"Four men came by on horseback. They had driven cattle over from Surprise to the railhead in Alturas and were riding home. Well, they got by. But one turned around and came back to help me. Together we pried the wire loose. He went on his way and I rode home. From the description of him my stepfather said that it was old Walt Hussy. Your granddad, John. I've had a soft spot for the Hussys ever since."

~

The disk we leased for this 150 horses in-hand is giving me fits. It has forty disks that clog by some whim I can't calculate, and pack in a turn or two. I stop and hack it out with a shovel, a bar, the claw hammer, even my pocketknife. I try every tool; still it takes precious time to clean each one. If I am not attentive or quick I'm dragging a steamroller. At lunch I ask my father-in-law, Walter, what I am doing wrong. He says it might be the metal the disks are made of, or maybe they have been tempered wrong, or set too close on the spindle for the kind of soil we have here, and suggests I lash a chain from the frame around the disk spindle loosely. As the disk turns the chain will cut and clean.

Mind you, I am a buckaroo. I would not drive this tractor no matter how many workhorses prance brightly inside the big, green engine if we did not need hay to feed our livestock through the winter—two tons for each cow to hold her flesh and keep her fit for calving—160 days of hay. Our work is husbandry to animals who work for us. By necessity that includes farming. It is the most distant point from the cow's hide unless you count mechanics: oil drums, compressed air, trays of wrenches, sockets, skinned knuckles, bins of rusty bolts used and used again, and above the workbench a pair of swallows. Their bodies of spooled copper wire and swipes of green-black grease swing on a light cord. They are the ground. They want to nest above the screwdrivers and the pipe threader. I ask them nicely to find a joist and bridging in the barn. They can't speak. They have mosquitoes clamped in their clown faces.

I rummage the shop and come up with enough chains and bits of chain to jerry-rig Walter's remedy on sixteen disks. Even then, the odd one will snatch some weeds and clog. But it is an improvement, and I work on through the afternoon, watching thunderheads build, darken, and flap on Patterson Peak like sheets on the line. This storm is the little boy playing at ambush. He scampers south, around and up the east side of the valley, kicking up dirt into messy billows, tossing fizgigs of lightning here and there. Alkali crosses my tongue before the dust storm hits, and when it does the field is obliterated in a vicious whirlwind of dirt. I hold the tractor steady on an imaginary point out ahead. On the turns I reestablish the line, but it's memory work. I ignore the storm blasting against the windshield. My mind is split between keeping the cut straight, watching the disks for packing, and hurrying to beat the rain when something catches my eye in the path of the left front wheel. I stamp hard on the clutch as something blows away and is gone. In the next instant my mind recalls the thing I had seen: an odd banding of colors, shadows, the ruffle of weeds, stems. From the vision I reconstruct a killdeer laying over on the ground as a heroine tied to tracks leans in terror from the oncoming train. I throw the gearshift into neutral and stand up in the cab. Less than a foot from the massive tire, a second away, are four darkly speckled eggs, tear shaped, snug in a hollowed scrape of small rocks and clods. Dirt, weeds, and rain pelt the glass inches from my face. I am stunned to think I saw her at all. Wind rocks the tractor in gusts. The clutch of eggs disappears in dirt blown by, then reappears. They will chill quickly in this storm without her sheltering body. I back the tractor ten feet and pull around the nest.

On the next pass the female killdeer is back on the nest. She rivets her attention on the tractor as it comes closer. But this time the tractor, wheels, noise, dust, digging disks pass sixteen feet from her. She turns on the nest with it, feather skirts blow over her head, wings in that broken arc—a disgusted mother with her hands on her hips warning me off. She does not abandon her claim. Each round, danger is another width of work away. Soon I have difficulty sorting her out from the other features of the blank oval left fallow in the turned field. My eyes pick through the tufts of blond grass and small stones for a curve that is her body settled once more over her eggs. The killdeer is the neighbor standing on that uncut sod, defiant and nearly indistinguishable from the dirt itself. For a lifetime, he crouched over his foolish claim on this same land against the impossible foe—time. The world swept around him, battering his faith with plagues of loss and failure. He stood his ground alone.

I finish my work before the rain sweeps down. Luck is with me.

↬ The Neighbor

1

THE DOGS DIDN'T EVEN BARK WHEN HE DROVE IN OUR FRONT YARD, struggled from behind the steering wheel.

Standing up he's stooped, ready to step under the low cellar door. His is always a view of the long horizon. I wonder if he remembers how it was to look up at the sky.

He asks if we would like to buy his cattle. They're just too much work. We've seen them, he says.

We've seen them, all right. Every morning hay is scattered in the stackyard, phantom tracks meander through the flower bed, under our bedroom window.

They've been busting out, he says. Gettin' breechy and nothing he hates worse.

His lane fence is completely gone in places. A pallet or odd board dangles from wire strung to rose briars. He cobbles it up when someone calls to complain.

All of the cows are bred up, he says. Some spring calvers but the rest have big calves on 'em.

They're bred up, all right, by a gang of two-year-old bull calves he didn't get cut. His bloodlines have thickened considerably.

John said we'd only be interested in the open heifers. When they matured we would breed to a bull bred to throw small calves a heifer could birth on her own.

The two men shake hands on the deal and I catch myself straightening my back and looking up at the plain blue sky.

2

Happy with the deal he turns his truck around in our yard.

At home he tells the wife, They bought the heifers. We'll weigh them Wednesday. They smile, nodding at each other, satisfied.

He goes out again before dark, starts the tractor, and leads his cattle in from grass with a bale of lush alfalfa dribbled from the wagon. In his stooped way he separates the heifers off and looks them over. Eight head straight English. The price was under market.

He forgot he pays no freight, pays no sale-yard commission, pays no beef promotion, no brand inspection. As my father would say, "He can't stand prosperity."

He chums the eight fat heifers into a smaller corral closer to the barn door. Thick flakes of green alfalfa stagger across the lot. They rip off mouthfuls, eyes shut on this lovely new taste, lips painted green. A sudden change from native grass to this hot feed is flirting with danger, but he'll chance it. He wants every bogus pound of gain. He drops a block of salt beside the water tank, spanks his hands together, and goes in to his own supper.

Dawn slips across his field, stutters, nudges at two heifers grotesque in death, bloated like poisoned pups on the neighbor's need.

3

He says, Don't worry about paying for the six heifers until the fall. He won't need the money until then.

We won't brand the heifers until we pay for them, John says.

He asks if we want to run any cows with his since we're taking the heifers.

We'd have to put a bull with them, John says. Need to get them bred up.

That's all right, he says.

This year, he has no herd bull for his cows.

He doesn't know how he's going to get his calves branded. There's just the woman and him now.

We take his iron—the 35—home with us, next morning drive his cattle to our corral. His are hen-skin thin in some places. We brand, castrate the bull calves, vaccinate, the works. Drive them back home.

4

Summer seeds harden into yellow fat. Frost lies down on the backs of the heifers. They are young cows now bred up to calve in the spring.

The neighbor drives into the front yard. He says he has a lot of feed left. The price has come up. He has decided not to sell the heifers, after all. We can bring them home. And move our cows and bull anytime.

We watch him drive out. I look at John, not sure what he'll say. He breaks into laughter. We sit down on the grass and laugh. We lay back on the grass, still laughing. We hug each other and laugh and then we just hug and watch a small bunch of specks flying south over the bank of black willows.

✎ Water Will Find Its Way

I GREW UP AT THE BASE OF THE DIABLO MERIDIAN, A POINT FROM WHICH California and Nevada are surveyed, mapped, locked into certainty. As a child I rode with my parents following firebreaks and ranch roads up shady canyons, across hot, grassy ridges, to the top of Mount Diablo. The mid-summer mountain was shaped soft, gold of filaree past flower, black-green of live oak gathered where long roots could tap water within the adobe soil.

I tied my horse as they had done and went up the rocky steps of the sum-mit platform. I do not remember wind, though there surely must have been wind. Mount Diablo rises from the level of the Pacific to nearly four thou-sand feet in a scant twenty miles, and although the western side rolls its broad shoulder to the moist Pacific air, the broken face of north and north-east pipes wind up or sucks it down to the valley floor.

My eyes followed the highway far below that connected our small town to others as my mind traveled the road past our bus stop, the field where Hap Magee's Longhorn steers loafed and shaded, Sally's house in the canyon, the bridge, my school. I saw, in fact, my home place as my memory had it mapped, captured into resolution, and felt reassured.

Minding their instructions I took the mounted telescope in my hands and pointed it north, past all I knew. They told me I could see snowcapped Canadian mountains if I looked far. Snowy mountains danced above the blue and tan ocean of land. Then they turned me south and said the mountains I could see now were in Mexico. Again, snowy mountains. Perhaps their information was wrong and the mountains were not beyond our borders. But for the first time in my life I touched my eyes on distance, looked beyond my perception of existence, held within my sight an expanse of country and people living lives I could not imagine. The world leaped out and away from where I stood. Gripped by possibility, I was pinned to the earth and yet free. Never since have I ever seen so far, never have I felt as sure.

⊕

Years passed, school finished, work, marriage, all laying out in order as was the rule, steady as the earth. But there are exceptions to the rule. I learned the raw truth of change when my marriage ended and divorce rolled under me like an earthquake. A world I thought solid and predictable went topsy-turvy, and I spun like a compass needle at the equator. No one could console me. I was alone for the first time in my life, and being alone was all I was fit for. Like a blind person reaching for bearings in the unknown I grasped scraps of a job in a flower shop, a two-room cottage on a ranch, and a stable for my horse to reconstruct a life. Caring for him let me care for myself, and routine steadied me: up in the dark to ride before work, straight home to ride after work. I haunted the hills without seeing them. My horse carried me across the landscape of my grief.

Again I rode to the top of Mount Diablo. But even from that highest point, that promising place of reckoning, a haze rose above our country towns that divided and doubled like cells into cities. I could not see home.

⊕

Wind shook the big oaks, and leaves rained down into the yard of my bungalow. I was raking them into piles when I heard the phone. It would be my friend Nancy asking me to dinner, or Mom or Dad. It was John Hussa. He said it was time to go to the desert.

I was raking leaves. What desert?

Nevada, he said. Did I want to come help them gather? Ten days to two weeks. He had asked my husband several times, but he was always too busy. Now, he said, I'm asking you.

When?

⊕

The first week of October my boss at the flower shop gave me time off. I turned my big horse into a pasture, and threw my bedroll and duffel bag into the Ford Falcon I had bought for two hundred dollars. It was an abused

'60s economy car: ashy red paint, sun-peeled dash, pinged windshield, spinning antenna, horse-blanket upholstery, full ashtray, and dangerous exhaust emissions. I did not try to fix it up or make it better. It was what it was. The directions John gave me on the phone were simple: turn left at Reno, turn right at Cedarville, go to the end of the ranch road. It was a map I could follow. I headed toward the extreme northeastern corner of California where the Hussa Ranch headquartered in Surprise Valley. Yet, I was a loosely wound ball of string rolling through that dark night. I told myself, just lay down that string as you roll and, like Hansel and Gretel, you can find your way home.

I met the predawn light on Donner Summit. At the roadside vista view I let the thin air chill my road-dull brain into motion. Tires spun wet up off the slick road hissing up storm after little storm as trucks and cars sped past. Everybody was definitely going somewhere. Where was I headed? The visitors' information window didn't open till June. It was up to me. I snapped a bite out of my apple.

꩜

My father's inheritance fit under one arm: a print of *The Pharaoh's Horses*—the elegant heads of three horses racing under a turbulent sky hung on the walls of his family's homestead house beside the John Day River, and then on ours. His father, Elza, freighted for a living and worked horses all his life. His brother, Ben, ran wild horses off Rudio Mountain and sold them for dog food. Dad recognized the horse as more than a beast of burden or source of protein. He revered their grace, intelligence, and ability, and understood the link from the sire and dam. He thought he could raise good horses.

In a photograph, my mother is riding bareback on a gray gelding rearing up, just as she taught him. Her young face was joyful. Unwilling to appreciate the peace she knew in riding free, her father called her "horse-crazy." She met my father at a rodeo dance and, in him, found someone who understood her. Like wild horses, they ran away to marry. They spent their lives raising and training horses of certain bloodlines to prove a horse of perfect conformation could be athletic, too. There was not a day in their lives without horses.

I grew up with horses in paddocks and horses in pastures surrounding the house. There is a memory, perhaps my first, of holding onto the rail of my crib, a horse just outside the window, stubby baby fingers flexing to reach it.

My first hurt came from a horse when I tried to shinny up the feathered leg of our old gelding as I'd seen my brother and sister do. Twelve hundred pounds of him stepped on my bare foot. Mom carried her shrieking two year old to the house, set me on the kitchen counter, foot in the sink. I watched my blood leaking out of me for the first time, sliding toward the drain, mixing with water. She cut off the dangling nail, saying Popeye didn't mean to, he just didn't notice my little foot. Then she cradled my face in her cool hands and said she hoped I would forgive him and we could be friends again.

When my brother and sister went off to school and left me alone I sat within the shade of the mares' grand bellies and napped in the pasture grass among their foals. Popeye let me push him to a tree stump or rail, and I rode Indian-wild through the lashing limbs of the woods. At the bus stop, his broad back let me lie back and dream. When no one else had time, horses walked toward me with lowered heads, or waited, looking back. Not for sugar. For me.

My culture was the horse culture. We gathered at shows, clubhouses, arenas, lessons, and lectures. We rode for pleasure; we rode to perfect an idea or movement; we made work for the sake of training. We developed trails, camped out, and enjoyed the company of those who counted horses among our friends. Our commonality was not social or economic or academic. Horse sense, courage, and the pure ability to ride breached class boundaries without exception.

That was who I was, what I was. I did not know what kind of people I would find ahead.

⋄

John was up in the dog box on top of the cab of the '52 International snub-nosed stock truck. He looked up when I drove in. Smiled. It was worth the drive for that smile. I tossed up buckets, bridles, saddle blankets. Slung the latigo up to him, and he yanked the saddle right out of my arms. I felt like he pulled me up, too.

Ike, Richard, Highpockets, Dandy, Ace, Rowdy, Cuba, Poncho, Raspy went calmly up the chute into the truck, found an order, hip to head, as was their routine. John pulled the stock truck through the gate. I closed it. He climbed down, grabbed a bridle off a peg in the barn, and we stood there while he checked off his mental list. Chaps? Yes. Okay. Warm coat and gloves? Yup. Flashlight! he said. Got one? Got one. He looked over at the house. Okay. Guess that's it, he said. I went around to the other side and climbed up into the cab. He looked at the house again, then up at me, and climbed in. The cab suddenly filled up with the two of us. We started out. Compound low.

John took the turns slowly, letting the horses get their footing. The stock truck was not built for speed, anyway. He stopped at the highway. Looked both ways. Everything I knew was west. He turned east. A crawl of disquiet pricked in my belly like my first day of school when I got on the wrong bus to go home. I remember looking around at the rows of faces and not finding one I recognized. John had been a friend for years, but I knew his outline only as my husband's friend. They met at Cal Poly—both there for college rodeo more than academics. John married his high school sweetheart. After eight years, and a daughter for him, we were each on our own. He stared hard ahead, trapped in a private memory. Then, he caught my eye and smiled weakly.

"I was in a wreck right here." He pointed to the bar pit. "Last spring. I can't get by here without thinking about it. Bill picked me up, we were going to Wall Canyon to scatter bulls, little skiff of snow on the road. He was fishing under the seat for his gloves and got a front wheel off the edge of the road. The truck rolled. I busted the windshield out with my head. Killed my best horse. Goblin." His eyes were on the side mirror as we left the spot behind.

The road curved onto the causeway. He glanced south, at the pasture fence on the shoreline; my eyes followed his. "That's the last fence you'll see till we get to our country on Badger Mountain, seventy miles straight ahead. All this country's open. We run on the Sheldon, about three hundred square miles."

"Three hundred square miles, just your cattle?"

"In-common range, with two other ranches. Close to two thousand head, in all. You'll meet the others in the morning."

"We're going to ride three hundred square miles?" I asked, still stuck on the number.

"Twice. We cover it twice." He paused, his eyes moving to the road as he gathered speed, the rearview mirror, the country, a glance over at me, then he went on, "Gather, separate out loads for each ranch, and haul them home in trucks; that's how we do it now. The cattle start drifting toward the valley early in the fall; no fences to stop them. They accumulate below our ranch on the salt grass.

"When I was a kid every night after school, I'd ride the lake and gather up our pairs and put 'em in our field. That was in the fifties. In October, at the end of the grazing season, the men used to go out to camp and ride for a week to start the cattle this way, Nut Mountain, through the Massacre Lakes country, Long Valley, '49. They'd turn all the extra saddle horses loose at Badger, and the horses would hit a long trot for home. I'd hear them coming up the road before light. Mom or I'd let them into the field when they got here. The men would go back out every day to pick up the tail end of the bunch, and riders cleaned the country a few miles on each side of the road coming this way. All up and down the lake, this would be going on. Down at Eagleville the Home Camp and Duck Flat cattle came in by the Murphy Place. Up at Fort Bidwell the cattle came from Barley Camp on Bidwell Mountain and from out toward Mosquito. The Lake City bunch came from Sand Creek and off the north end of '49 Mountain. Every community would hold rodear and separate out the different ranches' cattle." His arm moved in a way to show me his universe. "All those men ahorseback working together, thousands of head of cattle, for weeks every fall. It made good hands, good bridle horses, and kept men honest. I grew up with it that way."

As an afterthought he said, "Now we truck 'em instead of drive 'em. Saves time. I guess time's gotten more important."

Deep sand dunes of brittle gold lay in the waning light under the Hays Range ahead. Off to the south a dust devil whirled, tight at the core, loosening at the top until it blew apart and spun into nothing.

෴

A small sign said NEVADA where the truck bumped off the blacktop road and onto dirt. I looked back at the one facing the other direction. CALIFORNIA, with a golden poppy. NEVADA, nothing. Not exactly a warning; a simple statement of fact. Nevada, now. You should know.

It was up to me to figure out what Nevada might be about. Not poppies.

෴

The engine wound down as the road turned north and climbed the grade. John shifted down and down using the red button on the stick shift, splitting the gears to accommodate the steep pitch of the hill and the load of horses. As we crawled up the bench he pointed out the charred bedsprings of a burned-down brothel in the brush disappearing behind us at the state line. "Town women got blamed for starting the fire," he said. "Gossip was the women were suspicious of their men always heading out east to check their cattle, so they got together one night and burned the cathouse down.

Some said a bar owner in town paid a buckaroo to get rid of his competition. The town women took it on the chin. It made a better story."

Over the first string of hills, the skeleton of an old hotel stood on a little flat, doorless, windowless, torn down to the studs after word got out that a sack of gold coins was found stashed over a doorjamb. The number "49" is painted on a big lava boulder beside the Oregon Trail. Weather eroded the rock away and left the numbers standing up from the rock's face nearly an inch. Hard rock. Harder country.

He stopped the truck at '49 Summit to make sure none of the horses had gotten down during the steep climb. Over the open-topped truck they were all heads-up looking east, breathing in the smells of the country ahead. I did the same. Below us the road disappeared into a deep-pink sandstone canyon. Beyond the canyon, a long valley eased up at the edges into purple and indigo hills. A small lake winked up north. Not a light. Not a car. No sign at all of people. In the center of the valley a banded sandstone mesa stood up six hundred feet. Painted Mountain, John said. Lifting and erosion had delivered colored bands of sediments from the bottom of the sea. I looked into a place I didn't know existed.

The dawn of that day broke for me on the high Sierra. The same sun lowered across the Nevada desert. Painted Mountain took on the last of its light. The road going out east turned across the flat. We drove into that approaching night.

⬧

A half-lamp moon shined through the camp-trailer window. I woke cold and thinking of food. The apple on Donner was used up. Curled like a sow bug inside the soft nap of pajamas and flannel sheets, I hugged my knees and hoped stillness would preserve the warmth I generated, and I dozed again, dreaming about the jackrabbits' crazy, darting race across the road in the truck headlights. At the base of a sharp hill John slowed to miss one, and it cost him the speed he needed to reach the top. The engine dropped in tone as forward speed wound down on the brink of a stall. He cussed softly and, watching the dirt road glow red in the taillights, backed down the grade. The horses scrambled for footing. The truck shook and pitched. He made a run at the hill, splitting gears, engine winding high-pitched. We crawled over the top.

It wasn't far now, he said. In minutes a fence corner appeared in the headlights. Horse pasture, he said. Then, willow clumps in the lights. I located the cabin by the smell of smoke. Uphill. Lights out. We pulled through the gate. They went down the chute browns, bays, sorrels, and palominos, and disappeared into the dark.

⊸

"GET UP YOU LAZY BASTARDS!" a man's voice boomed out from the cabin door. I shot out of bed, grazing my head on the upper bunk. Upright, jeans and shirt, socks and boots, coat, I opened the door and stepped into the Milky Way. Night draped close as a circus tent over the poles and pegs of the foothills, and stars, so close, so many, I reached up, turning, dizzy with their brilliant, winking colors. I could almost feel them on my face like rain.

⊸

Bar of soap, wash pan, frozen to the table, I cupped my hands under the spring pipe. Never had I felt water as cold and still liquid. I washed beneath the cabin windows glowing with lantern light, laughter boiling over inside.

And then I stood at the door. First-meeting kept me from grasping the doorknob. But I was five hundred miles from home. I stamped frost from my feet on the porch, waited a moment, then stepped inside to a crowd of strangers around the dimly lit kitchen and the wood cookstove they called Bertha, huffing with heat.

John was holding a half gallon of Black Velvet in one hand, cup of coffee in the other. A little too early, I said, and took the coffee.

That's why you need it, said Bill, the anvil-jawed cow boss and author of the buckaroo wake-up call. Louie, who rode for Bill, and Frank, who worked for the Hussas, sat beside him on the backside of the long table. John and I crowded in beside them. We were the circle crew. The five of us would ride all the outside country.

Across from us on the shippers' side sat Mark (Bill's brother and partner in the Heryford Ranch), Walter (John's dad, partner in the Hussa Ranch), and Charles (who worked for the Harris Ranch). They would help gather today. Tomorrow, and from then on, they would stay inside to work out truckloads for each ranch. The hired cook, Jane, who was married to Charles, fixed them a hot lunch every day. They took afternoon naps and rode gentle horses. The shippers were scorned as old men.

The circle crew, on the other hand, packed no lunch, rode the outside country, trotted all day long, tough, the ace pilots of buckaroos, the elite.

Of course, I knew nothing of cow-camp politics that first morning, but it would become obvious in the days ahead.

Jane dished up breakfast at the stove, and the talk faded for a while as platters of bacon, biscuits, potatoes, gravy, and eggs passed hand to hand around the table. The fragrance was a meal in itself.

Frank ate quickly, refused a second cup of coffee, and went out before sunrise to wrangle the saddle horses while the rest of us got into coats and chaps. As we went down the long hill to the corrals all together, talking, there was a muffled hammering sound of hooves on the cold ground. I stopped. Suddenly seeing the horses in their wild gallop, before the wrangler, I knew I was in the right place. The others went on talking. They had seen this many times, horses spilling off the high rim and down that long, steep hill, jumping rocks, dodging brush, dust rising up a storm around them as they came up the meadow, throwing their heads playful, kicking, rearing, bucking as they ran, splitting through the willows, Frank right behind. So many horses in one bunch coming and coming, every size and color, flowing around the gate, into a current in the round corral, and Frank on his big, bald-faced sorrel, slowing up, stopping, bringing the gate around. And the horses continuing in their flow, mixing, heads up, lunging, nipping, or calm and sure of the day ahead. They were an eye-dazzler blanket woven of sun on horse hair, muscle, and sleek hide thrown out in morning light.

The horses gathered into the big corral at Badger Camp were ranch horses. Most were cold-blooded, feather-legged, and plain-headed, with flint-hard hooves. Born to the desert, they inherited a mastery of the country and were able to carry a rider twelve, twenty hours, exist on bitterbrush leaves and bleached grass buried under snow, and travel miles to water. Valuable in a different way from horses my parents raised. In the high desert the pedigree of the horse did not matter so much as its willingness and character.

The men entered the corral one by one, to catch a horse from his string of three or four with a spare if one got hurt or pulled a shoe. Each man fit his horse to the day's work ahead, and each horse was ridden in rotation with two or three days rest in between. There were four horses, all geldings, in my string. Rowdy was a quarter horse, bright sorrel, pretty, the only registered horse. The others were just good ranch horses: Dandy was lanky, seal brown; Highpockets was a big palomino, better than sixteen hands high, who, John said, would keep my feet out of the brush; and Ace, a waspy palomino with a reputation for bucking Frank off and breaking his leg.

When our horses were caught and led out, the gate was thrown open, and the cavvy let out to rest and graze the day away.

A cold breeze sucked down the draw at Badger Camp. Dandy's mouth felt warm when I slipped the bit across his tongue. Some of the horses humped up, using uneven ground, the grit of a jacket zipper, or the press of a spur as an excuse to play the bronc. Not Dandy. He moved quietly beside John's horse, Cuba. We lined out up the canyon, two by two.

৵

Badger Camp is tucked up against Badger Mountain, sixty miles from Surprise Valley. The country is dominated by the mountain's size, and by the geological features it presents on all sides. Shaped like its namesake, it looks squat, determined, as if rising up on all fours, ripped from the hide of earth, not as a range of high peaks, but as one mass in a posture of power.

Badger Summit (7,188 feet) is nearly twice as high as Mount Diablo, yet Nevada's basin-and-range geology limited my vision to a radius of less than two hundred miles: the Warner Mountains of Surprise Valley seventy miles to the west, Summit Lake Mountain fifty miles south, the Steens a hundred and fifty miles northeast, the Pine Forest Mountains a hundred miles east. The vast sweep of country within my sight was concentrated in its form, distilled down to the first thought of land, free of the mark of man, primitive, independent, whole. I thought of Africa's vast plains and, although the country had been settled for more than a century, I felt as explorers must.

That first morning we rode the north face of Badger, its benches and clearings, knobs and long sidehills. We checked for cattle at springs and in the dense, shadowed mahogany thickets. Bill and Frank trotted west as far as Domingo Spring, crossed the Flat into the north country, and swung toward P. B. Spring, while we picked up the cattle dotting rocky outcrops, scattered over every mesa. In that frosty October air the cattle threw their heads up when they saw us and ran down the mountain like water, spilling out on the flat. They numbered in the hundreds and strung out on the shortcut trail for a mile. Small calves, old cows, bulls sifted to the tail end like the dust. We drove them ten or twelve miles around the base of the mountain toward camp. I watched the men trimming the sides, one going forward to bend the cattle, to keep them from drifting off the trail. No boss shouted orders; they all knew how far we had to go. We eased back on the hills but kept them moving, always moving toward camp.

Late in the afternoon the last of the cattle passed into the holding field. Bill closed the gate, mounted, and we started toward camp. It felt wonderfully free. We were glad, the horses seemed glad to be quit of the bawling herd. All the aches I nursed—ragged throat, thirst, and hunger—were forgotten. October was soft on the hills. Shadows fingered across the flat to the foot of Blow Out Mountain. The horses dropped their heads and hit a swinging walk, all of us once again two by two in the track. Those in the lead eased into a trot as we got closer to camp. John came alongside, reached over, stripped Dandy's bridle off, and handed it back to me. Dandy squirted forward, encouraged by John's play. Bridle in one hand, reins in the other, I let him lope along until he realized he was alone. He stopped and nickered to the horses coming behind.

⊸⊘

Range cattle were different from the cattle I had handled before. Being away from fences and people they absorb wildness. I learned to sharpen my eyes to an odd shape or shade of color that was cattle far away. I learned the brands and the earmarks. Before I moved a cow, I made sure her calf was alongside. Not having seen a rider all summer, a cow might trot off and leave a sleeping calf. The clues to detect a wet cow are as subtle as clean teats, or bag hair wet to ringlets by a nursing calf. A wet cow brought in alone would have to be turned out the next morning to find her calf. It was a waste of time and left the calf vulnerable to coyotes.

The influence of the Spanish vaqueros brought north by Miller and Lux, Pete French, and others was in evidence in the men's vocabulary. *Buckaroo* is an Americanization of the word *vaquero, lariat* from *La Riata,* and *rodear,* which means the gathering up of livestock for working or sorting, becomes *rodeo.* We held rodear on a dry lake bed. Little bunches of cattle came from Martinez, Five Mile, the Ray Perry Field, off the Rock Springs Tableland, out of Sand Canyon. Alkali's cattle were all single-iron cattle. I was not thinking about strays. Bill and John entered the herd. The rest of us held them in a loose bunch. Suddenly one popped out. I put it back. Another shot out. I galloped hard to turn it. Bill gave the next one a push from the herd with quiet words, "You can let this one go."

The lightbulb snapped on. Embarrassed, I thought, "Can't you men just tell me what you're doing?" Truth was, if you are ahorseback, it's your job to pay attention. There is nothing more useless than having to respond to questions that could be answered by simple observation. From then on when we rodeared I watched what the men were doing and read their movements. By understanding their purpose I could be of help. Eyes— those of man and horse—held the key to the work.

The horse was simply a tool to some of the men, an extension of their own speed, endurance, and strength. The challenge for John was in teaching the horse to think, to take the initiative. He had observed horses, both wild and domestic, mastering each other, bossing, and he devised exercises to improve on their natural tendency to dominate and gave them the cow to boss. It was very simple really. The horse followed the rider's hands to the critter to be separated, and once it was pushed free of the herd, the horse established an imaginary line the cow was not allowed to cross. John gave the horse the tools and the confidence to think on its own, and it quickly took over from his hands. Once the horse was able to move free of John's direction, its reaction time was equal to the cow's.

As John and his horse worked cattle in silence on the broken ground of the desert, I watched a dance. The horse directed its attention at a certain cow as a predator would. It was natural for the cow to feel uneasy when he moved into her comfort zone. She worked to the edge of the herd until he stood between her and the other cattle. His intensity intimidated her. He had reduced her options. She must continue to move away or challenge his ability to keep her away. None of it was done for prize money; never was the movement of the horse more beautifully natural—athletic ability expanded by intellect. Work was what set these horses apart from others I'd known in my life.

I have forgotten so much of schoolroom lessons. Dates and facts drop from memory, leaving room for that first time in Nevada. For two weeks the world would not matter. This was the world. I was to discover longing for a place and a way to live.

The days were made of connecting each ride onto the next, the whole map of it constructed by those circles of going out, gathering in, riding back. I went where water raised, looked there for cattle and found tracks of antelope and deer, rabbit and mouse, and always, bits of obsidian. Storms blew over and changed the light, the colors. Valleys splayed out, hills slipped into complex draws, rocks wrinkled up from ridges or were spit out in cobbles, looking like zippers on the short grass. Solid rock split open into a sudden gorge wild with purple dogwood and bloodred rose briars, opening beyond into more open country. Sage grouse flushed, invisible before flight, invisible after. Hawk nest sewn to deer bed, to cow trail to knots of granite, bulge of pocked lava sewn to caves and blowholes gouged by wind, mahogany tangled dense and unyielding sewn to a trim of precious water—making whole the gown of the country.

Dust of cattle being pushed rose like smoke way off. Soon many bunches joined and swept forward in a crawling herd. At the end the country is known. Not every aspect, but generally. The other takes longer.

I had to give up every idea of distance. There was no glimpse of the desert in a bright opening ahead. It was all desert in every direction, never as far as I thought when John pointed to a pale, blue ridge receding behind others more distinct, saying we would meet there in an hour and we did. When we started toward camp I could see Badger Mountain ahead, but rode and rode as if on a treadmill. Obedient to its reality, distance ignored me. I could not control it, so I let it have its way and learned to let the day be measured by the work, not by the sun.

John kept me inside the circle at first. Soon he was able to send me to a far place, trust me to look at the country between, and meet him. He said to look back every once in a while, pick out some landmarks in case I got lost. Things always look different going back than they do coming.

I gathered the country on my own, chose my own path, kicked the cattle toward water or the trail to camp, and rode on. Suddenly I would see him, a drop of dark movement in the distance, a speck. When it appeared again it was horse and man, then bay and plaid shirt, then close enough to touch.

John sent me to the beauty places. Easily, in another kind of distance, I rode beneath the sea that once lived on the land. The sky became the water. Winds blew as tides. Ravens dipped in the breeze as gulls do, calling, flying straight on. I was a beachcomber gathering days to me, a hole drilled in each to hang about my neck until I was worn and smooth as they. On the desert floor, I found treasures of another time, sunken ships in single-room cabins settlers built and abandoned generations before. I learned a new country and a new way of living so different from all that was familiar I might well have been beneath the sea.

⊖

East from Five Mile I rode over the brushy, dry tableland of sandstone—pink and tan and the stain of rusted iron. John turned west through the deep wash into Sand Canyon. I let Ace trot free, skirting the steep-sided draws and scattered junipers. The air was sharp with the smell of wild onion crushed under the gelding's hooves. Suddenly, we broke out on the rim of a deep canyon filled with a desert lake, ducks and geese floating in the early light, aspen along the narrow shoreline against the pink cliff walls and a little bunch of range horses grazing at the water's edge. The stud dozed in the sunlight spilling over into the canyon. Black mane tangled forward along his shoulder, and his blue roan hide was scarred with a record of old battles. Two mares, a yearling, and a late-summer colt nipped grass. The brown mare looked up. Then they all did.

⌘

On another day John sent me to Chinatown. The name intrigued me. Beyond Mitchell Troughs a south slope opened out into a green lava flow twisted into tubes, pipes, and convoluted patterns like a rumpled pan of brownies. I was in it, picking my way through the coils of lava rope before I recognized the character of the place—physically being on a point of transition—force and tension not yet diminished. Sound was absorbed. Shrubs and wildflowers were crimped to bonsai, diminutive, enchanting. Mature aspen and mahogany were shoulder high, a natural occurrence in miniature. It was a place out of time or, more precisely, the beginning of time.

⌘

Trails skirted the rough western face of Badger Mountain and dropped into the grassy meadow below Cottonwood Creek. It began as a trickle wetting the sand at the base of a high cliff, increasing, meandering a wide canyon toward the lower country.

Obsidian litter circled the creek. Chips glistened in the light high up on each side. Indian campground sites everywhere. The country must have been a desert for a long time. Water meant life. I don't think I truly understood that before.

My home country at the base of Mount Diablo expects no rain during the months of summer. But the Pacific is just over the first low range of hills to the west, and storms sweep into the inland valleys from October until May, inches a day soaking in, sprouting thick stands of wild, red oats. When rain comes it is abundant, and the soil expands.

One day's storm there may equal what the Nevada desert receives in a whole year. The volcanic soils are too porous to harbor that moisture. So, dew is a water source, catch pools are a source, damp sand under an overhang is a source, every spring is known and counted on by man and animals alike.

The antiseptic taste of bitterbrush is said to keep one from wanting water. I chewed a stem and felt my mouth respond with wetness. Still, I wanted water.

I took the apple from my jumper pocket. Strangely exotic, its red-and-yellow roundness fit the cup of my palm, fruit of a fertile valley, out of place here. I put it back.

When we split up one morning toward the end of the ride John told me how to find the Last Supper Cave. There would be a warning posted at the mouth of the cave against disturbing the site. It was officially under study by university anthropologists, had been since '68. But as long as I didn't touch anything or pick up anything in the cave, I could go in.

I nearly missed it; the mouth of the cave was not noticeable from the trail. I left my horse and climbed up the rocky path. Warning ribbons fluttered from the boundary wire. I stepped over, feeling a little like a trespasser. The cave was as big as a two-story house, and the view from the mouth was to the southeast where Hell Creek flowed toward Virgin Valley. Water, food, and medicine sources, willows for basketry, brush and limb wood for cooking fires were all close at hand, and its placement high on the side canyon gave an open view of the rocky, brushy breaks, making the Last Supper Cave defendable against intruders.

An information bulletin nailed to a post reported that ". . . fragments of sagebrush bark cordage, twined basketry, and reed matting were found beneath the blown dirt at the site, and projectile points named for the Great Basin—Desert side-notched, Eastgate, Rose Spring, Elko Eared, Northern Side-notched, and Silent Snake-stem types—identified a 9000 year old community of native peoples. The remains of domesticated animals and bits of glass from medicine bottles indicated that the site was used into the 1900's—occupied through many generations."

The iridescent sheen of freshwater mussel shells in the tailing pile caught my eye. I dug some from the gravel and dung and dirt, and held the shells of mussels that once nourished the people of the cave. My thumb slipped into the cup of the shell. It could be a scoop, a spoon, an earring. Holding the tool, the ornament, I longed to know the community of this place alive with people, their joyous noise, their daily labor. But I understood by then that the land is independent of us; we were all disregarded, as the people of this cave were forgotten now. We are the blink of an eye. Passing through was merely that—passing. When I left the desert it would not miss me. I would miss it.

⊕

We were riding fast now on the second swing around the country, checking for cattle wherever there was water. We stopped at the gate to Cherry Springs. Two bay horses watched us from above the spring.

John told me to go on up to Billy McCluskey's, then follow the ridge behind the house down to Dave's, and meet him in the Yellow Hills. He was going to ride Hoo Doo and the Fountain. Watch for the wire, he called back.

I tied my horse to a fork of the cherry tree and walked up the hill to check the spring box before I got a drink. Billy piped the spring down to a trough so cows could drink and not tramp in the spring. The overflow fed a meadow he had fenced for his horse pasture. Rock cairns braced the corners. Rusted wire held tight and the fenceline ran true.

His house had been built in the '20s, under a ridge to protect it from the north wind. In those days, control of water meant control of the range. Billy and Dave Beebe squatted on springs for their boss, Harry Wilson. Now, leaves from the chokecherry trees blew in the broken windows. Swallows' nests daubed under the eaves in May were abandoned.

Shapes of cans in Billy's dump described the necessities of his household: five-gallon coal-oil cans were square, one-pound Folgers coffee cans were round and squat, condensed-milk cans—round with two neat punctures at the rim, one to let air in, the other to let milk out—Prince Albert tobacco tins, an elongated can, snap flap top, and painted red when they were new.

I sat on Billy's little porch, remembering my cheek against the Bull Durham tobacco pouch in my grandfather's shirt pocket, the stain of tobacco on his fingers, the comforting smell of it on his clothes, paper disks fluttering from drawstrings.

The mountains in Surprise Valley gleamed with snow in the distance. I wondered if Billy walked out onto that porch at night, tapped tobacco into the trough of trembling paper, and, as he twisted the ends, thought about being where people lived. Did he miss someone or was he content with no light in the world but stars, no sound but coyotes yipping and yodeling around, or a nighthawk's quavering song, or wind's little rustling in the sage?

⊷

The door was still on its hinges at Dave Beebe's place. It opened out. One room. The front window looked east. There was no glass to separate the image from the air. Cot along the south wall, table and chairs across from the cookstove of plain cast iron, fruit-box cupboard hung above the little wash table. The house was made of sandstone blocks Dave chiseled from the ridge, set into walls without mortar, abutted against the back wall of the hill's own rock face and into which he carved a fireplace and bored a chimney. He and Billy bumped a wagon some twenty miles to Summit Lake

Mountain where they cut cottonwood poles for a roof, furniture, and the long horse corral across the swale. I wondered how it looked with the head-high brush grubbed out and beaten down by horses being driven in, one small band at a time.

Dishes and cooking stuff were still in the cupboard, can opener on a hook, coffeepot hanging by the bail as if Dave would be returning. All of it, including the stove, would be gone in a few years. Desert homesteads and ranch houses were respected. But in the years after Billy and Dave died new people traveled the desert, treasure hunting. Hunters camped in the houses; tore the boards off the barn, and cut up juniper posts for firewood. They tossed the lower legs of butchered deer and whiskey bottles in the brush. They did not know the stories and couldn't help but take things away. It is a trait they easily recognize in rodents that carry shiny things into a nest; they call them packrats. They call themselves lucky. Soon Dave's house would be only walls, no roof, no door. Loosened rocks tumbling from the walls would roll to the desert floor and regain their first identity as rock.

No matter, Dave's fireplace mantel carved with horses running like those he and Billy drove toward the trap would always be on the face of the hill. I closed the door and rolled a rock against it to keep winter out—for now.

&

Zero degrees has a certain feel. No one wanted to read the thermometer that morning when we saddled up. We didn't need it verified.

Spanish explorers called Nevada the northern mystery. Although the word means "snow-covered land" they must have mistaken alkali salts for snow. Nevada receives less precipitation from snowfall than any of the contiguous states in the Union. But when snows come, the Spanish inspiration is fulfilled. The desert expands with purity and muffled sound. Each step forward breaks away from all that falls behind. Each step is the first step into mystery.

Late the afternoon before, going toward camp, we cut the tracks of a bull, but it got dark before we found him. As individuals, bulls reflect a major investment for the rancher. After the cows are bred up they sometimes pull off alone like buck deer, keg up, and winter-kill if not found.

Bill said we should give him one more try. The trail we needed to follow was under nearly a foot of snow that had fallen during the night. We rode to the last place we had seen the tracks and split up to look for the slightest depression in the snow that hinted of tracks. We scanned the brush for shapes of black or dull red—colors that also belong to the land. We looked in every stand of trees, every tumble of rock, every shadow held crisp against the white. In the mahoganies deer watched us pass by. They were finely drawn in gray, brown, charcoal-blue beneath the rough-barked trees, as if painted on rice paper.

On top of Badger Mountain mist and snow blew into a swirling white-out. Rowdy's tracks filled in as quickly as he lifted a hoof. It was a sensation of riding on clouds.

Blown snow obliterated the terrain. Distance was reduced to only what I could conjure from memory. To find my way I had to remember how the mountain looked only days before when we rode in shirtsleeves. I had to trust the compass I was given years before on another mountain. In the end, I found my way not by what I could see, but by the map experience had drawn in my mind.

I let Rowdy have his head. Horses know where camp is. He slid down an icy ridge, scrambling to keep his feet, and dropped into a pocket protected from the wind. I looked behind. His tracks were plain in the snow. Sky was up; earth was down. I was not lost. I could find my way back.

Rowdy jerked his head toward a movement in the trees ahead and nickered. John rode toward me. I wasn't the only worried one. Bill and Frank found the bull and drove him toward camp. John came back to find me.

⌘

The next morning was a little warmer. We hauled out to the far southern point of the range to save the horses extra miles. Someone would retrieve the truck later. All five of us were jammed in the cab, double-decked, rough road, heads hitting the roof on every bump. Silly antics. Jokes. Coats off, hot in the truck, cold when we got to Five Mile and stepped outside. Above Summit Lake Mountain the sky of hot apricot bled to saffron, and in the background a huge cloud was spun round, funneled upward. Higher, a layer of overcast was combed neatly by winds, as if a harrow had passed over them. I thought of a '50s civil defense drill, schoolroom tables against the windows, children huddled underneath, arms clamped to protect our necks, listening for the all-clear.

What do you think that is? I asked Frank, the one with the bet-winning eyes. (How many points on that buck, Frank? At four hundred yards.) He shook his head. But the color. Isn't it a strange, sort of burnt color?

No radio in the truck. No radio at the cabin. No way to know until the work was finished. I worried some great wrong happened. The jaundice cloud hung stationary.

Bill split the riders. He sent me toward the Potholes. We were to meet in the late afternoon on the road under McCluskey Spring. No way to know the condition of the world from here. Just get the work done.

My all-clear was in the brush below Ten Mile Spring. A cow bellered. Dust blew in a whirlwind. I rode down to take a look. The cow was wild, spinning and charging to keep a coyote away from her newborn calf. Two more coyotes kept just out of reach, circling to draw her from the calf, darting in and out as a team to expose it to their killing advantage. I happened along just in time to tip the balance to the cow and calf.

Suddenly she turned and charged Highpockets, my horse. She slammed hard into his chest, broke away, rushed back to her calf, and whirled to face us, ready to fight. I was glad she didn't have horns. I pulled back to let her calm down. The coyotes waited and watched me. To them I was another predator moving in on their meal. The horse was one big predator too many. They turned and disappeared in the brush.

I kept well away while the cow nursed the calf, and then I pushed the pair toward a bunch of cattle in the draw below. The calf's raw cord dangled and caught around his hind legs as he doddered along. Confused, he fell farther behind. The high brush threw up too many obstacles for a newborn calf.

I decided to try lifting him into the saddle so I could keep up with the cattle. The moment I grabbed him, he bawled and the cow came charging. We played peekaboo through Highpockets' legs while I tried boosting him, an eighty-pound, noodly-wet calf, onto the saddle. The old horse stood steadier than I should have expected with the cow banging into him and the calf bawling and struggling. I took my rope and put a loop around his feet, lifted, held until I got the calf balanced across the seat of the saddle. Getting myself aboard was not a cinch. But Highpockets stood and let me clamber up.

The cow finally gave up and trotted toward the bunch, and Highpockets carefully picked his way along behind. The calf relaxed against me. I forgot the poisonous-looking cloud. I came along just at the right time to keep one little guy stretched across my lap from being coyote breakfast. The big stuff of the world was on its own.

⊕

Bill, John, and I loaded our horses and drove northeast to Rock Springs to trade cattle with the MC buckaroos. The MC, headquartered in Adel, Oregon, bordered Alkali on the north. Range cattle can mix with the neighbors' cattle, and when they do ranchers meet and trade strays.

The MC cattle were already gathered when we arrived at the Rock

Springs camp. Buckaroo tents were anchored around in the rocks and brush; creamy white canvas under a broken blue sky; rodear, horses, buckaroos, sagebrush fire.

The MC cow boss invited us into the cook trailer to eat dinner and introduced us to Dee, a friendly, dark-haired woman stirring gravy on the gas stove. She laughed easily and seemed happy to have another woman in her kitchen.

Dee's job was simple but hard. She packed and moved camp ahead of the men's work and cooked three meals a day for a dozen hungry buckaroos. She said it was a good job but intense: no time to call her own, no place to get away, living in such close quarters with the men. There was always a buckaroo or two who offered to share his bedroll with her. She didn't fool herself; their longing was plain-old lonesome and homesick, and not to be mistaken for romance. Besides, there were the wives and girlfriends to consider.

After a Sunday in town one of the married men told her that his wife said she was "darned good and tired of hearing about how Dee made cakes and stuff for them every day out there in the desert on that contrary old cook-wagon stove."

Next Saturday night when the buckaroos were getting cleaned up to go to town Dee gathered them up for a talk. "Smarten up, you guys. You keep bragging on my cooking and there won't be a woman in all of Lake County that will speak to me. You've got to help me out here. Now, when you go in tonight you tell your girls that I've been letting you down in the dessert department, that I burned the only batch of cookies I made all week. Tell 'em I need a little help out here!"

Sure enough, Sunday afternoon a pickup came dragging a dust cloud across the flat, and pulled right up to the cook wagon. Inside were two wives Dee knew well. On the front seat between them were pies, cakes, bread pudding, and cookies. As they unloaded the sweet-smelling desserts they said Saturday night all the gals got together at the Adel Store and worked out a schedule so every week the men would have desserts. They patted her shoulder and said they all knew it wasn't easy to turn out pastries in a cook wagon out on the range, for goodness' sake.

Dee laughed just thinking about how she narrowly averted a social disaster. After a few weeks the dessert delivery slowed down and she went back to her regular practice of taking three pie requests every morning. We hit lemon meringue day. I think of the MC camp in that rough country on the north side of Catnip Mountain. Dee in her kitchen trailer. Lemon

Meringue Pie. Toasted tips of each meringue swirl raised above that tart-sweet filling. I stepped outside into storm clouds curled over the desert, tipped with rose. Under that sky I got on my horse and rode toward the cattle gathered against the rim.

We work out the Alkali cattle. There was not a loading chute within miles, so the strays had to be roped out and dragged into the truck. They were big, soggy cows. In the middle of the job a young buckaroo moved his horse to head a cow, and the horse bogged his head and bucked down through the rocks. The buckaroo threw his arms wide like he expected to fly and sailed off that horse. He slammed down unconscious or dead. We froze as the men galloped to where the boy lay, jumped off their horses, and gathered around him. After a while they helped him to his feet. He slumped down by the big tent as if he'd walked a hundred weary miles. The cow boss told us the boy was epileptic and the bucking horse triggered a seizure. It had happened before. Buckarooing was dangerous work for a kid with a problem like that, and the cow boss worried but didn't have the heart to let him go. The kid worked hard and the men respected his courage.

ꙮ

On the way back to Badger Camp, John and Bill's conversation told me the ride was done. They would reride the whole country again in another month. For now, it was over.

While John wrangled the horses I stuffed my duffel with clothes smelling of alkali and sage and horse sweat. I packed my late-night poker face, hoarding and losing stacks of chips, passing the wine jug. I packed squaw wrestling with Bill at Fish Springs, and Louie laying across the road in front of hunters' rigs to bum a beer. I packed someone nailing my cinch to the saddle-room floor, and us throwing Bill in the water trough at Ten Mile. I packed a hunter camped at Devaney asking us if we'd seen any decent bucks while we watched an even four point pass quietly behind him, between his Coleman stove and his cot. I packed John carving our names on an aspen tree above Hell Creek. I packed us sitting on Mary Pruitt's bench beside the stream that ran past her cabin door, and I packed Mary Pruitt.

The drive in was quiet. Both of us were tired. Both were wondering what was ahead. I wanted to spin a cocoon of wild silk around us against the passing of time.

Night was coming on. I looked over at John, he at me. I asked him to tell me how fast we would have to drive to keep up with the sun, to keep it from setting.

I stood on the top of Mount Diablo all those years back and learned the arc of the sky. I accepted what I saw to be the world in its entirety. I could not imagine liquid beneath its crust nor the pressures of heat and cooling, the building up and the wearing away. I did not understand the gift of water. I could not conceive of change.

The desert country had a different arc of sky enveloping a raw grandeur. I had never gotten to know a country as intimately, spending day after day in its company alone. My affection for the desert was won as friendship is, slowly growing, with elements of respect and admiration for small treasures, glimpses of complexities, gratitude for simplicity, communicating as much in silence as in conversation. In learning the desert the telescope turned inward and gave me time to learn the landscape within. My idea of home shifted.

From the ridge above Long Valley a star had come unstuck from the sky and fallen onto Nevada. It burned faintly against the dark hills. John said it was the light at the Washoe County road-maintenance yard.

Oh. A light. The first I had seen in two weeks aside from the faint lanterns glowing in the Badger cabin. I was emerging from a dream, one light at a time.

I looked back over my shoulder and took note of the landmarks. I felt certain I could find my way back.

✎ The Neighbor

5

NIGHT NEVER LEAVES HIS WINDOWS. MORNINGS ARE COLD. THEY ARE hungry for meat. The neighbor drives into the yard and waits in his car. John puts his sandwich down and goes out without his hat.

His forehead is Irish white. His cheeks and throat are browned with summer. His dark hands rest on the neighbor's door as he says hello.

The neighbor asks if John would butcher a steer for him for half the meat. It's been on grain ninety days. Should be good. Anytime it's handy. No hurry.

John looks hard into the deal for the loophole hanging above his head. Seeing none, he agrees. The next morning before there's a light in their kitchen window we go ahorseback, drive the walleyed steer out of his corral, across his fields to our gate, to our corral. By six his steer is hanging on the gambol. Blood puddles around our boots.

At eight he drives in. He says when John butchers the steer he should cut the oxtail deep—veed into the haunch—so there will be plenty of meat for soup.

It's too late. We've finished butchering his steer. The beef is in halves, clean and still as the cross beam it hangs from, the tail cut square. They must make do on that or organ meat.

Which half are you going to take, front or hind? His eyes are steady with the question.

Split 'er down the middle. We'll each have stew meat and steaks, even-steven.

He nods and looks at the hide stretched on the fence rails dripping pink-ish water into the dirt. Rank-smelling offal has been hauled down creek for scavengers. The head is skinned out the old way—cheeks, tongue, floating in icy water with the liver and heart. The brain was hacked out of its chamber of pure-white bone. He hobbles toward the skull, but the name he called all summer from the granary gate burned like bile in his mouth. He looked into the lidless eyes and made a hasty sign of crossing before he turned away.

6

At the meat market the butcher asks, This your beef, John?

No, he says. My neighbor's. He gave me half for butchering it.

Which half do you want?

Split 'er down the middle.

We'll let 'er hang a while, then I'll box it just that way.

A month or so later there's snow on the ground. The neighbor follows the county plow up the road, into the yard, rolls his window down. His breath glitters, frozen around him.

John walks out of the shop with a pair of jumper cables in his hands. He was going to start the feed truck. The neighbor leans away from John as if he already feels the red cable clamped on his cold, red ear—positive to positive. An apology slips over the sharp edge of the glass.

Remember when I said, "The woman went through all the meat and said she couldn't find any steaks, just hamburger and roasting meat? You musta got away with all the steaks. We got no steaks, a'tal." Wal, we looked again. There they were clear down in the bottom of the freezer: T-bone, sirloin, chuck, round, New York, just like you said. I'm sorry, John. I hope you're not mad at me.

He wasn't mad. It was too late to get mad. And besides, he had a soft spot in his heart for the crippled old man.

↦ Neighbor Boy

THE NEIGHBOR'S PICKUP WAS PARKED ON THE TURN IN THE LANE. HE
was wrestling a pallet from the back of his truck. Fixing fence, I chuckled.
I stopped behind him and got out. Never gushy, his greeting was hidden in
his quick blue eyes. I reached out and took one end of his pallet, crawled
through the rose briars and held it in place while he threaded baling wire
around a post and twisted it up tight.

When Bobby came home he would fix it right, he said. This would keep
'em home for now.

I remarked on the work Bobby had done the summer before, steady
through the heat, day after day, resetting posts, stapling wires up fiddle-
tight, burning out ditches, and farming straight through till it was too dark
to see. Every year he spent his vacation time helping the folks out.

The neighbor said it was too bad I never knew Marvin. He was a good
son, too.

Marvin? I knew Bobby lived in Minnesota now, and David, the youngest,
worked for us one summer before he died. But I didn't know about Marvin.

↦

The ten-year-old boy pumped his brother's bike up the hill to town. A
sound-truck speaker splashed a man's voice back and forth, directing partic-
ipants of the fair parade to the elementary school yard. Main Street was

filled with the parade crowd, and people lined the sidewalk. A red ribbon fluttered on Mr. Arnold's shirt. He flagged cars to stop or go down Garfield or park behind the gas station. Two guys in a Dodge sedan honked and hollered at him to let them through. He told them to go around. The parade was starting and Main Street was closed.

Weeks before, the light-company men rigged Modoc County Fair banners, pole to pole, across the street. All month long the banners swayed and snapped, and the words appeared and disappeared with every change of the wind. The town was all dressed up in flags and streamers, something he'd been waiting to see all summer, yet it was bittersweet. Fair came at the end of haying, right before Labor Day and the beginning of school.

People hurried along to get a good viewing place, on car fenders, lawn chairs along the curb, talking, pushing in and out of the bars. Music carried down the street.

Nine o'clock and hot already. Kids were everywhere; little ones by their folks; older ones played around. Some had balloons. When he saw the sunshine on the balloons—red, blue, white, gold—he wanted one of his own to tie on his handlebars, to let it float above him like a friend. Maybe he would buy one at the fair. He felt the heavy coins in his pants pocket against his leg from pop bottles he picked up along the road. He stopped at the crossing. A kid across the street hollered, "Hey, Marvin." Mr. Arnold waved at him to hurry, the parade had started.

The school band came up the street silent, just marching. Their shoes scuffed like the beat of a single drum. He could feel the sound vibrate in his chest. A horse pranced along in front of the band, and sparks shot out as its iron shoes struck the pavement. The stripes of the flag draped along the horse's neck, folded into a spiral. Cowboys and cowgirls from the rodeo carried flags, and a clown riding a little mule played a big brass tuba, only instead of music, confetti blew out of the horn onto the street. Behind him people rode in open cars and on the backs of trucks or wagons, waving and calling to their friends. The parade stopped when it got to the post office, and the nervous horse stood quiet and the band instruments came up shining and full of music.

> Oh, say can you see
> by the dawn's early light
> what so proudly we hailed
> at the twilight's last gleaming

Marvin's whole day was the fair. Tilt-a-whirl. The Hammer. Everything sparkled and spun. When he quit feeling dizzy and sick he ate three corn dogs and a Nehi orange soda pop. He caught up with some of the kids from school, and they poked through the booths on the midway together, tossed Ping-Pong balls at goldfish in bowls stacked up in a pyramid of fishbowls, and threw baseballs at milk bottles. He won a whistle.

Behind the Boy Scout booth they all laid flat out on the cool grass like puppies, observing each other, maybe how one had grown taller, and remembering each other after having lived apart for the whole of summer.

A couple of the older kids said they were waiting around until the carnival was over. When the roustabouts started breaking the rides down they would look for money in the grass. One of the boys said his brother's friend found a silver dollar once and one of the carnies saw him and said "Give it!" and grabbed the kid's wrist hard. But the kid broke loose and ran. So if you find something be cool and keep your mouth shut. Another one said his uncle could hit a silver dollar in midair with his .30/30; he'd seen him do it. They never did find the dollar. One said, aw, he never hit it at all. The first one swelled up, said he did, they all heard it go *zzzing*. And then they got talking about guns and what kind, and who had a hunting license, and who was going to deer camp, and where.

It was still early. Horse races were going on the main track, and there was a baseball game on the big field. Marvin was having a great time and he didn't want to go. But before his father agreed to his going to the fair alone he made the boy promise to be home by five for his chores. Marvin asked a passing man for the time. It was 4:35. He hurried off without saying good-bye, bought a balloon, picked up his bike from the pile by the gate, and cut across the parking lot.

Marvin put his feet up on the handlebars and coasted down the long hill toward home. Warm wind flapped the shirttail around his tan back and belly. Cards clipped to the struts clicked against the spokes in a purr. He held out his arms, then his legs, balanced just on his seat. It almost felt like flying. A loop of string pulled against the right grip dragging a blue balloon behind his speed.

⊸

The arena announcer called the last heat of chariot horses to the track. Despite it being the last event of fair week, the grandstands were still full and the beer stand was ten deep. Chariot races were a favorite at the fair. After the movie *Ben Hur* came out, meets popped up all around the West. It was the number-one country sport for ranchers who had never driven a team to do anything but haying, or on a feed wagon. Homemade chariots were a bolted, chopped-down fifty-gallon drum on light axles and a pipe tongue welded to the frame. It was something new to work on all the long winter besides balky tractors and haying equipment, and racing kept their interest in driving horses alive. They designed aerodynamic bodies, the lighter the better, painted them up, greased the harness. Some of the guys hauled to winter meets in Oregon and Idaho where sharp-shod horses pulled chariots down icy tracks, and come summer you could watch hot-running horses, bred for the quarter mile, sprint the dry lake bed.

Vern Smith drove his team away from the trailers and onto the back track. His horses were fast; his chariot was light. He drew up on the inside rail. Good spot. He intended to win the purse this year. Vern wrapped the lines around his hands in what he called his suicide hold as he drove the horses up into his slot. Three other teams came alongside, nervous and pushing to go. The starter held his flag until they quieted down. He wanted a square start. As the last team came to the line he dropped the flag, and the horses went off. Vern's team shot to the lead, low and fast into the first turn. He braced hard into the force pulling him. It was dangerous and wild flying behind the horses, nearly out of control. A team of browns gained, then the grays pulled up beside him. By the second turn they were all running dead even. Three-quarters up the backstretch Vern's inside horse stumbled, lunged, and nearly went down. Vern fell back, all his weight on the lines holding the team together. The sorrel horse leaped forward on three legs until Vern pulled them into the ground. The sorrel fell forward, face down on the track, its right front leg flopped and twisted halfway down the cannon bone. The sledgehammer of it hit Vern in the stomach, but he held the lines tight and said, easy, easy, to the horses. Cowboys ran from the infield toward the team, grabbed hold of the bridles. They unhooked the sorrel quickly, quietly, all the time saying, easy, boy. Easy. The people in the grandstand were standing silently, watching the back track where the cowboys huddled around Vern's team. The announcer told them it was bad, to look away. But they could not.

Somebody pulled Vern's trailer alongside the horses. The men held each other wrist by wrist, and lifted the horse into the trailer.

They all felt lousy. But there was only one thing to do with a broken-legged gelding, and it needed to be done right away. Somebody shoved a bottle of whiskey at Vern. It shook in his hand as he took a deep pull. If the sorrel had gone down, the bay horse would have rolled under the chariot, and Vern would have been thrown forward, the whole thing somersaulting after him. Damned lucky it wasn't him with a broken neck, someone said, handing the bottle his way again.

Vern reached in the truck, pulled his .30/30 down from the rack, checked the magazine, threw the rifle on the seat. His face was grim. Without a word, he climbed in the truck and started it up. As he crossed the track the announcer asked the folks in the grandstand to give him a round of applause. "For what?" he growled to himself.

Past the barns. Out onto the highway. At the intersection a guy waved, another hollered, "Where you goin', Vern? The party ain't over. Quittin' early?" Vern cut every man's hair in the valley one time or another and some of the women. They liked him, told him half their business, most of their secrets, and all their stories. Had they known he was going across the lake to kill that dandy sorrel colt he raised out of his good rope mare, they would have felt sorry and watched him pass by without a word. As it was, he didn't see them or hear them. His mind was ten miles ahead where he'd level the sights and drop his colt in the greasewoods. Dead.

⟁

Marvin saw a silver glider slant down over the trees at the Ricksteiner Place and swoop out over the playa. He put his feet on the pedals and stopped, spitting gravel aside. The glider arced upward. Long, slender wings looked exactly like the balsa ones he carved and painted and wired into a turn above his bed. Without thinking, he sailed past his turn and straight on toward the lake, drawn by the plane as it flattened down and settled onto the playa. He dove the bike off the causeway on the lake road, across the glitter of broken glass, and bumped along the alkali and salt-grass flat toward the pilot just climbing out of the cockpit, cars and people ganged around. Never before in the long years of the '60s had he been happy to see the lake dry. This was different. Just a quick look and then he'd git for home. Marvin rode straight to the plane resting on the white glare.

He laid the bike down and pushed through a crack between people with his body still smelling sweet of cotton candy. No one told him not to touch the plane. But the pilot watched him as he might watch himself in a mirror. A stub finger light as breath drew along the wing's long reach. He turned and walked back until he could see into the cockpit at the narrow seat, crouched until he could see out the windshield. The dark mountains on each side of the playa east and west formed a rifle sight, a groove for the glider to shoot through into so much sky.

There was a second seat behind the pilot. A man with a bottle of whiskey in one hand pushed him aside and climbed into the plane. He jammed a twenty into the pilot's shirt pocket, held his hat on the back of his head with one hand, tipped the bottle back. He offered it to the pilot. The pilot refused and shoved a paper sack at him and said, "If you gotta puke, use this!"

The tow car started slowly down the flat. The slack rope reeled out, tightened in a hard line. The plane rolled forward. Marvin jumped on his bike and peddled alongside the glider, faster and faster until he was even with the pilot's window. The balloon dragged shoulder high.

↢

Time, what do we know of it? the pilot asked himself. No telling where he was headed. His was the life of danger, the vertical edge of chance every time he strapped on a plane and rode it into the sky. Safe flying was diminished by mathematical equation with each entry into the dream he dreamed as he flew, that he had the right to enter the sky, that there would be promise holding him aloft. There was nothing else when he was in the sky, just flight. Being up there. Touching nothing, only air. Crossing a border he could not define.

Sometimes as he did his preflight check he wondered, would this be the day? How does fate work, after all, if it takes possession of the lives of children, like this boy, just outside the plane window, turns them toward safe jobs—shoe salesman, cowboy, teacher, gas jockey—while others, like him, sought the dangerous excitement of flight? He could not remember a time he was not possessed by light lingering in the sky.

Years back, when he was living in Farmington, New Mexico, flying a little biplane duster along the San Juan River, he had seen a Navajo ceremony, a sand painting created on a hogan floor.

The ceremony was to begin at dawn. He drove in dark hours, unsure of the country, the turns. The honored invitation of a Navajo mechanic at the hanger made him press on until he smelled the smoke of a piñon fire. He unrolled the window, let its sweetness into the car. Up ahead, a hogan set against a sandstone bluff, an arbor to the side, pickups parked near the corrals, and sheep feeding beyond appeared in the predawn light. His friend waited for him just outside the hogan. They entered together. Immediately he felt the familiar embrace of low ceiling and circular walls, and he was absorbed into the silence of creation.

A painter sat on the earthen floor in the center. Pots of pollens, cornmeal, sandstone, crushed flower petals, crushed rock, and charcoal were beside him. Color trickled from between the old man's thumb and fingers in steady strokes. As the painting developed the pilot felt locked into the mystery of creation. Understanding lingered like piñon smoke, penetrating yet elusive as a delicate balance was achieved, the direction elemental, opening east. Sun. Moon. Without knowing he'd done so he gasped when the painter's brown hand swept the sand painting away. A shattering in his chest was followed by a sense of peace. Forever after it was the calm of the enclosed circle, the dignity of the ceremony, the painting above the line of the plane when he flew. It kept his compass true, going forward, and all that he wrote with the body of the plane fell in on itself behind him, as if he had never opened the air, as if he had never been.

The pilot waved at Marvin as dust billowed up behind the car, the glider lifted, the rope came loose, and the plane went up at once like a bird. The boy remained, both feet on the earth, watching the white plane turn, pull the evening sky beneath it, write silent arcs like perfect penmanship above the earth. The glider was a white swan finding the right layer of air where swiftness moved in a stream. It flew weightless, sure, the most beautiful thing Marvin had ever seen.

He dreamed what he would see if he were in the plane. First, the valley flat and wide beneath him, and the playa connecting into a chain of three long, glassy, dry lake beds, rough mountains to the west, and deep sand dunes on the east, the high desert reaching far out and beyond sight. Then, he would see how the two highways into the valley made a cross in the middle of Cedarville, one arm shorter, one longer. Headlights would be crawling along the roads. In town, the carnival rides, the midway, would be bright with colors beneath the trees and people like ants down there. Maybe the pilot would loop-d-loop above the fair, bank one wing, and slide east from town, and the kids would look up and somehow know it was Marvin up there. When the plane leveled he would look for his house, white, two story, in the grove of big cottonwoods, his room on the upstairs corner. His dad would be coming in from the barn, from chores. Oh, no! Chores. Marvin's eyes came down from the sky. He jumped on his bike and went as fast as he could toward home.

❧

Vern never saw the kid on the bike. He came out of nowhere. He was just *there*, popped up from the lake road in front of the truck. The sound was impact, death happening, the moment that—no matter what is said or what is regretted—cannot be reversed or changed.

❧

Time. What do we know of it? Is it a blue balloon rising through the sky?

⤏   Oat Crop

THE NEIGHBOR FIGURED THE SEED WITH A STUB PENCIL ON THE FENDER—
eighty pounds to the acre—all his last year's grain crop harvested, sacked,
stored in the tin granary, to plant this sixty-acre corner field. It was a cold
spring—that last one—and dry to boot. Lucky to turn off at all.

Now that he's dead, I'll be using his old drill—the green paint's rusted
through clean down to the iron. It was converted in the '30s from a team of
horses. I hook it to our wheel tractor I call Trigger because it rears up when
I start off.

I top off the gas, check the oil, radiator, service the drill, grease all the
zerts, every moving part, check each feed funnel, and set the gauge to
trickle down oats onebyone onto the seedbed ahead of the packers.

Every sack I leg, belly, grunt, arm wrestle up to the drill box, and fight
the sacker's knot. Finally, it ripcords, spilling hard, blond, slippery seed
with a whoosh. I smooth them even over the holes, pluck up a single oat, roll
it on my tongue, soak it in my juice, bite down for luck, toss it in the box.
Oats that came out of this ground are oats going back in today.

⤏

Trigger's iron seat's already butt-blistering hot when I kick it into gear, eye-
ball a straight line to a fence post or gully or sagebrush. Trigger rears up. I
spur him a lick and go steady all dayandtomorrowandtomorrow, back,

forth. At the row end, I stand on the inside brake, lock the wheel, and Trigger comes hard around compass-wise, combing an empty loop in the dirt that will drill out on the final round.

I cherish those flaxen oats laid out under this pieced pattern of loam and clay. They will awaken with the first rain, sprout, thread toward the sun, sweetening, ripening past milk to soft dough, nod heavy in the wind, and each will multiply itself by twenty—unless it turns off dry or cold or early rain rots the seed. But we can't *not* try. Hell! It's mostly luck anyway—all of it.

I wear the sun in my eyes and sleep with its light. I eat the dust and feel its weight in my bones. Hours fall behind me like these rows. I stop to fill the drill box again and again. School bus comes down the lane. Little sprouts packing lunch buckets and color books get off and play their way home. Bus turns around, goes back for the big ones.

Early spring I prepared the ground, combed out the tangles. Today I plant the seed. I'll tend it just as the old man did and watch the field come up through summer, hip high, dollar-bill green. When the oats ripen we'll pull the combine into the field. The reel will gather to it, the shaker will pass the seed along to fill the sacks row for row:

> A measure to feed the stock when snow lays on.
> A measure saved back for next year's seed.
> A measure to mark my passing over the land.

↬

Blood sister, I am to these fields.

√ Mapping Bodies of Water

WE LIVE AT A SEAM WHERE DESERT IS QUILTED TO MOUNTAINS. IN
Surprise Valley two unique regions of climatic invention run smack into
each other. The Great Basin reaches west only this far. The Warner Mountains, a broken tip of the Cascade lance, is the opposing force. Volcanics have
shifted the boundaries epoch after epoch, creating a complicated geologic
pattern. Scraps of Pleistocene, Miocene, Oligocene are sewn on the valley's
face.

Lake Surprise defines the seam. But its waters are not eternal. Five hundred feet high on the eastern hills under a dust of spring snow, ancient wa-
terlines show up plain as pencil marks on a doorjamb marking a child's
growth. Fish spawned in those deep and pure waters. Several million years
ago things changed, geologic things, cataclysmic things that altered the inflow. Since then, spring runoff has been the only reliable source. Streams
and creeks the length of the valley feed through alluvial fill of foothill
country to a highly mineralized lake never more than a few feet deep. Water that reaches the playa becomes at once unpotable, amuddle with salt-
tolerant microscopic creatures.

Native people tell of a giant serpent that lived in the lake. They say it
carved the shore with its tail as it curled to sleep. When the waters dried up

the serpent followed the receding waters south to Pyramid Lake where it disappeared and was never seen again.

Science has supported the Native American theory that Lake Surprise was an arm of the Great Basin's Lake Lahontan. But recently another theory has been put forward suggesting Surprise was an independent body of water, singular, spreading from this basin only as far as Duck Lake, a slightly higher basin to the south. Denied rivers and an outflow, Lake Surprise is ephemeral now and mapped as an alkali sink. Three sinks, actually, separated twice by land bridges. Seventy miles long, all together. Water comes and goes Houdini-fashion. Bring on the rain and we will have a lake, abracadabra! Dry winter? Shazam! Dry basin.

To fully understand the boundaries of the lake you must study not only the geology, not only the scientific record, but also the precise nature of its value in human terms. Negative space. Poetry.

⟜

The two regions of mountain and desert don't always react compatibly to the forces of weather. The rain shadow cast by the Warner Mountain fault block extends tremendous influence over the landmass to the east, robbing it of moisture. Conflict can be felt when they arch against one another, stiff legged, bristling, creating a dry wind. Or perhaps, I read it wrong and it's not war at all, but passion in their meeting as sea air cools, pushing inland over the snowcapped peaks. Meanwhile, the warmer desert ground flow draws beneath. Tension results where they meet and mix hot with cold, and writhe and spin a wind.

I entertain myself by exploring such theories as I work to finish drilling the field before the storm cuts loose. I keep an eye on the sky into the morning. The light breeze in the early hours has hardened into wind. My hands are a poor woman's barometer, joints stiffening with pressure, tight on the tractor wheel.

⟜

Lake Surprise reflects a heavy roll of cloud lying in a trough formed by contrary winds. For now the cloud is still squeezed off, a string of sausages, one over each of the three lakes. If it stays split, we will be all right. If it adducts, tightens, jelly rolls, darkens from pearl to granite, granite to moleskin, moleskin to lead, if it turns the volcanic gray of Mazama ash that settled out of the sky seven thousand years ago, if it becomes the tumbling gray of pigeons that nest in the abandoned slaughterhouse, if it flaunts the unspoken shade of gray that is the water under its belly, we are in for a blow.

Often in spring red-tailed hawks ride the winds that spill off the mountain escarpments unimpeded, unmet by opposing winds. They hover like harriers above the high trees, slightly flexing the angles of the tail, the arc of the wings, while the stem of their body holds steady, and cause children to note the magic of soaring. But the winds of this March day are not soaring winds. Hawks, starlings, blackbirds, sparrows are nowhere in sight. The horses and cattle are not bucking and running silly, signaling the weather change. They are holed up in the willows, bunched, heads down, tails to the storm they sense will come.

The dust storm increases in force, sweeping topsoil across the field in wave after wave. At times I can't hear the engine over weeds and dirt hitting the windshield. I try to ease my grip, but I worry the tractor will be blown over on a turn. When it doesn't make sense to stay I park the rig on the lee side of some outbuildings and go home.

⌁

John calls it the wind cloud. He knows its ominous pallor as the petals of the wind rose unfold. He remembers the smell of it, like plants we call compassweed or fiddleneck, or dodder.

In 1972, such a cloud formed and blew. The wind gauge at Doc Gilbert's office broke when wind pushed the needle into the red past one hundred miles an hour and the weather glass shattered. It was that strong and stronger for one entire day. We collected our seven-year-old daughter, Katie, from school midmorning and witnessed violent gusts turn a trailer house inside out, pitching belongings to the wind as it cartwheeled across the pastures toward the lake. That was in town. At our place on the open expanse of the lakeshore the wind raged unchecked. We brought the dogs into the safety of our porch and from there watched a steel water tank get up and over a fence, a wagon tip over, the haystack come apart like feather pillows, a slab of roof-tin machete a path across the barn lot. Flying limbs shattered two windows. John fought his way out to the shop between gusts and brought plywood to cover the holes. It was a heroic act, if not foolish.

One of the big cottonwoods, more than one hundred years old, six feet through at the base, blew over. Limbs missed the house by twenty yards, and we did not hear it, we did not feel it, so intense was the wind. John thought it best to get away from the windows. He lit his grandmother's kerosene lantern and placed it on the table. We sat within the clutch of its light. We played Monopoly, and we played, for Katie's sake, at not being afraid.

The wind slackened into a monotonous drone during the night. The same weary phrase repeated again and again until the desert surrendered, and the wind went on. A sigh, a calm, stirred us from our chairs, and we went in a line as battle-fatigued soldiers, all of us together, collapsed into bed.

I woke at dawn. The wind still blew through my mind, swirling tattered memories of the storm like leaves. I opened the door. The massive trunk of the fallen tree filled the yard. Limbs meant to reach eighty, ninety feet into the sky, limbs that spread above our lives, limbs where the red-tail returned to nest each spring lay shattered across the yard, across the road, crushing the pasture fence.

Katie brushed by me. She stood with her hands on the root mass that had been wrenched from the ground, staring hard down into the ragged pocket in the earth. She pointed to the water a few inches from the surface. The water was dark. Clean. It had never seen the sky, she said. It rose through layers of earth to nourish the tree. It stood at a level. Who would it serve?

She knelt, lowered her face beneath the reach of the roots, and she drank.

⌀

In that wet spring of the big wind, Lake Surprise filled and flooded over the road. When it came spring-turnout time we intended to drive our cows across the causeway to our desert range, but the two miles of asphalt disappeared at the lake's edge. We knew the pavement was six inches under the water. The cattle were not as sure. They sniffed and spooked at the waves slapping up their legs. Ahead, reflectors marking the road edge rattled and wobbled in the wind. Brine shrimp and horseshoe crabs, awakened from suspended animation deep in the mud by the inflow, darted and dove around the cattle's hooves. The cattle turned back. John quickly rode his horse through the herd and took the lead. The cows watched his horse and followed, strung out behind the single rider in a long line across the water. From a distance, the crossing appeared to be a ranch country reenactment of a Bible story.

That summer the state road crew widened the cut in Cedar Pass and hauled the dirt in belly dumps to raise the causeway four feet. It was the last time our cows crossed the lake on faith.

⌀

Lake Surprise has been full of water for five years. Before that it was dry for ten. Diaries of emigrants on the Oregon Trail tell us it was dry in the early 1850s when they crossed Goose Lake. During the drought of 1932 their wagon tracks were visible in the rock-hard lake bottom like the scraped lines Native people thought were made by a serpent's tail.

To make things worse for the settlers, the Great Depression cut the dry country deeper than wagon tracks could. Surprise Valley ranchers had no control over the climate, financial or natural, and many were left in ruin. There was no hay to put up. They had to cut their numbers, sell—if they could find a buyer—on a rock-bottom market.

My father was working on a sheep ranch in '32. The boss called him to his office. Across the desk, he handed over a .30/30 carbine and a carton of shells, and told him to go out to the feedlot and kill the sheep. Dad was a teenage boy, a little wild but not cruel. He did not take the rifle. The owner back east wired orders, the boss shouted. Do as you're told!

He said he shot a few. Rage at the boss made him shoot some more. Then the blood and the cries of the sheep made him dizzy. Vomit twisted his mouth. He looked into the pen. Sheep, just like his dad's. He dropped the rifle and walked three days to get home.

↢

Lawrence Parman, partner in the Parman Ranches of Surprise Valley and northeastern Nevada, said their company bottomed out in 1929. Three-year-old steers were worth four dollars. No one wanted wool. They got a bill from a warehouse in New York City for wool storage.

Lawrence went to trapping to feed the family. In '32 he sold his hides to a buyer set up across from the train station in Gerlach. The buyer paid him off with a draft written on a bank in Reno, eighty miles away. Nobody in town could cash it. Lawrence didn't know if the draft was any good, but he had to take the chance. He crossed the tracks where a train chugged idle, taking on water, slipped between boxcars, and tramped the train into Reno. Hanging under a speeding train did not worry him; trading the hides from two hard winters of trapping for a piece of worthless paper did. He jumped off the train when it crossed Virginia Street and went directly to the bank. The draft was good. He got a few small things for his wife, and bought a ticket on the next train back to Gerlach. Lawrence straightened his shoulders when he said that he "rode home—like a gentleman."

At Gerlach he piled some grub on the counter at the general store and handed over a twenty. The storekeeper looked at the bill as if it were yen and said, "You'll have to take the whole twenty dollars' worth. I ain't got change."

The economy of the country might have been mired down, but at twenty-three years of age Walter Hussa and his chum Herb Wood refused to be depressed. They elbowed over a picture of a canoe and smoked and figured. At P. B.'s lumberyard they pulled out some clear box boards to form the bulkheads, cut green willows for the ribs, bought canvas for the skin from the Johnstone Store, and together, in the back of Hussa's Meat Market, constructed a two-man sailboat, never mind the drought.

In 1935 the weather started. Snow lay on before Christmas. People tunneled through drifts from the house to the outhouse to the barn to the woodshed. The school bus was stuck all winter down long lanes, ran off the main roads, got buried in the bar pit. It rained right through April, tore out fences, marooned livestock, swamped corrals and stackyards, silted in ditches, and the runoff filled Lake Surprise as it had not for years. Walt and Herb were ready.

Tippy Tim was not yare. They launched it in their swimming trunks and spent more time flipping over than sailing. After *Tippy Tim*'s maiden voyage a gang of them drove down south of Eagleville to soak in the Squaw Baths and steam the alkali out of their hides. And they had fun.

A crowd gathered along the causeway whenever they saw the canoe go through town tied on Hussa's panel truck.

While *Tippy Tim* was unceremoniously throwing its sailors in the drink, Walter partnered up with a real carpenter, Morris Warden. They sent away to *Popular Mechanics* for plans for a shallow-draft rocker bottom boat able to handle the shallow lake, gathered up some one-by cedar planking, and ordered some brass fittings. Walter's mother sewed up canvas sheeting into a sail on her Singer.

Alkali Ike was an unsinkable sailboat that would seat fifteen passengers on the deck. Indeed, the passengers came in handy when the wind died and left them stranded twenty miles south of Cedarville. They took turns poling the boat toward home. A string of headlights along the causeway was their lighthouse. Their names were launched across the water with hoots of laughter and every verse of "Abdullah Bulbul Ameer." The sailors finally put ashore at two in the morning.

The gang built surfboards, with ropes and handlebars, tied them to a twenty-foot fir pole wired to the back bumper of a pickup, and surfed along the causeway. For a while they did forget their troubles. Townsfolk did, too, as the lake came alive with buckaroos, sheepherders, ranchers, and young women looking gay and sophisticated and pretty nearly foreign, adrift under billowed sails on the chalky-brown water.

☙

The dry up began again in the 1980s. Each year started out with garden soils turned and manure spread thick. Fields were prepared, grain or alfalfa seed drilled, in faith that storms brewing up way out over the ocean would be coming in like cows for milking. In faith we looked ahead to winter snows and spring rains that would come to release us, renew us, the way it used to be, the way it was supposed to be. The weight of each dry day took its toll as we slipped into a poverty of drought.

In the first year, while we bitterly mourned the dry landscape and feared fire, we tried on Walter's attitude, using the playa for a playground, golf driving range, speedway, bike track. His sailboat was reborn with a new twist: land sailors or sand sharks, sailboats on wheels. Great Basin dryland sailors sped down the lake bed under brightly colored sails. Some of us exercised our young horses and ourselves, or rode motorcycles, or whatever we could imagine. We drove the eastern shoreline to gather up fence posts spit up by frost, ripped out by wind-driven ice, and left scattered. We pried out staples and tangles of wire swollen with minerals and salts, stacked the heavy posts on the wagon, rattled home. We rebuilt the fence. Strung new wire.

As consequence mounted, hope vaporized with the rain clouds. The drought years bunched and stretched to eight. We grew quieter, withdrawn. We refused to say its name as if speaking the word would call it home for good.

There was nothing to do but wait. But wait for what? Answers to prayers? Which was the right prayer? Or was there weight in collective prayer?

Children were conceived, born, and lost their first tooth without feeling a steady rain on their hair. The word *umbrella* could be crossed off their spelling lists. Wading pool doubled for a bath, and then Mother dipped the water on her limp garden plants. Dishwater was saved in a pail, bubbles scooped down the drain, the rest poured out on roses or fruit trees. No need of rain boots or slickers, or wooden boats. Puddles?

Geese, ducks, avocets, curlew, cranes veered away to other refuge and abandoned us like the storms that snagged on the mountaintops, crossed overhead, thinning, gone. Bluebirds, northern orioles, yellow-headed blackbirds, meadowlarks sang in other valleys. A cock pheasant paced a path along the chicken wire where my hens shamelessly rolled beads of water down their throats. I set a pan out for him. Quail died off. Deer panted in the hot shade and came into the calf lot at night. Their moonlit shoulders leaned toward water in the trough. Swans flew above us through the night, high and fast. Their whistling cries drifted through the open window above our bed, sounding, for all the world, like a ghost rain.

‹⊳

Worst of all I hated the death of trees. Native grasses would come back or could be reseeded, but not the trees shading the park, the hospital windows, Main Street. Tree houses, planked and nailed, could not hold limbs in place. They fell and fell, or someone cut them before they dropped on a house. Sweet sawdust of locust, crack of poplar, here and there. Working up the wood distracted the eye from the sudden bald view and the mind from missing cemetery trees. Matrimonial trees. Century trees.

The old ranch houses in the valley are defined by stands of poplars and cottonwoods. I have heard old-timers say that the government issued seedlings to homesteaders, free for the asking, to be planted as windbreaks. The political construct was this: a tree is a commitment, a row of trees is a claim, several stands of trees defines a community, a community forms an outpost to be seen from a distance, secure and permanent, strengthening the claim of the western territories in the name of the Union. All that is beside the point now. Across the expanse of open land the staggered rise of tree rows and underlayer of orchards populate the valley in generations just as the human ones do. They are the visual deed of trust.

‹⊳

Oaks were indigenous to our valley in the Miocene when this world was flat. I've seen the art of their leaves etching stone, veins logically spidering outward from the stem, shoveled from the earth at the base of the mountains. But there are no oaks growing among the juniper and pines now, not in modern times. Too cold. Too high. Not enough rain.

Settlers tried to make this valley look like those left behind in Ohio or Missouri, or Virginia, or Tennessee. Oaks would make it more like home, especially in the fall. I know of four pioneer oaks that have survived.

In the 1800s an acorn was carried back to Surprise Valley from the National Arboretum in a coat pocket by William Cressler, one of Cedarville's founding fathers. He planted a small arboretum beside his house on Main Street; the oak and a grand maple remain.

A few years later a scarlet oak seedling was brought by Dr. Kober from

Berkeley to Fort Bidwell and planted at the front gate of his niece Elsie's home. In the fall it can be seen for miles, mistaken for fire.

The Dodson family planted an orchard on their homestead in the mid-1800s when they migrated from their home country in Arkansas. The Dodsons' pin oak is in Alice Hicks's field south of Cedarville. Sheep graze beneath its brilliant purple-red canopy.

There is a scarlet oak in a Cedarville yard, one of eight acorns started in 1966 by the whim of Susie Murphy.

The oaks outlive the people. They are a pin on a map that connects a name to a place, a story we keep on telling of putting roots down, enduring.

I have planted oak number five in my yard, a seedling of the Kober oak. The first year it had five leaves, the next, seven. Last year the freeze turned eleven leaves red-gold. This year twenty-two. I protect it with wire and mulch in the winter. I pour water at its base and talk to it admiringly, as I do the colt born only yesterday out my side door, as a tutor, that it grow up sturdy and bright, agile and willing. I speak to it as I would to my heir.

Where Streams Flow Together

THE NEIGHBOR IS BURIED IN THE CEDARVILLE CEMETERY NEAR THE place where the waters of North and South Deep Creek join. No water ran on the day of his funeral. Snowmelt was done by the end of May that dry year, and the tumbled rocks that were lustrous under its spring flow were dull-gray cobbles in September.

Was it cruel to bury a man, denied water's gift of life across his land, in a dry hole near enough to hear its mocking noise for all eternity? Or was it just? That, for all his struggles and prayers and coyote tricks, he could finally know its sweet, rushing sound?

Two of his sons lay in plots beside him, one was a boy's length, the other, a man's. Some families seem marked for sorrows.

The gathering was small. Only John and I stopped by the family home afterward. And then, when I stepped onto the porch and knocked at the kitchen door, the old woman greeted me, took the salad bowl from my hands, thanked us for coming, and closed the door again.

As I turned to go I noticed a blackboard beside the hats and coats on hooks, rubbed off, but I could read faint words of good deeds—a psalm handwritten some past day in light-blue chalk.

The neighbor's Sunday devotions were common knowledge to all those who saw him in his regular pew at mass. But I was surprised to see a scripture where he would sit to pull off his boots and think on the day that had been. Was it written as thanks for free water that flowed from under *his* neighbors' fence to sweeten his land all those years? Was he right to think free water due reward for faith, for daily labor, for living cloistered and independent?

From that day on I knew that in the house across the field they accommodate God's will on a blackboard by the back door, a psalm to start the day or end it, a reminder to accept the portion dealt from life's unlevel spoon.

Morgan, his upstream neighbor, held first-flow rights to the main channel coming from Cedar Creek and, regular as a clock, tended the irrigation system, walking the two-mile maze of ditches running through the yards of town, across the park, under the streets in narrow culverts, across woodlots to his corrals where the water ran the checks across his fields. He kept the ditches cleaned out and running fast, even in the winter when it meant walking daily, at first light, to break ice dams and prevent backing up and flooding. The water ran by gravity flow, no pump, no cost, but his devotion.

Ice would fill Morgan's deep cross ditches, build in sheets across his meadows, hold in wells above the ice, freezing, thawing, inching down the fall of the land toward our downstream man, sliding under his wire. Water does not know that fences have a name.

The neighbor was ready: ditches burnt out or freshly plowed, transecting the land to fully appropriate the gift of providence. Then his meadows would freshen with the spring flood. Dormant seeds soaked and softened and split their skins. Radicle and cotyledon wormed down and up to dark and light—all things making use of both, as the blackboard kept him mindful of. And into summer the ground doled out moisture to satisfy the root, to flesh the leaf, to fill the sleeve.

A simple man, his needs were just: pasture for his cows, a bait of decent food to feed his rough-cheeked children gathered 'round the kitchen stove with books, and toys, and handwork. His rooms were small and did not need much wood to heat them. The pines he planted as a lad kept snows from shouldering up the walls. He filled his plate with beef he raised and picked his teeth with gratitude for free water that gave him yet another year.

Until the drought. Then eight long years of drying up and dying bored through his skull to lay reason to the why of it. Midway in those years Morgan closed his head box, turned the water, let it flood the channel, let it carry to the lake because he tired of cleaning out forgotten toys of summer and paper sacks and weeds that dammed the city culverts, and damned him when townsfolk drew their miseries out in one long breath. He took his share in spring but none in winter. It was not enough to cross the land—to reach the man downstream.

The drought laid on, year after year, and no rain fell except in numbers he could count like stones across the road. Meadows parched. Soil blew off in dust. The ponds cracked open. Moans of the drought shook above the ground in waves.

If his house went up in a blaze volunteers would come in the clanging and screaming fire truck, water tank and hoses, cars in a long line behind, townsfolk straining to help. But it was his land that was dry as tinder, gray as ashes, and no one came.

He pumped the house well to keep the orchard living. The towering cottonwoods around the house put out leaves like lilac, small and cupped to gather dew. In that last year of his life, gray bones of branches clattered in the winds. He weaned calves as light as leppies to save the cows from falling off.

The blackboard was rubbed clean, and in its blankness it was the prophet. The upstream man learned the sin of not looking past his own fenceline. The believer lived downstream.

⊸ H2O

ON A DAY IN LATE JULY 1999, DUNCAN METCALFE LOWERED THE SECOND
section of the drill bit through the hole in the flatbed trailer and braced it
between his knees. His colleague from the University of Utah and friend
Don Currey matched the hole with those in the sleeve coupling and slid the
cotter key in place. This final set on the shoreline of Lake Surprise in California would complete the third core sampling.

Nasty dun mosquitoes came off the brackish water in the sun's reflection.
The small company of instructors and students had been at their project for
nearly two weeks. They'd given up swatting, given up repellents, ignored
the irritating insects for the most part. The core samples were the focus, the
key to understanding archaeological remains unearthed at the King's Dog
site a half mile east, as the crow flies. Duncan hoped the geology of the
Holocene and the late Pleistocene history of Lake Surprise would help him
develop a context for the humans who built the long lodges, unique to the
area, at King's Dog. Yet none of them knew what to expect; each hole produced different ratios of lake sediments, salts, mocha-brown clay, the green,
then black, organic goo. They had become used to seeing distinct changes
from stratum to stratum. Radiocarbon dating of the organic material in the
core would reveal a time line Duncan could work from.

The final section was locked into place, and the auger wound down
again. Twenty-five feet was the limit, and at that level they would be look-

ing twenty to thirty thousand years into the past. The procedure was reversed, the sections drawn out, uncoupled one after another. Midway in the fourth core sample a six-inch band of purest white appeared.

"Mazama." Don said. "Completely uncontaminated, just as it settled on the water. They used to think Mazama ash didn't reach this far south when it blew. But here it is, seven thousand years. For ash to be this pure there must have been at least thirty feet of water in the lake at that time, and it had to be calm for the ash to settle. King's Dog must have been established after Mazama blew."

Then he smiled. "There must be an underlying layer throughout this whole valley, completely undisturbed. If there was a pharmaceutical use for pure volcanic ash, we'd be millionaires."

A Suburban stopped on the causeway a quarter of a mile from where the crew worked. Two men got out. They skirted the powdery crust on the shoreline, wound through the salt brush, hacking and slapping at the mosquitoes and black flies, making their way toward the rig.

Duncan groaned. "So much for knocking off early." His crew was used to visitors. Local people stopped by, curious about the crew, the odd-looking Acker drill on the flatbed trailer and the tent pitched alongside. Normally he didn't mind, but it was the end of the day, cleanup would take another hour, and they were all weary. Visitors would delay that by precious minutes. His private beer-and-bath mirage started to fade. Lowering his head to the work he ignored the strangers coming closer.

When Duncan looked up again he was startled to see the men only feet away. He wiped his hand on a pant leg and held it out, repeating his welcoming speech while the others kept working. He knew the questions that would come and had the answers ready. But the two men caught him off guard when they introduced themselves as geologists from Los Angeles. They were wondering what he knew about the flow of groundwater in this valley. They were looking for a surplus to export to southern California. Duncan withdrew his hand, said curtly he knew nothing about the groundwater of Surprise Valley or any other valley, and turned to help Don and the students load the truck.

᠅

It is time for all the heroes to go home
if they have any, time for all of us common ones
to locate ourselves by the real things we live by.

—William Stafford, "Allegiances"

The real things we live by. I was about to learn what those might be. In 1987, a drought settled on California. Its power increased on the eastern slopes of the mountains, in Surprise Valley, and ate into us for six long years, searing all ideas from our brains, save one. Rain. But it would not come. Clouds teased at the mountain peaks, then dissolved into thin air. Within that landscape of hopelessness a project forked and slithered toward Surprise Valley. It promised, by all accounts, to steal whatever water lay pooled beneath the soil.

This is the story of those years, as close to the facts as I could write it. Data and details and names are sometimes tedious and confusing. But it is important to consider the manner in which people of power in this country attempt to solve our greater social questions, and the forces that can be applied to the methods of reaching those solutions. As a schoolgirl I learned the theory of supply and demand—two kids and only one Dream-Sicle left in the Good Humor Man's refrigerator box. The issue of an increasing need for water in developing urban areas and the competition for the water available has not been judiciously addressed.

⟜

Lavelle Dollarhide's voice trembled as she talked about Nevada's Silver State Water and Power Project (SSWPP) to pump the water from under her land. Befuddled, confused by the process, she confronted documents spread on her kitchen table for which she had no reference in her daily life, written in a language that was complex, arrogant, dismissive, mutated from the graceful language she learned to write in a forward-sloping line.

"They don't have the right to do that, Linda." She picked up her cancelled check as if to show it to me through the phone. "I had to pay an attorney to fill out the protest forms. It cost six hundred dollars. He said it's bound to cost more. Why? So they can build more houses? Reno's an anthill now. What are we gonna do?" I wished I could sweep those troublesome papers into the fire and reassure her, somehow bolster the woman I had known for nearly twenty years, who held her family's ranch together after her husband's death and kept the operation humming.

Lavelle and her husband, Adrian, had survived hard times on their Eagleville ranch at the south end of Surprise Valley, a cow/calf operation with meadows, brush fields, hay land, and grazing permits spanning the California-Nevada borderlands. In the mid-'80s when the doctors told Adrian he was losing his battle with cancer he insisted Lavelle sell her flock of sheep. He didn't want to leave her with lambing and shearing plus tending the herd of cattle they had built together. Shortly after the eighty head of ewes were sold and shipped Adrian died. But his death was not the worst of it.

Nevada's water-importation plan announced in 1987 put the Dollarhide Ranch in jeopardy. If the plan succeeded and water was aggressively pumped and exported to Reno, the land their people had settled and worked since the end of the Civil War would raise nothing, would be worth nothing. Was it Lavelle's destiny to see Surprise Valley dry up and blow away, and was it all to come to an end on her watch?

I tried to answer her first question—why? Washoe County was playing a water power game hedged against a future need. It was happening all over the arid West: identify the resource in decline—water—and bank it for the future.

Water has no loyalty. It is an element that will comply. It will climb a rope if the right engineering is applied.

Water is not bound to parcel entitlement. If someone sells their groundwater and puts a pump on a pipe, water will crawl toward the pump under property lines, under state lines, out of the neighbor's ground and their neighbors' until the pump is shut off or the aquifer is empty.

Banking water—laying legal claim to water by private companies or municipal or political agencies or the federal government to service a future need—may appear logical, like many theories developed in isolation, far away from the land and all things affected. But tampering with the environment comes with a price tag. In the case of Washoe County's ambitious plan, the complex and unique community of the high, cold desert from Reno north to the Oregon border, millions of acres, thousands of square miles, could be altered, perhaps permanently. If the plan fails, or the social conscience finds the cost too high, can a living place be started up again?

There is no need to ask Lavelle or her neighbors for a drink of water; they understand thirst. They respect the value of water in a dry country and protect it for the community. A visitor would be served up a glassful at their doorstep and told the story of their own weather station. Over the years old-timers like them noticed a snowdrift that formed a perfect upside-down triangle on the east face of Bald Mountain. If the triangle doesn't break before the first of June everybody will have irrigation water out of Eagle Creek. If it breaks before and shrinks, they will all be short of feed for their livestock. So they administer their water rights with the conviction of a ditch rider: each one gets their share, but no one takes too much. Greed would cause the whole of the system to fail.

To Lavelle's second question—what are we gonna do? I had no answer—yet. People unwilling to accept the authority of Washoe County over the land's water were just beginning to stir.

⌒

The rooster quail sits high on a bush to guard the covey feeding in the thickets below. If a hawk passes overhead he gives a cry of warning. Ralph Parman, also a native of Surprise Valley and a third-generation rancher, was our lookout, though none of us knew it. From his retirement home in Reno he watched out for Surprise Valley.

On a morning in the spring of 1987 Ralph noticed an article in the *Reno Gazette-Journal* that described Washoe County's proposed water-importation project for metropolitan Reno. An inset map was knotted and veined with proposed well sites, reservoirs, power stations, and pipelines coming together in a single black artery terminating just north of the city.

Few people reading the morning news would have given the article much thought. But Ralph cut his teeth on the ranching business in the California-Nevada high desert. Parman Brothers' livestock, like the livestock of all Surprise Valley ranchers, flowed across the borderlands as water flows beneath it, and Ralph understood the climate and the demands on the limited water supply. The newspaper article worried him the way a circling hawk would worry a rooster quail.

Ralph tucked the clipping in an envelope with a note addressed to Bettie Parman, his niece and secretary of the Sand Creek Grazing Association, advising her to look into the matter. It was his opinion some of the proposed wells were sited on the association's range.

⌒

I have kept two boxes boldly named "H2O" in the cellar all these years. They hold the research papers, maps, files, clippings, and logs of our twelve-year journey through the Silver State Water and Power Project and its many successive aliases. Two boxes are the archive of the project that asked so much of us. In preparation for writing about that time I carried the boxes to my kitchen table. I opened the first. A shining black spider had tatted the lid to the stack of papers in the same way I have attached myself to this valley. To get at the documents I had to disturb the web of silk defining the spider's territory. It was surprisingly strong, yet when I used force the fragile web was ripped apart. Inside among the pages ordered in a system I have forgotten were documents of a project designed to do the same to me, to all of us living here, and to this piece of country known as the Empty Quarter.

⌖

The *Reno Gazette-Journal* article that worried Ralph had unveiled Nevada's Silver State Water and Power Project. Applications had been filed in October 1986 with Peter Morros, then Nevada state engineer, to "appropriate all the unappropriated water in Washoe County." All the water in the county from Reno to the Oregon border flowing beneath the land's surface to the unplumbed depths, in interstate aquifers and shared basins, was being claimed by Washoe County. Assignment of those applications to Washoe County precluded those of any other.

The accompanying map had a complex rash of fifty-two well filings, including four within the Surprise Valley Basin in California, two of which, as Ralph suspected, would affect the Sand Creek Grazing Association. The plan detailed a storage system to power the project with the very water that was being pumped to town. Water would be pumped uphill into storage reservoirs, and the energy collected by the downward rush would provide the power required at the next pumping station—a great looping superstructure draining the desert, moving its water toward the faucets of the Truckee Meadows.

Washoe County commissioners predicted that the Truckee Meadows Basin (that is, the Reno-Sparks metropolitan area) at the turn of the next century, like Los Angeles at the turn of the twentieth, would be on the verge of a water deficit, with demand and supply nearing an extremely critical situation. Their number crunch somehow justified desertification of northern Washoe County to support growth demands in the Truckee Meadows. To anyone who lived and worked in the semiarid environment deemed the "areas of origin," the idea was at first ludicrous and then chilling.

Surprise Valley's annual precipitation (ppt) has been recorded only since 1894, a reasonable time frame to form a scientific conclusion if the data are valid. An average ppt range—from 1894 to the present, dependant on meteorology—is somewhere between six and twelve inches. There also existed a study that indicated some of the irrigation wells in the valley were pumping fossil water, and that there was not enough ppt to replenish the discharge and balance the aquifer, let alone support exportation, especially in drought years. Spring runoff is manipulated through irrigation systems for maximum utilization and recharge and minimum loss.

Washoe County is drier yet. One-third of Washoe County receives only four to eight inches' annual ppt, and the other two-thirds between eight and fifteen inches.

Prior to filing the SSWPP applications, proponents of the project reported to Washoe County commissioners that the ppt data-collection station in the Virginia Mountains on the edge of the Smoke Creek Desert, directly west of Pyramid Lake, had been shot up by deer hunters. So, in order to develop projection figures they had substituted ppt data from a fire station at South Lake Tahoe—in the high Sierra. The variance between the two stations' average is notable: *four to six inches ppt in the Virginia Mountains versus forty to sixty inches ppt at South Lake Tahoe.* From the onset, the project was conceived on a set of data that misrepresented the facts by overestimation of annual ppt and, therefore, a corrupted computer model. It was clear from the start that if Washoe County developed the SSWPP based on the ppt data from South Lake Tahoe, the result would be groundwater mining. Yet the commissioners accepted the bogus statistics presented to them, and they filed applications with the Nevada state engineer to import that drawdown into the Truckee Meadows.

The application went on, "The diversion is anticipated to exceed the perennial yield of the basin for limited periods of time. This limited duration over-pumpage will provide a supplemental supply of water to augment the quasi-municipal use of surface water during droughts or other short-term emergencies and to fill reservoirs. This water will be commingled with other waters appropriated by Washoe County to serve a county-wide population of 500,000 by the year 2030."

✧

My home, Surprise Valley, is not named on maps until after 1860. Bound by the Warner Mountains on the west, it lies within the rain shadow of the tilted fault blocks forming the Warner Range. To stand on their nearly ten-thousand-foot peaks and look eastward from that extreme western lip of the Great Basin is to look into the heart of a dynamic environ with a dramatic geologic past. The land here has been submerged by a saltwater sea and freshwater lakes, emerged from more than one ice age, endured violent volcanic action, and an epic three-thousand-year drought. Now it is a high, cold desert, classified semiarid in the northern region and arid in the south.

The peaks rake moisture from the sky, leaving the valley floor primarily dependent on snowmelt for recharge of the aquifers. In the fifteen-mile-wide crease between the Warner Range and Nevada's seven thousand–foot

Hays Range, rainfall gradually diminishes, west to east, from an annual average of fourteen inches to six inches, dividing the valley—actually a closed basin where water drains inward—into three distinct zones.

Beginning at the western foothills, a fertile alluvial band gathers rainfall and snow for recharge, acting as a groundwater reservoir supporting four agricultural communities: Fort Bidwell, Lake City, Cedarville, and Eagleville. The rich, loamy soil decreases or is contaminated by salts as it nears a central playa where runoff pools during wet years. On the eastern side of the playa, a wider and dryer band of salt- and alkali-affected desert soil, sinks, and sand dunes begins, supporting a sparse covering of shad scale, saltbush, rabbitbrush, greasewood, some willow, and a few junipers.

The California-Nevada border runs north-south along the foothills of the Hays Mountains on the east side of Surprise Valley where both states share the valley's hydrology. There is also a suggestion that basins to the north (Warner Valley in Oregon), east (Long Valley, Nevada), and south (Duck Flat, Nevada) may be connected through a latticework of faulting and the north-south-trending Walker Lane fault system. In essence, it is a porous zone where groundwater could collect in an extensive subterranean basin, and an underground channeling system that may enable water to move southward from the northern basins.

During the Pleistocene epoch the Surprise Valley basin was the site of a vast lake with a depth of 550 feet. Over time Lake Surprise began evaporating, and the sink filled with 6,000–7,000 feet of materials eroded from the Warner Mountains. Today all that remains of the ancient lake are three ephemeral lakes, separated by land bridges of alluvial fill, constituting the spectral fingerprints of their mightier ancestor.

It is by these land bridges, and around the north and south ends of what was Lake Surprise, that all valley ranchers drive their cattle to and from summer grazing on the public lands in Nevada. They are dependent on the public lands for their livelihood, and the four valley communities, total population about 1,200, are dependent on the ranchers.

꙳

Bettie Parman picked up her uncle Ralph's letter at the post office and immediately telephoned her small band of community activists: Sara Gooch, Sophie Sheppard, and me. We gathered around Bettie's kitchen table waiting for Bettie to tell us what had her so worried. Even with a plate of Bettie's Tootsie Bombs on the table and the Parmans' stock dog, Timmie, curled asleep at our feet, it felt like a war room.

Bettie knew she could count on us. Together or independently, we had worked on other projects to protect or enhance living in the isolated valley: defending the airspace over Surprise Valley that the air force thought suitable for low-level training missions because "nobody lives up there, anyway"; participating in a group application to get PBS television service brought into the valley; and lobbying for the formation of a tax district to support the reopening of our community hospital when an absentee management group let the doors close. But we didn't think of ourselves as activists. The activists on the TV news were pushy, strident people who had obviously been raised by the Huns. We were just part of the population who mind our own business, for the most part.

Back in the '70s someone pulled a house trailer in on Main Street in Cedarville and set it up as a beauty shop and residence. Nobody liked it. It stuck out among the Victorian houses and the charming brick buildings built in the 1860s like a tattooed sailor at the prom. We frowned every time we drove by, thinking maybe we ought to call a town meeting and talk ordinances. But I guess no one really wanted to establish a committee of their peers to decide about how things should be done in the valley. A couple of years went by and the house trailer was gone. Things have a way of working themselves out. However, when the California Department of Corrections cast eyes on Modoc County for a prison site and the board of supervisors saw a prison as positive economic growth, the people stormed the courthouse, forcing the supervisors to take the issue to the voters and abide by the decision.

If the accumulative effect seems intolerable to the majority, the people will come forward and develop a process.

Bettie took out the clipping. "Just look at *this!*"

What she read to us outlined a plan to drill deep wells in the desert, tap the aquifers, construct artificial lakes, and leapfrog the water from basin to basin until it reached Reno. "To green-up how many golf courses, wash how many fancy cars, run how many hotel showers, flush how many toilets?" she asked, slapping the article down on the table.

It was a joke, right?

"No! It's not a joke!" she said.

But we didn't know anything about interstate transfer of water. We didn't know about water law.

"Well, we better find out, and damned fast," she said as if our brains were powered with thirty-watt bulbs. "Says here, 'Washoe County officials expect the population to reach a half a million by 2030.' They don't even have water meters! Vote 'em out every *time!* But they want to suck us dry? Now that's just not right! If Surprise Valley water runs the gutters in Reno, it'll be over my *dead body!*"

⌁

In a foothill field the Hussas have owned since 1913, North and South Deep Creeks run high in spring, dwindling midsummer. The Brush Fields are rocky, gravelly, alluvial, showing evidence that the creeks meandered, cutting the banks, spinning a new course where the flow was blocked by debris. After the first flush of spring runoff the water moved slowly, recharging as it went. The first valley settlers in the mid-1800s divided the water. The courts heard disputes and adjudicated rights were decreed, tied to the land, as elemental as the soil. Neighbors protected their water rights and cooperated to develop and maintain irrigation projects, headgates, and diversions to ensure maximum benefit from the life-giving resource.

When the California Department of Water Resources (CDWR) was established its governing code plainly defined a primary responsibility—to put water to beneficial use. In the state of California it is against the law to waste water.

The Hussas' brush field was a healthy environment for spring calving. The parcel was divided into four lots, each with livestock water in the ditches as provided by the decree. Despite the heavier ppt in the foothills the sandy soil drained and did not harbor bacteria. Young cattle are especially susceptible to the ravages of bacterial scours.

Cottonwoods and juniper grew along the creek bank with an understory of chokecherry, wild plum, mahogany, elderberry, serviceberry, and gooseberry in nature's random pattern. Pines followed the body of the creek for a short way, bitterbrush and sage in the openings. The natural habitat provided protection and feed for deer, rabbits, gray squirrels, quail, Steller's jays, flycatchers, vireos, northern orioles, wrens, a few Canada geese, and mallards.

In the '60s, P. B. Harris, a neighbor and co-user on South Deep Creek, approached Walter Hussa with a plan to put his water right on their shared ditch in an underground pipe so he could eliminate loss to evaporation and soaking the ditch. Water adjudicated to the Harris Ranch would be diverted into a pipeline buried four feet under the Hussas' brush fields. Walter agreed to the project. Construction began immediately. It didn't take long to realize the mistake. Before the pipeline, the ditch loss was shared. With the Harris pipeline in place, P. B. took his measure at the diversion and the Hussas absorbed the entire ditch loss. But the real harm took longer to realize. As soon as the spring runoff was past, the Harris share went down the pipe, leaving no surface water, no livestock water, no recharge, no evapotranspiration.

The shallow-rooted shrubs were the first to show the effects. Soon the trees began dropping dead limbs in the creek bed. The old channel was littered with dead wood. Noxious weeds and thistles moved in to fill the niche. Plant life was restricted to the most drought resistant, only those able to exist on the scant moisture that comes in winter. Wildlife moved on to other canyons.

I saw the effects of the exportation of water from a tract of land on a very small scale, and I recognized the unemotional science. If water is pumped out of the ground and transported elsewhere the landscape will be altered. The effects are dramatic and irreversible. They cannot be mitigated by guzzlers or wildlife stations. If a climate is classified semiarid, any amount of water removed will alter the environment.

⌐

"Owens Valley," Sara moaned. Why not? The precedent had been set.

"Well," Bettie thumped the newspaper clipping, "what are we gonna do about it?"

What indeed?

Nevada, the driest state in the nation, had developed a comprehensive and exacting body of water law. Anyone owning land in Washoe County could protest the applications on grazing land or the impact it would have on their business or both. Anyone could protest in support of the public lands and the environment. California, on the other hand, has no provisioning law for groundwater, offers no protection to landowners like us from the usurpation the sswpp represented. And we, as Californians sharing a hydrologic basin, had no legal basis for complaint simply because we were worried. We needed scientific data to support our protests.

We sat around Bettie's table, draining the last of the coffee, hoping inspiration was a side effect of caffeine overload. Slowly a plan of action took shape. Our first move, we decided, would be to contact the Nevada state engineer's office to see what recourse was open to us; second, educate ourselves; third, enlist the help of experts; and fourth, get the word out to the community.

The first item, as it turned out, had a very heavy "other shoe." Sophie called an emergency meeting and said that when she telephoned Morros's office an engineer told her that anyone opposed to the sswpp should file protests to the applications. Write in for the protest forms, they can be copied, follow the instructions, don't forget the twenty-five-dollar filing fee for each application you protest, the deadline is May 28th. Two weeks away.

We lived in a rural county with a weekly newspaper. There were only four of us to mount a campaign.

"Better get busy," Bettie said, passing out blue T-shirts she had designed. The fronts were screened in a flowery script: SURPRISE VALLEY GARDEN CLUB AND TERRORIST SOCIETY.

Accepting the shirt would be taking an oath to fight the Silver State Project—dubbed the Silver Snake—to the end.

I did not want this job. None of us did. The thrust of the Silver Snake was about mining a resource without regard for consequence—robbing Peter to water Paul's golf course. It was not about advancing the community; it was about being drafted to defend community. And in order to defend it, we would be forced to take up the arms of activism, deal with powerful agencies and corporations—all of this without their experience or resources or support. The process, we knew, would cause divisions within our own valley. It would take us away from our work in the solitude and isolation of our home places.

I guess it would be fair to say that none of us were shrinking violets, yet none of us were ambitious for a role in politics, or hoping to see our star light up the night skies. Each in her own way shunned notoriety, a walk up the salary scale with full benefits, a trash compactor, two hundred TV stations, the trappings of "normal" life other people can't seem to live without. Conveniences of society, resources of urban living, had no relevance to us. A simple life in open country did.

We avoided like poison soul-deadening bureaucracies, the foot-tangling crawl of organizations, verbal jousting, monthly meetings where common sense is not necessarily the goal as the same agonizing issues arise again and again without resolution. We wouldn't go. We were not seeking a cause through which to elevate ourselves in the eyes of community, nor did we want to police the proposals of people driven by greed or the perfume of personal gain. We had already read too many Environmental Impact Statements (EIS), and developing comments on them was not about creativity. Unlike the salaried proponents of the sswpp, we would not be paid to see this through to the end, not paid to attend countless meetings, write countless letters, and on and on. Besides, the impact on home life, family, sanity was simply too great. No one could reimburse us for time: the seasons came and went—the work of home, school, art, ranch would not wait.

Who were we kidding anyway, to think we could stop a project with political backing and powerful supporters? Four women from the sagebrush flats? It was laughable. I could imagine the amusement we provided in Reno boardrooms. And, win or lose, when the dust settled, wouldn't we come away changed? Sophie's magical watercolors could not glow with light if anxiety was layered in. Bettie's bright garden rows would not flourish without a constant flow of water and her gentle hands working the weeds away, and Joe needed her baking Tootsie Bombs or cherry pies when he came in from the corrals. If Sara's mind ground on the question of whether, in a few years, her students would have a valley to come home to, how could she teach them to dream of college and a job that could be theirs? And what of my poetry?

Bettie eyed us dead level. No one else was volunteering for the job. What could we do?

❧

Until I had held the newspaper clipping in my hand I did not fully appreciate the concept of water as a commodity, that it could be sold, bought, and transferred without regard for its source. I had seen the movie *Chinatown*, but until I heard the wolf scratching at our door I didn't understand the history of Owens Valley as it touched people. Like all of history, I needed to hear their cries, their stories, to know the sorrow.

Mulholland's project, responsible for ruining the Owens Valley, was promoted to Los Angeles under the patriotic banner, "the greatest good for the greatest number." The initial intent might have been valid, honorable even. But, in fact, the hard kernel of the project was greed. The greatest number had no real meaning at all, faceless figures never more important than the profit they represented. And the greatest good was a mutable goal. Implementation of the plan to import water (defined, for the social conscience, as *excess*) for the singular purpose of augmenting dwindling supplies in the Los Angeles basin was the initial thrust. An unspoken secondary benefit was profit from development that the water made possible and that required secrecy to keep the money and power base deep and narrow. Small players were satisfied with small money, while an exclusive second tier became very rich by shortstopping the water, detouring it to the San Fernando Valley to develop thousands of acres. The ambitious ones at the pyramid's top were driven by the lure of greater power. Money, after a certain point, becomes merely an accessory.

The master plan was protected with ruthlessness and cunning: suspicions answered with lies and deception; detractors bought off; friends, neighbors, family members divided, one against another. Force was applied to the fearful. Violence spilled out the frayed edges. Perpetrators who were once enemies found themselves bound together in a conspiracy of wrongdoing. Ruin, for some, was inevitable. And before it was finished, even the price of human life came into question.

In March 1928, the Saint Francis Dam built by the U.S. Army Corps of Engineers, designed by Chief Engineer Mulholland to contain the flow of water from the Owens Valley River, gave way. A wall of water and mud, initially two hundred feet high, swept death and devastation all the way to the sea. The *Los Angeles Times* headline reported the tragedy with an elitist attitude typical of the thinking that had ruined Owens Valley in the first place: "450 Killed Excluding Mexican Laborers."

⟜

We were suddenly arms and legs sticking out of a rolling snowball of documents, laws, draft legislation, and agendas caused by a project that threatened to change our lives—had already changed our lives. Our husbands gave up regular meals, folded clothes, everything they'd come to expect from a wife. Dinner conversations took on the timbre of a lecture hall. They got used to us leaping out of bed at night to jot notes by the light of the refrigerator door. Or maybe they didn't. But if John was impatient, it never showed. He knew what I was doing must be done, and he had neither the time nor the temperament for it. When my brain ached with statistics and rebuttals, I would steal out to the pasture and catch my mare. We would ride out to check our cattle, or load the truck with salt blocks and salt the cattle, or stack hay. Cleaning the chicken house was a relief. Anything that smelled of dirt and sweat was the real work and reinforced my fearful passion to protect our home place.

We consumed stacks of data as though cramming for college boards. The Terrorists were regulars at every meeting. I spent whole days on the telephone with legislative aides, asking pathetically formed questions, rarely able to give an intelligent response to theirs. I couldn't understand half of what they said. I had no experience. I faked it, thinking if they just kept talking I'd catch on. I was emotional. I whined. I got angry, then pleaded for help.

One day, frustrated with the process and not having a head for protocol, I telephoned David Kennedy, the head of the California Department of Water Resources, Peter Morros's counterpart in California. I garbled my ten-minute speech about the SSWPP (soldiers and tanks at the state line, drill bits sharpened, hoses uncoiled like sidewinders). His secretary put me on hold. I was willing to wait for (I assumed) the big boss to calm down, regain his composure. I expected indignation, immediate action, maybe a satellite bearing a warhead tipped ever so slightly toward Reno. Her stainless-steel voice came back on the line. She suggested I call the CDWR in Red Bluff and speak to the north-district chief, Wayne Gentry. Should I tell him what I told Kennedy? Dial tone. I rang the Red Bluff number and got the person who takes Chief Gentry's calls. After my abbreviated five-and-a-half minute speech, he passed me on to an assistant who made the mistake of pausing between "hello" and "good-bye." For Chief Gentry I shrink-wrapped my plea into fifteen seconds. Silence on his end. Then I felt his long arm reach through the phone and give me a "good dog" pat on the head.

"Don't worry. If they pump on the Nevada side it will *not* draw from the west side of the valley."

His tone said, "Everybody knows *that.*"

⊸

We got the name of an attorney. He sounded sane on the phone. He flew in to the Cedarville airport to meet us. His girlfriend wouldn't get out of the plane. She kept her eyes glued to the runway and the door locked and repeatedly asked if there were any Indians around here.

We pointed the attorney up and down the valley, to the mountains and then to the state line. He wanted the job. What was the job, exactly? We said we hated to leave his girlfriend in the plane, but we had lunch at the house. He said she was okay. After lunch he asked if we had a magic marker. I found one in the junk drawer under the sink. He needed a piece of poster board. Had that. He said we needed to make a chart to track everything— vitally important—and he ruled squares on the poster board. Seven rows across, five rows down. When he finished it looked very much like a calendar. I said I had a calendar. He grimaced and said this was a FLOW CHART. We needed one for every month. I said it looked like a calendar.

"Always use a STAPLER," he told Sara. "Do *not* use paper clips. *Always* staple. I *hate* paper clips."

I think that was about it. The lawyer and his girlfriend flew away. I hoped they found somewhere to land.

⊸

Geographic isolation sweetens the air of our valley with birdsong and the mating squabbles of geese. Cars and trucks and tractors pass up and down the valley on errands we can nearly identify by knowing how ranches lay out or who works in town. They are us; we are them, more or less. We have one paved highway entering the valley from the west, ending on the east side at the Nevada border. Until the Washoe County road crew paved the dirt road coming into the valley from the south in the '90s, there were no roads passing through. The airstrip was developed for small private planes: hunters, absentee owners, mercy flights, and the federal trapper flying predator control, although Governor Reagan landed his jet here when he was running for president, and Robert Redford dropped in for some fuel one day. No trains, no busses bringing strangers, bringing news on a regular schedule, no bundle of newspapers. Some of us subscribe to outside papers, but mail-service delays delivery at least one day, and the SSWPP proponents did not send press releases to the newspapers of the surrounding communities that would be affected by their project. So, the very quality of isolation that we cling to and ardently protect led to our ignorance of the Silver State issue.

If not for Bettie's attention to Ralph's letter I wonder if anyone else would have taken the *Reno Gazette-Journal* article seriously. A child could recognize the scarcity of water in the Nevada desert, and everyone was aware of steadily declining groundwater levels. We might not have known the average ppt level was a paltry 7.5 inches over the past five years, but we darned sure knew the drought was killing us. In all fairness, the dollar drought had our serious and complete attention in 1987. We were still scarred and bleeding from the recession and sky-high interest rates of the early '80s. The national economy barely had a pulse, and its weakened condition translated into very hard times in the country—again. Bankers, who in the '70s and early '80s handed out loans like feed-store calendars, reacted to the big-city panic and swarmed over Surprise Valley in the mid-'80s, forcing foreclosures on all marginal accounts.

This wasn't the Hollywood cliché of the villainous banker forcing one old rancher and his pretty daughter to pay up or else and the community gets Roy or Gene or a bunch of hungry Broadway actors to put on a benefit barn dance to meet the note. These were family operations that, for the most part, grew out of homesteads and use of the open range in Nevada, ones who could not stay in business without operating loans. The rout took the country. In the mid-'80s in Modoc County alone where calf sales are the number-one economic figure the cattle census dropped by fourteen thousand head and continued in a downward spiral into the '90s.

Ranching operations historically operate on borrowed money to pay the monthly bills because they have one cash crop, beef ready for market once a year, in the fall when the cattle come off the desert-range permits and calves are weaned from their mothers and sold. Once a year they get a paycheck, the bank cosigns it and takes its share (or portion thereof), and the rancher gets what's left over. If, as in the '80s, the market price has dropped and the feed is sparse and weaning weights are low, then the beef check won't cover the bank note. The balance due is carried over to the next year's loan and the rancher falls behind, and he hopes like hell for a good year to bail him out. Maybe the good year is delayed out there over the Pacific where storms brew up and decide which way to go. Then our rancher is in trouble, and before long the bank owns him clear down to the ground.

The economy of the Surprise Valley has always relied on agricultural prosperity for steady growth, and when it failed, the towns folded up like a bouquet of wild roses. Bank and drugstore moved out, John Deere dealership shut down, dress shops, fabric shop, butcher shop, saddle- and shoe-repair shop, hardware store, mill and lumberyard all closed. With heads buried so deeply in survival we were people who had no time or energy to look for any more problems to solve. Overburdened we were, yet we were the only ones who could save ourselves from the sswpp.

With less than two weeks to the deadline for protests, we organized a meeting at the Cedarville Community Church Hall, contacted a few people, who contacted a few more, taped a sign on the barrel people used as a bulletin board, and set it in the middle of Main Street. We let the news travel via the rural chain letter and got busy baking cookies as was our habit for social gatherings.

We stood at the door greeting our neighbors. They looked worried and confused as they got out of their cars and trucks and came up the stairs into the hall. These were not pampered people; these were good people. Nothing fancy about their clothes, their homes, or their operations, older folks who reminded us of our parents. Some were our parents, third-, fourth-generation ranchers, who learned to trust only what they could do with their own hands. Maybe they sent their children away to find a "better life" outside of the valley, but *they* chose to stay as true stewards of the land who took the work of animal husbandry as something honest and honorable. The cost of doing business challenged their good sense, but still, they held on with the optimism of tomorrow's sunrise: better prices, free water, good grass, fat steers. Why, then, were they so often the pawn of some economic or land-use policy that, on a turn, kept them in business or dumped them out like chaff? And now, we were going to have to tell them they were facing a fight to keep the water under their own soil.

Sara was our spokesperson. She introduced us, the committee the Modoc County Board of Supervisors appointed as an advisory group on the development of the SSWPP, and Pam Townsend, Modoc County planner. Pam was fairly new to Modoc, and most people had had no reason to stop by the county planner's office. They would now. Pam would prepare protests to the SSWPP applications on behalf of the county.

"Water is Topic-A in Reno," Pam said as she walked to a California-Nevada map overlaid with the proposed project from pump to pipe to hookup in the Truckee Meadows. The scope of the project was overwhelming on such a scale. "Last winter was Nevada's sixth driest on record. If we have another dry winter we are going to see hardships imposed on people we have never seen before. Nevada has the strongest groundwater law in the nation, and Washoe County has a plan: the Silver State Water and Power Project. The estimated cost: $262 million. We've all heard of cost overruns. Estimates usually double before the project is finished.

"California has no groundwater law, but it does have a reputation among western states for strong-arm tactics when the issue is water. But this is not a California-Nevada fight. Forty-three of the eighty-seven ranchers in this valley own property in Nevada. They do not think of the borderlands as separate states but rather as one region straddled by their lives. We object to taking water out of these rural basins to supply Reno, which has no water metering or controls on growth. In reality it's a problem of very inadequate laws and regulations."

Sophie had invited an attorney and water specialist from Inyo County who knew the history of the Owens Valley in detail. Owens Valley lay a few hundred miles south of Reno along the eastern slope of the Sierra. Slides of historic *before* photographs showed us a lovely, long valley very much like our own. And then the *after* view lit the screen with the stark truth of a wide, dry flat, a finger of Death Valley. This was destruction of a magnitude none of us could imagine. He asked for questions. There weren't any. He sat down.

When the lights came up Pam spoke into that quiet of hollow hearts. She described the process by which we could file protests to the applications. "The official protest is the only power we have. It requires a response. It can't be ignored. I have the forms. Gary Wooten, advisor to the Surprise

Valley–Vya Resource Conservation District (RCD) board, or I can help you fill them out. Each one has to be notarized and accompanied by the required fee. I am available to anyone. Talk to me now or call my office for an appointment."

The silence was the heavy silence that comes over a planeload of airline passengers in a bad storm who have just been told to sit down and buckle up. But a few moments later, the audience stirred back to life. This was not, after all, a situation in which they were completely powerless. One by one, our neighbors stood and formed lines to sign up for workshops or took a list of water attorneys who would fill out protest forms for a fee. Some went to the map. I watched their eyes touch the portion that was their land or their grazing allotment and wait there as though looking into the face of someone lost to them. One by one they seated themselves around the Sunday-school tables, their knees and elbows knocked together and their heads bowed over papers. In their awkwardness of first steps I felt the beginning of hope.

⟿

Sophie started calling us ankle biters. It was easy to recognize those qualities in ourselves. We were in a constant whir, yapping at one person or another through letters or phone calls. Gossip began to trickle back that we were taking it all too seriously. We asked Pam if she thought this SSWPP was just a fishing expedition. She reminded us that though Lassen County borders Modoc at the south end of Surprise Valley, it butts against Nevada nearly to Reno, seventy miles from the county seat in Susanville. A mere seventy miles from the fangs of the Silver Snake, its writhe of pipes and acrid breath of welds struck. They were all scared in Lassen; the threat was serious, and the supervisors and planner had been fully engaged in trying to stop the SSWPP from the onset. If implemented, the SSWPP would obviously affect the California valleys nearest to Reno first, moving north to Honey Lake Valley, and then on to Surprise Valley. That is, all California basins sharing hydrogeology with Washoe County had the potential to be drawn down if Nevada's project was allowed to go forward.

She suggested we invite the Lassen County supervisors and county planner, Bob Sorvaag, to come up to Surprise Valley, meet with the Modoc supervisors, and let them address the public at an open-house meeting. Smiling, she said sometimes people need to get pushed off their stoop.

On a balmy evening we stood outside the Surprise Valley high school gym as cars pulled into the parking lot. The people from Lassen arrived. We talked while we waited for our supervisors to show up. Folks filed past us and took seats in the bleachers. We waited a few more minutes. When it became obvious that none of the Modoc supervisors were coming, not even our own district supervisor who lived about five blocks away, we went inside and sat in the chairs set out for the Modoc dignitaries. Pam represented the county to the gathering.

Eve taught us women that there's more than one way to skin a snake. In a letter to the Modoc supervisors we requested a meeting in chambers, to include the Lassen County supervisors; their county planner, Pam; and the CDWR's chief, Wayne Gentry. We were hoping, with both counties represented, to force Gentry into a discussion as to how California would protect its groundwater from Nevada's exportation project. The presence of Lassen officials and Chief Gentry would be bound to impress our supervisors with the seriousness of the threat posed by the SSWPP.

The California-border counties immediately north of Reno had already signed a Joint Powers Agreement (JPA) and were shaping the language of a groundwater district to manage and protect an aquifer they share in common with Nevada much in the same way Lassen and Modoc share Surprise Valley with Nevada. It was essential that Modoc join that JPA to form an alliance of real strength, infinitely more powerful than our one county standing alone on the skyline. In addition we were asking our supervisors to support our cause to the CDWR by requesting legal and financial aid from the state to offset expenses to the county. To date, all expenses had been paid out of the Surprise Valley Terrorists' shallow pockets.

The board issued invitations for their next scheduled meeting. They liked the idea of it being their party.

On the way over the mountain pass to the meeting, Sophie showed us a book, sort of a *Popular Mechanics* for kids, her son, Jason, had found. One of the chapters outlined a method of moving water over unlevel terrain. On the far side of a hill a tousle-headed, wacky-looking kid held a big hose that he had aimed at the summit. Water gushed out of the spigot and landed with a splat in a giant funnel that caught the water and drained it into another hose, where another kid aimed *his* spigot over the *next hill* ahead to *another* funnel. The project was titled "The Big Squirt." The Silver Snake had a new nickname.

❧

The brass cupola of the Modoc County Court House can be seen for miles. It has the kind of neoclassic beauty that can still evoke a flutter of patriotism in the heart of the most cynical citizen. Elms and rose gardens set off massive pillars. Within the rotunda a marble staircase winds to the second floor.

In anticipation of the large gathering, the supervisors moved the meeting to the courtroom. I had sat in the raised jury chairs along the north wall on two separate trials and remembered the serious nature of the proceedings. Granted, I was ignorant of the protocols of the board of supervisors' meetings, but I wasn't prepared for the casual chitchat of the members as they arrived and took their places, coffee cups in hand. We brought a serious issue before them. I expected more formal behavior in keeping with the place where the course of people's lives was decided.

The Lassen County people took chairs beside us, and we at once felt part of something larger, a coalition, a team. Chief Gentry sat across the aisle from us, briefcase on the oak bench beside him. He looked like a nice man. We hoped he carried the support of the CDWR in that briefcase. United, we stood a chance of protecting our valleys and the Nevada desert beyond.

The chairman waived the preliminary items and recognized the Surprise Valley committee. Sara presented our position on the SSWPP, saying that our concerns were threefold. First, as residents, dependent on the agricultural economic base of Surprise Valley, we wanted to protect the valley aquifers from being mined by the Nevada project. Second, we believed that a project of these proposed dimensions would deplete the aquifers of the Nevada desert that Modoc County livestock people relied upon for summer feed. Third, as environmentally responsible citizens, we wanted to keep the SSWPP from doing serious damage to the high-desert region of Washoe County.

She also told the board that we had contacted the Federal Energy Regulatory Commission, and to date, the SSWPP had not filed for a power project. This could mean that possibly Washoe County was drawing back from the original scheme to throw a net over the resources of water and power to reel in as much control as possible, and they were refining their focus, for the present, to the delivery of water.

Chief Gentry stood and, without so much as a nod to Sara's statement, gave a basic lecture on the geology of Surprise Valley. He rejected the idea that Long Valley, Nevada's aquifer (directly east of the Hays Range), interlocked with Surprise, and ended by saying water could not pass from west to east through the compacted sediment of the playa. Before sitting down, he offered calmly that the California side of the basin was in no danger of pumping done on the Nevada side.

I felt myself stepping outside my body into a *Saturday Night Live* skit: the face of Chief Gentry slowly inflated like a balloon, stretching and swelling bigger and bigger and bigger, towering over us like a Mardi Gras float until he burst and flew all apart—tatters of red rubber raining down, catching in our hair. Then someone coughed and the moment dissolved.

The supervisors stared at us blankly. The figure of authority on geology and water for northern California had stated clearly that we had nothing to worry about. Period.

Sophie and I were frozen in place. Sara jumped to her feet, waving a copy of the CDWR's "Northeastern Counties Ground Water Update—1982" and said, "It is the opinion of other experts and, is stated here, in your own handbook on page 64, that 'On the east side of the valley, there are extensive upland areas composed of sedimentary deposits of the '49 Camp Formation and of the overlying Miocene basalt. Topographic and geologic conditions are favorable for some subsurface inflow to the valley from Long Valley, Nevada. Farther south there appears to be subsurface inflow from the north end of Duck Flat, Nevada.' So then, Mr. Gentry, doesn't it logically follow that if water can flow in one direction, it can, conversely, be pumped in the opposite direction?"

The supervisors' heads swung to Chief Gentry. He stood again and did what might be called a water ballet—paddle, paddle, swish, splash, splash—around the issue. "Well," Gentry said, "if pumping drew water from the west side, it would be contaminated by playa salts and minerals and the pumping would be curtailed."

The spotlight Gentry danced in illuminated the CDWR's firm stand that it didn't want to be drawn, like the water, from the California side into a battle with Nevada. We were learning fast that politicians, and those who depend on politicians for their jobs, skim down the population figures of a howling county, and do a quick comparison to, say, that of Los Angeles, before responding. From our read of the current south-state news, Las Vegas and Los Angeles were locked in contentious negotiations over the Colorado River. It didn't take a CDWR engineer to interpret Chief Gentry's blind-eyed stance. The water of the north counties could be sacrificed to Reno if it would keep Nevada off California's back along the Mexican border.

I looked around the room at Modoc County's judicial presence, the pictures of our judges on the walls, the judge's bench, the Bible on the stand, all the trappings of justice. Wasn't simply being in the sanctity of the courtroom enough to expect, no, guarantee truth, whole truth? Perhaps not.

Pam was addressing the board chairman, asking formally for their signature of the JPA with Lassen, and that they request meaningful support from the county and the state. She had prepared letters for both our federal and our state representatives expressing concern over the scope of the project and requesting that a moratorium be put into place until a definitive study could be conducted for an equitable distribution of interstate groundwater. The supervisors voted unanimously to sign the JPA and to sign and send the letters. The meeting was adjourned.

I thought it was good form that none of us Terrorists mentioned that, as we walked through the parking lot, we noticed Chief Gentry getting out of a nice, new car with a license-plate holder advertising a car dealership in Reno—possibly just a coincidence. No need to jump to conclusions of conflicted interest or numbered Swiss-bank accounts.

Bob Sorvaag caught up with us in the hall. He congratulated us for being involved and said, "You don't know how powerful your voice is in a meeting like this. We're all being paid to be here. You aren't. Don't forget that."

It was the first time since the day we had read the clipping in Bettie's kitchen that I felt intense anxiety split somewhere in my gut. On one hand, we had found and established allies standing between us and the assault of Washoe County that had existed only in theory until that day. Modoc would be a part of the joint powers, and the campaign would be very different now. If the JPA could concentrate its efforts south at Lassen's border and stop the pipeline before the first shovel broke the earth, we might stand a chance, assuming California officials would support us. They always showed up at election time, pretending interest in issues that concerned us, and they accepted our checks at tax time. Now, unless we could conjure a way to get their attention, all interstate basins would be exposed to the Nevada water raiders.

↔

The next day we were in the car headed north to Oregon to appear before the Lake County commissioners. We were tougher and a little more savvy.

Oregon has a firm hold on water issues. The commissioners listened to us very carefully. Their concern was serious. They immediately drafted a letter protesting Washoe County's applications, and contacted Gov. Bob Smith to follow up at the state level.

In the past two weeks, we had written to every state and federal agency, every organization with an interest in the resources, the environment, the ranching industry, and the people within the scope of influence of the

SSWPP from Ducks Unlimited to the Fort Bidwell Civic Club. The file folder containing their responses was growing. But I guess we should have realized that a letter of agreement is (I hesitate to use the words *lip service*) not necessarily a mounted posse riding hard toward Modoc.

⮑

I figured people of the Truckee Meadows weren't concerned with the fiddlesticks of acquisition: the requirements of zoning, services available, laws, ordinances, restrictions, filing applications for streets, lights, sewage, water. Just build the house; they'll buy it. Give them work to pay off the mortgage. Development at any price. I was wrong.

Editorials and letters to the editor began appearing in the *Reno Gazette-Journal.* The opinion page filled with guest comments registering opposition to the SSWPP and questioning the purchase of agricultural lands for development, one parcel after another, when available resources were already overtaxed. They expressed concern that houses and pavement inched out from the city, that fertile valleys were being cemented beneath a Lego Land of houses and strip malls. Air quality was an oxymoron in the Truckee Meadows. Wood burning for heat was limited, but that was the least offender. Air and street traffic spewed a deadly looking pall of smog up highway corridors, and winter inversions pressed it into adjoining basins as far north as the Smoke Creek Desert. During peak commute time the streets became congested and the freeway interchange, nicknamed the Spaghetti Bowl, tangled.

The public voice was not demanding antigrowth but carefully planned growth with water-conservation methods, so the home place they loved dearly would not be sacrificed. The editorials and letters were proof that there were people in Washoe County who understood that the SSWPP was not about securing municipal water to maintain the current population; it was about power and money and unsustainable growth in the West—again. We knew we had to seek out those people and build a power base within the voting public in the heartland of the Truckee Meadows.

The Westerners is an organization of longtime Reno residents who are openly concerned about the changes in their community and the progrowth positions of their local politicians. Their president was a colleague of Sophie's parents at the university and an old family friend. He knew about our opposition to the SSWPP and invited us to speak at their annual meeting. We accepted and made our first sortie into enemy territory.

We dressed nicely. Sara helped us. Up till now we had no reason to worry about our image. In addition to serving as our fashion consultant, Sara was our final authority on grammar and spelling and our arbitrator of ethics and libel. What I know of the goodness that high school teachers offer the world I have learned from her: a shine that comes from opening young minds; a gentle willingness and patience; and a 220-volt bullshit detector that enables her to cut to the heart of any issue, to offer a swift rebuttal in any argument. Whatever needs to be said, Sara says it in an articulate, non-combative way.

Bettie wore a beautiful red dress and matching lipstick, and looked more like the president of the PTA than the woman in the picture tacked above her thirty-cup coffee pot holding up the front feet of an enormous dead porcupine, Winchester, over her arm. "The son of a bitch climbed up a snowdrift above the stovepipe collar and girdled my Jonathan Hale peach trees! I planted those trees to feed my family." She thumped the photo with a knuckle. That was reason enough for me.

A snappish energy surrounds Bettie, defying exhaustion, infirmity, and aging, drawing people as though she is a power source. She is the epitome of a ranch woman living two hundred miles from anywhere. If we want to eat next winter we have to seed, tend, harvest, can, freeze, dry, bake it now. Most of us work outside too, riding, haying, holding the cow's tail up while our husband pulls a calf, pulling it ourselves when he isn't around—or, in Bettie's case, welding.

I met Bettie in the adult-ed welding class at the high school. We were standing on opposite sides of the principal's girlfriend, watching her tack a black iron ring a foot in diameter to a four-foot-tall tripod with the arc welder. We closed our eyes when she struck the weld. When the hum stopped we opened them. Bettie smiled at me and said hi. We thought the girlfriend was making a planter and imagined ivy or geraniums. It turned out to be a dog dish for her Great Dane.

"Can't he eat off the floor like a regular dog?" Bettie asked.

The girlfriend said he was too tall.

Bettie snorted that horses were tall and they eat off the ground. She gave me a look that said let's go, and I went to check out her welding project. It was something for the drawbar of Joe's tractor. She said she took the class every winter to brush up her technique, because that's when she welded up all the broken-down haying equipment on the ranch. Her eyes were better than Joe's, and her hands were steadier.

She invited me come see her sometime. I went and stood in line behind a lot of other women, young and old, who came to tap into Bettie for a while, recharging their own imaginations or worn spirits.

Sophie wore a dress of somber tones, although you might have expected something more flamboyant, knowing she was raised in a home of artists— a painter father and a sculptor mother—and had studied at the Ecole des Beaux-Arts. But it was imagination and a gift for envisioning opportunity and possibility that Sophie was weaned on, not pretense and privilege. She was the first woman artist I'd met who supported herself and her son with her artwork—and, during thin times, with odd jobs like mowing lawns and caretaking the Lake City Cemetery. Her standards of performance and good behavior in others are never higher than those to which she holds herself. A failed painting gets the Zorro treatment and sent to "art heaven."

Just as incisive and unforgiving was her assessment of the volumes of paperwork that we now had to read and assimilate. When it came to deciphering the jargon of the EIS, the regulations guiding the California Environmental Quality Act and the National Environmental Quality Act, the fine print and the doublespeak, we knew we could count on Sophie. She was the one brave enough to telephone the Nevada State Water Engineer's office again. It was an incursion into enemy territory, but stacks of protest forms were mailed weeks before and no one had been notified of the hearing; we had a lot to prepare.

The engineer who answered the phone laughed and said, "Lady, it's going to take a long time to wade through this stack of protests. We've never gotten a response like this before."

"Really?" she said, innocence sugaring her voice.

"Usually we get one or two, maybe a half dozen. There must be 200 protests piled on the desk. We'll let you know." Pause. "It'll be a while."

"Actually," Sophie said, "I think the number is nearer 250."

❧

On June 5, 1987, shortly after our presentation to the Westerners the *Reno Gazette-Journal* ran an op-ed piece:

"Water Importing Is No Sure Thing for Reno-Sparks"

To the water-scarce Truckee Meadows, importation of water looks like a golden dream. But to people in outlying valleys, it can look like rape and pillage. When the cost is added up, it might look like rape and pillage to the Truckee Meadows residents, too.

Washoe County has filed 52 applications for ground water in

northwest Nevada, and this has led to a record number of protests being filed with State Water Engineer, Peter Morros. The 52 applications have generated more than 250 protests from the Bureau of Land Management and people in California, Nevada, and Oregon. including the California Department of Agriculture, the California Department of Fish and Game and the counties of Plumas, Lassen and Modoc.

At least one thing is clear. Populous areas have no moral right—and should have no legal right—to take water from areas which will be damaged by that taking. Landowners must be protected and so must wildlife.

All of this sends a pretty clear message to Washoe, Sparks, and Reno officials: Look for water if you will, but don't base growth expectations upon it. Regulate growth based on the water that the area has, and not the pipelines that might be no more than pipe dreams.

We were encouraged enough to write to Governor Dukmajien, demanding California come to our aid. He passed our letter off to CDWR director Kennedy who wrote that he understood there were "quite a large number of protests," he would keep his eye on the project, and we could contact Chief Gentry with any questions.

⊷

You know how it goes, darkest before the dawn? One morning in August John and I headed out on horseback to separate young bulls out of the yearling heifers they had been running with all summer. If you've ever tried to shut down a frat party off campus, it's similar. One by one we located the bulls and pushed them through the gate. They waited in the next field while we went back for the next one. In no time we had the whole bunch headed toward the corral. No problem. They trotted along in front of our horses, obedient laddies. We kept giving each other a "pinch-me" look.

"Well," John said, "I guess good luck can happen—just like bad luck. We ought to accept it and be happy."

Later that month old schoolmates who were home for a visit held a barbecue down the valley. John and I were invited over to meet Bonnie and Mike from Sacramento.

Bonnie shook my hand, looked me in the eye, and said, "So, what's news in the valley?"

"You'll be sorry you asked," I said. "It's a long and sordid tale." I had been boring people for months with the saga of the SSWPP until even I was tired of hearing about it.

"Try me," Bonnie said.

I gave her the scaled-down, four-second version: "Reno wants our water."

"How so?"

Okay, sister, I thought, *you asked for it,* and launched a full frontal assault. She listened with complete interest, never once spun the ice in her scotch, never once looked over my shoulder to see whose conversation looked more interesting than the one we were having. When I finished she asked a couple of questions about what kind of help we had.

None.

"You need to talk to my dad."

I followed her into the house, saying, "Your dad? Your dad, as in *father?*" She was dialing the phone.

"Why would I want to talk to your dad?"

"Hi, Daddy. Mike and I are having dinner in Surprise Valley with Judy and Mel. There's someone here I think you should talk to." She handed me the phone.

A voice from a long way off said, "Hello?"

"Hello," I said weakly.

"Hi. Jim Slosson here. What's news in the valley?"

And so began a conversation that neither of us knew would go on into the next century. Neither did I know that afternoon to whom I was speaking: Dr. James Slosson, chief engineering geologist of a consulting firm, former state geologist under the administrations of both Gov. Edmund G. Brown and Gov. Ronald Reagan, chief of the California Division of Mines and Geology, member of the Seismic Safety Commission, and author of numerous articles and abstracts on the geology of Surprise Valley.

Dr. Slosson listened carefully to my dog-eared explanation of the SSWPP, asked a few questions, and said he and his wife, Nancy Jane, were going to be in Modoc in a few days. They had a cabin in Jess Valley and would be happy to meet with the Surprise Valley Terrorists at the Modoc County Fair in Cedarville.

A week later a handsome couple came up the boardwalk behind the grandstands. Dr. Slosson flapped a file the size of our county phone book against his pant leg. His wife, Nancy, explained it was his resumé. He was interviewing for the job. Between us we maybe had two nickels. He didn't want our nickels. We hired him on the spot.

Dr. Slosson's best advice was given to us that day: protect the area of origin, demand good science, don't let them segment the project because once a pipe is in place it won't be allowed to run dry—and don't forget, not everybody is honest.

⊷

In September 1987, an independent firm, R. W. Beck and Associates, released a preliminary study of the importation project, "Phase I—Reconnaissance Study—Summary." Dr. Slosson wrote a review of the executive summary, finding "errors, lack of hard data, and gross over-estimations of ground water availability by greater than 50%." "Phase I" made no provisions for a project-wide cumulative-impact study, he noted, including requirements of the areas of origin and current water users. Those flaws nullified its recommendation to proceed to "Phase II."

"Reno/Sparks may create a Sahara of the west," Dr. Slosson concluded. "This project, as planned, can become the great human error of the century—but the casinos will grow in number and will flourish as a result of the project."

It was about this time that the power portion of the plan was officially abandoned, and for a while the project went forward as the Silver State Project (SSP). There was also a emphatic denial that Surprise Valley water was ever a part of the plan. Public assurances were made that the well sites applied for within the Surprise Valley basin were withdrawn.

They were not, of course. Sophie called the Nevada Division of Water Resources engineer she had spoken with before and read off the identification numbers of the well sites on the project map located within Surprise Valley. He confirmed that they were still among the appropriations held by Washoe County's SSP.

⊷

In October 1987, Travis Linn, moderator of *Silver State,* a television show produced at the University of Nevada, Reno, hosted a debate of the issues surrounding the SSP between Bob Jasper, acting director of the Washoe County Water Board; WestPac manager Bob Firth; Dr. Slosson; and me. It was to be our first public confrontation. Sophie, Sara, and Bettie appointed themselves my handlers and quizzed me without mercy until I left for the broadcast.

Dr. Slosson and I were early getting to the television studio. While he coached me on some pertinent statistics I stifled yawn after yawn—a nervous reaction I have to frightening situations. Travis Linn led us into the studio, chatting to put us at ease as the sound levels were set. I yawned again and the program began.

Mr. Linn gave his viewers an overview of the project and asked for our comments. Jasper and Firth spoke about the SSP as being just one of many options Washoe County was looking at for delivering water to the Truckee Meadows. They said it was a Nevada project on Nevada soil, and they couldn't understand why California ranchers were concerned. I had to keep reminding myself they were the front men for a project with a first-phase cost estimation of $90 million, a completion cost to exceed $400 million, and hang the details.

Dr. Slosson reminded the Reno viewers that the projected cost was grossly underestimated and the water available grossly overestimated, and that if the project failed the taxpayers would carry the burden of the accumulated debt up to that time.

Jasper didn't like that. "I totally disagree."

"Well, that's okay," Dr. Slosson said. "But you're wrong."

Jasper looked like he'd been hit with a Sunday punch. He recovered enough to sidestep discussing alternatives to the SSP, denying Surprise Valley was ever figured in the project. I tried to make it clear that the Surprise Valley well sites were still listed in the applications Washoe County held with the Nevada state engineer's office. Jasper changed the subject to a discussion of value exchange between phreatophytes on the Smoke Creek Desert and beneficial use. We got bogged down. Mr. Linn tried to steer us back to the project overview, but time ran out.

I wished I had thought to bring the picture of Bettie and her dead porcupine.

⟿

The next day I got a call from a Reno radio deejay. He saw the TV show and was interested in the controversy. He knew Surprise Valley and asked what he could do.

"Use your station to encourage people to attend the commissioners' meetings and read the paper. Help the people of Reno get the straight story. Ask them how they can, in good conscience, allow their elected officials to spend their tax dollars searching for water when Reno has no water meters or plans for metering water? Have them drive around town and see how many lawn sprinklers are running in the gutter. It's a drought, for kripes sakes."

The next day there was a new feature on his station called the "Sprinkler Report." He gave out the addresses of homes and businesses around town where the sprinklers were left on, and he encouraged people to call in if they saw water running on the sidewalk. Every day the list of "water hogs" grew. His idea was gaining attention.

Small placards appeared on dining tables in Reno's restaurants: "We're conserving and helping Nevada save water and energy during the drought. If you'd like a glass of water please let us know. We'll be happy to serve you!" As soon as the drought broke the placards disappeared from the tables, water sloshed from full pitchers, and the "Sprinkler Report" was canned. The crisis was over. So, apparently, was conservation.

⊷

Following Dr. Slosson's advice, we continued our letter-writing campaign to the California legislators and the CDWR regarding the SSP, the Beck report, and the United States Geological Survey (USGS) study to request their advice and to remind them that we were still in need of their support.

In early November, Chief Gentry responded to one of our many letters, stating that he hadn't received a copy of the Beck study (the report we had had for six weeks). In an attempt to placate our worries, he said that according to what he read, in the "Phase I" summary report (which we provided to his office), "they [Silver State] have dropped plans for pumping from Nevada's portion of Surprise Valley. The summary also stated that any pumping from a basin would be limited to keeping the poor quality water in the central parts of the basin from migrating to the wells. If this is done, then the chances of causing ground water to flow from California's portion of the basin are greatly reduced." (This now coming from the man who only a few months earlier stood before our supervisors and denied the basins were interlocking.)

He then outlined the summary plan to segment the project: Smoke Creek Desert, Duck Lake Valley, and, finally, the basins adjacent to Surprise Valley. This latter stage, he wrote, "is about 50 years away and might never be built. Besides, Surprise Valley isn't a part of the plan."

Were we mistaken thinking that Chief Gentry ought to be expert on the all documents pertinent to the SSP, especially those defining the scope of the project, and would read those documents with an inquisitive, even critical, eye? Why didn't he advise against allowing the project to be segmented beginning headfirst in the valleys nearest to Reno like a tapeworm burrowed in, sucking from the host land and growing out the back end, section by section? Wasn't he working for us? Where was the outrage that would speak to us of protection against the interstate transfer of California water? We felt like battered housewives who call the police only to hear the desk sergeant say they don't do domestic conflicts.

We hotly responded to Chief Gentry (cc: Director Kennedy and others), "[W]e are curious how you can make a judgment on the SSP without reading 'Phase I—Reconnaissance Study by R. W. Beck' which has been available to the public since October.

"Please get the 'Phase I—Reconnaissance Study' and count the number of times that Surprise Valley's groundwater is mentioned as available to the project. Sincerely," etc.

Dr. Slosson followed with a letter to Mr. Gentry (cc: Director Kennedy), "The report clearly states (Paragraph 3 on Pages 11–12) . . . that the plan proposes extraction from the Nevada portion of Surprise Valley. Since the eastern (Nevada) side of Surprise Valley is hydrogeologically connected with and geologically related to the western (California) side of Surprise Valley, extraction of water from the eastern side of the valley will affect the groundwater regime of the western side. Having been party chief for the original Department of Water Resources groundwater study, I believe I am qualified to express the opinion that inter-connection does exist and that pumping on the eastern side of the valley will affect the groundwater of the western side. The residents of Surprise Valley *should* be concerned and hopefully the CDWR will provide some assistance in the protection of their water resources."

Privately he said, "A guy named Newton sat under an apple tree in the seventeenth century and figured this out. Water held at a higher elevation will flow toward a lower elevation. What these guys need to do is go sit under a tree."

So, we were suited up in our wrestling slings, people shoving us at the California-Nevada tag team, saying, "sic 'em, go on, sic 'em," and us—ankle biters, no muscle, no might. Government agencies were unwilling to negotiate or even confer with the Surprise Valley Terrorists. Royalty only makes deals with royalty; they don't have tea with the serfs.

Okay. The problem had been identified, scientific data in hand, groundwork done. There remained one thing to do: establish an entity with which agencies could communicate. Dr. Slosson urged us to press for the legislative act creating the Surprise Valley Water District, responsible to and controlled by the users, residents, and landowners. The district board would be the entity we needed for negotiation. The district would offer us protection. Two-for-one.

Before our state reps would consider proposing such an act to the legislature they wanted assurance that local organizations such as the Farm Bureau and the Cattlemen's Association could be counted on for support. They wanted to enter the capitol with a consensus in their vest pockets, not egg on their faces.

Therefore, the Modoc supervisors expanded the advisory committee to include the District 1 supervisor; one member each from the RCD, the Modoc County Cattlemen's Association; the Farm Bureau; the Hay Growers' Association, RFD; at-large members from the four communities of Surprise Valley; and all other interested parties. The committee's goal was to study the issue and bring forth a recommendation to the people of the Surprise Valley groundwater basin of whether to pursue the formation of a groundwater district, independent by virtue of its closed basin geology and empowered by the California legislature, to act as a legal entity, in the best interests of all concerned. Once passed, the act could stay on the shelf, to be activated only if and when it was needed.

The meetings were *deadly dull.* Personalities, past and present, had to find their footing through generations of feuds, petty gripes, playground fistfights, and sweetheart rivalries. Within the makeup of the committee were individuals with a shadowed reputation of after-hours irrigation, meaning they could not be trusted on a shared ditch of water. Some powerful ranchers we needed refused to attend. Instead they sat at the big table in the Cedarville coffee shop and spoke out against the district. (There'll never be a meter on my well, by God!) Some came to the meetings and threw their weight around. Some newcomers had left regulations behind when they moved to Surprise Valley, and they didn't want to be forced to comply with pressures from any agencies, even a locally controlled one. Some were negative to the core and blocked every discussion. There were raised voices, silent irritations, and a shuffle of members.

We wasted time bringing the new appointees up to speed. Their questions were ones we'd already hammered and chipped our way through. Conditions already agreed on were reexamined by the new members, and negotiations began anew.

There was a shuffle of advisors. We suspected transfers had been requested just to get away from the frustration of meeting every Wednesday night. Heaven knows we wanted to, but there was too much at stake.

I can't say I didn't feel the teeniest bit of resentment toward John sitting in his chair with a book and a glass of red wine when I staggered in at ten o'clock feeling like I'd been dragged home behind a team of runaway horses. I had been out slaying his share of the dragons while he'd been riding his pretty horses across the pampas. Then he'd look up and say, "How'd it go?" I'd take a slug of his wine, sit down, and tell him.

And, of course, the public heard all the ragged edges of our meetings practically before we got home at night. One man's statement, "My twenty-five dollars an acre-foot water here is worth twenty-five hundred dollars in Reno. If I want to sell into a pipe and not farm that's *my* damned business!" stuck in every conversation like a burr. Despite the little annoyances, the focus had to be maintained.

One night our District 1 supervisor came to the meeting and triumphantly announced that he had had lunch with Larry Beck, Washoe County commissioner, and Bob Jasper, now assistant Washoe County manager, and they assured him that the Surprise Valley sites had been dropped, that Surprise Valley was no longer a part of the plan.

Deep silence.

Some members were staring down the long table at us with a—*Whaddya need? A signature in blood?*—expression on their faces. They needed to get home. They had work to do tomorrow. They had a life.

So did we. A trip to the dentist was a fiesta in comparison. As the original Surprise Valley Terrorists in it from the start, the first advisory committee to the supervisors, and out of respect for Dr. Slosson's efforts in the valley's behalf, we hadn't missed a meeting. We were the only women who ever attended any. All the smart ones were home scrubbing down the bathroom or ironing socks. It was hard to miss the fact that Surprise Valley was just beginning to emerge from the dark ages of male domination, and we were on the slippery slope of becoming bitchy women in the men's eyes. But we were remembering Dr. Slosson's words on the expectation of honesty. Sophie calmly told them she had called the Nevada state engineer's office that morning, and an engineer had confirmed that the Surprise Valley wells were still on file.

The speech began to feel like a sermon: we had to be responsible for our own environment, and we had to know that whatever happened in Lassen would be coming our way. Dr. Slosson's advice to protect the area of origin, not to allow the proponents of the SSP to sell the idea of a segmented project, must stay foremost in our minds. "Keep sight of the whole plan," he said repeatedly. Once the pipes were in place they would vibrate with the rush of water.

All heads swung back to the supervisor who gave a strawman-in-the-Land-of-Oz shrug. Tension faded; the meeting continued.

Following the exchange of letters with Gentry back in November we, *the women,* got called on the carpet. The acting president berated us in front of the committee for unprofessional-like conduct and ordered that any correspondence sent out heretofore must have board approval.

Sara, Sophie, and I got up, pushed our chairs in, and excused ourselves. (Bettie was one of the smart ones. She refused to sit through meetings at all.) We bustled down the hallway of the Forest Service office and slammed the copy-room door behind us before we exploded. How dare they? We had been involved from the onset. They were the latecomers. For four long years we wrote the letters, made all the phone calls, followed up, neglected our own work, our families, attended to all the boring meetings, licked all the goddamned stamps!

We tore into the next batch of correspondence that needed to go out, cheering ourselves with a Gary Larson cartoon of a dinosaur measuring himself against a ten-story sign. The caption read, "To attack this city you have to be *this* tall." About then, we felt *that* tall. We looked at each other. Sara chuckled, "They're all married men. They know the drill." We grabbed up letters, envelopes, stamps, stomped back into the boardroom, slammed them down on the table in front of the president, and went home.

We heard later that he silently signed each page in the stack, divvied up envelopes and stamps, and they all got to work. He adjourned the meeting early and stopped by the post office on his way home.

Chief Gentry called up and said he would be attending the next meeting in the company of another engineer, Bob Clausen, and Glen Pierson, an engineering geologist.

They didn't give us money, they didn't give us much, but from that point on our board had their attendance and their best advice that saw us through the process to the approval by the state legislature. And we understood, at last, the power of "cc:" on the bottom of official correspondence.

↔

I wonder how John and I made it through those years. We had tensions of our own. John's mother had a massive stroke that left her horribly damaged, and within a week my father died. After months of hospitalization and doctor appointments and therapy sessions his mother came home. We managed twenty-four-hour care at home for nearly a year on top of trying to keep the ranch running. My journal tells me how we made it through.

October 3: John and I are fixing fence in the lake field. It is late afternoon. Twenty-nine posts broken over, staples pulled loose, five strands of wire are on the ground. The cows mowed it over, who knows why. He is setting posts a hundred yards down the line. I string wire, hammer each staple across the grain at an angle so the cedar posts won't split. John's whistle stops my hammer midswing. He is looking across the field, still as the post he had just tamped solid. A pair of cranes—a pair—are a quarter of a mile away in elegant flight coming low across the meadow directly at me. Giant, gentle birds. I believe they are a returning pair we have seen for years, the pair that nested in the upper fields and range to feed a circular mile. We wait for their return every March. Spring cannot begin until they cross the sky in scribbled lines. And now, in the pearl of evening light, their wings beating even, straight on, stroke, stroke, keep coming, perfectly silent, long wings gracefully slow. The lowering sun is in their eyes. She leads. He is a half beat back and to her side, twenty feet away. They see me. He purrs softly. She bends, turns as a stranger met on a narrow path, shoulder away, her outside wing tips upward into his air, him so close. He lifts his head. His graceful long neck recoils, S's, to avoid clipping her wing, to accommodate her. In two strokes they are past me, angled slightly away, and again their flight gains a cadence. Wings in three-quarter time, one beat, two, three, four, five, six, seven strokes, precisely together, into the waning light. Seven strides. Then his longer wings, perhaps stronger, go opposite. In her draft, he pulls behind, their unison blinded from me now by the setting sun.

I look back at John. I expected he would have gone back to work. Cranes. Only cranes, this pair with us all season, night coming and so much work to do. But, no. His eyes are still on the cranes. He saw the male pull up for her, stay by her, and for seven strides find the same air.

        ☙

The next big meeting, an appearance before the Nevada Legislative Public Lands Committee, was held in the Carson City chambers in the fall of 1989. I met Dr. Slosson and Nancy at the Reno airport, and we drove to Carson together. The room was stunning, glowing of polished wood. The spoken word floated around and around, never touching down until all present had a chance to hear. It was a marvelous room. The men of the committee took their places. Dean Rhodes, committee chair and a rancher from the Elko area, respectfully greeted each person who came before them. It was an impressive assembly, and, even though the SSP was the last item of business on a full agenda, I felt something of true purpose might happen in that room.

Important topics were discussed throughout the afternoon. By the time they got to us it was four-thirty—a Friday evening and the committee looked weary and slightly disinterested. One member excused himself and left to catch his plane for home just as I took the stand. I had had all day to learn the procedure: wait for the question and answer it in plain language, direct and to the point. I would like to say that my appeal for sense and reason woke them up, stirred them to cancel the project, but if anything, it made them look sleepier. I took my seat between Dr. Slosson and our old friend Bob Sorvaag from Lassen County.

Dr. Slosson went over his notes with me. I suddenly realized he was conferring with me. It was like Santa asking one of the elves if he ought to skip Russia entirely because the big babushkas had been so *bad* over there. Then he was called to the lectern. Having testified before literally hundreds of august boards and committees he is not intimidated by the power of any office, and there is no price on his integrity. He has laughed in the face of bribery attempts and ignored thinly veiled threats targeting him and his family when his expert testimony stood between opponents and profit.

Dr. Slosson began by reviewing the science in Beck's "Phase I—Reconnaissance Study," namely, the overestimation of water available in the northern basins (that is, the disparity between estimations of the proponents and the actual yields). He discussed empirical methodology rather than analysis based on facts, the cost variance of the completed project as proposed, and the financial burden placed on the Nevada taxpayers by the project. By this time the legislators were not only engaged but also mesmerized, leaning across the broad oak table toward Dr. Slosson. Chairman Rhodes thanked Dr. Slosson for his insights and information.

Bob jabbed me in the ribs with his elbow and whispered, "Where did you get *him?*"

"Oh," I said, giving him my innocent Carol Channing eyes, "he's a friend's dad."

"How much do you pay him?"

Carol again: *"Pay?"*

After the meeting closed I introduced Dr. Slosson and Nancy to Bob. Bob casually asked, "Dr. Slosson, do you ever do any duck hunting?" They walked off across the parking lot talking golden retrievers and green heads. Water and geology and how to save a place would come later.

⊖

Of course, we were naive not to see through the smoke screen of the SSP. It was not a civic project of simple supply-and-demand economics. It was not floating a bond issue to borrow enough to expand services to satisfy growth. Investors whose dollars could provide curbside water service enabling development in the valleys adjacent to the Truckee Meadows were being given every political consideration. Big money shimmered in the distance like an oasis. It wasn't the water they wanted. Water was merely the means to the end. The end promised money and power enough to satisfy investors willing to risk venture capital to fund a start-up company in the water industry that might or might not include the purchase of permanent rights to water, to be sold or leased independent of the land it flows from.

Imagine a pipeline designed to drain the north county into Reno, mapped out on the wall of the Nevada state engineer's office. In the next room lots of guys doing the dirty work, risking their professional reputations for a little job security. Their work would funnel down to the wheel greasers who would take the midlevel cut. But the real money, like the mainline pipe, would be buried out of sight, underground, so that its location could not be pinpointed.

I read a book of poetry written by a man who lived in Owens Valley during the Los Angeles water project years. He wrote poems about his wife's garden, and his little boy going off down the road to school every morning, and the boy's dog waiting by the gate until school was over for the day and the boy returned home. Poem after poem written about neighbors, family, and the valley, until gradually the project crept into the lines. As the book progressed neighbors sold out and stopped at the gate to say good-bye, until it was him and his family leaving. He wondered in the last poem if the wisteria vine that draped the garden door still bloomed in spring even though they were not there to smell its sweet perfume. He didn't see it coming, any more than we did. He couldn't stop it. We were going to try.

⊖

Meanwhile the Truckee Meadows Project (TMP) pulled ahead of the SSP in the water-importation race. It was a parallel project to the SSP, but segmented (and seemingly less threatening), that would draw from California-Nevada interstate basins that came under the scrutiny of the United States

Geological Survey. Lassen had secured a three-year moratorium on the implementation of the TMP that allowed the USGS unimpeded time to study the hydrology of the Honey Lake Valley, an interstate basin sixty miles north of Reno but largely located in California. People of the interfacing California counties enlisted powerful allies among groups as diverse as the Sierra Club and the Paiute Tribe determined to protect the fisheries of Pyramid Lake. Press releases were backing up on the editor's desk at the *Reno Gazette-Journal,* and opposition to the project was swelling. Meanwhile there was a new twist to the old dance in the headlines.

In 1989 the *San Francisco Chronicle* featured an article in the "Business Extra" section titled "Big Spurt in Water Investment." It was reported that the Fish Springs Ranch at the south end of Honey Lake Valley (across the state line in Nevada) had been purchased in the mid-1980s for $2 million. Plans were to convert the "old cattle ranch" into an alfalfa farm. But the new partners "never got to do much farming. When they began to till the land, they found it had three times more ground water than either previously believed—water that could be worth as much as $140 million over the next eight years if they can transport it south to the metropolitan areas of Reno and Sparks."

If that were true the Fish Springs Ranch irrigation water could be diverted into a pipe, to sort of kick-start Washoe County's plans for development. For a price, of course. Washoe County could immediately have thirteen thousand acre-feet of water for $113 million ($8,692.31 per acre-foot—hardly a bargain).

Honey Lake residents who knew the ranch history began speculating on the deal the moment the sale became public. Openly they said it couldn't pump enough water to raise a decent hay crop. That's why the last owners sold out. But the new owners let the talkers talk, and only occasionally talked back. In an appearance before the Lassen supervisors in October 1985, one of them said, "We want a ranch, not a tax loss, we want a ranch that in fact will pay its own way and be a viable economic unit. . . . Sierra Pacific Power Company paid eight thousand dollars for an acre foot of water in Warm Springs Valley. If that's true, then the water rights I have at the end of Honey Lake Valley are worth about 128 million bucks, and that's a lot of money. . . . But I don't think it's true, number 1, and number 2 that's not what I'm out there for. I'm out there to try and build my farm . . . trying to be a good neighbor. We don't want to fight with you . . . and if we end up having problems . . . all you're going to do is drive us into the arms of the Sierra Pacific Power Company."

News of the proposed sale of Fish Springs water to Washoe County rico-
cheted off the *Chronicle*'s pages and hit the local papers. Lassen officials
were upset. The USGS had not completed their findings, and it was clear that
Washoe County was trying to slip some water in the back door. Washoe
commissioners called a meeting and categorically denied the connection to
the SSP.

Someone at the meeting stood up and asked, "If it's true that Washoe
County has no plans to transfer water from Honey Lake Valley to Reno then
can you please tell me what the three eighteen-inch culverts are for that
have just been installed under the overpass on Interstate Highway 395?"

↶

In 1990 the half-million-dollar USGS study of the TMP was presented to a
packed auditorium at the Lassen Community College in Susanville. We felt
sure Elinor Handman, project chief and geochemist, would conclude that
the proponents of the TMP overestimated the Honey Lake Valley water
budget. To achieve a figure even close to the estimates in the Beck report,
aggressive pumping at the Fish Springs Ranch would draw contaminated
water to the well field, degrading a productive aquifer along a hydraulic
gradient toward the well. It is old news that overpumping creates a cone of
depression pulling a plume of available groundwater toward the point of
pumping.

But Handman said nothing of the kind. In fact, there was no reference
made to the geochemistry of the groundwater at all. During the Q&A portion of the meeting Dr. Slosson asked about the water quality. Handman
replied that water quality had not been a part of her assignment. Dr. Slosson pointed out that her expertise was in water quality rather than basic geology and hydrogeology. She made no response.

At the time, we knew there were two artesian wells a short distance
northwest of Fish Springs Ranch known to be high in total dissolved solids
(tds). Hydrology consultants for the proponents of the TMP indicated that
they knew of the contamination but had developed a computer model that
they could utilize to "fence off" the "bad" water. Dr. Slosson laughed,
"Ranchers traditionally fence their cattle away from the neighbors' herds;
fencing contaminated water from good-quality water must be next to impossible."

Dr. Slosson had spoken with a geohydrologist from the CDWR and an en-
vironmental engineer with the federal Environmental Protection Agency
(EPA), both of whom were knowledgeable about the water quality of the
Sierra Army Depot at Hurlong, which was less than ten miles directly north

of Fish Springs Ranch. They told him that the preliminary reports from those studies indicated the wells contained arsenic and boron in dangerously high levels as well as other deleterious chemicals—contaminants of fifty-thousand-parts-per-million. One should expect that contaminants are usually a serious problem at military bases and especially at a storage facility of military hardware and vehicular equipment. They said, "Very nasty water can be expected."

There were many dangerous chemicals at the Sierra Army Depot emanating from various sources: deterioration of tracer bullets and mortar shells deployed on the range, white phosphorous munitions that were used to explode over enemy troops as a weapon, and solvents used to degrease vehicles and equipment in the motor pool. Old batteries containing very toxic acid were dumped into a sand and gravel pit at groundwater level. As conditions existed in the '40s and '50s disposal of these chemicals at the depot posed no threat to military personnel and public safety. However, these hazardous chemicals could be drawn into an aquifer and flowing via pipe toward Reno-Sparks, carrying the potential for cancer.

It was obvious Handman was making use of a limited study in her conclusion that the TMP could export fifteen thousand acre-feet from Honey Lake Valley, precisely what the proponents were banking on. Dr. Slosson was mildly surprised that Handman had sidestepped science and granted the TMP the green light where water availability was concerned and had ignored the issue of contaminants completely. He was familiar with the kind of blinders she chose to wear. For Bettie, Sophie, Sara, and me, Handman's report was, unfortunately, the triumph of experience over hope.

On the long, dark drive home from Susanville I thought of a Peanuts cartoon I had pinned above my desk. In a simply drawn square Charlie Brown faced his defeated baseball team, looking thoughtfully sad, and asked, "How can we keep losing when we're so sincere?"

↢

Dr. Slosson called, saying he had contacted colleague Dr. Alan L. Mayo, Department of Geology, Brigham Young University, a specialist in isotope testing to age water.

Water could be aged. The concept was fascinating. My world shot out in a new direction. I could hardly wait to tell John.

Dr. Slosson thought it imperative that someone perform the research the USGS did not see fit to do. Isotopic analysis would determine the age of the groundwater, and show the elevation at which the water entering the system actually becomes groundwater. The studies would also reveal water quality and identify the origin of the recharge source of the groundwater. (Amazing.)

Conclusions of the testing, initiated by the Surprise Valley Water Advisory at Dr. Slosson's suggestion, and supported by the Modoc and Lassen supervisors and the RCD, were the basis for an analysis of the USGS report on Honey Lake Valley. Cowritten by Mayo and Slosson and published in the 1992 *Bulletin of the Association of Engineering Geologists*, the paper, titled "The Application of Ground-Water Flow Models as Predictive Tools—A Review of Two Ground-Water Models of Eastern Honey Lake Valley, California-Nevada," brings into careful scrutiny the methodology of the USGS report as follows.

In the late 1980's Washoe County, Nevada, entered into an agreement with a private water development company to develop and export ground-water from the Nevada portion of the arid Honey Lake Valley to the rapidly growing Reno-Sparks area. The proposed project is known as the Truckee Meadows Project (TMP). Honey Lake Valley is 35 mi north of Reno, Nevada; but is located predominantly in California. Computer ground-water models of the valley were prepared by the USGS and the TMP proponents and presented to the Nevada State Engineer to evaluate the impacts of the proposed exportation of the 15,000 ac-ft annually from eastern Honey Lake Valley.

Mayo and Slosson concluded:

Both models have serious errors in their design and water budgets and are not useful as predictive tools. Both models place unreasonable and in some instance unbelievable constraints on the biology, geology and hydrogeology of the ground-water system rather than allowing the biology, geology and hydrogeology to constrain the models. However, the major problems with the two models fall into two fundamentally different classes. The USGS model exceeded the technical limitations of the model code and included large inappropriate adjustments to the water budget to compensate for these undetected errors. The TMP model used a water budget that was not technically justified or explained and placed the spatial distribution of recharge and discharge beyond the realm of hydrogeologic reality. . . .

The data base must be scientifically accurate—wishful thinking must not be incorporated. Both models for eastern Honey Lake Valley failed to meet these latter requirements.

❧

The decision on the TMP rested not with the legislature, or the governor, but with R. Michael Turnipseed, the newly appointed Nevada State Engineer. (Morros had been promoted to director of the state Department of Conservation and Natural Resources in 1990, and he, in turn, appointed Turnipseed to his old post of state engineer.)

In 1991 Captain Culver, the attorney representing the United States Army, contacted Dr. Slosson on the issue of groundwater contamination and the TMP. The army did not want to be held responsible for the contamination that would occur once the pumping started. Captain Culver joined Lassen County in requesting a hearing with Turnipseed to object to the TMP's application for permits to pipe water to Reno-Sparks. As water quality was one issue, Culver wanted the expert-witness testimony of Drs. Mayo and Slosson in the record.

The hearing on the Washoe County appropriations took place. When Drs. Mayo and Slosson gave testimony regarding the quality of the water the TMP proposed to pump, Turnipseed, acting as the administrative law judge, disallowed the testimony related to water quality because Dr. Slosson had not been able to produce the water-chemistry test results as background data. Dr. Slosson asked for time to formally obtain the records from studies by the federal and California EPAs. Turnipseed denied Dr. Slosson's request and disallowed his testimony since the test results were not available until a formal report was released.

Dr. Slosson said, "I do not know of a study of a military base that did not have a problem with toxic materials; it is just a matter of how much."

Again Turnipseed struck Dr. Slosson's statement out, saying the final EPA tests of the Fish Springs wells had not been completed; it was a study in progress.

At the conclusion of the hearing Turnipseed ruled that the TMP could safely export thirteen thousand acre-feet of water annually from Honey Lake Valley.

❧

In January 1992 Sophie got a call from someone in Reno who had been out hiking in the Never Sweat Hills, a little southeast of the Fish Springs

Ranch. The September before he stumbled onto a series of trenches on the playa directly south of the foothills that gaped open, like fault lines one expects to see after a major earthquake. Through the winter the fissures kept coming into his mind. He couldn't figure out what could have made the hard pack of the playa open up that way.

Sophie called Dr. Slosson, and he asked her to map the trenches. She took along her husband, Lynn Nardella. Lynn works for the Bureau of Land Management (BLM) doing archaeological transects; he understands natural and unnatural phenomena in the desert. A scientific transect of such a large area would require a crew. Lynn called some friends from the Honey Lake Valley area and asked if they wanted to go on a desert walk.

Five trenches lay within the whitish hardpan basin measuring from 50 to 240 yards long, 3 yards wide, and, in some places, deeper than the 4-foot probe Lynn carried. He said all five were cracks and not drainage channels; each crack disappeared into at least one greasewood hummock and reappeared on the other side. Sophie told Dr. Slosson that they looked like stretch marks on a woman's stomach after the baby has been delivered, and he told her to call Faith Bremner, staff reporter at the *Gazette-Journal.*

Dr. Slosson now had evidence to uphold his prediction: subsidence due to drawdown by the irrigation wells at the Fish Springs Ranch. The fissures were in all probability caused by a drop in the groundwater from the pumping rate of only five thousand acre-feet per year. In addition, two springs on the ranch had already dried up due to the current demand of pumping, and bodies of tui-chubs (the desert fish that Fish Springs was named for) littered the dried gravel. This gave credence to the objections that thirteen thousand acre-feet per year would not be a sustainable yield from that basin.

Faith ran Lynn's findings and photographs in the *Gazette-Journal* the following week.

But the big break for the opponents of the TMP, the one we didn't dare to dream of, came in the spring of 1993 when the *Gazette-Journal* broke a story that called into question the integrity of Nevada officials. The TMP was at the heart of the story. The article was subsequently picked up by the *Civil Engineering NEWS:*

"Engineer Blows Whistle on Water Projection"
   ... [S]tate hydraulic engineer Tom Gallagher, P.E., accused Pete Morros, P.E., of pressuring Gallagher's boss, state engineer Mike Turnipseed,

P.E., into accepting a higher projection. . . . Morros . . . took the action during a February 1991 meeting in his office attended by Turnipseed, deputy state engineer Hugh Ricci, and Gallagher.

. . . [A] minority partner in a company that hopes to make millions off the water-pumping project attacked Gallagher's credibility. "The water expert has strong ties to Lassen County, Calif. officials who are fighting the project," [he] said.

"The supposed 'strong ties' amount to nothing more than a casual friendship," Gallagher contends.

Turnipseed gave a boost to the $113 million project in March 1991 when he decided the county could safely export 13,000 ac-ft of water annually from the valley. That was nearly double the 7,000 ac-ft of water that Gallagher's draft report said could be taken from the valley without causing any harm to its underground supply.

Although Gallagher said he didn't realize it at the time, his finding was less than the 8,500 ac-ft minimum the county needed to make the pipeline project financially feasible. Gallagher, 35, who has been with the state water division for 12 years, said Morros exploded when he saw the 7,000 ac-ft number during the 1991 meeting.

Morros was upset with Gallagher's criticism of the USGS in the draft decision. When Gallagher tried to point out that expert witnesses at a hearing presented strong evidence that the USGS was flawed, Morros got even angrier, Gallagher said.

"He said, 'I'm still the boss here. I'm still calling the shots,'" Gallagher told the *Gazette-Journal.*

"He said, 'I know you guys are looking at this on completely scientific grounds but there's a bigger picture here.'"

What followed, Gallagher said, was a negotiating session in which Morros turned to Turnipseed and asked, "How high do you think you can go?"

"Morros and Turnipseed began tossing around numbers and in 15 minutes Washoe County had the water projection it needed to make the project practical," Gallagher said.

Turnipseed does intend to move Gallagher to a different position in the department, however. "He will be reviewing reports and not stay in a position to be writing draft rulings. We have certain laws and rules in Nevada as to what are public records and what are not and that clearly falls in the category of not being public records," he noted.

As for Gallagher, "Why should I leave? I didn't do anything wrong. All I wanted was for the taxpayers of Washoe County to know that there was a different professional opinion involved and it wasn't as one-sided as it appeared. . . . Whether I'm right or wrong or too conservative is not the point. The point is, there is a difference of opinion."

Turnipseed says there is a great deal of speculation on the future of the water project, "but the speculation is not as a result of our ruling," he said. "There are still some environmental issues outstanding that have to be addressed."

One year prior to Gallagher's coming forward Norman Tilford, professor of geology at Texas A&M University and executive director of the Association of Engineering Geologists, had published a paper written by Drs. Mayo and Slosson criticizing the groundwater flow models related to the TMP. The paper exposed the TMP projections versus reality and the sleight-of-hand tactics within the models, clearly describing the errors in the design and the inflated water budgets.

When I was a kid I remember being stumped by the maze on the activity page of the *Weekly Reader*. Start was marked at the entrance to the maze; X, in the center of the squiggly lines, was the goal. But too many paths leading nowhere opened before my pencil. I quickly learned that if I started at the X, the path out of the maze was direct and clear. I should have applied for a job with the TMP. We thought alike, for, as Slosson and Mayo pointed out, the model was designed by entering the desired result and working backward, adjusting the data to support the conclusion already in place despite the fact that it was beyond "the realm of hydrogeologic reality."

Tilford published the response of the TMP proponents (which amounted to an attempt to discredit Drs. Mayo and Slosson), followed by Drs. Mayo and Slosson's reply and a comment by Dr. M. D. Mifflin, geologist/hydrogeologist.

Mifflin supported the Slosson-Mayo report, concluding: "There is very little reliable data on boundary conditions and interbasin flow, and rather uncertain data on distribution of recharge. There is little justification for the modeling to determine exploitation impacts in most of the basins. It's pure show analyses at a high cost in credibility to all involved."

Tilford received unbridled threats by proponents of the TMP for running Mifflin's criticism of the project and the applied methodology. He told his harassers to go to hell. Threats were made against both Drs. Slosson and

Mayo, the militant members of the Surprise Valley Garden Club and Terrorist Society, and others who stood in the way of the project. Dr. Slosson said, "It's not the first time. It won't be the last."

The back-room politics were painfully obvious. Some of the Washoe County commissioners made public appeals in support of the TMP. Larry Beck went so far as to appear on televised ads that were paid for by the project's developer. Before the camera Beck walked across Fish Springs liquid-green alfalfa field to a six- or eight-inch pipe. As the camera panned to the valve gushing water, his voice-over explained the virtues of the TMP. The only thing missing was a bluebird perched on his shoulder and a swirl of butterflies about his head.

If there was not sufficient water at the Fish Springs Ranch to fulfill the option Washoe County purchased, one might ask, where would the water come from?

A *Sacramento Bee* article by Jane Braxton Little in May 1993 answered that question and raised others:

Neither the quantity nor the quality of the water has been proven, according to critics of the [Honey Lake Valley] project.

"Politically, it's just not acceptable to build a pipeline for $120 million with no water in it," said George Benesch, a Reno attorney who represents the Lassen County Board of Supervisors.

The chloride levels of the water proposed for import are "worse than the Dead Sea," said Bob Fulkerson, executive director of Citizen Alert, a Reno-based Nevada environmental watchdog.

The proposed Honey Lake water project already has been the subject of court rulings and proposed legislation. A bill, approved by the Nevada Assembly and moving rapidly through Senate committees, would allow the transfer of water from agricultural to municipal use without proof of its quantity or quality.

Washoe County officials had already spent $5 million on the water importation project.

"It's nothing but politics now and I don't think anyone is being told the entire truth," Lassen County Supervisor Jean Loubet said.

In 1994 the TMP began to shake and rumble. The project was in trouble. The proponents said there were twenty-seven thousand acre-feet of water a year available to the project. The USGS estimated the figure at plus-seventeen thousand acre-feet. Modoc and Lassen expert consultants estimated the number closer to seventy-five hundred. Washoe County had already sunk millions of dollars into the development stages of the TMP proposal. The commissioners wanted an answer they could take to their constituents. And the backers of the Fish Springs Ranch needed a scapegoat. The United States Army looked like a good target. A suit was filed against them, blaming failure of the project due to contamination by the Sierra Army Depot, and claiming that information was not forthcoming in a timely manner so that expenses incurred could be avoided.

And what proof did Captain Culver have that information was made available to the owners of Fish Springs Ranch? He called Dr. Slosson.

Why, yes, of course. Dr. Slosson was a child of the depression years. He learned to give attention to detail. He learned to save. From the storage boxes that his secretary fights continually with him to toss in the Dumpster, he pulled research records and an evidence list from court records, each page date-stamped with a court-record number from the hearing with Judge Turnipseed in 1991. The information was available, and Dr. Slosson's warnings about the water-quality problems and the limitations on availability were on record.

⊷

Anthropologists recognize three phases in the study of human habitation in the West as it applies to land use. The first period is that of hunter-gatherers living off the land, harvesting for their needs. Second is marked by the arrival of settlers who harvested the produce (loggers, miners, trappers, livestock growers) and sold it to make their living. Third, and most recent, is the phase of land-use regulation by those living elsewhere, possibly never having seen the region in question, having no real knowledge of the impacts to environment, society, or community resulting from their politically guided decisions.

The Surprise Valley Advisory Committee was probably never aware of that scientific theory, but they were derailing the third phase. At the local level they joined together to develop a collective project based on their best guess of what was right for the majority and for the environment. They were—at last—in control of their most important resource, not some nameless, ever changing agency east of the Mississippi River making an arbitrary decision about how to run their business. Perhaps without knowing it, the members matured through the process to realize that if they did not see the formation of the district confirmed by legislative act, who else would? Despite unswerving resistance from neighbors and fellow ranchers suspicious of any legislation that might impinge on their water rights, they hung together and continued to meet, reaching for reassurances from Dr. Slosson that their work was critical. They were aware through media coverage of water negotiations in adjoining California counties. They finally understood that Surprise Valley, as a closed basin, would benefit from making tough rules to protect the aquifer and insulate the users from outside interference. Dr. Slosson reminded them of the probability that in the near future the legislature would enforce federally mandated regulations to protect and disperse the use or sale or both of groundwater, and if there was no legislative act in place they faced losing control of the Surprise Valley aquifer. They pushed ahead to complete the formation of the district.

On December 8, 1994, Senator Leslie introduced Senate Bill 29: "An act to authorize the creation of the Surprise Valley Groundwater Management District, relating to water, and declaring the urgency thereof, to take effect immediately."

Bonnie Slosson, our old friend and lobbyist for the California Community College System, waited outside the governor's office, and when the bill was safely signed she called her mom and dad. Dr. Slosson and Nancy called us with the news.

"The folks in Surprise Valley owe you Terrorists a debt of gratitude," Dr. Slosson said. "But let me add a word of caution. Don't think it's over. It's never over."

Indeed, our celebratory mood proved fragile and fleeting. I suspect the advisory-committee members never gave themselves more than a one-handed pat on the back. Oh, their spouses were probably happy they wouldn't have to hear the grizzly accounts of the Wednesday-night meetings anymore. But I doubt if any of the members ever got together and raised a glass to a job well done. It's unreasonable to expect it. To be involved in a process of this intensity and see it through to the end is to be a survivor. Survivors rarely hope to relive an ordeal of suffering with buddies.

It is important to remember that the committee members were independent owner-operators. The western rancher standing alone is more truth than myth. Prior to the 1960s, it was the "damned weather" or the "damned neighbor handy with a long rope" that created the dynamic flux between success and failure. Mechanization changed the way business was done, and it also changed the essence of community and deepened the ranchers' independent ways. Instead of neighbors moving teams and wagons from ranch to ranch, men helping each other put up the hay, women joining forces in the kitchens to feed the men, there is one man on a piece of haying equipment alone in the field. Today even a rancher's best friends and neighbors, those called on for help and advice, are his arch competitors in business. Shell Oil probably doesn't call Exxon to give them a hand on their drill rigs. I bet Amazon.com doesn't expect Barnes and Noble to help get out a big shipment.

Ranchers share more than business. They share community, the school board, the hospital board, the farm-services agency, and Farm Bureau and Production Credit Association boards. They are linked in innumerable ways, maybe in-laws. Ranchers must maintain independence just as they must stop their work to give a hand to a neighbor.

These failed promises of agricultural lending agencies forced sales and restructuring or foreclosures of loans in the '80s and left many ranchers with a murderous attitude toward operating on borrowed money. Those who survived are cautious in the extreme, and resolutely self-reliant. Profit or loss in any given year teeters on a fulcrum narrow as a knife edge. New methods or experimentation with new crops are considered too risky by most. Any change, however innocuous, is something we agonize over. Stick-with-what-you-know is probably the primary economic principle for the single-family ranch.

Obviously, then, the legislative act authorizing the Surprise Valley Water Management District was a threat precisely because it brought into question ranchers' traditional ways of doing business. If the crop that has balanced your books, allowed your children a college education, or family health insurance is thought to be water exacting, its production heavily demanding on the water table, perhaps overdrafting the sustainable yield, what do you do? Hone the language of the act to protect the environment, go home, and continue pushing the levels of production? Or do you revolutionize your management, your vision, your operation, and take your knocks while the neighbor who opposed the burden of the district formation and told you—publicly—all to go to hell keeps his pump going, overflows his stackyard with tonnage, and tops the market with his steers? Where does that leave you?

The men who made up the advisory committee endured a process that tested them in an unfair way. Their position revealed their business strategies. What little anonymity they maintained in the tight community of ranchers was sacrificed. If the district was to succeed, they had to stop thinking as individuals and focus on a goal of protecting the valley and its water from themselves as well as from outsiders.

Old-timers in the valley as well as newcomers have condemned regulation in any form, from strangers *or* neighbors. As a result, divisions and hard feelings within the community may never heal. In the end, I would guess the men who passed the news to each other by phone that night of December 8th paused before sleep, wondering, "What the hell was that all about? Are we better for it? Did I do the right thing?"

⮥

On February 5, 1998, the twelve-year battle seemed to be nearing closure when the *Gazette-Journal*'s Faith Bremner filed the following story:

Nevada State Engineer Mike Turnipseed pulled the plug on the [TMP] plan last week saying, "The county isn't serious about using the water. I sent them a letter (in August) asking 'Where's your project and what are you doing?' They sent back a letter saying they're not really doing anything." County officials initially estimated they could pump 75,000 acre-feet of ground water from the rural valleys, an amount that was later revised down to 12,000 acre-feet.

But since both projects [SSP and TMP] were conceived, northern Nevada's water future has changed considerably. Under the Truckee River Negotiated Settlement, which U.S. Senator Harry Reid, D-Nev., brokered eight years ago, Reno and Sparks can get enough water from the Truckee River to continue growing for the next 50 years.

"Reno doesn't need the Silver State water," said Rose Strickland, a member of the Sierra Club. "The county's 20-year Comprehensive Regional Water Management Plan does not include the Silver State Project in its list of viable water supply alternatives."

"If you suck the Nevada side dry, the impacts just don't magically stop at the state line," said Lassen County lawyer George Benesch. "Despite Washoe County's claims to the contrary, Lassen County and Modoc County believe the two importation projects were tied together. If there's not enough water in the Honey Lake Valley, which I personally believe there isn't, it's not politically viable to say we made a mistake. They would go someplace else to supplement [the Honey Lake Valley project]. That's what I think would have been the ultimate role of the Silver State Project."

Just before Christmas that year I got two phone calls: one from Dr. Slosson, one from Bob Sorvaag. As a follow-up, Bob sent the following newspaper article, from the December 15, 1998, *Reno Gazette-Journal:*

"Firm Negotiating on Fish Springs Ranch"

U.S. Filter, a leading water treatment service provider is negotiating to buy the Fish Springs Ranch 38 miles north of Reno, the source of 14,000 acre-feet of water that could be piped into the North Valleys, Reno, Sparks . . . [and] add about 50 percent to the current water supply available for growth, said Steve Walker, Washoe water management planner.

. . . U.S. Filter, a giant in the field of water and wastewater treatment, has annual revenues of more than $2.3 billion.

. . . The Fish Springs Ranch would include 14,000 ac-ft of transferrable ground water rights granted by Nevada and validated by U.S. Geological Survey, the state engineer and the Nevada Supreme Court.

The 7,500 acre ranch has a perennial yield of 24,000 ac-ft. To keep the deal alive in bringing water to the Truckee Meadows, the company wants the Washoe County Commission on Dec. 22 to extend the county's option on the water rights until sometime next year. The county option, which expires Dec. 31, maintains the state water engineer's approval of the interbasin transfer of water.

Washoe County manager Katy Simon wants a deal sealed. . . . "In having a player like U.S. Filter, it builds confidence in the region for other investors. . . . It's a good investment in the future. . . . It provides for a stable source of water rights and allows for orderly development to occur."

"Orderly development." I suppose it's in the eye of the beholder. Currently if land developers purchase farm or agricultural land that is under a farming-only state program such as California's Williamson Act, they must wait out the ten-year period before beginning construction. Because golf courses are commonly granted agricultural status by many city and county governments, they are exempt from that restriction and escape the scrutiny of the environmental-review process. Golf courses pump between 1 million and 4 million gallons of water each night, depending on climate and soil type. (According to the 1998 USDA Farms and Ranch Survey, an acre of tomatoes or lettuce requires less than five hundred thousand gallons of water for the season.) A golf course in a semiarid to arid climate could easily use three times that amount per night during its initial growing-in period. Gray (reclaimed) water, if it is used, burns the fairway grass and must be leeched by freshwater, and in some instances the entire fairway must be replanted. Therefore the wide majority of courses pump fresh, drinkable water almost exclusively. What must be sacrificed? Something always is sacrificed when there's money to be made, whether it's public safety or seeing certain people as not as important, or certain land, or certain kinds of life as expendable. In this country money is the measure of success. Until the health of the earth that supports us as a species is recognized as the ultimate goal, we are destined to failure.

Early in 1999 the Bureau of Land Management completed plans to designate certain lands on their inventory *disposable,* to be offered for sale. The companion map identified the entire Smoke Creek Desert, leg two of the original SSWPP.

We thought of the BLM as an ally in the protection of the public lands. But this decision opened the door to developers. While the BLM gave assurances that their planned sales were currently under reconsideration, numerous transactions were finalized.

The history of Owens Valley may be repeated; the tracks are easily followed. Just as the buy up of Owens Valley progressed, many large Surprise Valley ranches have been bought up by absentee owners with no community ties. We welcome them as neighbors, their employees are our friends, and they can call us to help at branding time. Yet some of those owners are connected to development in the Truckee Meadows, and their parcels, both private and public, follow the ghostly pipeline that was drawn on the newspaper article sent by Ralph Parman to his niece Bettie back in 1986. Water rights are attached to those lands.

U.S. Filter was approached by Vivendi, a French firm, to negotiate the acquisition of their holdings. A purchase price of $6.2 billion was reported, making it the world's largest water-procurement company. By spring we heard that the U.S. Filter–Vivendi sale fell through.

On July 26, 2000, Fish Springs Ranch was in the *Gazette-Journal* headlines again. Faith reported:

"New Company Controls Water of Honey Lake"
   Controversial Project: No decisions on how to develop land.
   A California water development company has purchased the Fish

Springs Ranch in Honey Lake Valley, and along with it water rights that once belonged to Washoe County's controversial ground-water importation project.

Dorothy Timian-Palmer, chief operating officer for Vidler Water Co. of La Jolla, Calif., declined to say how much her company paid for the ranch and its 8,600 acres of deeded land and 14,109 acre-feet of ground-water rights. The deal between Vidler's new subsidiary, called Fish Springs LLC, and the ranch's owners, Northwest Nevada Water Resources Ltd., was closed June 28.

U.S. Filter Corp. backed out of an agreement to buy the ranch and its water last August when it could not finalize the deal under the original terms the company thought it had negotiated months before.

The company could decide to continue using the water for agricultural purposes or it could use it for an industrial project, power generation or an importation project to Washoe County's North Valleys, Timian-Palmer said. . . .

"We're very conservative," Timian-Palmer said. "We feel that if we did a project to the North Valleys, we would look at a maximum of 8,000 acre-feet."

"It's too early to tell whether Vidler has what it takes to successfully pull off an importation project to the Reno-Sparks metropolitan area," said Bob Firth, a local water rights consultant. There is demand for water in Lemmon Valley. That valley's aquifer is being over-pumped by about 3,865 acre-feet a year. "There are still problems that would be faced by a Honey Lake project," Firth said. "There's still the army depot, the tribe and the EIS . . . a number of hurdles they would have to get over first."

⊸

In May 2000, Dr. Slosson was in Reno for a conference. He wanted to hear a paper that was scheduled for presentation. He found the room and sat down not knowing the subject of the presentation under way. Fate, maybe, sent him to the room an hour early where he heard a master's of science thesis submitted by University of Nevada, Reno, student Nancy Moll. The abstract reads:

In 1990, the State Engineer of Nevada granted a permit for pumping and exportation of 13,000 acre-feet/year of water from southeastern

Honey Lake Valley south to the Reno metro area. This thesis examines the question of whether that amount of pumping is feasible on a long-term basis. A MODFLOW groundwater flow model was constructed for the eastern part of the valley. Data developed for an earlier model (Handman et al., 1990) was used, as was additional geochemical and well test data. The additional data led to a new interpretation of the eastern and northeastern boundaries of the model area, with the result that 8,000 acre-feet/year of water appears to be the maximum amount that can be exported on a long-term basis. Amounts greater than this will cause migration of saline water into the wellfield.

Ms. Moll's independent scientific research corroborates Dr. Slosson's. Her data upholds that of Drs. Slosson and Mayo. But that's no guarantee. There is still greed to consider.

Inside one of those file boxes from my cellar labeled "H2O," I found a typed "Letter to the Editor," dated May 1987, by Ralph G. Parman, titled "The Big Water Grab." Interrupting the typescript are corrections or clarifications by a careful but trembling hand. On that day so far in the past Ralph Parman wrote the following warning: "Taxpayers to take note of a scheme to steal our water from under our feet, and don't be fooled, you will be paying the thieves to steal the water they will sell to you."

What did Ralph Parman know? Why should he be believed? He was an old man, a rancher from Surprise Valley, a place beyond the border, across the fenceline.

Time proved Ralph right. Lacking the strength the fight required, he trusted his niece to defend the land he loved as home. And she trusted us. We set out into a strange land against an unknown enemy with little in our war bag. We were afraid. Sometimes, we are still afraid.

Again I read Faith Bremner's article, and as a citizen I look for assurance that the 1931 County of Origin Statute is upheld as originally written into law, that "areas from which water is exported must have their own economic needs served first." Too late to protect Owens Valley, I hope it will protect other valleys. Ours.

As a citizen, I search for words of respect for the principle of conservation: "You may use, but you may not ruin."

As a citizen, I search for a pledge that the concept of the public trust will be observed: "Certain lands and resources belong to the whole people and that the government, which serves as a guardian, has an inescapable duty to manage these properties well, including wildlife habitat, nature study, and simple beauty of scene."

The language of protection has been written into law by caring and conscientious people. But I have witnessed that written law provides no guarantee. If we call a place home, if we find safety and sustenance, friendship and community, we are responsible to reciprocate in kind.

Anthropologist Margaret Mead said, "A small, thoughtful, committed group of people can change the world. Indeed, it is the only thing that can."

I have memorized the words of our friends and advisors: George Benesch, "Politically, it's just not acceptable to build a pipeline for $120 million with no water in it," and Dr. James Slosson, "But let me add a word of caution. Don't think it's over. It's never over."

↠ The Antelope Kid

JOHN'S BIRTHDAY CAKE HAS BEEN BAKED IN THE WOODSTOVE AT THE Wall Canyon cow camp every year since he was seven during the spring gather, mid-June. Perfect, if you're a boy. Cow camp with the men, their talk and cooking, chopping wood and carrying armfuls inside, whistling.

The cramp of home was forgotten. No homework. No bedtime, no bed to make. No table manners, no foolish chores, and no sister. Society was men who talked horses and cows, and their stories were not made up. The more he learned, the more he wanted to learn.

Just at daybreak, the watery whap, whap of the sage grouse drumming in the canyon above the cabin would wake him. Slipping through the brush, the last part crawling, he would get a look at the cocks strutting for the hens. Later on in the morning, the chance of seeing antelope in the basin west of Badger Mountain where they came to kid in the short brush below Domingo Spring.

This was our first gathering together as husband and wife to move the cattle up onto Badger Mountain with the feed. John wanted me to see the things that he loved about the spring ride. He gave me the outside swing up Greasy Flat toward the sound he described, toward the basin where I might see courting and birth.

↠

The antelope kid exploded from under my horse, but not as a land mine detonated by weight—its survival instinct triggered before the hoof touched it. Horse, antelope shot in opposite directions. I got my horse stopped and pointed at a wobbling dot as it disappeared off the edge of the earth.

Heartsick, I worried all day long about the little antelope wandering the breaks, bleating for a tall blur and smell that was Mother and not finding her. Lost at the Washington State Fair when I was a kid, not wise enough to ask for help, I searched for a pink flowered dress and a pair of Levis in a forest of hemlines and Levis. On a Nevada desert rim I was as close to that old desperation as I had ever been.

I knew the doe would have been dehydrated from birthing, from cleaning away every trace of membrane, from giving down precious colostrum, thick with antibodies to neutralize the bacterial flowers in the baby's gut. Nuzzling under the kid's tail, the doe had stimulated the passing of dark, sticky feces, and memorized a scent, a taste that named this flesh hers alone. The kid, meanwhile, consumed from her udder the same tangible and intangible layers, scents as distinct forever as pepperwood from lily. The mother would have stood, then, nibbling the short grass while the kid folded, small enough for a pocket, at her feet. Standing guard she had turned her head, watching, every sense open. When she felt right, the need for water had awakened, and, leaving the kid sleeping, safely odorless, nearly invisible to predators, she had walked to a spring nearby.

It all worked perfectly, naturally, until my horse and I stumbled onto the kid. "It bolted and now it's lost somewhere," I told John.

"Don't worry. They'll find each other."

"You don't understand. The kid ran off into the breaks. The doe won't know where to look."

"Mothers always know where to look," he said calmly. "They go back to the beginning."

Impatient with his unconcern, I shot back, "Okay. Where *is* the beginning?"

"Anytime a mother and baby get separated they always, always, go back to the place they sucked last. It's built in. No question." He let that soak in a minute. "It's why we mother-up cows and calves every time we change pastures. If the calves get confused or scared they won't run clean back to where they were picked up. Wherever they nurse, every time, that's where they find each other."

How could I have lived so closely with animals all my life and not known of this miracle? To return by code to a shared place. A *place* could be significant. Safe. Important beyond the birth. Important through a bond of nourishment.

As we rode through the complex geography of the low desert we gathered the cattle left to graze at will through the spring. The weather had warmed, the days lengthened, the upland feed was ready to be harvested. We were going onto Badger Mountain. All day long the moving herd built as riders scoured the draws, the long valleys, the swell and swale, pushing toward the center. From a distant ridge shadows and colors moved before a funnel of dust, and in that mill—like the one of high-heeled shoes and boots at the fair where a small girl lost the hand that held hers, the hip she walked beside—the bond of cow and calf was tested. At last there was a fence and a gate thrown back. Bawling cows turned back, calves darted away or stood battered with confusion. Riders pulled away and held them loosely to give them time to order their thinking.

The process can take an hour, more. The elements of survival rise slow as cream. The cowman may seem to be doing nothing, sitting on his tired horse, watching. But he is playing the card game Concentration, matching a pair of jacks (brayford cow and the white-necked calf), a pair of tens (black cow that calved in the lake field and her black baldy calf), a pair of threes (straight Hereford pair). Good cowmen don't rely on numbered ear tags; they *know* their cattle. Good mothers search the herd, smelling every calf until hers is found and nurses. It went on until we were satisfied every match had been made. Only then we counted our work done and let the cattle graze away.

To solve any mixup a rider would go back to that gate the next morning and throw it open. Any cows with tight bags or calves hanging along the fence would go through and return to the last place they sucked.

A few years after the incident with the kid antelope the theory was tested again. The outcome was all the proof I would ever need. Mid-May we shipped a load of dry cows to the desert. They would calve in the low country. In June we would brand all the long-eared calves as we moved them up to their summering country. When the truck came up the road at first light we had already gathered the meadow and were pushing the cows into the crowding alley. We loaded the truck, sent it off, and rode to a field in the foothills to work out pairs for the next load. When we came in for lunch there was a calf bawling in the meadow we had gathered in that early-morning dark. One of the drys had calved during the night. We had mistakenly put her on the truck and sent her sixty miles east. Her baby bawled from the willows. There was nothing to do then. The trucker had unloaded hours before, and the cow could have been anywhere in the Yellow Hills. But John's faith in our cows was deep and abiding. He looked at his watch and did some figuring. "She'll be back by about two in the morning." At two-thirty the dogs barked. John got up, pulled his boots on, walked out to the yard, opened the gate, and let the cow into the meadow. Her bawl raised in pitch and excitement when the calf answered.

In those hours she had walked out of the belly of the cattle truck, allowed her mind to locate a direction, and started back through the day and into the night. She did not wail and wander circles from the chute gate. She was a needle charged by a distant point. While a world spun on around her, she moved through a tunnel of her own making. Steady, steady. Across the desert she sipped water from catch pools, snatched at bunchgrass, and went on. Over the treacherous barriers of cattleguards, she was light-footed. Up the mountain pass, she did not falter. At Lake Surprise, she walked the skim of water. There was no dotted line on pavement, no road signs for her. She followed the pledge of an internal map to a place anchored in an event revisited by the female of every nurturing species.

We—the rare breed—go to the baby's crib when it cries, hold the baby as it suckles because it is not developed fully at birth and cannot come to us. Later we call the child indoors, the family together, for meals and strengthen our comfort in communion—talk, nearness as nourishing as food. A *place* can satisfy our needs.

Nature gave us the right response. Like wild things we are born knowing, collecting important information about our surroundings while seemingly engaged with play. I imagine the alignment of chemicals within the brain to identify a place of safety, in short, family. If that alignment is interrupted the search may go on indefinitely entering quarters of danger and confusion and loss.

⌁

The antelope kid ran in alarm, frightened by a strange nearness that might have been fatal. Soon it stopped and lay down. When it quieted, the messages began again, wound in a thread as fine, as stout, as water's memory of its source—light's hot wink of ignition—a cant of sound from stone to seed, from seed to time and back, vaporous yet fixed, recalled ever after, to draw the kid on kindling legs to the holy ground where nourishment was given, and Mother, waiting.

❧ Water, Water, Everywhere

I'M FIXING DINNER. THE PHONE RINGS. IT'S GINGER HOPKINS. IN A VOICE deadened by tragedy she thanks me for the roses the florist left on her kitchen table—memorial flowers for their daughter Jody killed in an accident two days earlier.

It is one of those conversations we aren't ready for, difficult on both ends, yet necessary, and in the end, helpful.

I say I hope it was okay that the florist went into their house when they weren't home.

"Oh, sure," Ginger laughs softly. "You know, Ron and I never lock the door because sometimes we come home and there's a pie on the table, or a jar of jam. I don't want to discourage those people."

Thankful for the slight detour, we come back to the reason for the call. She tells me how beautiful the roses are and asks if I know the name because she'd like to order a bush for her garden. I don't know and we talk about rooting cuttings and how neither of us have had luck doing that.

But Jody is on her mind, and she moves toward her obliquely, beginning with a mother's tender memories of her girls. When they were kids one or all three might wake up one morning and not want to go to school. They worked hard and got good grades, which she rewarded with an occasional indulgence. They all piled in the ranch truck, dogs in the back. When Ginger drove past the bus stop and turned away from town, the girls would whoop and cheer. The desert roads took them to a new excitement each time. In the brush her girls became wild things, exploring dunes and swales, dried creek beds and rims above springs. Ginger prized purple medicine bottles and granite pots. Her eyes were sharpened to the least reflection of half-buried glass, the hint of a curve or color. Hours beat upon the sand while the girls practiced the jackrabbit's absolute stillness and the horned toad's invisibility, while they examined the delicate bitterroot hugged to the ground, or left tiny bites of apple for ants to come upon and taste and lug home.

Treasures were not necessary to the success of the day. Being together, clouds and sky, changing patterns of light on the desert hills. The day would linger in their long hair, on their clothes and skin for Ron to smell when they all washed up for dinner at the laundry tray. The air would be in their eyes and their voices as they crowded around Ginger in the kitchen fixing supper. And for her it was enough to think about the girls' shouts and squeals of discovery or to simply see their bright blouses above the brush. They shared time and place. Now they are grown and on their own, she feels their presence more in the desert than anywhere—and feels their absence, too, especially the one who will not be coming back.

I listen to Ginger's voice; imagine her bending over a weed tomorrow or next week or next month, seeing it tethered by its root, turned by the wind, circumscribing its full reach in the sand. "Compass grass," she thinks, standing, wondering where, after losing Jody, her next bearing might come from. But now Ginger is telling me about another day in the desert: a summer Sunday, driving out with Ron to check on the cattle they take care of for their boss, Lavelle Dollarhide. It's an outing many local ranchers take. Sometimes she throws a lunch together, sometimes not, and they putter around putting out salt, checking water tanks, generally looking around.

⌁

I usually drive when we go out in the country, Ginger began her story. Ron likes to look around at the condition of the feed, pointing out things, thinking as we go, planning, and I know the roads as good as he does. We were just going along when all of a sudden Ron grabbed my arm and shouted, "Stop! Back up!"

I slammed on the brakes and threw it into reverse, looking over my shoulder to stay in the track and out of the brush. I know Ron. He saw something he didn't like the looks of.

"Stop," he said again, but this time softer, and sad.

I turned off the key and slid across the seat, my arm on his shoulder, lean-ing around the brim of his hat to see what he saw. Three horses. But some-thing was wrong with 'em.

"Wild horses. *Dyin'* wild horses."

Just yards away from the truck, three animals wavered in the sagebrush beside the road. Three adult horses. Two mares and a stud. I've never seen animals that looked like that, not live ones. Their heads hung out at that an-gle any livestock person knows means the animal is sick, and the cords in their necks were bulged out with the effort of holding up the weight of their heads. Their eyes were shrunk up, dull as dried olives, and their hides were stretched over their bones like you threw 'em over a sawhorse, coated with dust, burnt and frazzled like they'd been set on fire. I asked Ron what was the matter with 'em.

"They're dyin' of thirst."

I scooted over and he drove, way too fast on that washboard road for the old truck. But he was in a hurry to check on Lavelle's windmill in the canyon.

A breeze moved around the blades, but they didn't turn. No metal squeaking. No thump of the sucker rod. Only thing in the tank was dried-up algae.

"What the hell? Somebody's shot up the damned thing! Look at that!" Ron shouted.

The blades and the tail were full of holes. Oil drained from bullet holes in the motor housing.

"Goddamned hunters!" was the first thing I thought. "What kind of haywire person would shoot up a windmill?" Ron was looking it over, checking everything out.

"It wasn't hunters." He folded the blade of his pocketknife and held out a handful of pebbles. "The intake pipe is packed with these. They didn't get in there by themselves. We've got terrorists working the country."

"What are they thinking of, Ron? It don't make any sense. This is the only water for miles once spring runoff's done. If they're wanting the cattle off the range, they gotta know there's more than cows use this tank. Every-thing. Everything in this country comes here for water. Birds, chuckar, but-terflies come to that little grassy place where the outflow drains. Rabbits, snakes, rockchucks, mice and rats and lizards. Look at the tracks. They come here expecting to find water. Good God, don't people know that?"

"Either they don't think that far ahead or they don't care. Well, we can't worry about it now. Let's go back and try to get those horses to Cook's hold-ing field," he said. "Maybe Wes'll let me leave the gate open until I get this mill fixed. When we get home I'll call the sheriff and the BLM range rider. They need to see this."

⊷

I listen to Ginger. Who is this person? I think. Ron's word surfaces: *terrorist.* There is no other. There are terrorists among us, even here, spreading suffering like cheat grass. We are tenuously balanced on the land as it is. Killing windmills changes all that. The windmill is killed; cattle, perhaps some of the wild things that know this place; and ultimately us, too. The windmill is killed; we become range cops or we move the cattle off, or haul water. But if we take the cattle home to the hay fields we won't have winter feed. We'll be forced to buy hay to carry them through, and buying hay will take the profit out of the thin margin we live on. The windmill is killed: we lose time and money we don't have, and so it goes. We get worn down, maybe go out of business, and who is the buyer? Absentee owners or corpo-rate ranches are the only ones with ready capital. They come into the valley, mine the resources, the money leaves, and they don't know or care that the Eagleville Civic Center needs indoor bathrooms or that the roof of the Fort Bidwell Church leaks. We don't see them in the bleachers at the basketball games, or selling raffle tickets for the Senior Center van, or walking up the hill to the Lake City Cemetery. Every family that leaves, the towns feel it. The high school enrollment is already down in the low sixties—maybe the terrorist's kids are in that number, maybe they're on the basketball team or working a shift at the snack bar. If the school closes and the kids are trans-ferred to Alturas, that's a fifty to one hundred–mile commute—over a mountain pass; teachers leave—money leaves. Our hospital is already tak-ing high-maintenance patients from the cities to stay open and to keep our seniors here at home. The drugstore closed. The bank closed. We're down to one gas station. The valley ranchers depend on summer grazing on the pub-lic lands. We hold on, hoping a new rationale will take hold and people who kill windmills will consider the cost to little towns like the ones in this val-ley. In my body, it's an old ache, and an old fear. It feels like looking at a cloudless sky and wishing for rain.

⊷

Ginger's voice draws me back. I see the horses: macabre sculptures of horses, whittled down to the thinnest grain of life. Dying of thirst takes a long time. If the mares had colts they would have died first as the milk dried up. The body slowly shrivels, abandoning the peripheral first, the least necessary functions, focus narrows, draws toward the core.

Ginger pauses. In a quieter voice she says she imagined them standing beside the tank waiting for the wind, waiting for the sound of water climbing up the pipe, to flow out silvery, satisfying. It is a patience death requires.

She shakes the image off and continues, "The stud seemed to fight off the death trance when Ron reached out and touched him on the hip and told him to move. No human had ever touched him, but he didn't flinch, he staggered and caught himself, following behind his mares down the road to a windmill on Cook's place. Weave-walking like drunks, they'd stop to rest, then go again. It took over an hour for them to walk the half mile. Any horse could cover that distance in five minutes."

In that hour Ginger said she and Ron asked each other questions neither had reason or answer for. Why would someone with a professed love for the land, whose catechism is the protection of the public land from range cattle, destroy the water source upon which wildlife is also dependent? How can anyone focus so tightly on their own politics that they would jeopardize the lives of innocent animals? What defense is there for cruelty?

Ron circled ahead of the horses and threw the gate open. His view was from the front then, and he was sickened by the sight of those pathetic creatures staggering blindly toward him. He reached out a hand to guide the sorrel mare through the gate. The others followed her, unaware of anything, least of all the tank of water. They drove like gentle horses. Worse, they were dead on their feet.

Ginger said, "We only allowed the horses small sips of water at first to keep the shock from killing them. Ron slapped them faces with his hat to make them get back. We both tried to turn them back. We shouted and shoved them away from the tank. But it was like pushing on a tree. We scooped water at them and splashed it in their faces, using the very thing they craved to turn them away. They just closed their eyes against it and pushed forward.

"Finally, we succeeded in turning them away and stood together, barricading the tank from them. We didn't know how long to make them wait before we let them drink again. It seemed cruel to drive them up to the trough and then drive them away. But they were jerky! So dehydrated that at first their bodies couldn't even absorb the water. It just *shot* out of their behinds.

"The old stud was in the worst shape. He started to go down, and I pounded on him to keep him up. But the sound was unbearable, hollow, as if my hand would go right through his hide. I let him at the trough again. His head dropped into the water like an anchor, buried up to his eyes, and he would not lift it. Ron grabbed around the stud's neck with both arms and yanked him from the trough.

'I wish that bastard was here to see this,' Ron said. 'He'd be proud, wouldn't he?'

We stayed with the horses for hours, letting them have a little more water. But the damage had been done. The horses had suffered too much, especially the stud.

It was starting to get dark. In summertime that meant it was about ten o'clock. Ron said he thought it was safe to leave them alone, and he had some phone calls to make. We walked up the road where we left the truck. We didn't look back."

⤳ Desert Lullaby

THE CALF WOULD NOT BREATHE. IT LAY FLAT OUT ON THE BLOOD AND birth-spoiled straw. I quickly milked the rubbery fluid from its mouth and nose to clear the airways. No gasp. No movement. I poked a straw into a nostril hoping for a jerk, a head shake. Nothing. No response. I had only a few things left to try. I covered one nostril and blew gently into the other, drew back, blew again. The narrow space between the ribs did not fill, did not flutter. The calf's heart was a frozen-up engine that almost starts—pump the throttle, play with the choke, body rocking with the motion you want as the starter grinds. Encouraged at any change in sound, you beckon, come on, come on, *come on!*

I jumped up, grabbed up the calf by its hind legs, swung it around and around, hoping centrifugal force would cast out the thick matter of death and fling it hard against the barn wall. Dizzy, I laid the calf back down and knelt over it once more, lifted the front legs apart like a bellows wanting the lungs to suck in air, slapped the ribs sharply as old-time doctors would slap a baby's bottom to bring forth life with a cry, and I watched its eyes go dull, as daylight leaving lets night in.

The first time I saw death happen it was a fawn beside the road. Mother stopped the car. I ran back. I lifted it, carefully folded the broken legs, and sat down on the crumbling asphalt. As I held the fawn against my young ribs, life disappeared.

My mother's hand was on my shoulder. She said we must leave the fawn in the grass nearby for the doe to find, so she would know and not search on. It was important to know even the worst news, she said as if she knew it to be true.

⇔

I could feel Katie beside me. Together we had hurried out to the feedlot and found a young heifer ready to calve. So excited with the adventure of birth we forgot about breakfast and school. As we walked the heifer to the barn I pointed out that the feet presented beneath her tail were front legs, coming right. She just needed a bit of help, that's all.

I tied the heifer to the fence and slipped the chains around the calf's front legs so I could pull when she pushed. Katie took up slack in the rope, and held the tail from slashing manure and urine in my face. But something went wrong, and the calf lay between us perfect and dead. I said maybe the umbilical cord wrapped around its leg and ripped off before I got the calf's head out and it suffocated. She said nothing.

I thought seeing the moment of birth would mean more than spelling words and math. I imagined Katie steadying a calf, wet and wobbly, minutes old as it searched for its mother's udder, never anticipating death would be linked to the lesson.

Katie's attention needed to be directed away from the dead calf. The heifer stood outside the circle of the overhead light, stunned by the sudden evacuation of the calf from her body, by the dullness following severe pain. Nothing about the past few hours spelled baby to her. There would be no gurgling cry to snatch her from depression. I told Katie we must milk her out and keep her fresh in case we got a calf to splice on her. She is the patient now. We must attend to her.

The heifer let us push her toward the stanchion. I leaned, overbalanced with my head in her flank, as I had seen John do to keep from getting kicked, held the bucket with one hand, milked with the other. She never offered to lift a leg. Touching her teats, wooden and hot with the swelling of first milk, smelling her light golden milk purling in the bucket, filled me with sadness. I kept at it a while, then realized Katie was bent over the calf again, stroking its silky hide. I pushed myself upright to straighten the ache out of my back, and asked if she could take a turn milking. She let me lean her forward, ball cap smashed into the cow's flank, and in that awkward stance, she grasped the near, front, teat. She balanced there, gaining a rhythm. A soothing sound of milk drilled through the foam.

While Katie milked, I dragged the calf outside, away from the barn door. John would haul it away when he came back from feeding the big bunch up the canyon.

↭

Katie was six when she came to live with us. On Christmas Eve, 1971, she stood between her father and me as the minister blessed three gold rings and married the three of us together. A week later, for reasons none of us wished to question, Katie's mother delivered her only child, all her clothes and toys, to our front yard, and left without a word. There was abandonment in that small pile of belongings. After we settled Katie in her bedroom upstairs, John and I celebrated quietly.

My father loved her from the first. Baptized Lynne Catherine, he renamed her Katie. He grasped her frail frame in a bear hug, took her to a chair, and sang a song he remembered from his young days.

> K-K-K-Katie, bee-utiful Katie
> You are the one and only girl that I adore.
> When the m-m-m-moon shines
> over the cow shed
> I'll be waiting at your k-k-k-kitchen door.

This gay, new name was Dad's way of giving us a chance to leave behind the old failures and start over as a family. We trusted that he could be right.

↭

The milk? The cats could have it, I suppose. Or the dogs. Even the hens. The calcium would be good for their eggs.

What about the lamb? Katie asked.

What about the lamb?

Yami. Could he have the milk?

Of course. Yami. Until we find a calf for the cow.

Her head bent over the bummer lamb, reddish blonde braids replaited by the morning sun, gleam bent this way and that.

↭

John didn't want the lamb. Cow outfit, not a damned farm. I saw it differently. Every morning Katie propped her chin on her fists over a bowl of mush going cold, or cold cereal soaked up into mush. She was used to a different schedule, meals, rules. We went slowly, but firmly. Still, the getting up and ready for school was difficult. I thought back to my young days when my older sister and brother went off to school and I was left to play alone until the bus brought them home. A small, white goat appeared in my father's arms one evening. She soothed better than my dolly—rapid heart, warm breath, legs of springs, tasted, touched, smelled everything. Curious. Clever. Comic. We forgave her when she pawed open a sack of oats. We laughed when she butted heads with our little dog, Mutt, and bucked and scampered silly. In the apple-tree swing she sucked the fringe of my pigtails while the wind rocked us from side to side, and I learned to read the silence of her eyes.

❧

One Sunday after feeding we delivered a brown gelding John had been riding for a rancher in Oregon. After lunch John saddled up to ride the horse for Ed. Katie and I wandered over to take a look at Ed's flock of heavy ewes in a pen near the barn. An old gentleman was tending the sheep. We helped him carry buckets of water and hay to the ewes and lambs in the jugs. He told us that the little ones get mixed up, so he kept each pair in a separate pen until they locked on the ewe, solid. Twins were more of a worry than singles. Always jerked off a triplet. Only two faucets. One would always be late to the supper table. Two big lambs were better than three skinny ones. Sometimes, one was better than two. It was his job, he said, to see to it they were up and sucking right away. In cold country a wet lamb could freeze down before the ewe gets to her feet.

What do you do with the bummer lambs? I asked.

Get rid of 'em fast as I can. Raisin' bummers is too much like work.

You wouldn't have any now, would you?

He smiled.

I put the lamb on hay in the saddle compartment of the truck and closed the door. Katie sat between us looking happy—a kid with a secret. Her dad didn't seem too surprised when she stepped around the truck with the lamb in her arms.

John couldn't deny the change. She galloped down the stairs in the morning, shook up the measure of powdered milk in the bottle, popped on a nipple, pulled on her cap and coat, and was out the door. Yami was the best stuffed animal she could have had. His soft ears and fuzzy face nuzzled into her neck when she held him, with or without a milk bottle in her pocket, and he followed her like a puppy. What Katie needed, the lamb was sure to give.

After chores she galloped into the kitchen, wrestled her dad for the last piece of bacon, pulled on her school clothes, jumped on her bike, and raced down the lane to the bus stop. Her teacher rewarded the change with a row of E's on a card that had only reported U's and S's.

After the heifer (now named Bridgett) came into Katie's chores she had to plan a little extra time for milking. Yami squalled and paced his pen while she perched on the milking stool. She told him to be patient, he was a sheep and this was a cow, and besides, he was too short to reach her faucets! But one morning, exasperated with his racket, she grabbed him up, shoved him into Bridgett's flank, and said, "Go for it, Shorty!" Yami obliged her common sense. Front feet on Bridgett's back hoof, neck stretched like a snake, he closed his eyes and nursed as if he'd finally found his way home. Katie took him away when his belly puffed out like a baseball.

The next evening she was ready to surprise her dad, but she was the surprised one. When Yami burst through the gate Bridgett looked around and mooed.

Human-interest photographs in the newspapers show us: Cat Adopts Rabbit, Dog Suckles Raccoon. I marvel at the unreasonable need to care, and yet, motherhood has more to do with caring than birthright.

Bridgett never offered to stick her foot in the bucket, or kick, so Katie left off the hobbles. The next step was to try her without the headlock. That worked, too. The young cow responded to the smell of her own milk passing through the lamb. She nuzzled her little baby, licked his wool upswept into a punk do, and chewed hay contentedly as he nursed.

When the time came to turn them out we drove them down the long lane of cottonwoods to the pasture gate. Other first-calf heifers already turned out in the field with their calves were grazing peacefully until Bridgett led her "calf"—Yami—toward them. They broke into panic and stampeded to the far corner of the field, whirled, and stared back over their shoulders, walleyed. It was hours before they settled down.

⋄

Katie's sheep and cow numbers grew into a herd of her own from her start with Yami and Bridgett by the time she left for college. She sold some to cover expenses and kept some. I took on the extra work of the bummer lambs. The number varied from year to year. Sometimes splices relieved my work. Sometimes, as with triplets, there just weren't enough faucets to go around. In the afternoons I lifted the lambs out of their pen and took them for a walk. Exercise, grass, and sunshine were reasons enough to spend time in their company. Left at home again, I was lonesome for Katie. Her lambs cheered me in the same way the little goat had.

One day I led my nine bummers through the gate and into the pasture where the main bunch of ewes and lambs grazed. I was wishing my bummer lambs could join the outside lamb-gang in their wild race spectacle across the pasture and know that excessive joy. The lamb races would start out easy enough. A handful of the older ones would scamper and buck through the ewes toward the willows. Lamb after lamb would tag on as the racers flew past. Before long the entire bunch of three hundred would be streaking over the rolling banks of the creek as far as the bridge, piling up on the end in a mass collision, whirling around, and racing back in a dead run. It was a woolly Boston Marathon through rush-hour traffic. The races happened twice daily—early morning and late afternoon. I timed my chores to be on hand. I led guests out for the entertainment. Friends drove down from town, parked on the roadside, and watched and laughed. I could have sold tickets.

The event was under way when I led my bummer lambs through the gate. But before I could introduce *my* lambs to *their* lambs, the ewes became alarmed. Alert for their own protection from coyotes, they flushed away when my strange, tall form came across the field, until my lambs, scampering beside me, called out a sound that in sheep language might have sounded something like "mother." The ewes stopped and turned. I sat down on the ground so my height wouldn't intimidate them. My lambs pushed about me, climbed into my lap, nibbled my coat collar, fingers, hair, and said again, "mother, mother." The whole flock gathered around me, centering their curiosity on my little family. Breath of alfalfa hay and new spring grass puffed against my face. Noses touched my skin, clothes. They studied my eyes as they would one of their own kind. They smelled *my* lambs, then me, arguing with the information they gathered based on their experience of being sheep. They tried to see through the trickery, tried to make my shape and smell add up to *sheep* as it did to *my* lambs. I felt I had fallen into a rabbit hole and tumbled a long, long way down. And, although there are places in this world we are graced to enter, we must not stay. One by one, the ewes reached satisfaction—without proof—and wandered off to graze. The races were canceled for the day.

How were the sheep to think about the lambs and me, the cows think about Bridgett and Yami? How were the women of the community to think about me and Katie? How was I? What is my relationship to Katie's life, to the lives of animals? What determines the boundaries? What is acceptable? Was I making a circus act of the proven structure of science? Or do I pass through the architecture of nature, giddy as a migrating butterfly, cross-pollinating as I go?

The lambs were weaned and sent out to join the flock where they could learn to live in an animal society, not a half-human one. If I happened on them when walking the fields, a head would pick up, setting their bells stirring like wind chimes, and they would come trotting for a rub. The whole of the flock would stop eating or rise from rest, holding quiet as our worlds embraced.

Yami and Bridgett spent the balance of their year together, grazing side by side among the cattle. They made a language between them. Much of it was mute. When the lamb wished to, he nursed. When the cow lay down, he curled into her and let her body break the sharp desert wind aside. They drank where the water opened from the swale and widened into a clear pool, never startled by their reflection.

⤙ New Mown Hay

1

I MOW THE MEADOW. I MOW THE TIMOTHY. I MOW CLOVER. I MOW THICK, leafy alfalfa. I mow pungent sage and wormwood, red-top, yarrow, bird's-foot trefoil, blue stem, quack grass, flaming brome. I mow up something smelling like witch hazel, and something smelling like honey. I mow up weevils, beetles, ladybugs. Butterflies spin up from the header, from the scissoring sections, pirouette in the updraft. I mow up squirrels and mice and voles and shrews, green frogs and grasshoppers, canary grass and devil trails, cowlicks lapped by the wind's long tongue, deer beds pressed flat in curving slumber. The bitter smell of badger seeps up from deep squirrel holes and catches on the reel. Four rounds cut out the land, then back and forth, north to south, south to north, laying out windrows behind like mares' tails combed out long and slightly wavy all day long until it is done. And when light bends the reflection on my slanted front window I mow up black birds, cow birds, gray and white gulls, hawks and buzzards soaring. I mow up ranch pickups, stock trailers, compact cars, and big-deal eighteen-wheelers passing on the road. Thank goodness it's summer or I might get a school bus or two. I mow up a vagabond strolling, long lines of willows lingering by the creek, a wash hung out to dry, a barn's hot tin roof, a whole mountain, thunderclouds building, and lots of blue sky to bale up into crackerjack bales so when winter comes and the wires snap this day will lay out on below-zero snow at the feet of our cows and horses smelling of sunshine, saved up, returned to the earth.

2

Through my swather's wide front window I have a view beyond the thick grasses falling before my sickle. Neighbors are in their fields making hay all around me. A baler there, and over there. A bale wagon stacking hay down there, beyond the silver poplars. Another swather in the canyon's mouth and a combine harvesting oats over there. All at our own work, in our own way, yet parallel, almost like a team. I keep at it. Lunch is an apple and water. After noon a few gulls fly in.

3

Across the fence from where I cut grass into lanky ropes of hay cows watch as I pass, spreading noise out behind. Down the bench of a fault line where water turns upward to the surface is the sloped land where, one afternoon in the fall, Mr. Jones died.

I stop the swather and cut the engine. Haying means machines. I accept the obliteration of natural sound to hammering and clatter. But as the engine settles into *not* working, the noise drains slowly out of me. The vibration lessens. Silence reclaims me.

4

Mr. Jones and his wife worked digging out water holes for their stock. The eight-year drought would slip into history once the rains began at the end of the month. The land would live again. But just now the cows couldn't wait, and who could know what was to come?

They rode his tractor across the fields. She stood on the drawbar in a pair of his old rubber boots, one hand holding onto a shovel, the other, her husband's wide leather belt. He sat the seat, slick as gut and wobbling loose on a worn bolt hole. They bounced and lurched over dried-out hummocks, greasewoods, and gaping cracks in the hard, baked ground, working their way from one seep to the next.

He stopped on the bench. They got off and thrashed into the willow brush, ditching water through heavy black muck into a pool where cows could get at it. They worked most of the afternoon, pounding the mud loose from the shovels on the sod. Finished, they clambered out the way they came.

He sat down on the drawbar to catch his breath, let the air get into him. The sun was still high and hot. She leaned on the shovel, weary, worried what would become of them. Everything was dying: the trees, the fields, the land. No rain. No rain.

He climbed onto the seat, pushed the starter with the toe of his mud-caked boot. The motor ground and caught. Said, Get on! She did.

He started off the slope. She grabbed his shoulder, in a rough voice said to back around! She wasn't going off there! He said, Done it a hundred times, woman. She said you'll kill yourself. He shoved the throttle forward. She let go of his shoulders, one foot on solid ground, the other coming off the draw-bar as if she pushed the tractor away. The old man nosed it off the ridge. The rough ground jerked the front tires, the wheel from his hands, and pitched him off the seat like a rag. The lugs of the high tire took him down and cleaned its feet on his back.

The ambulance came across the field turning lights—no siren. She said, I hope they don't start a fire in this here dry grass. He said Ow,Ow,Ow when they rolled him, slipped the clam shell underneath. It took six of us to lift him. The stretcher came up—thimble weed, poverty grass, in its teeth.

She said, I told him he's crazy to go off there. Told him he'd tip that thing over and kill hisself. Look there, if he hasn't gone and done it.

5

I drink warm water from the plastic jug in the toolbox. A red-tailed hawk soars above me. The same one, or a daughter, I have seen in this field for years nesting in the locust tree at the old homestead on the knoll above the granaries. Now she swings down to claim a squirrel between the windrows. Ravens pluck up field kill. Gulls swallow dark, furry mice whole, alive in one gulp. Blackbirds work the windrows for insects. Even the lovely red-tailed is an opportunist. She lifts off, squirrel swinging heavily. At the nest in the locust two young hawks shriek and hop, excited.

I lie down on uncut grass until the service is over.

⟡ Stone Trees

In the Shoshonean language Pah means water or waterhole. The Pah-Utes are the Water Utes taking their name from their rarest and most precious resource. They live mainly in Utah and Nevada, the two driest states in the Union, and in those regions water is safety, home, life, place. All around those precious watered places is only space, forbidding and unlivable, what one must travel through between places of safety.

—Wallace Stegner, *Where the Bluebird Sings to the Lemonade Springs*

NOW I CAN CONFESS TO ONCE FEELING SORRY FOR THE HIGH DESERT east of Surprise Valley. It was immaturity, I understand that now, wanting the world to be right, fair. Learning the desert in daylong rides showed me the past within easy reach of my imagining. Evidence of change was obvious. The gift of rain had been taken back. In the steady drying up, species, both wildlife and human, moved out toward the next water hole, and on, and on, if they could make it. Anthropologist Kay Fowler told me that there was a whole stratum missing in this region, a layer of earth—time—blown away during a three thousand–year drought. Three thousand years.

All day I found no cattle. I saw three desert big-horned sheep that had escaped their enclosure, several small bands of horses. No cattle. John would meet me at Mud Springs. I had some ground to cover.

The basin I crossed ended abruptly against a basalt rim, and I found my-self in a fallen grove of trees, slash laid out on a sandy ridge, or the sandy ridge eroded away from the long-buried trees. Stone trees. Petrified. I came on them by accident, riding up a crease north from a spring, watching for cattle in the high brush. Nothing goes unnoticed in the desert, but I couldn't remember anyone mentioning this place. I felt the thrill of discov-ery, and then gratitude the ridge was far enough from a road that specimens had not been carried off in car trunks and pickups to line a flower garden or be cemented into a wall.

A need to touch the trees overwhelmed me. I got down, hobbled Dandy to graze or rest, and walked within them. The petrified forest was exposed over several acres of the barren hills. One trunk stood upright, its roots still gripping the ground. As erosion happened and the supporting sediment loosened, upperstory and main trunk must have lopped off at fractures. Glassy segments lay out as if whipsawed into rounds. I measured the length of one solid log, two feet through—fourteen long steps. Beside it, twigs small as matchsticks and limbs of every size scattered away from it down the slope.

I wandered up the ridge, across to a second ridge, the swale between, knowing I had fallen behind. John would be watching for my dust. Yet, at peace in the company of the ancient things, I could not make myself go. At first the chunks of wood, faced with black, silver, orange lichen, interested me for the sake of their age and their preservation. But epochs mingle in this desert. Fossils work to the surface at differing rates. Near here we found bones of the Miocene, Pleistocene. I needed to put this forest in context. What were these trees? (People say they are redwoods.) In what epoch did they stand? (A paleobotanist dated leaf fauna specimens found in the Warner Mountains at 33.9 million years.) What kind of creatures slept within the shade? (The tooth of a bear dog was found five miles south of here.) If it were here now would I be afraid? (Yes.)

My eyes got sharper. At the base of a trunk, a gray-green mass looked like small branches laced together. I picked it up carefully and, turning it in my hands, read its construction. It appeared to be a nest. I sat down, cradling it in my lap, holding encapsulated time. I thought of a packrat. I thought of a hawk. It may have been neither, just a pile of limbs torn loose by an ash fall. Then I noticed one twig bore teeth marks of a beetle or a ro-dent. Another had a hollowed-out knot and bark pulled away in a papery roll I had seen on living aspen. The rings went wavy, some mere shadows of growth, others fat with abundant rain. I counted rings. I've forgotten the number. It had no relevance to the crack in time I had entered.

I unhobbled Dandy and took one last look, imagined a forest, a wood, noisy, verdant. Breaking light. Wind in a dance and sway through leaves. High overhead, heavy underfoot, openings swimming in sunlight, branches alive with fruits, flowers, nuts, insects, birds. There would be lilies in the still water and creeks flowing into valley lakes. Perhaps a river.

It felt like a graveyard, and I felt a graveyard's sorrow.

⌣

John and I went to a reception a few years ago for a friend who received an honorary degree from the University of Nevada, Reno. Molly Flagg Knudson was there. I had heard she was being treated for skin cancer. Too many years of Nevada weather on a ranch woman's face.

I first heard Molly speak at a Nevada Women's History seminar in 1982. She was well known in northern Nevada, regent at the university for many years, breeder of fine registered Hereford cattle, horsewoman, respected by the livestock world as much as the academic. One glance told me this was a woman I could believe. She had the carriage, the confidence, that comes with doing the work she spoke about with ease and humor, as at home with urban women admirers as a herd of her own cattle. She made me think of a horse of mine that did not shy from bones in the grass. She did not shy from bones as she spoke about the challenges of being the only woman for miles, working all day, every day, with two men: her husband and one hired man, trucking the bulls off to sales, and laying a trap with the brand inspector to catch a cow thief. I bought the book she wrote about her Grass Valley Ranch out Highway 50 near Austin, and reading it made me feel less alone.

I suppose the friend told me about Molly's health to prepare me or so Molly wouldn't be embarrassed by my reaction. She was across the court-yard, friends circled around her. She turned her lovely face my way—red-dened by the treatment, her nose was carved down to the cartilage. I felt a knife twist within me. Must we give it all away? I had heard Molly left her beloved ranch, her place in this universe that needed her, as she needed it. It was said that there was love lost and no need of staying. And now, this maul-ing of her rare beauty?

I needed her young, energy charged with the workings of her Grass Val-ley Ranch. I needed her at the end of a dirt road just off the Loneliest High-way in America. I wanted to ride with her, see how she managed her cattle, hear her reasoning for herd sires, when to move the cows to grass, and watch her stroke her dog's head while she talked. And if I couldn't, knowing she was there would have been enough. But that time is gone. The ranch was sold. She is alone now and living in town. Dogs, horses, cattle, hills left behind.

Molly chatted and charmed, gracious as always, as if unaware of the unconventional line of her profile. I watched her, knowing if it were it me I would hide out, unable to endure the failure of flesh. Not Molly. In a moment my attention lifted from her nose to her face—alive with the same spark I saw on our first meeting. I could hear her voice. It was bright, like water.

⟿

When I went away from the desert after that first ride I took with me the beauty places John showed me. The Five Mile Field where waterfowl tracked the algae of the deep lake, and aspen leaves dropped on the water. The bonsai garden of Chinatown. Cottonwood Creek's lush meadows. I thought back on them, pleased in a way. Those pretty pockets of another time were still holding on. But they were not the desert. The desert is beneath those delights. It stands pat.

In some past time the climate was temperate, moist. There was a deep shadow of redwoods and threaded wind. Cones held out on long stems. Needles fingered into fans. Paths meandered wide as the stride of deer. In open lands grasses grew like wheat. Now that same land is covered in bitterbrush and sage. Its time of abundance exists in memory.

Stone trees lay under the skin of the desert where bald hills drop abruptly into gorges or gradually run onto flat bottomland. Hills are brushed and swept as if down to the very earth itself, spare and smooth. The far point in the distance is the same as where I stand. In every direction—any movement, any cast shadow, any change, any shape is in plain view. The life of ease is gone. Seeds are harder. Animals exist on less fat. Tougher. Resourceful.

Do the stone trees mark a loss? I think not. This is what it is now. At first I thought it was courage that brought Molly to the reception. But, of course, it was not. Molly and the desert are the same. It is beauty of a different measure.

⟿

I took a visitor into the Nevada desert. It might be considered the locals' idea of *the guest test*. I drive without being a tour guide, without a sales pitch about what we will experience. Why should I, after all? It can be learned only one human soul at a time. If they pass the test, they will be invited back. If they exclaim, "What the hell is this?" well . . .

This chattering woman beside me was dressed for the desert. Her bright colors could be spotted from an airplane at thirty thousand feet. She was used to tennis courts, golf courses, and mountain bikes. She had looked across the valley at the desert but never wandered over. This was something new.

We crossed the state line, bounced on the abruptness of pavement ending, and went a ways in silence. I was absorbed in the particular desert aroma coming up through the floorboards, greeting the old haunts of horizon, of distance, of late-afternoon light. I turned down a side road, and then another, bumped and swayed, dodging the worst of it, thinking to stop the truck and walk into the sand dunes where blue-green chalcedony oozed up in a long, low dike. I thought the person beside me was seeing what I see every time I enter the desert. I thought her gasp was awe. She stared through the windshield at the sudden view of Long Valley, the road across it disappearing beyond Painted Mountain. In a frail voice she asked, "Where does this road go?"

Go?

↝ Nesting

THE YELLOW JACKET COMES THROUGH THE OPEN DOOR OF THE SWATHER, legs hanging like a paratrooper about to land. But it does not land. It lurches toward my face, reconsiders, and bumps against the windows on each side as if saying, "Here? No, not here. Here?" I try to turn it back outside, keeping one eye on it, one on cutting close to the fence without breaking a post over.

I have just begun to cut the lower meadow. The sun rising over the '49 Mountains is directly in my eyes. My dog, Rita, is trying to find a comfortable place among my feet and the foot pedals, levers, and the brake. As if that isn't challenge enough, I have a marauding wasp inside the swather cab with me.

I am trying to keep a straight line; the baler man doesn't like to chase wobbly, weavy windrows. The mechanics of his machine eats hay in a straight run and kicks out bales in orderly rows for the bale wagon to retrieve. It makes sense and it's efficient. Besides, there's an old ranching tradition I've learned: leave no poufs of uncut hay sticking up in the field; keep the line straight and even; if you break a section—the blades that scissor-cut the hay as it feeds into the header—fix it right away or there'll be a telltale line of uncut hay trailing the swather. These slip-showing proofs of inattention are noted by the neighbors and marked against you in idle coffee-shop conversation. Besides, I sleep with the baler man, and he often brings my morning coffee to me in bed. I don't want to mess that up.

I am also watching for holes and ditches in the field. Our fields are un-leveled, native land, and we harvest the wild grasses for hay. I have tried to memorize the slight tilts and undulations, the natural swales, the run of the irrigation ditches that move the spring runoff to dry corners, and the alkali sloughs that can swallow a wheel. Experience has taught me the hazard. But the exact location of the holes is a mystery, a surprise hidden in high grass. Suddenly a wheel drops and the swather is stuck. Haying stops. It's a mile walk to the house for help. John has to leave the job he is doing to pull me out. One dose is enough. Trouble is, the header is twelve feet wide, and we cut out the land the same way every year. If you got stuck before, chances are . . .

Now, you might be thinking, I ought to just close the door if I want to concentrate and keep the livestock out of the cab. Well, the air conditioner hasn't worked since the mid-'70s and, on a day like today, you can fry eggs by ten o'clock. The door stays open—and the yellow jacket is still bumping around the glass. I sling a grease rag its way, trying to drive it toward the door. It ignores me, lurches upward, and disappears into a vent in the air conditioner. After a while, it drops down bungee-jumper style and flies out the door. Good.

By midmorning I am cutting the fourth round of the land, on the far side of the field, when another yellow jacket flies in the cab. I am used to mos-quitoes, moths, butterflies, green-heads, dragonflies, even praying mantis coming in for a visit. But I particularly distrust the cranky disposition and sting of a bitter wasp circling my head. It rises suddenly and enters the air conditioner. What's going on? What's in the danged air conditioner? Could this be the same yellow jacket? Soon it drops down and is gone out the door.

Although the New Holland design engineer must not have had a dog that liked to ride in the cab, it's my bet that he had small children at home. The ground speed lever has a picture of a tortoise, for slow, and a series of notches moving toward a rabbit doing wind sprints, for fast. I'm traveling halfway between—loping rabbit—three notches higher than I could cut this field last year. This year, no rain has fallen since April. The country is dry. The feed is short. The plants hold no reserve moisture in their roots for recovery. Still we need to cut and bale what we can. John says it all looks good to a cow when there's snow on the ground.

He comes across the field on his motorcycle to see how I'm doing and to tell me he has to take some tires into town to be fixed. I wipe my sweaty face on my shirttail and ask him if he will take Rita back to the house. She's been restless all morning. It's already in the nineties and easy to imagine her on the grass in the cool, shady yard. She wants to stay with me, but I don't think she realizes her options. He lifts her onto the bike and streaks off. Later I see his truck go out the road. A few minutes after that Rita comes galloping down the field, tongue lolling, tail wagging, panting her particular dog smile. I stop. She leaps inside.

Throughout the morning the wasp returns with its load of mud, locates the vent, and leaves. The back and forth of cutting hay, the repetition of lever, petal, windrow lets my mind wander. It's the part of the job I really like. I can accomplish the work with the split attention of the woman who sews, or weaves, or assembles computer optics: alert, yet in a half trance, able to direct my concentration elsewhere entirely for the whole day. Above the grind and roar of the old engine, I usually begin with my list of things to do and work downward (or upward) to the deep shadows of the rough Warner Mountains and the flat cloth of the desert where the most in-significant shadow lifts whole ridgelines or canyons into view.

I have grown into this place. A few years back I worried when I had to leave it, thinking something would happen and I would never get back. I left long pages of instructions for Katie in the event the feeling was right. At the place where the road turns out of the valley I would stop the car, get out, pick a sprig of sage, twirling it in my fingers, breathing the rush of scent, and memorize the way it looks, the way it is, before going on.

The yellow jacket returns. I've lost count. Its determination makes me think it's building a nest that was started while the swather stood before the shop door, waiting for a part to come in the mail. There are hundreds of these wasps buzzing around the pipe rack and the bolt bins. They daub mud in every available hole, including glove fingers and sprinkler heads. They drive us crazy with their dogfight maneuvers around us as we work in the shop. This one must have flown away from its nesting spot and, when it re-turned, found the swather going away, down the long row of willows toward its job in the lower field, and buzzed out, Hey! Wait up!

I continue to greet the little paratrooper as it flies in the door. I am amazed that wherever the swather is in the field, going whichever way, it zeros in on the thundering yellow-and-red machine, reel turning like a Fer-ris wheel, sickle bar clacking, me in the cab and the dog, ignoring all that, driven inexorably to its nest. The wasp seems to live for the motto Chief

Dan George spoke in Clint Eastwood's *Josey Wales* film: "You must endeavor to persevere."

It takes four days to finish cutting the lower field. Rita rides beside me every day, and every day the wasp finds us, flies in the door, enters the vent, and flies out. Each night I drive alongside the dry creek and the stand of willows, happy to have another day of work finished.

⤺

I was born on Oregon's high desert. After learning the medicine smell of the doctor's room, the warm sweetness of breast and milk, Dad took Mom and me home. On the way they opened the car window—it was September—and I breathed in the smell of sage. Did I know it then? No. But I know it now.

I found no religion in church. The desert baptized me. So sure, the open country repeats itself many times, east to west, basin and range, running not long with the sun but crossways. Shadows lean in and then away; they yield to the passing of time.

For me, home is this valley and our house built squarely between mountain and desert. For Rita, loyal in her desire to always stay by my side, and for the yellow jacket adapting to the unusual nature of its nest-2000, home is a moving target.

Fire Hall

Sophie Sheppard | | |

The Road Home

MY SON, JASON, BURIED HIS BELLY BUTTON UP ON THE MOUNTAIN ABOVE
Lake City. He chose a tree just under the rim of rocks where the turkey vultures nest. Under the tree he scraped away the forest duff and dug a small
hole. In it he placed the jerkylike piece of tissue that had been his physical
link to me just thirteen years before. Although I didn't ask him about this
private moment, I think that he probably buried with it the yellow plastic
clip that was stuck to it, the little clip the nurse had used to pinch off the
flow of my placental blood to him just moments after his birth.

My artist parents had made Jason a cradle board when he was born. They
patterned it after a Kiowa cradle, with the two long, picketlike boards that
protruded above the beaded leather hood. My father stained the wooden
stakes turquoise and hammered brass tacks into the wood as decoration. My
mother hung an old beaded Kiowa bag from the edge of the hood that
would shade Jason's newborn face. Round, covered with tiny seed beads,
that old bag must have come from my grandfather. In it, I had placed that
scrap of Jason's umbilicus that had dried and fallen away from his body during that first sweet week of his life. Jason loved his cradle board. If he were
fretful, I would place him in it and lace the thongs that held him snug inside
the leather wrap. He would quiet then, secure in that tightness that must
have felt familiar and womblike to him. The beaded bag had swung and
trembled near his face, out of touch, for even his little arms were bound

inside the cradle board. Later he had asked for the story of his birth, and I told it to him, many times as one does with stories for children. I must have told him that, perhaps, someday he would want to choose a tree that would serve as a sort of guardian when he took that piece of flesh that had connected us and placed it inside the earth.

That summer when Jason turned thirteen and buried his birth cord, he decided to pack into the mountains by himself. I suppose that for him it was a sort of vision quest. He looked small under the huge pack he had prepared for his solo journey into the mountains. He had even tied a cast-iron frying pan onto the load, not yet having mastered the art of lightweight packing. Young and going for comfort in camp, he did not worry about extra weight on the trail. And so he disappeared that afternoon, walking away from our house, across Main Street, and up out of town on the steep canyon road into the mountains.

I watched him and understood. During my own childhood, my parents left the city limits of Reno often for long camping trips into the heart of the dry sagebrush country. Always, when we were out in Nevada, my father would gather us about him.

"Listen," he would say to us. And we would. I remember in the stillness of the desert that my collar brushing my neck as I turned my head seemed deafening, my own heartbeat thundered, a whisper shouted. In that way, without words, he taught us about *place*.

That sense of place barely existed inside Reno's city limits. I could show you the house where my family lived; we could peek through the window into the small bedroom my brother and I shared on Primrose Street. A postwar tract house built next to hundreds of others in what had been a pasture. A house with tiny rooms. A kitchen little more than a galley. A bathroom only as big as a closet would have to be and still contain a sink, a tub, and a toilet. For years—until my parents added a studio to the house—my mother squeezed her sculpture stand and clay into a corner of the kitchen between my brother's high chair and the little stool and table where I ate.

Even though the houses all shared the same floor plan, the interior of our house differed from the others that surrounded it. My father's paintings and my mother's sculpture jostled for space between the walls. And then, there was the beauty outside of our home, outside of town, that surrounded our family each time we escaped the city limits to the places where our father took us camping or fishing. We ran through the sagebrush, camped near streams, and there my father seemed completely at home. You see, before my father taught art at the university, he had been a cowboy, good enough to ride the bulls at Madison Square Garden, good enough to compete in national rodeos. And the ranchers I knew from our trips deep into the heart of Nevada figured higher in my cosmology than the lawyers, doctors, and college professors we knew in town. I tried to walk bowlegged like the cowboys I knew. My mother never quite understood my ability to wear off the outer edges of my boot heels in record time. I carried a Bowie knife. I dreamed of sagebrush; I wanted to be in that rough country where we camped on our long weeks away from town.

That is to say, except for the contents of our own house, the town of Reno was not a place I associated then, or now, with beauty. Nor was it, in my child's mind of the 1950s, associated with security. After all, at school we learned to duck-and-cover beside the long rows of desks when the fire bell rang. And on certain occasions, my father awakened my brother and me in the middle of the night and led us from our beds. We sat waiting on either side of him on our back-porch steps in our pajamas, his arms around the coats draped over our shoulders. When it happened, the light always flared first. The double green flash across the sky. To the southeast. There was no sound. But seconds later we felt it. The soundless rumble. The cement porch steps growled silently beneath us, cold in the predawn quiet.

We heard the grown-ups joke at the faculty parties, the ice tinkling in their glasses, about the bomb shelter with a picture window that overlooked the Truckee River—the shelter and the huge house just above it having been built with the new Nevada wealth they scorned. And Reno was where from my top bunk, I could pluck the curtain back and watch the big searchlights mounted on top of the Mapes Hotel. Every night of my childhood, these batons of light swept the sky, announcing the arrival of yet another movie star in town for a gig in a casino nightclub and, perhaps, a hasty divorce.

⊕

To visit us now in Surprise Valley, you will have to start from Reno, that town of my childhood I eventually grew away from. Friends from Reno call to ask how long a drive to expect to our valley. We tell them this isn't a question with a simple answer. It has taken us five days, we say, when we have chosen the dirt road that skirts the Smoke Creek Desert and indulge every bit of our curiosity to stop and wander at will. Or only three or four hours, if we stay on the pavement, following the old Valley Road from Reno at seventy miles an hour.

Highway 447 north from Reno threads through the valleys that lie along it on a north-south axis. It links them like jewels on a necklace. Pyramid Lake will be the first to dazzle our friends. Sometimes cobalt, sometimes turquoise, Pyramid fades to silver and pewter in the winter, and a silence overtakes it: the pelicans are gone, lifted by the thousands in long, white flights, heading south with the fledged nestlings they raised on Anahoe Island.

The road floats up and over the old sand dunes that separate the Pyramid Lake basin from that of Winnemucca Lake. Swooping bands of ancient beaches circle the playa, the dry lake bed left behind when the lake's water source from the Truckee River was diverted early in the century to water the farms of Fallon, draining the huge fishery in just three short years. But sometimes after heavy spring rains, an enormous puddle pools there, pearly pink with salt deposits.

Just after the road touches the edge of the playa for the first time, we pull off on the dirt track that leads up away from the highway to the old tuffa deposits. We take our first rest stop there, getting out to stretch and explore the rocks where the petroglyphs are etched deep into the rough surface of the tuffa.

Back on the highway I stick my arm out the window. The dry desert wind pushes my hand into flight as the playa flashes by. The road climbs then, up and away from the lake over the long swell that divides the Limbo Range from San Emidio. We glide down the pavement to the edge of the Black Rock and the Smoke Creek Deserts, linked by the Gerlach peninsula. A tiny railroad town grew up here, raw and rough, with hot springs and bars. Gerlach perches on the brink of surrealism, that limitless expanse of the Black Rock Desert at the edge of town. We stop in Gerlach for a beer or a Coke and say hi to Bev at the Miner's Club.

After Gerlach, the road follows the northern edge of the Smoke Creek Desert to the west and winds up the sharp, steep curves of Gerlach Canyon through the break in the Buffalo Hills. At the top of the pass we stop again because from here we can see the mountains of home. My husband, Lynn, gets out and stands silhouetted against the broad backdrop of those mountains. Pale blue, the same shade as his faded Levis, the mountains cup the northwest boundary of the Great Basin, guarding our Surprise Valley from the rest of California.

But to get home, we still have to cross the twenty-five miles across Duck

Flat, or Duck Lake, the name change dependent on whether the year has been wet or dry. The big, flat valley blurs by. We slow for the curve at the north end, where the water is, watching out for the cows that will have congregated there, hidden by the sharp curve in the road and the big sage. We wiggle down through the last canyon, down into Surprise Valley.

The staccato slap of the tires crossing the cattleguard is the only ceremony that marks our passage from Nevada into California. Here, suddenly, are the first irrigated fields. Here it is that in the early summer the dry desert air softens, moister, permeated with the scent of wild roses or, later on, with the sweet pungency of freshly cut alfalfa. It is the smell of home. It is here that County Road 1 turns to the north and begins the long sweep up the flank of the Warner Mountains, through the four tiny towns and the fifty or so small ranches that lie in the lee of the mountains.

I know we are home because the waving begins. It is especially noticeable after having driven almost two hundred miles, passing only two or three cars during that whole long stretch after Pyramid Lake. This greeting from each of the cars we pass is what I suddenly realize I've been missing.

When we had first driven through the valley years before, I wondered then if it were the sign I had been waiting for, the sign that we were home. For years before we came here, I had dreamed a recurring image. I was a passenger in a car. We were driving slowly, slightly uphill, just entering a small community. In my dream I don't recall faces or features, but I recognized the smiles and the waving that greeted us.

⌁

We had driven up from Reno for a barn dance that our friend Roger was throwing at his ranch just north of Eagleville. This was the first outing where Lynn and I admitted we had become a couple in the year we had known each other. Both of us were on the brink of change, knowing that we would start a new life together with my son, Jason, wanting it to be somewhere rural.

The road dropped us down from the canyon into the valley and carried us across the cattleguard at the state line. It was late afternoon, early September. Through the windows of Lynn's old red delivery truck, we smelled the cut alfalfa, lying in long windrow spokes of mown hay that rotated by us in the fields on either side of the road. I looked out across the oxidized red paint of the hood, and from behind each windshield of each car we passed flashed a wave. We waved back. Someone here must have an identical '50

Ford truck, a twin to ours, we said; the wavers must be mistaking us for that person. But this was not the case. Because you always wave back in Surprise Valley. We learned that early on, and more.

⟶

In January when the heater barely mists the inside of the cab with whispered warmth, waving is problematic. I drive and wave right-handed for a while, my thumb wrapped around the steering wheel until the cold numbs it. Then I jam my right hand into my coat pocket and drive, waving left-handed, until I have to switch again.

When they were in high school, my son and his friends had what amounted to a comedy act, imitating our neighbors' various and distinctive waving styles. But soon after they started driving, they began trying to find a personal wave of their own, as young girls will experiment with handwriting, practicing the addition of flourishes to capital letters, dotting their *i*'s with tiny, round circles or hearts. The boys watched more experienced drivers and hunted for a gesture they liked enough to modify and make their own.

My next-door neighbor, Carol, is a pilot, and she drives like one. Both hands grasp the wheel firmly, at ten and at two o'clock, as she was trained. When she passes, eight fingers flash simultaneously, thumbs locked on the steering wheel, never relinquishing control. Some of the older men in the valley are war veterans. Their waves are salutes: fingers held together, thumb tucked to palm, their hands arc brusquely forward and up. I can see their shoulders square as we pass. And others cannot muster more than a backhanded flip, a sort of brush off, a wave in name only that satisfies the bare minimum required of our valley's greeting while on the road.

On the way down County Road 1 to Cedarville, I often come up behind the dilemma of a slow-moving vehicle, usually a pickup truck, and usually driven by an older neighbor. I back off on the gas pedal and slow down, enough to put a respectful distance between me and the truck ahead. Usually I won't pass, but drift slowly along, a good quarter of a mile to the rear. To pass would be bad manners. Notice would be taken. I know from experience that the neighbor will have a ribbing ready for me the next time we meet and will tease me about my hasty ways. If for some reason I have to hurry, have to pass, I do so slowly and carefully, ducking my head and waving as I come abreast of my slower-moving neighbor.

I have noticed lately that people don't wave as much anymore. The cars are newer, the colors and shapes less distinctive; we don't recognize one another as easily. But whenever we drive one of our old trucks—the dump truck, my '48 Chevy, or Lynn's Scout—no one passes us without the wave.

At the intersection in Cedarville, we still wait politely for the other car to go first. It would never occur to us to honk in impatience. For these are the people we live with, the larger extended family of community here in this valley we have chosen as home, home for the rest of our lives. Manners, old-fashioned manners, bind us, restrict our impulses of the moment.

The waving is a phenomenon of our sparse population, I think. Not many cars pass on the length of the road through our little settlements. All that surrounding space outlines each person's image clearly. We wave in acknowledgment of that delineation, just as we mark on the map of our minds the exact placement of each lone tree along the desert highway. And, too, we wave in the knowledge of the future encounters we may have with the other person we pass. The waving, that sign of civility, will have built a bond that will hold us together in a time of need. That is our community. Although the civility may cause us to temper our speech, it opens our hearing; though it restricts our freedom, it binds us. Slowly, bit by bit, the manners of living together in this valley with its four tiny towns open my mind.

✎ Owl Creek

I TELL PEOPLE WE CAME HERE FOR THE BEAUTY. BUT I ALSO CAME HERE because I no longer knew how to live in the town where I had grown up; that town, Reno, had grown up, too, differently than I might have wished. I had moved from Montana back to Reno the year I divorced. My ex-husband and I had chased nontenured teaching jobs from university to university all over the West. My son, Jason, had lived in twelve houses in his eight short years.

I was ready to settle down in one place and raise my son. The Reno I moved back to from Montana didn't resemble the Reno I had grown up in. I had learned Reno and the landscapes around it as a child, to see it, to know it, as my artist parents did. Perhaps I expected it to stay still the way art stays still. Even as a child I seemed instinctively to understand what my parents were up to, translating the apparent world into art, fixing feeling and movement and moment in ink and paint and clay. I wanted the mountains above Reno to be the same as they had been when I was a kid exploring those wild places on horseback.

But in 1980, I could no longer find my way into those mountains. On days when the walls pressed in, I needed to be where I could walk from the house and be alone, on land, not cement, climbing to a place where I could look out. Now the mountains were covered all over with streets and expensive big homes.

How could I afford to be a painter and earn enough money to raise my son in Reno? I would have to get a job, full time. I would no longer be able to work at home and see Jason off in the morning, tease him as I always had as he headed off for school: "Have fun. Sleep well." I would no longer be there when he came home to hear about his day, to tell him about mine.

In early February each year I dreamed of a garden, but how could I afford the yard where it would bloom? My freelance art wouldn't even pay first and last months' rent in a bad area of town. Reno ran on money, money with a capital *M*. How could I give my life to what I loved here: my family, my painting, and my garden?

That year I met Lynn at a ranch south of Reno. He had lived there for ten years. I noticed right away how Lynn put his feet on the ground when we walked in the sagebrush. He walks like a big cat. I know that sounds lame as a reason to fall in love with someone. But it was the symmetry, grace, and balance of his steps. It was clear to me that here was a man who was paying attention.

⌘

Roger's barn floor came alive under you, undulated with the music, defeated any effort to stand still, to resist the dance. The big double doors of the barn had been thrown wide open to the dusk. Light from the one bare bulb above the door cast gold on the horse manure that littered the corral outside. People milled around waiting for the band to start. John and Mary and the crew from Gerlach and Smoke Creek tuned up their electric guitars, the keyboard, and the drums. The Smoke Creek Irregulars, they called themselves, often playing on an old flatbed truck in the middle of the desert somewhere. Tonight they were playing for Lynn's friend Roger. Rock-and-roll, good old rock-a-billy-knock-your-socks-off transcendent dance music.

No one waited around looking bored when they started to play. Live music is a treat in a place this remote, and people love to dance. Kids, parents, and grandparents, cowboys, rednecks, and hippies all danced together, raising a fine dust that smelled faintly of horse manure and of the sweetness of Bridget, Roger's black-and-white milk cow, relegated for the night to the outer corral. Parents circle danced protectively around the smallest children, sometimes lifting them to their shoulders. We pulled the shyer children from the sidelines into a long line dance that snaked in and around the other dancers. Lynn danced with his hands lightly touching my waist, breaking every once in a while to dance freeform, his steps loose with the music.

Winded and sweaty, we sat out a tune or two on the hay bales that lined the walls and looked up into the big hayloft, empty that night of the pigeons that usually roosted there. Old harnesses and horse gear hung from the rafters, laced together with cobwebs, dull with the dust of who knew how many decades.

We had made our camp for the weekend at the old Mallet place on the west edge of Roger's pastures. Roger's swather had broken down in the middle of that third and finest cutting of alfalfa hay, the hay so prized by the dairymen of California's Central Valley that they pay a premium to truck it all the way from Surprise Valley. At the barbecue that afternoon, Lynn had volunteered to help Roger fix the big red machine, so while the rest of us danced on toward morning, they worked in the old mechanic shop down the lane from the barn. Every hour or so, getting progressively dirtier and greasier, they would take a break and come to the barn to dance a few numbers with us.

When I think back about that night, I think of the two men at work on the swather, passing tools and having the kind of close talk most men can have only under the pretense of doing something else. Lynn must have told Roger about us, his worries about starting a new relationship with a woman with a kid, and about the changes coming to the ranch south of Reno. He must have told Roger that both of us wanted to live someplace, say, like Surprise Valley. By dawn, the swather was running, the barn floor was quiet and empty again, and Roger had offered to let us live in the old Mallet place.

⌁

The house, really little more than a shack, had stood empty and abandoned for many years. Occupied for short stints in the summer several times in the recent past, it was more a camp than a house. We learned that the Mallets had given the place their name at the turn of the century, raising a truck farm there, hauling their produce to Reno on the old Valley Road. They had even grown watermelons over against the big south-facing fossil-lake dune that protected the place from the north winds. I could visualize another garden there. I would plant it the next spring.

We ignored the mess inside the house where the chickens roosted, flying in through the broken windows. We ignored the pungent heaps of packrat detritus in the corners of the kitchen. We ignored the west wall of the kitchen where there had once been a window. Now there was a gaping hole. But we saw none of that, only how well the little house was tucked into the grove of big trees. Jason and Jay, Roger's son, were already building a fort over by the creek. We stood outside in the yard. We looked up at the Warner Wilderness. Lynn said, "It's a little fixer-upper with a view, isn't it?"

I said, "Yes."

⌐

We lived there our first year in Surprise Valley with an outhouse, no running water, no electricity. Jason hauled the ten gallons of water that we used each day from Owl Creek across a complicated series of bridges and ramps of his own device. Over the weathered board highway he made, he brought the wheelbarrow twice a day, each time with a full five-gallon bucket, although simply carrying the buckets from the creek to the house would have been simpler. He was nine; his joy was in the possibility and novelty of things, not necessarily their practicality. But this was as it should be, and Lynn and I, occupied as we were with the practical, welcomed my son's sense of whimsy. One day, halfway through his chore, Jason was stopped in his tracks by a new kind of thought: "Each one of these buckets is what it takes to flush a toilet once," he announced. Then he smiled at me, loaded the empty bucket into the wheelbarrow and headed back to the creek.

We cleaned and scoured. We fixed the broken windows. Roger brought the backhoe up. He and Lynn dug a new hole for the outhouse, rolled it to its new perch on some logs and filled the old hole in. I stapled burlap feed sacks over the walls and the ceiling. I hung pictures there and in the house. We put a good supply of reading materials in the outhouse, which faced east to the morning sun and the Hays Range, cobalt blue in the morning, Mars red in the late-afternoon sun.

All that fall I cried when I contemplated the piles of scrap wood that we would have to use to patch the holes in the old house walls. Lynn's cardinal rule, then and now, has always been "No debts." We would make do with what was there. Often he was detained after dark by the myriad chores required on the ranch, traded for our rent. And on those evenings I learned to saw, with a bucksaw at first because it seemed easier, and then with an old carpenter's saw. I developed a keen eye for the exact board in that pile of scrap that would patch each hole.

By winter we were in. I worried that our supply of winter wood was thin. We didn't yet know the lay of the land, didn't know where to gather our firewood easily. I knew that was information people would not part with readily. But the house itself was fit and snug.

We bathed down the road in Roger's sweet-water hot spring. The snowflakes fell around us hissing into the steam. On clear nights the moon bounced on the water in front of us as Jason splashed and we looked out over the whole south end of Surprise Valley. Lynn showed us the constellations wheeling through winter. I would slide down in the water next to Lynn and Jason and listen to the family we were becoming, bathing together outside under the stars.

Back at the house after our baths, we'd light the kerosene lanterns for our reading and Jason's homework. The dim light seemed to make us sleepy earlier. Our rhythms shifted and slowed. We were never sick. With an outhouse, the last thing you do at night and the first thing you do in the morning is to go out to pee. I knew the phases of the moon.

That year my mother asked me if Lynn were the one for me. I told her that in my mid-thirties I was less starry-eyed than I had been at twenty. I was still wary and still grieving over my failed marriage with Jason's father. But I remembered what my mother had said to me once when I was a teenager. I had asked her how I could tell if a man were to be my husband. She told me, "A really good relationship with a man will make you feel more like yourself than you have ever felt before."

In my mind I couldn't separate being with Lynn from being in this place. And in this place I felt more like myself than I had ever felt before. I decided that was good enough. Geographic compatibility had a lot going for it. Maybe I would be able to do all of the things that really mattered to me here in this place, here with Lynn and Jason: become a family once again, love my family, be with my family, paint, grow a garden. It all seemed possible.

∝

Roger winter-fed his cattle in the big field between the Mallet place and County Road 1. He and Lynn would appear every morning around nine, Roger in the truck, Lynn on the back of the feed wagon, whacking open the big hay bales with a hatchet and throwing the flakes down to the wake of cows that followed them in their slow arc around the field. Every school day before the feed truck came I watched Jason walk through that field to catch the school bus. The cows stood, spread out across the snow. Later they would bunch together when they heard the hay truck coming. From my vantage point at the my worktable I could easily pick out the Angus bulls half a mile away, their black shapes massive next to the smaller cows. I watched Jason approach them, wanting to call him back. But I didn't. Roger and Lynn had taught him to stand his ground in front of the huge animals. I watched him, a tiny dot in the distance, move among them, how those big bulls backed off from his approach.

Roger and Susie went skiing for a couple of weeks that winter. Lynn recruited Jason to drive the feed truck for him. I wondered about the wisdom of this arrangement when I saw Lynn piling all those pillows behind Jason so that his short legs could reach the clutch. He peered out the windshield from under the arch of the big steering wheel. One day after feeding the cattle in the deep snow of that winter, Jason and Lynn seemed particularly attuned, content with each other's company, reluctant to come from the snow back into the warmth of the little house. Later Jason told me how he had accidentally popped the clutch. In the truck's rearview mirror he watched horrified as Lynn was jolted, toppling from the top of the bales stacked on the wagon. Jason said Lynn didn't say a word to him. Jason stopped and waited until Lynn had climbed back on the wagon to the top of the bales. He told me he would never pop that clutch again.

⌣

One night in January I went to Jason's room to give him an extra kiss before I slept. His bed was empty. Through the frost on his window I saw his fresh tracks in the snow and the snowflakes swirling in the glow coming from the open outhouse door.

I grabbed my flashlight from the table, thinking that maybe he had suddenly felt sick. But no. Inside the outhouse Jason sat, holding his own flashlight over the book on his lap, reading, his pack boots unlaced, snow blowing in through the wide-open door.

"Aren't you cold?" I asked.

"Oh, yeah," he said. He didn't look up from his book.

"Do you want my coat?"

"Oh, okay," he said, laconic, indulging me now, obviously hoping the interruption would end. I tucked my parka around his shoulders and left him alone with his book and his flashlight in the storm.

Ten minutes later Jason came back inside and pulled his boots off, leaving a little heap of snow on the mat by the door. I waited until I heard him settle down, stepped quietly into his room, and gave him one more kiss goodnight.

❧ Bouquet of Forks

IF I PUSH WITH MY THUMB AND FLEX MY FINGERS, I CAN MAKE A SHARP staccato counterpoint to the ring of each utensil Bettie lets fall, one in front of each gray metal folding chair. We circle the tables in unison, Bettie on one side, me on the other. I carry a bouquet of mismatched stainless-steel forks, she a rosette of spoons. We click each spoon and fork into place on the worn, waxy Masonite surface, mine on the left of the paper napkins, hers to the right. This time we had set up only four of the long tables stacked against the community fire hall walls.

"Most of her friends have died, so it won't be a very big funeral," Bettie had said. "I doubt if there will be more than forty people." The old wood creaked as we unfolded the metal legs, fitting them into the window catches bolted to the underside that some fireman had jerry-rigged long ago. We heaved each of the heavy tables upright and placed them in rows, stepped across the fire-hall linoleum.

I watch Bettie as we work together. She is the same age as the one for whom we are preparing the fire hall today.

❧

Here, when there is a funeral, the whole town comes. First to arrive are the older women, vestiges of the Lake City Ladies Club that was disbanded a few years ago because most of the younger women have jobs and no longer stay at home. At the potluck funeral dinner everyone will file in together: the women unfamiliar in dresses ordered from catalogs, the men's hatless foreheads glowing pale in contrast to the tan of their freshly shaven jaws, the younger people that I won't recognize. I will search their faces to find the features that resemble those older ones I know gathered there in the hall. These young ones will be the family members who have moved out, out to the bigger towns, towns with more jobs, and who come back to visit during the county fair, for marriages and for funerals. Subdued and on their best behavior, the children's eyes will widen in anticipation at the number of cakes and pies arranged at the end of the big serving table set up in front of the kitchen.

These days it is Bettie, her friend Noreen, and I, younger than they by a generation, who show up before the funeral to clean the town's fire hall at the bottom of the hill below the cemetery. We set the tables, put flowers out if it is the season for gardens, and wait for the containers of food to come. The work reminds us of the potluck fund-raisers that dot the calendar for the various civic groups in the valley. We enjoy one another's company. We tell each other stories about our families and catch up on the valley's news. But we know that later, when a member of the bereaved family walks into the kitchen, we will stop our conversation to hug them, to pat their backs and murmur our words of sympathy.

Bettie, who is chair of the town cemetery board, guides these potlucks for the funerals and for the fund-raisers. When something is needed in the community, she is the one who comes forward; the rest of us, whether friends of her generation or of the two generations after, wait for her to determine what needs to be done, to direct and organize. It is she who salvaged the community canner after the end of World War II. The big machine could steam and seal two hundred cans at a time. Bettie dismantled it and stored it in one of the Parman Ranch barns should the community ever need it again. She is the one who always will take on the work of whatever needs to be done. Even among these infinitely practical women, women who rarely discuss a project, preferring to simply jump in and share the doing, Bettie stands out as the one who does the most. All of us accept her strong lead.

Lynn and I worked for Bettie at the Lake City Cemetery our first five summers here after we had moved off Roger's ranch at Owl Creek. We had come to this big valley seeking the isolation. Eighty miles long with four tiny towns. Only twelve hundred people. The valley's pristine beauty unspoiled. On a practical level, though, we couldn't eat the landscape. We had a family to support that Roger's ranch couldn't sustain. We found a house and moved to the smallest town, a village really: Lake City.

The weekly Alturas newspaper, our only local publication, rarely listed new jobs. We took any work we could find.

We heard the Lake City Cemetery needed a part-time caretaker. And Bettie pointed out to Lynn that he would have the use of the cemetery tractor, an ancient machine that was always getting stuck in reverse. Lynn never gets angry at recalcitrant machinery. He simply choreographed most of his moves to keep the tractor moving in a forward trajectory. But when he hauled the excess dirt away from a new grave and dumped it onto the rubble pile below the hill, he would have to back up, knowing it would then be stuck in reverse. Lynn would sit slightly slumped in the tractor saddle and patiently jimmy the gears however long it took until they popped into place and the tractor could move forward again. After work he parked the big, red-and-yellow Ford tractor in amongst the collection of trucks that surrounds our house. Some run. Some don't. Those that don't we keep for spare parts for the ones that do. I liked seeing the tractor there in the lineup, parked companionably next to our old, yellow Chevy dump truck, knowing how well the two would complement one another when a neighbor needed gravel hauled in.

Our first job for Bettie was to smooth out a new grave that scabbed the green of the cemetery lawn. The raw dirt humped, rough and stony, dumped where the backhoe had buried the casket after the funeral. We raked and picked out the rocks. We shook the sod that lay mixed in with the soil at the side of the grave, and we fitted the jigsaw pieces of green together over the mound we had made tidy. We hauled off the excess dirt, the rocks, and truncated roots to the debris pile hidden in the big sage and mahogany thicket at the edge of the cemetery where deer would come to bed down in the winter. Together, Lynn and I wondered how much higher than the lawn should we leave the new plot? How far would the coffin and contents settle over time? Lynn shrugged, and we patted the last piece of sod into place on top of the mound.

Bettie laughed when she saw how we had heaped the dirt, a foot and a half higher than the surrounding green. She told us not to worry, that there wouldn't be much settling. She told us that her husband, Joe, always waited until everyone had left the cemetery and the community potluck in the fire hall before he filled in the grave; how he waited, sometimes long into dusk for a solitary mourner to leave, until he was sure that no one was there. Only then would he fire up the ranch backhoe. When he had replaced as much of the fill dirt as possible, he would raise the heavy bucket of the big, yellow machine and let it drop again and again to pack that dirt down.

Every ten days in the summer we dismantled the big aluminum irrigation pipes and laid them in neat rows along the edges of the grass to begin the three-day process of mowing the cemetery. I couldn't reach the riding mower's pedals with my short legs, and I had a tendency to collide with the headstones. Once I ran over one of the irrigation pipes, the mower blades shredding the thin aluminum into shrapnel. After that, I was relegated to pushing the hand mower. But, as Lynn noted, trying to soften the demotion, the cemetery tenants never offered a word of complaint about our services.

We chose our favorites among the names chiseled into the old stones: I liked the sound of Icy Fink, while Lynn preferred the oldest name in the cemetery, Wilkerson, barely etched onto the rough, undressed stone from the mountain above. We took note of those headstones that never bloomed with the fake flowers on Memorial Day. Lynn would save the best of the plastic and silk flowers salvaged from the year before, flowers we collected during the major cleanup every spring to ready the cemetery for that weekend in late May. He would walk among the stones and carefully decorate the graves that had been ignored. Only then would he consider our Memorial Day chores completed.

◦❯

In the corner of the fire hall, the stove puffs out a little smoke as the fire we have built begins to warm the chill air of the building. I watch Bettie move down the row of chairs opposite me, intent on her spoons. Her shoulders slope now. For the last five years she has dislocated a shoulder almost every spring, usually lifting the big bags of planting medium to start up her greenhouse.

The spring after we moved here, I learned that Bettie was the woman who raised flower and vegetable starts for the valley gardens in the greenhouse she had built on the Parman Ranch. When she saw my truck pull up in front of her house, Bettie crawled out from under the tractor, eyes bright, long legs encased in oil-stained jeans. She put down the wrench in her hand and invited me into her kitchen for pie and coffee. After that the Parman's stock dog, Timmie, never barked when we drove up to the house. Instead she pulled her lips back and seemed to smile, her eyes looking almost human because so much white showed at the sides of her irises.

The second visit I found Bettie in the kitchen, the air sweetened with the scent of the fifteen hundred cookies she was baking. By then I had learned that when Bettie makes a pie, she always makes twenty, one to eat, and nineteen to put in the freezer, to pull out in the winter for the constant stream of visitors who surround her kitchen table.

The third visit, Timmie thrust her cold nose into my palm as I walked to the house. Inside, Bettie lay on the floor rewiring a circuit. She told me she had done so much of the wiring on that old house that she hardly bothered anymore with the extra safety of pulling the fuses when she had an electrical fix-it chore to do. I told her that all I knew about electricity was that it shocked. Always when I left she gave me something—extra produce from her garden or a plant, saying it was left over in the greenhouse and that it would just die if I didn't take it for my garden.

Bettie welcomed Lynn, my son, Jason, and me, newcomers into this tight-knit little community, and she was the first. Most stood back, watching us carefully, waiting to see what we were about. Much later, Bettie told me that she, too, sometimes still felt like an outsider in the valley even after half a century of residence. I knew she had moved here in the forties to marry Joe. To the ranchers in Surprise Valley, belonging meant that you had been born there. Would I ever feel like I truly belonged?

⊕

I painted a portrait of Bettie last month, my first oil. I painted Bettie against a Prussian-blue and zinc-white background, the same blue as the brightest stone in my grandmother's turquoise bracelet, a piece of jewelry that I always wear. Dressed in jeans and a green sweatshirt, she looks out, her eyes round and expectant behind the reflection of her glasses. Gray-going-white hair that she cuts short, herself, before the bathroom mirror, frames the perfectly round top of her head.

She is seated in a yellow armchair. Her hands are big, capable, and strong. Her hands cradle the pie in her lap, offering it. A cherry pie. I know, because I painted it and because I can see the shiny, bright-red cherry juice leaking, dripping from the woven lattice crust. I like the painting. I don't know what I'll do with it. I imagine that I'll give it to Bettie someday, but for now, it will stay stacked against the wall for a few months until I can experiment with the mysteries of varnishing an oil painting.

⊕

As we set up the fire hall for the funeral dinner, I think of Bettie's painting. Click, jingle, and glide. Click, jingle, and glide. Around the tables we circle, the two of us filling the still air in the hall with our improvised percussion. We have finished with the clatter of the folding chairs. This time I have lifted the ugly gray chairs from the rack in the back of the fire hall, two by two, so Bettie is not tempted to do any of the overhead lifting that dislocates her shoulder.

I think of what Linda said when she saw Bettie's portrait: how complimentary I had been to Bettie in the way that I had painted her. Her comment caught me by surprise. I thought I had rendered a faithful likeness; after all, everyone who saw the painting knew it was Bettie. So today, I find myself looking at Bettie, looking hard at her, not into her, but just at the surface. I realize Linda is right. For the first time I see Bettie's wrinkles, their depth, how many line her face, how her cheeks droop at the corners where wattles are starting. My eyes hover over the stoop of her shoulders. I see the deliberate way she plants her feet on the floor, surely different from the way I saw her climb out from under the tractor the first day I met her, long legs swinging easily. I notice how the skin on her arms sags, is wrinkled and soft, but the underneath, the sinew of her forearms, is still hard. The image I carry of Bettie in the eye of my mind is the Bettie I painted.

As the funeral party arrives, I stay in the kitchen, hot in the bustle of all of us trying to do something when there is nothing left to be done. In the hall, the conversation softens. Everyone eats. The kids come back for seconds at the dessert table. Later, one by one, the chairs grate on the linoleum as people rise from the tables full of ham and beans and Bettie's taco salad and pie. I plunge my hands into the hot, soapy water as one by one they push their paper plates into the old galvanized cans set up at the door, lined with the big government garbage bags, salvaged after the last forest fire.

I hear the chunk of silverware dropped into the stainless-steel bowl filled with hot water and dish soap, the clunk and scrape of each spoon and fork. I know I won't have much washing up today. Bettie was right.

◈ The Lake City Ladies Club

WHEN BETTIE INVITED ME TO A MEETING OF THE LAKE CITY LADIES CLUB
for the first time, I almost laughed and refused. Me? A liberated, degree-
bearing modern from the college campuses of the seventies? I was a woman
who had thrown out the gender roles of the past and probably a good deal of
manners besides. I had a little trouble seeing myself crocheting doilies to
raise money for the Ladies Club, the auxiliary to the men of the Lake City
Volunteer Fire Department. Could I picture myself balancing a teacup on
my knee and making polite conversation with women who called themselves "Ladies"? The thought made me a little nervous. Although we didn't
advertise it, I was not yet married to the man I lived with in our new place
in Lake City. Lynn was not Jason's dad. We had three different last names in
our family. How in the world had I imagined that I would fit into this tight
little community of tradition?

When we knew we had to leave Owl Creek, we were advised to look for a
place in Lake City. The properties were smaller there, we were told, more
affordable. The name, Lake City, is misleading. Most years the lake that the
town is named for is bone dry, blown white by the prevailing drought. And
Lake City didn't exactly qualify as a metropolis either, with its sixty-two
people and forty-two dogs. All the better, Lynn said: this would be a good,
safe place to raise Jason.

The house we found—actually the only house in the valley that we could afford—was on a quarter acre of land, a south-facing parcel fringed on the north by big Jeffrey pines. Later we saw the old photo that had been taken of that parcel in the 1870s. The house was new and raw looking then, but those huge trees were the same size a hundred years ago as they are now. Those trees would deflect the north wind from the garden I planned, like the garden that bloomed in my dreams every February from the time I was a child. *Good dirt,* Lynn said, irrigated by water from the creek next door. *This was the place for us,* he said. I wasn't so sure. I wasn't sure of this two-year-old partnership that Lynn and I had. And I was having second thoughts about living in such a small and remote community. I had not yet made friends with my neighbors.

But Lynn knew what I needed to hear. In my recurring dream, winter becomes spring overnight. The world is in full blossom. Fruit trees are frosted in pinks and whites, and given voice by birdsong. Dahlias and zinnias splash yellow and red everywhere, petals crisp beside lacy yarrow. The breeze is warm. I wake hungry for new growth, wanting that garden of my dreams.

We bought the house.

‹›

Over the years Bettie had built the complex of hothouses and lathe houses on the Parman Ranch, adding on to the first little greenhouse she built for herself and her own garden. She could never resist starting plants for others, and eventually she called her thriving business the Lake City Gardens, supplying valley gardeners with plants and earning enough to buy Joe a new tractor for the ranch.

As I sipped a cup of coffee poured from the big electric pot that always steamed at the end of her kitchen table, Bettie laughed as she looked outside to the snow blowing by her kitchen window. "How on earth am I going to be ready to plant? I have a shipment of three thousand seedlings coming this week." My annual dreams of the magic garden had begun. I almost begged Bettie for the chance to help. Timmie followed us down past the milk barn into the pearly light of her hothouse. It was the largest she had built, using the windows she had salvaged from the high school renovation of several years before.

We unrolled the old mold-stained plastic that she had stored along the north wall, and from it we pieced together a tent to cover the planting table. This was what Bettie called a "girl job," meaning we used lots of baling wire and staples and nails to stitch the tent together. It's funny how a woman can sew, even with nails. But the tent would hold together for the month or two when the plants were tiny, saving her the cost of heating the whole greenhouse for those first early seedlings.

We hauled several of the big seventy-five-pound bags of planting medium from the mountain of them stacked in the old barn and wrestled them inside the greenhouse from the back of the truck. Bettie pulled out her pocketknife and slit the first bag open down the middle. Moist dirt poured from the belly of the bag. We scooped it into the shallow beds on the planting tables, spreading it smooth with our hands. She handed me the box of seed packets; most of them folded over, frugally saved from the year before.

We planted one row each of all the varieties of warm-weather vegetable starts and labeled the little white plastic sticks with permanent markers: three types of eggplant, five different varieties of tomatoes, and the ten or fifteen different peppers she tries each year. Because they sprout so quickly, we would wait a few weeks to plant the flowers, cabbage, broccoli, a few seed onions, and what she calls "culliflower."

Bettie told me, "Wait till all the snow is melted off the Hays Range. A garden won't do any good in this country if you transplant warm-weather stuff much before the first of June."

Inside the greenhouse Bettie's sure, steady voice continued with her instructions. I took my coat off and hung it in the corner. My fingers tingled warm in the dirt while outside the snow still skiffed cold and white across the corrals.

I knew that Bettie didn't really need my help except for the few weeks when her shoulder was out. But it didn't matter. From that first day in the greenhouse on through spring, I would drive up to the Parman Ranch every chance I could, Timmie greeting me with her semblance of a smile. When the shipment of trays that she had ordered arrived, we transplanted the tiny sprouts from each tray of four hundred thimble-size cells into the larger six-packs. Tenderly, so as not to break any of the seedling pansies, petunias, and marigolds, we tugged each little stem with its hairlike roots free. I crooked my forefinger and scooped a hollow in the planting medium in each cell of the black plastic six-packs. One by one we tucked each tiny seedling in until we had transplanted all ten thousand of them.

⁀

I dressed up that day for my first Ladies Club meeting. It was suddenly important to me that Jason's new community see me as being a real mother on their terms. Tea, coffee, and a gooey, sweet dessert were set out among the china cups and plates on the lace tablecloth on the dining room table at Phyllis's house. A dozen older women from our little town and a few of the outlying ranches sat on the sofa, the blue Barca-lounger, and the extra straight chairs that had been pulled away from the dining room table and brought into the living room for the occasion. Bettie wore a dress, hose, and patent-leather pumps. I, too, had on a dress. Bettie introduced me to the circle of women and suggested I sit on the chair next to Ferrol, the oldest woman there.

The conversation veered from small talk to the subject of the Easter Ham Dinner, the annual fund-raiser for the Lake City Volunteer Fire Department. This meeting of the Ladies Club would be the main planning session. Bettie had told them I was an artist, so there was no way that I could avoid volunteering to make the signs for the event on colorful construction paper. In addition, since I had a kid in school, I would get the information about the Ham Dinner into the only local paper, the *Hornet's Buzz*, mailed weekly by the high school journalism class free to all the box holders in the valley.

Peggy, the secretary of the Ladies Club, read the minutes in rhymed verse, each word starting with the first letter of the name of the woman that line was about. Jean reminded everyone how the Ham Dinner was always done, each year following the previous in exactly the same way, it seemed, from time immemorial. But most of all of that day, I remember Ferrol and how she fooled me. I was the youngest one and Ferrol was the oldest, in her mid-eighties. She sat with her feet crossed at the ankles, long, slim legs clad in sheer nylons, knees pressed properly together. The gold handle of her cane she clasped in her hands in front of her knees. She wore a skirt, the neat rows of pleats precisely ironed. Bettie commented on her mint-green hand-crocheted sweater and asked for a copy of the pattern. Ferrol's white hair was fixed carefully in soft curls. I had watched how haltingly she had entered the room, how she had sat down with difficulty, so I fetched a teacup of coffee and a small plate of cake from the table for her. I made sure to jump up and help when it was time to pick up the empty plates and carry them to the kitchen. Of all of them gathered there, Ferrol embodied the reason I was on my best behavior, the reason I was watching my language.

After the Ham Dinner planning session the talk shifted to the subject of the long winter, of hay stacks dwindling, and the coming relief of getting the cattle back out onto the range. They talked of who would ride and who would truck the cows out to Nevada.

Sweetly, Ferrol looked up at me. I could tell she had been a tall woman, but the hunch of osteoporosis made her tilt her head up like a bird when she talked in her soft, contralto voice. "The worst part about buckarooing with a bunch of men," she said, tipping her head up toward me, "is finding a place in all that short sage where you can pee."

Suddenly I heard myself belly laughing, a sound I had not expected to make that day, belly laughing with all of those women, wiping the tears from my eyes. It was the first of what I would find I had in common with the Ladies Club. For me it was enough. I knew then that I would be all right.

⟜

Bettie's regret is that she doesn't get to ride with Joe; her son-in-law, Nate; and her daughter, Carol, when the rest of them go off to buckaroo in Nevada. She stays home to mind the ranch. But, by being left behind, tethered to the home place, she discovered another kind of freedom.

"If you want to get something done, wait till they," meaning the men of the house, "are gone. Then, start. By the time they get back, you'll have so much of it done that they won't be able to talk you out of it."

This was the way to handle "girl jobs," she told me, like the planting tables she and I had cobbled together, and like the greenhouses she built. My friend Linda learned about girl jobs from Bettie before I did. With her father-in-law, Walter, she tore out the walls between the kitchen, the dining room, and the ranch office. By the time her husband, John, returned from wherever it was that he had gone that day, the walls were down. Linda's remodel was well on its way.

One day when we knew Lynn would be camped out in Nevada for some time, Jason and I ripped up all the old, ugly carpet and linoleum from the floors of our house. I had already talked Lynn into taking some of the walls down with his chain saw. Later, when I was sick of trying to keep the bare plywood floor clean and sick of mopping and having it smell like an old, wet dog and look no better for the process, Linda told me how to lay the new pine boards for the floor in tight. She told me how to wedge each satiny plank even tighter to its neighbor before I nailed it down, using a chisel for leverage.

The point of what Bettie has taught us about girl jobs is not about what we can accomplish without men. It is about the pleasure of what we can accomplish ourselves.

I had seen Bettie's spinning wheel in her living room and the skeins of yarn drying by the stove when I went to the ranch to help in the greenhouse. I had asked her to teach me to spin then. One day in late spring, she called and said that she'd be over to pick me up. Tom Espil, a sheep rancher down in Eagleville, had a bunch of colored fleeces that he had saved for her. We drove down to Eagleville slow and steady in her big, gold Buick.

The fleeces were lumped, greasy and dirty in their burlap wraps, and corded with brown twine. The heat of the dusty barn intensified their smell: sheep, lanolin, and manure. Bettie leaned down and pulled out a lock of wool and snapped it fast between the fingers of both hands. If the sheep had been sick or malnourished during the growing season, the lock would break. I picked out a blue-gray fleece. It had a pearly sheen to it. The lock I tested snapped satisfactorily between my fingers. Bettie picked out a dark one for herself, almost black.

Back at home I put a sheet down on the floor. We unrolled the fleeces, picked off the tag ends, the tangles of wool wadded with manure and dirt. We discarded the worst of the dirty stuff. She handed met a shiny new flicker brush, wood with stiff metal bristles, the kind the 4-H kids use to fluff up their lambs for the fair. She showed me how to hold the wool tight in my left hand against a square of heavy leather to protect my leg from the sharp wires of the brush; to flick out the dirt and hay and seed from each lock, one by one. "You clean all of this and I'll show you how to wash it. Then, you'll be ready to learn to spin."

Each summer evening after supper, I'd clean wool out on our back porch. The dirt and grease from the wool left my fingers black and sticky. I punctured the forefinger and thumb of my left hand repeatedly with the stiff wire bristles, but when I washed my hands the lanolin from the wool had made them smooth and soft.

On the Friday before Labor Day, I helped Bettie pack up her baskets of raw wool, rolags, those long clouds of clean, carded wool, bits of yarn taped to a poster board next to the pressed samples of the plants she had used to dye each colored swatch, the sweaters and hats she had knit from various batches of spun wool. She had invited me to the county fair to help set up her spinning display in the little historic section called Louieville where various old-time crafts are exhibited. We crowded all that, her spinning wheel, some drop spindles, and a couple of Navajo spindles into the car. She had asked me to bring my little flicker brush so that I could be cleaning raw wool as part of her spinning demonstration.

Kids shrieked on the gaudy rides set up on the fairground lawn behind us. People wandered by on the boardwalk and stopped to chat with us and watch Bettie spin while they nibbled pink spun sugar and sipped soda pop in wax paper cups. I cleaned wool. Bettie spun on her russet-colored wheel. Kids stopped, transfixed by Bettie's whirring wheel, and leaned forward to see how that cloud of wool managed to turn into yarn. She always asked any kids who seemed interested if they would like to try. They did and she pulled them around to her side of the wheel, patiently guiding their little fingers and laughing with them when the inevitable tangle of fibers resulted.

But when she spun, it looked so simple. The fluffy wool almost looked liquid as it slipped though her fingers to emerge as yarn before disappearing into the little whirling orifice to be wound onto the bobbin. During a lull in visitors to the booth, Bettie asked me if I would like to try. A friend, Tina, who already knew how to spin, had told me that I would have to find four or five hours where I could be very patient and forgiving of myself to learn to spin, a time when I could maintain a sense of humor. Although this was neither the time nor the place, I said I'd try.

The wool zipped through my fingers. Too fast, too fast! I would feel it start to flow and spin into yarn for just a moment, but then the fibers would pull apart and the yarn would break. I'd have to stop and fish the end back out through the orifice, web the fibers back together like Bettie had shown me, and start all over. When she needed the wheel to demonstrate again, I relinquished my place on her stool, telling her I wished there were a way to slow the process down.

"There is," she said. She bent over and rummaged in the heap of things that lay beside her on the rough boards of the Louieville porch where we sat together. She pulled out a long, smooth stick, pointed on both ends; the stick inserted through a wooden wheel the size of a dessert plate, the counterweight. She handed me the Navajo spindle.

I learned how to roll the spindle on my thigh and let the wool slip through my fingers with just the tiniest bit of drag. Miraculously it wound itself into a yarn, lumpy, thick, then thin, but yarn just the same, and obviously handmade. All afternoon, I practiced with the spindle. At the end of several hours I had managed to spin a little hank of the lumpiest yarn in the world. I was so excited that when I got home, I sharpened a long piece of doweling, drilled a hole in a piece of kindling, shoved the dowel through, and Voila! I had fashioned a crude spindle for myself! The next day, I did take Tina's advice, giving myself four hours to laugh at my efforts. At the end of it I was spinning a passable yarn.

⟜

Bettie has taught a number of us to spin. We like to collect together on a winter afternoon to spin and talk. The first sunny day of early spring, we gather on my back porch. The sun is low in the south, but its warmth is cupped by the porch. Tina comes—a vegetarian and environmentalist as was Lynette—and Bettie and Linda, the ranchers in the group.

The talk turns to grazing, and cows. *Uh-oh!* I think to myself. Isn't that forbidden conversational territory among us? There are so few of us living in this place that we always take care to invest in our friendships, not our politics. But this warm afternoon, something strange happens. For two hours we talk about what we all know could turn a lovely afternoon into an argument. We talk about the grazing on the public lands. We talk about the future. We talk about our kids and whether they will be able to find work and stay in the valley when they are grown. We talk and find that our thinking is remarkably similar in spite of the political chasms that we had thought carved up the space among us.

For Gandhi, the spinning wheel was a potent unifying symbol for an independent India. He also used it as a meditation device. Maybe the slow turning of the spinning wheels in the sun on the porch slows us down as well and allows us to span the polarities we think stand among us. As we spin, we hear ourselves speak our desires for Surprise Valley. The labels that we have secretly attached to one another no longer matter much. What matters is the fact that we all live in this place and that we care about it, and how well we coax the fibers to twine and bind and hold.

I think of the Ladies Club when Bettie, Noreen, and I get together to clean the fire hall. Every year we talk about starting it up again, about reinstating the Easter Ham Dinner, but we never do. Peggy's funeral was small. Eva is in a rest home in the Central Valley near her grandchildren. Madeline moved with her husband down to Cottonwood to be nearer the big hospitals when her health failed. So did Dorothy and Ollie. Bettie will be seventy-eight this fall.

⟜

One day several years ago as I entered her yellow flowered kitchen she chortled, "Come over here and look!" She bent down and lifted a small cardboard box. I was always happy to see her latest project, "girl job" or otherwise. She put the box on a kitchen chair and pulled out some of her hand-painted china tiles. She set them in rows, four wide and four high, on the kitchen floor. Pieced together, a wreath of delicately painted yellow roses twined with wisteria circled the tiles. In the center of the wreath were the words:

Bettie Parman
Born October 2, 1923
Died ———

"Isn't that pretty?" she asked. "I just didn't want Joe and the rest of them to get me something ugly."

◦

Petunias and salvia line the entrance to Bettie's garden. Strawberries shelter under the big peach tree. Tomatoes, peppers, celery, and chard stand in perfect rows, crowns of beets purple beneath deep-green leaves. Bettie's garden is the biggest I have seen. And it is always tidy. In the summer, when you visit, she'll link her arm through yours and say, "Come and see my garden."

Some of what Bettie harvests she will put into one of her four freezers. Some she will can, the jars lining the shelves in her legendary basement cool room. Some she will give away. Much of the fruit in the pies for the Ladies Club desserts came from her garden. Some of her produce she will take to the farmers' market, held in Cedarville each Friday afternoon on the shady side of the hospital. Nurses will bring the elderly people out from the convalescent wing and park them in their wheelchairs beside the tables stacked with homegrown produce and baked goods to spend an afternoon in the shade in the company of the community surrounding them. Bettie's table is always loaded.

Each time I visit the Parman Ranch, I vow I will care for my garden with the devotion Bettie gives to hers. But if her garden is a testimony to vision and order, mine subscribes to something closer to anarchy. Bettie's rows are tidy; the flowers and vegetables consort with their own kind. I have weeds—and not a lot of control. I have a propensity to let my cosmos volunteer in the middle of the rows of sweet corn. Calendulas pop up with the spinach, marigolds wander through the tomatoes, my flowers and vegetables all mixed up in a sort of exuberant garden stew. But when I look closely, most of my vegetables are big and healthy, too.

I love to push the corn aside to make my way to the center of the patch.

Hidden by the tall stalks I stand and listen to the bees hum in the middle of the incessant rustling of the corn leaves. Or I lean close to the tomatoes so I can see distinctly each golden whisker growing on the leaves and stems. I find the round yellow spiders that hide camouflaged on the yellow irises in the spring. And despite my weeds and the chaos of my plantings, when Bettie comes by in the summer, I link arms with her and say, "Come look at my garden."

✤ Fire Hall

WE HAVE A SECOND PHONE IN OUR HOUSE. MOSTLY IT SQUATS, SILENT, gathering dust at the far end of the bookshelf by the east window. Behind it, a dog-eared list holds the names of the members of the Lake City Volunteer Fire Department. The phone is an old beige Princess model that Lynn pieced together from the box of salvaged phone parts stored in the white shed, along with the other detritus he considers indispensable to life in Lake City.

It's easy to recognize the difference between the ring of the fire phone and that of our personal one. The wiring to the fire phone trips the big siren mounted on the pole above the red roof of the fire hall on the hill under the cemetery. The whir of the siren whines, gathers speed, climbs in pitch, ripping into the quiet of our town. If none of the three of us with fire phones in our houses makes it to the phone before the third ring, all the dogs in Lake City, all forty-two of them, begin howling in unison with each scream of the siren.

When I do get to the phone, I answer, "Lake City Fire Department." Most of the time, when I pick it up it is either a wrong number, or a salesman asking to speak to the fire chief. I am annoyed then—for myself, for the dogs, for the napping children all over town, and for everyone else who has been slammed awake by the siren, that high-decibel announcement of crisis and danger.

"When you call this number, you set off the emergency siren all over town," I say. "You need to call the chief at home. He'll be out in the field, so try him later, at noon." Then I give them Johnny's number.

The callers always apologize, especially the salesmen. I secretly delight in this small revenge for having disturbed us all. And I take secret pride in the sanctity of my position as a member of a volunteer fire department, the group that most symbolizes for me the community that I have found here, a community that is palpable in my gut. The fact that we have only ourselves to rely on.

But, sometimes, the voice on the other end is not an insurance agent.

July and August sear the greens of early summer; grass and leaves turn ocher. It is then that the first whiff of smoke will pull me from the house out into the dry heat. I pace up toward the mouth of the canyon, down to the fields, sniffing, seeking the origin of the elusive puff. Usually the smoke comes from forest fires far to the west of us, fires that can mask the sun for days and paint it red. We have the most beautiful sunsets then, although the smoke reddens our eyes. The ruby light is like a painting by Turner. But the odor of smoke makes the light seem glaring; the burnished landscape looks apocalyptic to me. The horses and cows graze in it normally enough though, somehow knowing that such fires are far away and hold no threat to us here in the valley.

Lynn works now for the BLM as a field archaeologist. Jason moved back to Lake City after college and married Michelle. For a few years they lived just down the street from us and worked for the Forest Service. Range fires and forest fires on the public lands took the three of them from home for long days and nights. Instead of attending to their normal duties of biology and archaeology, they were pressed into the ranks of firefighters. Alone at home, I listened anxiously to the scanner in the kitchen, relieved when I could identify one of their voices in amongst all the fire chatter and hear that for the moment at least one of them was safe.

Sometimes fire burns nearer, and we watch it on the rim of the valley, burning through the sage to the east, or the timber on the west. We watch that it comes no closer. In Lake City, we are the most vulnerable to fire of the four valley towns. Here, the timber pokes a long finger into Lake City and crooks it along the creek as if to reach down through the narrow mouth of the canyon and pull us into the mountains. Or point the way for fire to burn right down into the town.

In the last few years we have been lucky: the daytime calls have reported only grass fires. When more than one of the three of us with fire phones answers, one starts calling at the top of the list, the other from the bottom. If the third catches the call, that person makes a fast run up to the fire hall to sound the alarm, to open the big garage doors, to start up a truck, and to wait for the department members to show up, one by one, as they are pulled from the field or a job by the warning of the siren wailing out over the valley, or by a phone call telling them of fire.

An August day: I hear the first ring of the beige phone from my garden where I am picking tomatoes. And then the siren kicks in. Pete and Feather lay their heads back, muzzles in the air. As if they remember their genetic coding, they howl like wolves in unison with the telephone and the siren as I race to the house. I don't bother to kick off my muddy sandals at the door. I grab the phone. "Lake City Fire Department." I am out of breath.

"We have a grass fire up at the old Parman place." The speaker is as breathless as I am. "On the west side of the road."

"We'll be there," I call into the phone to the click of them hanging up, the line already silent.

The west side of the road is the uphill side, the mountain side, the side where all the timber is. We know what can happen if fire gets into the dry August timber.

This day, I am the only one at home to answer the fire phone.

I gun my old truck with a cold start up to the fire hall and park it off to the side of the tarmac apron to keep it out of the way of the engines. Urgency makes me nervous, shaky. My heart pounds. For the umpteenth time I think, *stay calm, stay calm,* and know that I am the wrong person for this job. I lean on the siren button, an old doorbell salvaged from who-knows-where and installed by one of the men. I listen to the siren start to blow and pick up decibels, unbelievably loud in the still day. I am embarrassed that I am the cause of such a noise. I'm always afraid of being seen as a hysterical woman. I know that it is good to be calm in an emergency. But how can I stay calm with the sound that I am making? I lean on the little black button, and the sound that surges out in four long waves is surely hysterical.

I wait. A short pause. I lean again. Four more long screams blast out of the horn-shaped loudspeakers at the top of the pole above me. Another momentary pause and then, again, I push, and the alarm shrieks out over the town. It brings them in.

First Gary's blue pickup slides to a stop in the gravel next to mine. He helps me open the big heavy doors, too heavy for me to lift on my own. The garage door hangs precariously overhead at the entrance to the bay where the old '46 Ford is parked, a beautiful storybook fire engine with only fifteen hundred original miles on it. I keep my eye on the heavy door. I am sure that it will fall and slam one of us on the head. Gary heaves himself into the truck, the mainstay for the department, and starts it up, a complicated process of knobs and switches, clutching and gas. I scrawl the location of the fire on the blackboard that hangs hot in the August sun next to the alarm button just outside the Ford's bay door. I punch on the alarm again. Four more blasts of the siren.

Timothy shows up next, his red-and-white pickup bristling with the tools he uses as the current keeper of the cemetery. He moves slowly, but it is deceptive, for the sharpness of his eyes shows his attention to the moment. And then Jeff. They fire up the chief's blue one-ton. Scotty jumps in and the trucks head north, on County Road 1, each with the two people required before a truck can roll.

I wait as the others straggle in. Ferrol shows up, and Clevon and Anola. All too old to fight fire, they ask and talk and wait at the edge of the tarmac.

Inside the truck bay, the phone rings. I catch it before the siren can do more than whir. "Lake City Fire Department," I answer.

"This is Shanks. We have a grass fire up in front of our place. On the west side of the road." I lean on the siren and cram the new information about the second fire beside the first on the little blackboard.

Bucky and Jim pull up. I tell them we have another fire. They start up the small tanker and head north.

The phone rings again; the siren whines. This time I hear, "This is the Sheriff's Department. We have a fire reported on County Road 1, about three miles north of Lake City. It's on the west side of the road." I lean on the button again. More people show up. The siren this often is not a good sign on a hot August day.

We already have two trucks out. We're supposed to keep at least one on standby at the hall. Another truck leaves. I ask the sheriff to notify the BLM fire station in Cedarville. The sheriff tells me that Garth has already sent one of the big, acid-yellow government trucks.

A few minutes later the phone rings yet another time. "We have a fire. It's a grass fire, on County Road 1, down by Bullen's on the west side of the road." I mash the black button and the siren shrieks again. We call and the Forest Service is now in on the act. They, too, send a truck. As our department keeps arriving, one by one from outlying ranches, people grab shovels off the rack in the truck bay and jump into their own trucks. We have sent all we can.

Once more the phone rings. A fifth fire is called in, just down the road from the last, on County Road 1, on the west side of the road. The BLM sends another engine. We listen to the radio crackle as ours and the others report in. People talk in little knots outside the fire hall. Some of us mouth the word *arson*. Someone must have set those fires.

We are lucky. The fifth fire is the last. Because it is an absolutely still day, not a breath of wind, all the fires are contained, put out before they can do more than scorch some power poles and fence posts.

↔

It is the sheriff who spots the hired hand from the White Ranch on his way from the leased ground to the home ranch a few miles away. On his slow journey south, his old tractor has farted and popped, blowing out hot bits of exhaust and smoking diesel, igniting little fires all along the way, all along the west side of County Road 1.

When one by one the trucks pull back into the fire hall, the jokes fly, a relief from the fears that a stranger or, worse yet, one of our own has been deliberately trying to start the world burning.

It is a man's world again on the tarmac. They drain and fold and store the long canvas hoses. They back the trucks into the appointed slots in the bays. I go home thinking that it is at this moment that I belong most to the community. The rest of the time we try to remember our manners. But in emergencies we have only each other to rely on here. There is no one else. And today we are able once again to keep our own community secure, safe from harm.

This Mano, That Metate

A FEW DAYS AFTER CLARENCE DIED, HIS WIFE, JULIA, AND THEIR SEVEN children burned his belongings in the yard. I suppose that, as Paiute ritual instructed, they gathered some of his things, things that he touched every day, things that he was attached to. Or those things, perhaps, that he would need in the afterlife? What did they choose? I imagine them moving from room to room of the house: a certain chair, that shirt, yes, and the basket so-and-so wove for him.

I imagine it is the end of the day when they are done choosing and build the fire. I wonder after they light it if they speak the Paiute language or stand together silently in a circle, watching the fire burn orange, the colors fading from the day.

I don't ask Julia to tell me much about the burning. It is a private thing, and I know what my people have taken, and are still taking, from Julia's people without understanding anything and usually without asking. This morning she called to ask Lynn and me to come to her house to get a few belongings of Clarence's that she has picked out for my husband. So I sit in a chair at Julia's kitchen table beside Lynn, looking out the big window, and I wait for her to tell me what she wants to.

Modoc County Road 1 in California bends sharply to the east at the edge of the Fort Bidwell Northern Paiute Reservation, and for at least twenty-five years from their house on the hill overlooking the turn, Clarence and Julia have been the first to see any visitors to the reservation coming from the south. The kitchen window holds the whole sweep of Surprise Valley, so vast only Upper Lake is visible, the other two playas lost behind the horizon and the curvature of the earth down the long middle of the valley. I think to myself that they really do see the big picture from here. This is the place the Paiutes call *Yamosza*, the northern end of our valley. This is their home.

Julia tells Lynn and me about her heart and her chest pains, about the helicopter that had flown her out to the hospital a few days after Clarence's memorial. She tells me not to worry; she is resting and eating well again. Today she presides at the head of her kitchen table; the small and birdlike widow I saw at the service for Clarence is gone.

But her fingers stray to the ragged edges of her hair. It is much shorter than usual. "I need to get a permanent," she says. "We all cut our hair off." *In mourning for Clarence* is the part she does not need to add, the part I understand.

Julia's granddaughter Amber pulls herself to her feet from her teenage slouch in Clarence's big Naugahyde armchair. The curtains in the living room have been pulled shut to block the day's glare on the big TV set in the corner. She stretches. "I am going now, Grandma," she says.

"Okay. Tell me when Cheyenne is coming to stay," Julia calls out as Amber goes through the front door.

"Amber has been here for a week. Then Cheyenne started whining that he wanted to go stay with Grandma," she laughs, "so I told them it was his turn to come after Thursday." I am happy the grandkids are taking turns staying with her, happy to know she is not left alone.

We sit together and share stories about our memories of Clarence. The window looks out over the half-burned, charred pile in the yard. We talk a little about the burning, and she tells us that she has given away a lot of Clarence's things to his children and friends. I tell her that I think burning possessions makes a lot more sense than survivors fighting over the scraps left behind.

Julia mentions she has given Clarence's prized collection of Conan the Barbarian comics to their oldest son, Jerome, always referred to by Clarence as his number-one son. I imagine Clarence poring over the comics. He always claimed he did not read. I never knew if he was joking or not, but now I think of Julia telling us that Amber had stayed with him at the hospital so that Clarence would have someone to read the menu to him. She tells me he was going blind, a result of the adult-onset diabetes that claims so many Native American elders. Yet, Clarence was the tribal storyteller. Now I suddenly realize my error—and the cultural bias carried so deep I hadn't even known it was there: that stories and reading always go together.

Some of the stories Clarence told us he asked me to write down. I loved the way he told them in ever widening circles, around and around, each time around picking up something new and pulling it in. I taped them and then I wrote them down exactly the way that he told them. He asked me to try to get them published, but each time we were ready, he came by our house, and over coffee, eventually, he would let me know the family didn't want them to be printed.

Each time Clarence stopped by, he said that those white families who figure in the Paiute histories, they know the stories, too. Some of their past is held in heart wrenchers, in the terrifying memories of the Paiutes that rub against the cowboy stories and the forty-niner stories and the stories of the settlers who came from the east. Those white families, he said, still live here. And I could see his fear.

‑‑

It was a Friday. Julia called in the dark of early morning.

"Clarence is gone," she told Lynn. He had died just an hour before in the Redding Hospital ICU, having never regained consciousness after two emergency surgeries the week before.

The following Monday, a long line of people filed into the tribal basketball gym at the reservation—so many people that the service for Clarence had to begin while we were still waiting at the entrance to sign the guest book.

Inside the gym, Clarence's family, friends, and acquaintances had already filled every folding chair in every one of the rows set out on the polished wood of the court. Lynn and I saw a couple of empty spaces high up in the bleachers. Whispering excuse-me's, we worked our way up, sat, and leaned our backs against the cool, tan-colored wall. So many people. At least four hundred. And among all those faces, almost as many Anglo as Paiute. I was glad for Julia, glad for Clarence that so many came.

Down on the court up front, Clarence's cousins played country western songs on twangy electric guitars. On a long folding table were Clarence's mementos and photos, most from the army or from sports. In the first row was Julia with her seven children, the two men and the five women, all grown with families of their own. Julia sat between her two oldest daughters and looked very small, the others spread out next to them, her youngest son at the far end of the row.

I sat next to Lynn, thinking how appropriate it was to have the service here in the gym, remembering how I met Clarence.

⌒

When the little red Datsun pickup stuttered up to our house, the noise pulled me to the front door.

"Is the boy ready?" Clarence called out the open window. The volunteer coach had kindly stopped by on his way down from Fort Bidwell to pick up my son up for sixth-grade basketball practice in Cedarville.

What I saw was a broad Paiute face, an enormous grin, and as Jason opened the passenger side door, I saw Clarence bend over, reach down, grunt a little, tug, straighten up, and toss his left boot out the window. It sailed up and back and landed in the pickup bed behind him, immediately followed by his other boot.

"My feet hurt," he called out in explanation. Another grin and the little pickup roared and sputtered away, muffler hanging loose.

Lynn and I have never been sports fans—all that fuss over a *ball?* And while we did not dutifully attend every one of Jason's basketball games, I had a sense back then, sixteen years ago, that Jason was not particularly gung ho about his sports career either.

We saw the reason on the day Lynn and I drove over to Alturas for the intramural tournament, the season finals.

The teams from the smallest rural schools were scheduled to play first. Jason's team from Surprise Valley was surely the smallest of the small: only four boys out of eleven sixth graders attended his school that year. To make a complete team Clarence had recruited some of the girls and even a few fifth-grade boys who stood a good six or eight inches shorter than their smallest opponents.

I knew Jason would be watching for us in the stands, so I tried to hide my smile when the kids filed out onto the court. But I could hardly help it. They looked so *little,* so disoriented and helpless out there on that great plain of varnished wood under the harsh fluorescent lights. Especially the girls who stood slump shouldered, toeing the floor, not looking up. Looking up would have meant seeing that the other girls in the noisy gym were wearing cheerleader outfits and shaking their big pom-poms, rehearsing for the main events later in the day.

This will be over fast, I thought. *We'll be back home in no time.*

The whistle blew and the game started. Both teams were clumsy and slow, but Jason's was clearly the least coordinated. Down on the front bleacher sat Clarence in his cowboy hat, scuffed boots, and faded blue jeans. He was short of stature but had the massive shoulders, barrel chest, and slim hips of a man much younger than his sixty years. He didn't seem worried. He wore a big grin. He was obviously enjoying himself. The minutes passed. Neither team was scoring much, but when it was all over, somehow Surprise Valley had won.

Before the next game started, Clarence called the kids all over to the bleacher. They leaned into his words with the anxious determination of a tone-deaf choir about to go for six-part harmony. But when the kids bolted back onto the court they wore grins as big as Clarence's.

Now I noticed the kids were rolling the ball instead of dribbling. A good thing, I thought: in the first game none of them had been particularly proficient at keeping the ball bouncing in a planned trajectory. And then I noticed something else: the kids were having *fun.*

So Lynn and I settled in for the long haul, and Clarence's little-team-that-could kept winning. Three games and two hours later, they had the title for their own league.

But now Jason's team would play the larger schools in the district. Schools with more than one sixth-grade class, schools with big, muscular boys who lived close enough to town to stay after school and practice. These boys looked balanced and familiar with the basketball. These boys swaggered and sneered. They were obviously going to smear the motley team from Surprise Valley, the team with girls, and little fifth graders. But soon into the game—soon into every game—a sort of desperation would take over the apparently stronger team. They messed up. They couldn't score.

Clarence just sat on the bench and grinned. He laughed out loud. He laughed when our team got possession of the ball; he laughed when they tripped and lost it; he laughed when they rolled the ball instead of dribbled it.

And he laughed when they won. Game after game after game, he laughed.

I asked Jason later how they had managed it. I had half convinced myself that Clarence had performed some sort of Native American hocus-pocus, but no. Jason said Clarence had simply told them to pick out the best player on the opposing team. Their only goal was to make that one player *mad*. Clarence knew they would win if they could accomplish that one thing.

⊷

When Clarence told stories, Julia's hands would lie still as if they listened as well as her ears.

He told the stories of his childhood, his family, and his friends; he told the traditional stories he remembered the telling of, and the stories about the time before people. He told them to the children, to anyone who asked. He said once that it would take four years of storytelling just to get to the place where human beings showed up, if those traditional stories were told properly; four whole years of evenings, listening and learning about animals like coyote and hummingbird and rabbit and wolf before you even *thought* about the two-legged kind.

Sometimes Julia would tell stories, too. She told me that when she was ten, she and her little sister survived three months of winter, living alone in their house. She told me they would not have made it through that bitter winter if the storekeeper hadn't given them food. But these stories she pulls out from between her teeth with effort and with anger, so I don't ever ask her for them.

⊷

Our second year in Surprise Valley, Lynn and I came to know another couple who, like us, were newcomers. The man was Caucasian and worked for a time at the reservation. His wife was Native American of southwest and northwest tribal heritages.

One evening over dinner, the woman explained her scorn for the Paiutes, this tribe so unlike her own sheep people and salmon people. She described a shopping trip to Klamath Falls, how everywhere they drove the Paiute women she was with said this was the place you could get good milk shakes, this the place for good fruit, that one the place where the pie melted in your mouth. All they talked about was eating. How stupid she found these Paiute women and their incessant recognition of where to find food!

I kept my mouth shut. But after dinner, after that evening, I thought about this woman's words. Lynn and I had started our long forays out into the empty Nevada places that lie to the east of us. Whenever we would take a day to park the truck, to wander out and explore until thirst and hunger and dark drove us back, I would look at the obsidian glinting on the ground, and I would look at the sage, at the creosote brush, at the thin stands of Great Basin wild rye and the few patches of rice grass. I would marvel at the livelihood that the Paiutes had been able to find here where I knew I would surely starve if left.

I thought about what that woman had said about the Paiutes she had traveled to town with, and I thought how absolutely appropriate it was for those who had lived here more than a century ago, before the big wagons lumbered out of the east, before the diseases and the guns and the laws took it all away from them, how appropriate it was for those people to know absolutely and to share the telling of those good-food places. All the traditional names for the territories of the different Paiute bands honor the principal animals that sustained the people of that region: the cui-ui eaters, the rockchuck eaters, the jackrabbit eaters, and the deer eaters.

Lynn and I have come to know a few of the native plants, and we have dug and tasted their sweet roots. Now we can see more of the garden that is still hidden here. We have been lucky enough to take the freedom to wander, to learn.

Over the years friends from Fort Bidwell have told us some of what they know, some of what they remember being told to them: how their parents were afraid to leave the reservation. Sixty and seventy years ago their parents were told the bounty for a Paiute found off the reservation was fifty cents; jokingly, of course, but it was one of those jokes that clearly told them where their place was. They listened to their parents who told only of the old special places but did not take their children there, afraid as they were to leave the reservation.

↦

There is an old picture I have seen reproduced in an issue of the *Modoc Historical Journal*. It is a picture of the Fort Bidwell Indian School students, taken in 1934. At the far right in the back row of children, ten-year-old Clarence leans against the white clapboard wall of the schoolhouse. His black hair is cropped short and shiny. He squints into the winter sun. He grins into the camera.

In front of the bib of his denim overalls, he cradles his right hand in his left palm. Clarence liked to tell me that he learned English the hard way, that he would teach me to speak Paiute the way he learned English. He learned English by going to the Fort Bidwell Indian School and getting his hand broken. On his second day. For having known and spoken only Paiute until the day before, the day before his right hand was struck and broken by his first white teacher. Because Clarence didn't understand the English instructions spoken to him on his second day of school.

The other Paiute students tip their heads down out of the glare of the sun. They remember Clarence's second day at the school, too, each of them in the picture, standing in the snow of that 1934 winter day.

‹›

Julia told Lynn that her kids had taken what they wanted; she showed him what she had kept for him: just a few things, but special, like one of the surveying tools that Clarence had used when he worked for the Forest Service. Julia also wanted Lynn to have the videotapes he and Clarence had made a few years before in an attempt to stop some of the looting of Native American graves and archaeological sites—looting that is ongoing in the valley.

Yesterday I watched one of the homemade videotapes. The camera jiggled when it panned the width of the valley from Eagle Peak on the north to Bidwell Mountain. Then, jerkily, it zoomed in on the dirt mounds made by the looters, heaps left after they had screened the soil for artifacts.

Lynn and Clarence had stopped first that day to film a dune-village site on the east side of the valley near some hot springs, a place that most certainly had been inhabited year round. The whole large, hundred-acre site is now a tumultuous jumble of shoveled holes, caved in excavations and screened dirt humped in piles to the side. Burnt bone fragment, both thin-walled bird and thick, large ungulate pieces, mingles with bits of charcoal in the sand. Fire-cracked rock, broken manos and metates, flakes of shiny black obsidian, and colorful chert litter the ground. There are no whole, unbroken artifacts. The looters have stolen all of those.

Even though it is illegal, a traditional Saturday-afternoon pastime for many Anglo families in Surprise Valley is to go out and look for arrowheads. To most it is a hobby. The arrowheads they bag will be artfully arranged in a frame, in the shape of an eagle perhaps, and displayed on a living room wall. Others will sell the artifacts in an illegal but poorly monitored and lucrative market.

In the video Clarence points and names the things on the ground. "See, over there they threw away these two pieces of this platter, this metate." He picks the pieces up and cradles them in his hands for a few moments. He puts them back gently, exactly where they lay. "They were probably digging in a grave. The metate is broken. That is what we do with things when someone dies," he says. "We break their things, or we burn them."

I listen to the timbre of his voice on the tape. The broken sound of his voice speaks his devastation over the desecration of this place where his people once cooked, split willow for baskets, played with their children, flaked stone tools, ground seeds into meal, danced, sang, slept, ate, lived, and died.

Later in the tape Clarence attempts some humor: he pretends to be a Paiute on the hunt for Anglo artifacts. "*I* know!" he says. "Let's go back to Lake City! We can dig in the cemetery there! I know which grave! I know which one to dig! I saw the diamonds on her hand." His joke is like a knife, driving home the dishonor of all the thieves who have looted this old village site.

All through the tape I watch Lynn wander with Clarence, pointing and bending and picking up things to look at together. Now it is my husband's turn to speak: archaeologists and geologists, they sometimes see a bigger picture than the rest of us do. Patiently Lynn explains to the camera what the artifacts can tell us if left in place. "If an artifact is taken from the site," he says, "it is like a page torn from a book. The story needs the other pages, the context in which the artifacts are found, intact, if a whole story is to be told. How did people make a living here?" Lynn asks. "What was the climate like? What can we expect from the future?"

Suddenly, watching the tape, I see from Lynn's perspective. I see the beginning of an answer to my question: do I really belong to the community here? At first, though, my answer comes in the form of more questions: Which community is it that I belong to? Do I belong to the ranching community that for the moment claims the definition of community in this valley? Do I belong to the community of Clarence's people who claimed it once and who live here still? Do I belong to the growing Hispanic community moving in to harvest the garlic that is replacing some of the alfalfa in the fields recently bought or leased by big, absentee agribusiness speculators? Or is the community here even more amorphous than I realize?

Isn't any community just an odd assortment of strange and disparate individuals who happen to share the same space? The family shares a house. The families share a village. The villages share a region. In Lynn's archaeologist's eye, cities grow and die. Settlements and cultures ebb and flow over time. We all share the world. At best we are lucky if we can share a vision of how it is that we plan to continue our community, all parts of it, into the future.

It is whatever place we are in that forms us. Like it or not, it is this place and its rhythms that should shape the community that occupies it. If this community doesn't listen to the place, then the community's tenure here will be short.

I know then that Lynn and I will be here, in Surprise Valley, for the rest of our lives. The seasons, the shapes and smells and sounds of here, surround us. The special friendships shared here, those are the belonging that I have found. I belong to this place; it doesn't belong to me. That is the order of things that finally makes sense to me, watching the tapes that Clarence has left behind.

⟁

One day when Clarence and Julia were sitting with us at our kitchen table instead of theirs, Julia told Clarence he and Lynn should try to find that rock where the water is inside, where you can dip it out, and no matter how fast you dip from the water inside the rock, the level always stays the same. So later that summer when the hills had turned hot and they thought all the mud dry and the roads open, my husband and Julia's husband set off together. Clarence said he thought he could find the way.

The road was overgrown, barely visible as it threaded through the sage and the lava rock. Frequently it disappeared altogether, and they would stop the Scout to sweep the sage with their eyes, scanning for the track that Clarence remembered. Then, finding the faint trace, they would resume their progress, the truck barely crawling through the rough country. Clarence told Lynn how his father had talked of this place, how the old people had maintained it, kept it hidden, never revealed the secret place of it, the secret of that water in the high lava country where the springs were far from each other and the walks from one place to another were dry and long. It was the one place his father had taken him to see when Clarence was very small.

The truck crept along, lurching up and over the rocks hidden by the heavy growth of brush. Finally, Clarence lifted his left hand, fingers outspread, palm facing the windshield. This was the place.

Together they left the truck, Lynn a few paces behind, to the side, as they walked up the gentle rise to the outcropping of the black, lichen-encrusted rocks on the skyline. It looked just like all the others in that country, undefined, one pile of rock indistinguishable from the other. Undefined, except that this one might have a litter of shiny black flakes scattered in the center where the rocks ringed the hard, chalky soil. That one might have two rocks, one stacked carefully on top of the other, so long ago the lichen had mortared the two together. These were signals that Lynn understood, showing that this or that outcropping had been chosen for some reason now invisible as the spot to stoop, perhaps, to take one of those palm-size round flakes of obsidian from a fiber bag or a basket, and sit to press the small, refined tertiary flakes from its edge with the tip of an antler; to fashion it into a point for killing or a blade for scraping; for whatever purpose that, to Lynn's trained eye, is presented by that particular heap of scab rock, a purpose long forgotten.

When Clarence and Lynn reached the outcrop, there were head-size and larger boulders scattered randomly, the larger bedrock chunks embedded deep in the hardened basalt that underlay the thin, light-colored soil. Clarence pointed to one large, flattish stone that overlay another in the jumble of rocks before them.

"That one. Lift that one off."

Lynn bent and grasped the rough surface on each side of the rock and lifted. The big stone tugged free, and underneath, in the hollow of the bottom rock, the sky quivered, reflected in the clear water pooled there, still, quiet, and cold. They dipped with a cup Clarence had brought, and tasted the coolness and cleanliness of it. They dipped and dipped and always the water level stayed the same, the wet ring at the edge of the tiny pool memorized by the stone.

I listened to the story that Lynn told of that day, and I wondered: Had the old ones known then that we white people were coming, that water here would become something to be owned, to be controlled, to be bought, and to be sold? Or was it simply that this place taught the old Paiutes the preciousness of water and to protect it against the dry times that will surely come again?

♻

Another one of the Paiute attributes sneered at by the woman we knew: she said the Paiutes had no word for *family*. I kept my mouth shut then, too. Would she have listened if I had contradicted her?

Ethnography and archaeology tell us that the Paiutes lived in small bands. They rarely collected in big tribal gathers the way the peoples of gentler landscapes did. This meager land could not have sustained them if they had. Would she have listened if I talked of how those small, nomadic family groups survived because of the careful way they moved over the ground? If I had told her that the Paiutes did not need a word for *family* because most everyone an individual would see in a lifetime was, by simply being there, a family member? Clarence spoke about children taken in and raised in the Paiute way by people to whom they were not tied by blood in the way we know it, but who were never called by other than family names and who were never considered other-than-family.

Now that Clarence is dead, I remember this again, how large the idea of family can be, and I think of how we went with Clarence one day to the top of a mountain Lynn knows. My husband wanted to show Clarence an obsidian source. To help his understanding of what he sees in the field as an archaeologist, Lynn has come to be proficient at replicating obsidian projectile points.

I have complained on occasion that Lynn isn't the type to bring me roses. I forget all that when I am in my garden and I find one of the thin, sharp points he has made and hidden there. He tucks them under the big leaves of squash plants, or hides them at the edge of the tomato row as a surprise for me to find, and for the kids who come to visit us.

Clarence, on the other hand, made blue arrowheads out of Milk of Magnesia bottle glass. He called them poison arrowheads and said that if you get hit with one of them you will shit yourself to death. Occasionally Clarence came by the house to borrow one of the obsidian points that Lynn had made. Clarence teased us. He called us Anglos "the boat people." And we teased him back; we said, *Look. This old Paiute has to come to the boat people for his arrowheads.*

Gradually, Clarence became interested in using obsidian instead of colored glass. When the University of Nevada archaeology students came up here every year for their field school, Clarence kept his sense of humor intact by salting the sites they were working on with his "new and genuine Paiute arrowheads": some made of ruby glass, some of milk glass, some of kelly-green wine-bottle glass, and some of black, translucent obsidian.

That fall day up on the mountain, Lynn and Clarence busted up big obsidian cobbles together, collecting only the results of those that split apart just right. I listened to their mutters of satisfaction when they whacked off one of the big, flat, round flakes they would take home with them.

But the obsidian source was our second stop: the first was at the end of a detour Clarence suggested, up and around the top of the mountain, homing in on the trail he remembered. We found the track, winding to the peak where the big cliffs face east, overlooking all of Surprise Valley. We got out of the Scout and stood transfixed above a flight of sandhill cranes, trumpeting their hollow, ratchety calls to each other, wheeling on a thermal current below. We watched as they rose higher, higher still over us until we almost lost sight of them. Then lining out in a big V, the birds slipped out of sight, over the top of Bald Mountain to begin the first leg of the long flight south to the Central Valley and their wintering ground in the rice fields there.

That day thirteen years ago, Clarence had looked hard at me, hesitated and then had chosen his words carefully. "How old are you now?"

"Forty-two," I told him.

Clarence shook his head. "I'm sorry, but that means you can't come with us. You'll have to wait here."

I turned away then so I would not see where Lynn and Clarence disappeared over the edge of the scarp that jutted out over a ledge and the pines, little pines of great age, twisted by the winds that had stunted them.

I pulled my drawing supplies out of the box in the Scout and walked down in the other direction to where the big cliffs turn and face north up toward Bidwell Mountain, hazy and pale blue in the distance. I sat down on a rock to draw and lost myself in all of the space below me, funneling it through my eyes and into my hand and onto the paper tablet on my lap.

Later, I heard their voices coming up the cliff with the wind as they returned. I heard Clarence tell Lynn to take fat, animal fat, to the place they had been and to burn it there from time to time. I heard him tell Lynn that the younger people on the reservation were not interested in this old stuff. I waited until I heard the groan of the Scout's sticky driver's-side door before I turned around, shut my tablet, and stood.

✎ Chicken

I WALKED DOWN OUR STREET, SOUTH WATER STREET, ALONG THE EDGE of what serves as Lake City's town park, a city block–long strip of over-grown land on either side of the south fork of Mill Creek. Early summer, early morning to Jason and Michelle's place, only a hundred yards from ours. Twice a day I went, through their front gate, around to the back to the chicken yard to let their two hens and the rooster out to scratch and dig for bugs and seeds, luring them in each night with corn tossed into their run.

Jason and Michelle were living temporarily in Burney, eighty miles away, working as environmental monitors for a fiber-optic cable installation through the heart of California, jobs that paid more than the only jobs available here: seasonal-temporary work with the Forest Service or BLM. I knew they were talking about starting a family, buying a house.

The chicken coop doubled as a woodshed, and I noticed that only four tiers of wood remained stacked in the corner against the wall. The kids would not need to cut their winter wood in the fall. This winter, they would come back to the old house where they were married two years ago only for visits, only for an occasional weekend.

Our woodshed was not empty either. It was an easy winter last year, and we didn't burn all we had gathered. Lynn is fifty-eight. I am fifty-five. How many years will we still insist on going up into the mountains above Lake

City to cut dry lodgepole to load into our yellow dump truck? The truck is neither licensed nor insured. We drive it only three times a year up that tortuous, winding canyon road. At home Lynn splits the rounds and I stack the wood in the woodshed on the end of the big shop we built the summer Jason was thirteen.

Eighty miles to the west of Surprise Valley, Michelle and Jason were watching what amounts to a rope of light being laid down under the ground, a rope that can carry a seemingly infinite number of images and pictures and data over miles of empty land. At the end of that rope of light might be a house like ours or this one my son and his wife lived in. I realized suddenly that in this high-tech computer age Jason has never known a house with central heating. He has lived only with wood-burning stoves. He and Michelle might well choose not waking to a lifetime of winter mornings like those of Surprise Valley's, down to twenty below and colder, when a person builds a fire fast and then hugs the stove for the first couple of cups of coffee. The two of them were swinging somehow on that rope of light between worlds: between the remote, rural lifestyle and ideology chosen by parents who came of age reading Gary Snyder and Wendell Berry, and the larger world outside our valley that is their inheritance as well.

In a way I have Lynn to thank for Jason's adaptability. Lynn values tools. He hates dogma. He sees no contradiction in the fact that our only heat comes from a woodstove and that a computer links us to the world. Both are tools, he says, and each is appropriate to our particular place and time.

Jason and Michelle's house was called the rat house by the town before they fixed the foundation, tore out walls, built a kitchen addition with lots of glass and French doors. Jason planed the old wood floors and polished them until they gleamed, Michelle planted flowers and a garden, and they had a wedding in their big backyard looking out on the pastures and valley beyond. They needed to leave here to find work, their own place in the world. I was trying to accept this decision.

෴

Jason's ax and chopping block were near the entrance of the chicken house. But those tools were not for the demise of these chickens. They would enjoy natural deaths. I knew this because I know my son.

Four years ago and just out of college and working for the Forest Service, Jason was living as a bachelor in the old rat house that had not yet been renovated. He still ate many of his meals with us at our house, and he shared my garden. Jason had always loved to help me in the garden. When he was three he hauled the weeds I pulled from the rows to the compost heap off to the side. All summer, back and forth on his knees, he crawled, behind his yellow Tonka truck piled high with wilting dandelions, chicory, and button weed, spluttering a loose-lipped approximation of the appropriate diesel-dump-truck sound effect, revving up when he had to push the truck up over the little rise of each row he crossed on his way to the compost heap. He helped to dig the potatoes, pick the peas and tomatoes, pull the carrots, and braid up the onions and brightly colored Mandan corn to hang on the wall. In January when the cob would loosen its hold on the kernels, we rubbed the kernels off, rattling, into a stainless-steel bowl and took them out to the shop where we ground them into meal for our cornbread.

We had a largely vegetarian diet then. The vegetables we ate came from dirt we tilled and tended; I was pleased that Jason was growing up knowing this.

One day, when he was close to turning four, though, I cooked a big pot roast. The smell of it had filled the house all afternoon, exotic and intoxicating in a way cooking vegetables could never be.

Sitting in his chair that evening, Jason started in enthusiastically on the unusual meal before him. Suddenly he lifted his spoon, waved it back and forth in front of his face, and grew thoughtful, chewing. "Sophie, where does this meat come from?" he asked.

"It came from a cow," I told him.

He ate a little more. He waved his spoon. "Sophie, how do you get meat off the cow?"

"They have to kill the cow."

He pushed the pieces of roast around on his plate with his spoon, examining them closely. He took another bite and chewed it slowly, considering. "Then we should thank this cow for giving us its body so that we will be strong."

✧

Four years ago, the year that Jason turned twenty-five, he and I decided to raise chickens. Not chickens to lay eggs, but chickens for meat, for us to grow, to butcher and wrap and put in our freezer for winter dinners. Bettie told us to get the white kind, Cornish Cross chickens. "Butchering size in eight weeks," she said.

I called the Co-op with our order: fifty chicks. Almost one chicken dinner a week for a year. Fifty Cornish Cross chicks. They would be delivered to the Co-op, and I could pick them up on Friday. That gave Jason and me the week to clean out the old shed behind his house. We started the job on Tuesday and found rotten walls, decayed sills, a door that wouldn't close, all hidden under the mud and junk surrounding the shed, a host of big fix-it jobs. We sawed splintery boards, pulled from the scrap lumber pile down at the edge of the field, and hammered them into place. But the chicken house wasn't ready by Friday. A cardboard box would have to do.

I cleared off the big table in Lynn's leather shop and put the box there, sides cut down so we could reach in to feed and water the chicks. It was risky business putting it there because Lynn had adamantly refused to participate in our chicken business. "No livestock!" he had said. He had once raised a pig, a pig for meat. Every morning the pig had come to the edge of the pigpen to be fed and snuffle and to gaze at Lynn with its little eyes, little pig eyes that looked so human. While Lynn drank his first cup of coffee, they had communed. Every day. Until the story was over. It did not have a happy ending. And so Jason and I knew better than to try to change Lynn's mind.

Friday was hot for April. I drove over the mountain to Alturas to collect my chicks. Hopelessly small balls of the palest yellow fluff, smaller than my fist, they peeped and scrabbled in the box on the backseat of my little blue car. I had to stop on Main Street in Cedarville to go to Page's Market, but I parked across the street so the car would have the benefit of shade. As I killed the engine, I saw Celesta in the rearview mirror crossing the street to meet me. Her face appeared in the window.

"Hi, Soph. Ooh! You have chicks. I can't believe it!" She knew Lynn's opinion about raising livestock.

I was happy to see Celesta, the daughter of close friends, a family who adheres to a strictly vegetarian diet. They raise chickens, but for the eggs, not for the meat. Embarking on the first day of my adventure in animal husbandry, I was deeply ashamed in my core to have Celesta, a young and pure innocent—and a vegetarian besides—witness to the sacrificial future of my chicks. It was a future I had ignored until that moment. I had thought "chicks." I had thought "meat" neatly wrapped and in our freezer, but I had jumped the bridge between the two thoughts. I hadn't made the connection. Well, I was connecting the two now, and all at once I was unsure.

Finally, home. In the big box, the fresh wood chips smell of the chopping block by the woodshed. The little chick watering dispenser, brand-new and pristine, a scale of tiny bubbles collecting on the red plastic. Little red chick feeders, full of chick starter. Scrabbling and tiny peeps leaked from the boxes we carried into the leather shop. The cats followed us, eager. We shut them out.

One by one, Jason and I lifted the tiny handfuls from their carrying boxes and placed them on the wood chips. We switched on the heat lamps and watched the chicks discover the three-by-three-foot universe that surrounded them. Every five to ten minutes I would run out to the leather shop to check on my brood. I tried to keep the bridge between chick and the freezer in mind as I peered down to watch them scratch in the litter, peeping, eating, sleeping, and pooping tiny chick droppings.

Four days later, I gloated over the top of the box, proud of their obvious growth under my care. I felt almost maternal. Then suddenly, I perceived myself as the giant troll in a Nordic folktale, waiting for the captive children to grow, feeling their legs and arms fattening, drooling over them, calling them "my pretties."

The smell helped harden me. A big cardboard box filled with fifty chicks accumulates a strong ammonia smell fast. And for some reason, this breed, these white Cornish Crosses, looked reptilian. The chick faces had the beady eyes of a snake or a lizard. Nothing about them reminded me of Easter chicks.

Then one sickened. Not moving, it huddled in a corner, not eating, not drinking, head hanging low, feathers ruffled out untidily away from the little body. The tiny wattles and comb turned purple. I removed it from the others, brought it inside, and put it near the warmth of the woodstove in its own small box. The efforts to feed and help it drink gentled my eye. The bridge looked more difficult again, the crossing from chick to freezer looked less negotiable as I tried to save this one.

The next morning I looked in the box by the stove. The little body had stiffened already, stretched out on its back, skin blue under the first pinfeathers. I buried it in the garden down by the yellow plum tree, just then blossoming, the branches misted white with the first promise of fruit.

I went to the library, sat at the computer, and scanned: *Chickens, diseases of.* I brought three books home and was overwhelmed with worry. So many diseases. Most were fatal, at least to a significant percentage of infected birds. So many of the diseases were communicable to humans.

Jason and I stepped up the work on the shed. Now that the chicken house was finished, we could move the chicks and build the fenced yard around them.

The birds had doubled in size in the eight days since I had picked them up at the Co-op. When we released them into the comparative vastness of the eight-foot-by-ten-foot chicken house, they huddled in a corner, the space too new, too large. But within a day they were exploring their new home, waddling jerkily over the whole floor. For the most part, they slept, huddled under the lights, two pools of growing chicken flesh, partly covered now with the first pins of new feathers poking through the fluff.

Each week another chick died, listless at first, wattles and combs darkening from healthy orange to purple. After I buried the fifth one, I called the county extension agent and got the number of a lab that specialized in chicken diseases at UC–Davis. The people at the lab told me to double bag the next one to die and mail it to them for a necropsy.

Within two days I was rummaging in the shop for a box that looked the right size. What had been a chick had become a chicken, close to full grown before it had turned purple and volunteered to be a specimen. I had found it that morning stretched out on its back in the litter of the chicken house, stiff and cold. By now a dull detachment over its fate had set in. I wrapped the dead bird in three plastic bags and packed it in the cardboard box padded with rumpled pages from our weekly county newspaper.

When I opened the door of my car for the drive into town, it felt like an oven in the early-June heat wave of that week. It was Thursday. Would UPS be able to deliver my package by the next day, Friday? Otherwise, my package would reek on a shelf in the UPS office, waiting in the Sacramento heat until the lab opened on Monday for delivery.

"No," Kim answered. "Our trucks won't get to Sacramento until tomorrow. Then it has to be sorted for delivery to Davis. It probably won't be delivered until Monday."

Back out I went to the hot sidewalk and turned up the street to the post office.

"Hi, Marge. I need to send a package Express Mail. Will it get to Davis tomorrow?"

"It should," she replied. Mercifully, she didn't ask me what was in the box. The postage was twenty-five dollars, but it was worth it to find out what was killing my chickens.

Monday morning the call came from the Davis lab. "Your chickens have round-heart disease. We don't know much about it, but it seems to be caused by oxygen deprivation in the egg stage at the hatchery and gives the animals a predisposition to congestive heart failure. That chicken of yours had a heart as big as a golf ball."

It wasn't contagious, then?

"No. But I'd cut my losses if I were you. I'd butcher those chickens as soon as possible."

The detour was over. I was approaching the bridge.

⟁

When Jason got home that night we talked. We knew better than to ask Lynn to help us. We hadn't lost any hens, so we figured they must be less susceptible to round-heart disease than the roosters. *Saturday,* we said.

Saturday we would butcher, we would kill, we would chop the heads off fifteen roosters.

We decided to do it out in the flood sand that had washed down with the winter storms that year, out behind Jason's house where the big cottonwoods had begun to tip over, one by one every few years in a strong wind.

Still not wanting after fifteen years to seem a newcomer, a townie, I was embarrassed to ask any of our neighbors how to gut a chicken. We had a book and we read it and looked at the pictures. We would figure it out on our own. I sharpened knives.

We knew how to kill them. Simple. Catch them, put a cord noose around their legs, and hang them upside down for a few minutes until the blood rushed to their brain. It was supposed to drug them, I read. Hammer two nails close together on the big stump. Put the chicken's neck between the two nails and stretch him out by his feet. Whack his head off with the hatchet. Simple.

The hatchet. I had forgotten the hatchet! I asked Lynn if he had a hatchet we could borrow. He reached up to the shelf above the workbench in the shop for the one that he had already sharpened for us. This was his one concession to our grisly enterprise.

Saturday morning I awoke. I lay still for a few minutes as is usual for me, reviewing my plans for the day. Normally I leap out of bed if I anticipate a new project. On this Saturday I was tempted to roll over and sleep some more, to forestall the inevitable. That afternoon Jason and I backed my Chevy flatbed into the shade at the edge of the designated killing ground. We made sure that the chickens in their yard couldn't see it. Compassion, I guess. I hammered fifteen nails straight up along the back edge of the truck bed. Each one would receive the leg noose of a headless rooster, to hang there and to bleed. We wanted no macabre barnyard dances for this bunch of roosters.

Next to the chopping block, Jason set up the table with cutting boards, five knives honed as sharp as I could get them on the old whetstone taken from the jumble of my biggest kitchen drawer. I had large canning kettles, bowls, buckets, and the huge colander that hangs in the back porch of Jason's house. The hose, with extensions, stretched from Jason's well clear out to the sandy patch in the shade under the cottonwood trees. We filled the buckets and kettles with cold water.

Fifteen nooses waited, tied from the thick twine that Lynn had used to weave the seats of our kitchen chairs. We were ready.

I took the first noose, a gallows loop. I placed my wrist through it to keep my hands free to catch the first rooster. I forced the rusty bolt back from the hasp on the chicken-yard door and stepped into the pen. The chickens were used to our comings and goings. I fixed my eyes on the nearest rooster and slowly stepped toward him, arms out to the sides to keep him centered in my path. Slowly I moved, then grabbed, feeling the predatory pounce in my movement. Grasping his thick, yellow shanks, I lifted and turned him upside down, fumbling with the noose as he beat his wings against my thighs, frantic to escape. The other chickens scattered to the far corners of the yard.

I closed the chicken-yard door behind me, my captive squawking, six pounds of terrified rooster fighting to right itself as it hung from the noose in my hand. My feet sought the path to the shady place, fiddlenecks and foxtails sticking in my sandals, irritants already.

The only way we could hold the rooster's head firmly in place was to place him belly up, head between the two nails on the stump, looking us in the eye. It seemed the baleful, reptilian eyes knew what was coming. I turned my head, pulling taut on the noose around his leathery, yellow feet, tension enough to keep his head in place between the two nails.

Jason picked up the hatchet. I held my breath and waited. I heard Jason take a big breath.

Thwack! The hatchet chopped. Nothing happened!

"Shit! I missed!" Jason sounded incredulous. Once more I averted my eyes.

This time when the blow came, I felt the quick release of tension. The full weight of the chicken fell to hang heavy from the noose around his shanks. I felt the sudden stillness. Then the tremor started. Too slowly, I moved to slip the noose over the awaiting nail at the end of my truck. The violent flapping almost jerked the noose from my fingers. This rooster who had fattened so fast he could barely waddle flew headless into his death hanging upside down from the back of a green Chevy flatbed truck.

Back and forth I went to the chicken house, my sandaled feet stinging from the fiddlenecks growing beside the path, feet filthy, sweaty, coated with dust, and spattered with chicken blood. I returned each time from the chicken yard with a fat rooster, the noose fuzzy around the scaly, yellow legs. Each rooster fought being carried upside down. Each pair of yellow eyes watched my own, every step of the path to the stump.

The killing went on and on, fifteen times. Fifteen times, Jason wielded that hatchet, resolute now after his initial miss.

The afternoon sun backlit the row of white wings outstretched in a sort of poultry benediction. Thirty wings hung upside down, limp, fully open, white feathers translucent, anointed with scarlet. Fifteen heads with vermilion wattles lay in a pile by Jason's feet.

Some we plucked. Some we skinned. The first few we gutted, exploratory, experimental, feeling our way to hearts, gizzards, livers. The slim sack of bile, slippery, was hard to cut without damaging the liver with the bitter green juice. Yellow chicken legs, thicker than my thumb, were chopped off and added to the pile of heads.

I had crossed the bridge. The carcasses now looked like meat as we placed them in pans filled with cold water to be carried into the house for a final washing, and to be wrapped for the freezer.

Jason lugged the big kettles, heavy with rooster bodies, into the kitchen for me. I reached in for the first one, and my fingers sent a pulse of shock up my arm to my heart. The water was hot, from the body heat, the last vestige of life in these birds that had never flown except for that desperate and bloody and fruitless flight behind my truck.

One by one I rinsed them, picking off the remaining pinfeathers. I cleaned the livers and the hearts. One by one I cut open the gizzards, peeled off the gizzard skin, wrinkled and tough, loose like the skin of a scrotum. I thumbed out the gravel and the ground-up green food and rinsed them clean. I shoved necks, hearts, gizzards, and livers into sandwich bags. Each bag I stuffed into a chest cavity, then bagged and wrapped each bird in turn.

Jason labeled the packages for the freezer. His speech grew elongated and drifted. Finally he sat, as though suddenly drunk.

"It was so much killing," he said.

A month later we butchered the hens. And three months would pass after that before we thawed any chicken for dinner.

That spring morning I watched Jason and Michelle's chickens cakewalk with hesitant half steps out the gate of their run into the backyard full of flowers that the kids had planted behind the rat house. The rooster strutted and flapped his wings, feathers gleaming, wattles heavy. On guard, he stayed between me and his hens. Then later, yesterday evening when I went to shut them in for the night, only the rooster and one hen came to my call of *Chick, chick, chick* and the scatter of scratch. Rather than hearing the usual contented crooning from their roost that signals a settling into evening, they were silent, perched back in the corner on top of the wood-pile. I debated. Late for a meeting in town, I couldn't wait for the other hen to find her way back home to roost. I decided to leave the trapdoor at the top of the ramp and the gate to their yard open.

In the morning, the chicken house was silent. I smelled it first, the strong odor of skunk. When I opened the big door to peek in I saw the carnage. The rooster torn apart. Blood everywhere. The hen missing. The trail of gray feathers led out the trapdoor, down the ramp, out the chicken yard, into the field beyond. There was so much blood mixed with the feathers that I didn't bother to follow the trail any farther.

Later that day, Lynn came into the kitchen. *I cleaned it all up,* he said. *I took what was left of them out across the lake. It will make some coyote really happy.* I was grateful that he didn't blame me for leaving the door open.

I waited few days before I called Jason and Michelle to tell them what happened to their chickens.

I think of all that when Jason calls some weeks later. He tells me he and Michelle are looking at some land to buy, a few acres near Nevada City, five hours away. They think they can afford it with what they have saved from their work this summer.

Jason tells me he misses it here, but he wants to buy this land with Michelle. *Remember when I buried my belly button?* he asks me. He wonders whether I think it ties him irrevocably to this valley.

If burying your belly button links you to anything, I think it means simply that you are connected to the earth itself, this whole big planet. No, I wouldn't worry, I tell him, knowing that I have to leave this door open.

✒ Airspace

FIFTY YEARS AGO, JOE AND BETTIE DROVE HOME FROM TOWN WITH THE
kids, Carol in the backseat curled under a blanket, and two-year-old Nina
asleep on Bettie's lap. Bettie told me it had been good to see people that
night. The late spring had kept everyone holed up at home too much. Getting out to a party was welcome. The Parmans had enjoyed themselves in
Cedarville.

The headlights swept up across the junipers at the rise, at the head of the
big alluvial fan where the Parman Ranch starts and spreads down, down to
the hot springs labeled the Mud Volcanoes on the map, down through the
marshes, and down all the way to the alkali lake, the northernmost of our
three valley lakes. The lights shimmied as they made the turn across the
cattleguard into the lane. The car wound down among the cows and big
boulders toward the cluster of house, chicken yard, tack shed, corrals, and
hay barn. The headlights brushed out the shapes of the cows and the four
big bulls. Their shadows walked wavering and stark along the face of the
rock wall, the rock wall that ran all the way from County Road 1 to wrap the
east and north sides of the big field closest to the house.

Past the wall, the car bounced down the ruts to the cluster of buildings.
Bettie smelled baby shampoo, ice cream, and salty little-girl odor from
Nina's head, nestled sweaty in the corner of her arm. The dead weight of

the child stirred when Joe parked in front of the house and shut off the engine. So as not to awaken her girls, Bettie opened the car door quietly and stepped out gently. But the cold night air weaseled in through Bettie's arms. Nina stiffened and clutched, awake.

As Bettie straightened and lifted the child, she heard a sudden sharp intake of breath through the sweet baby lips. She looked down in the dim light and saw Nina's wide-eyed stare, straight up, at the stars, the big stars that she had never before seen until this moment.

Bettie stood there for a long time, holding the child in her arms while the two of them drank in the sight of all those stars, shining, bright new jewels for a two year old's eyes. Together they tipped their heads up at the absolute wonder of the high desert night, a night with no moon, when the unbelievable luck and miracle of being here on this planet, in this valley, alive, was never more clear.

⤙

When we camped with Jason and his friends out east of Surprise Valley, over the border into Nevada, we drew straws to see which of us, the grownups or the kids, would sleep on the top of the old red truck. There, Lynn had welded a rack that doubled as a cargo carrier and at night served as the rails of a rooftop bed. The short straw meant you were one of the lucky ones that night. You climbed to the top of the truck. You took the binoculars. You crawled into your sleeping bag and lay there, looking, sometimes with the naked eye, and sometimes through the lenses that seemed to bring you just a little bit closer to the stars.

Up on the roof of the truck, a weird sort of vertigo inevitably grabbed you, as if you were falling, falling up through the sky and into the stars.

One hundred miles south and east in the Black Rock Desert where our family often camped when Jason was growing up, the sound of the air was all we heard. It is the same now, although we have noticed in the last ten years that in spite of the silence and vastness of the Black Rock, the glow of Reno, over one hundred miles away to the south, pulses on the horizon.

But no glow from a city fuzzes the clarity of our night sky and the solitude here at home in our valley. We are far enough from anywhere urban for that. A moonless night is truly dark. Except for the starlight.

When friends visit from the big towns, we like to take them out to the other side of our valley, out across to where no one lives, out where there are no lights. We stop the truck. The engine, losing its heat, pings and clicks in the cold high-desert night. We say, "Get out. Look up." The door whines open. Then we hear the same catch in our friends' breathing as they tip their heads back and look up, the same sound that Bettie heard when her baby Nina first saw the stars, half a century ago.

⤶

We have a friend, Jonas, who has made many portraits of rural Nevadans. He photographs his subjects outside, and they all carry the reflection of the burnt landscape glare in their eyes. Their look is slightly crazed, the look of having seen too much light.

And I wonder if this isn't the reason people raised in the desert do so poorly when they leave, move to a place with average rain, cloudy skies, and light that is tempered by water vapor in the air. There simply isn't enough light for them in those softer places.

I thought of Jonas's portraits that day, one of those days when I went out to Nevada with Lynn. I thought about how the intense light changes your vision. And the sounds of the desert, too. When you walk out into Nevada on a hot July day, the high-pitched buzz of the cicadas half hypnotizes you. If you walk long enough, and it is hot enough, the shadows start to jump and quiver. Purple, they dance and trick your eyes.

Lynn spends long days surveying for traces of past peoples indigenous to this place, doing his archaeological fieldwork for the BLM. I go with him whenever I can. The best time to catch the glitter of a site littered with obsidian flakes is when the sun is low. Walk facing the sun and the reflection from a projectile point will pierce your vision from many yards away, long before you can really see the small object.

After the long walk facing the low sun to the west, eventually, you have to turn and walk back to the truck. The sun warms your back, the skin on your face tight from the heat and the dry. One evening after a long day in the sun, I made that turn toward the east.

All day I had heard the incessant song of the cicadas. All day their uncontrolled flights up out of the sagebrush had startled me. The big insects lumbered, seemingly blind, inevitably striking me in the chest or the face as I leaped away from the whir of their wings that sounded so much like a rattlesnake's warning buzz. That evening, returning to the truck, the blue shadows jumped and flittered long over the sunlit ground burned almost red. I followed my stretched shadow. It undulated over the low sage, wavering, but steadily leading me on. Suddenly, I noticed a glow crowning my head on that impossibly long shadow. A halo!

I watched. The halo stayed with my shadow. I stopped. It followed, remained, encircling my shadow head. Curious, I edged through the sage closer to Lynn, a hundred yards away from me on his own trajectory back to the truck. I fell into step behind him, narrowing the distance between us. He halted for a moment, bent down for a closer look at a yellow chert flake on the ground. When he straightened, I was standing close behind.

Do you see it, too? I asked, feeling unsure, feeling foolish. *Do you see the halo on your shadow?*

Yes, he said. *I do.*

But it isn't only such miracles of space and light that we see. The openness of the desert makes some people uncomfortable. It is true that there is that risk of exposure, both to be witnessed and to witness. Not much can be hidden in the desert.

❧

The jets had never come at night before. Nor had they come to town.

It was a summer evening. We were enjoying a barbecue at our neighbors', Hugh, Sara, with the kids, on their deck that looked out over the valley. Everywhere, that peaceful, just-before-dark mauve glow and the whistle of the night hawks diving down out of the sky, falling, falling to the fields, then swooping upward at the last minute above the willow patch. Soaring, diving, swooping again.

It took a moment to figure.

Two military jets spiraling toward us in a screaming dogfight, a tight vortex just above our little town. The horses in the fields panicked, bolted, tried to outrun the sudden wall of sound that had surrounded them. They ran toward the teeth of the barbed-wire fences. Two-year-old Madeline opened her perfect pink-rosebud mouth, but her fear could produce no sound until Sara picked her up and cradled her. Even then, we couldn't hear her cries, masked by the howling jets.

Always before it had been in daylight and only when we were across the border in Nevada. One time when Tina and I and the children were riding back from the hot springs together in my pickup, I could see the three blond heads reflected in my rearview mirror. Jason and Tina's two girls sat in the truck bed, side by side, close to the cab. Creaking and rattling, we slowly bounced along the back road from Eagleville out to the Long Ranch on the Nevada side of the valley. Tina and I, deep in conversation, were enjoying our time together.

Then the sound hit, at first barely audible over the complaints from the chassis of my old truck and the rumble of the worn engine. It seemed to come from no particular direction, was just suddenly there, an engulfing roar swelling louder, too fast for my senses to absorb. I glimpsed the jet coming up over the horizon, coming at us, low to the ground. At the exact moment that I saw it, the pilot must have seen us, for the jet took aim, veered, and dove toward us, head on. My body took over and I drove the truck off the gravel road down into the thick creosote brush. By then the jet had passed us by and my logical brain had engaged again as the roar receded behind us. I knew the jet wouldn't have hit us, but as it was happening . . . it was all too fast, too loud, too much. The kids were a little shaken but unhurt. I shook my fist ineffectually at the dot in the sky. And I got angry. Very, very angry.

It wasn't the first time. One autumn morning out on the Sheldon Antelope Refuge, Lynn and I had carried our first cup of coffee up a little knoll above our camp, seeking the early-morning sun. We sat sheltered, leaning against the rimrock, above the frost, warming. Suddenly the desert morning silence turned into its opposite, the sound too loud, coming from where? from where? I remember looking down in disbelief, down from the knoll onto the top surface of the wings of the jet that was strafing our camp in mock combat, down over the pilot's head clearly silhouetted in the plastic canopy of the cockpit. There was something in his posture of a teenage boy crouched behind the handlebars of a fast, sleek motorcycle. Yet the sudden, overwhelming power of sound from his terrible screaming machine could not possibly be compared to a motorcycle. The jet was, after all, a very expensive machine designed for killing. At the instant of our understanding of the nature of this beast, the attacker was already gone. That time, too, we had shaken our fists at the departing speck in the sky. Don Quixote. Pathetic. Other military jets had buzzed Lynn's old red truck, the truck that we called the Tomato Can, because when we camped in the bed we made in the back, we felt like tiny cartoon mice tucked in all cozy inside a cartoon soup can. But that morning on the knoll I hadn't been as fearful or as angry as I was the afternoon on the dirt road. That morning it was just Lynn and I, just two mice; that morning I didn't have three children tucked in the back to worry about.

Everyone we knew who went out into Nevada to camp or to buckaroo told similar stories. Of camps used as targets in mock but nonetheless scary attacks from the jets. Of being knocked to the ground by a wall of sound. Of cows scattered over the scab rock, of horses bolting and losing a rider.

We began to hear those strange folktales that circulate when a topic becomes a hot item of discussion, the rural counterpart to urban myths. Our favorite was about the jet that had harassed a sheepherder and his herd for several days in a row. I imagined the pilot of that jet, chasing those sheep for the sport of it, slavering like a feral dog over how he and his machine could make all the silly beasts run and scatter. On the third day the sheepherder was ready. He drew a bead with his rifle on the tail of the speeding jet as it mock strafed his herd. He fired.

The story went on to tell of the sheepherder's arrest—and subsequent release. Seems the bullet he had fired had entered the jet at a horizontal trajectory, thus proving the flight had been at the sheepherder's eye level when attacking the flock of sheep and had therefore been flying illegally.

The equivalents of folk remedies were devised. One instructed how a person could bring a low-flying military jet down with a silver Mylar birthday balloon. All you had to do was to release one of those birthday greetings just below a jet that was strafing your camp, or your cows, or your sheep, or your town. The rising helium-filled balloon would activate the radar and fool the jet's computer into thinking there was an imminent attack from below by a heat-seeking missile. Then the jet's automatic evasive action would take over, causing the pilot to lose control.

Of course there were several logistical problems with this line of defense. No one I knew hiked around the desert with a helium balloon on a string. Then, too, we meant the pilots no physical harm. We just wanted them to stop flying illegally. And to stop using us as their targets.

✧

A few weeks after the incident on the knoll, Mary, a friend of ours who lived in the Smoke Creek Desert, called. She asked if I had heard the rumors about a new proposal for a military takeover of airspace. She was worried and I knew why. The jets were worse on their edge of that desert one hundred miles to the south of us. I had heard a rumor and didn't know what to make of it. We promised to let each other know if we learned anything more.

By then low-flying jets screamed down over the Warners and strafed Surprise Valley regularly. These jets flew well outside the low-level flight paths to which they were supposedly restricted. These jets flew well below the minimum altitude levels required by law. Our next-door neighbors, who operate the tiny airfield in Cedarville, told me of a jet that appeared out of nowhere, flying right through a morning instructional flight over the airport. There had not been an accident—not that time. And when they had called to complain to the military bases within flight range of Cedarville, none claimed the transgressor pilot and jet. The rules were in place to protect us, but it seemed impossible to find any way to enforce them.

Shortly afterward, Citizen Alert, a fledgling environmental organization from Reno, called to tell me that the air force was proposing a Military Operations Area, known as an MOA in the official parlance, just to the east of us. The MOA would extend from the Hart Wildlife Refuge in Oregon, down over the Sheldon Antelope Refuge in northern Nevada, and over a portion of the Black Rock Desert to the southeast. Citizen Alert sent us a copy of the one-page "Categorical Exclusion" prepared by the air national guard. The "Exclusion" claimed exemption from any environmental analysis. We scanned down that one meager page. In it was no mention of the treasures we know in that area, no mention of the towns, of the ranches dependent on the Nevada summer grazing. Nothing about the antelope or the sage hens. And nothing of the big silent sky over the high sagebrush steppes that open to the east of us.

A jet strafing the desert there would be as much a sacrilege as a hoodlum roaring around inside Chartres cathedral doing wheelies on a dirt bike. But with the exception of the Native American Sacred Places Act, our culture has yet to give legal recognition to the idea of sacred place in nature. After all, how could a wild, unimproved place deserve the same protection afforded a religious edifice?

We let our neighbors know about the MOA. We called all the friends we consider neighbors a hundred miles to the north, a hundred miles to the east, and a hundred miles to the south. We worried that the ranchers, often fierce in their patriotism, would think we were Commie-pinko-ratfinks in opposing the American military. I asked Bettie for her opinion. She told me more stories of cows scattered, of horses bolting while ranchers were out buckarooing in the rough country under the proposed new military airspace. My friend Pat, a teacher and local historian, told me of the flyboys and their flight-training runs during World War II and how they had strafed the antelope herds with live ammunition, decimating the pronghorn population in the Sheldon Refuge. How even then, during the height of fervent patriotism in the area, many in the valley had found the slain antelope hard to overlook and forgive.

I thought of all the empty fifty-caliber casings we had seen out there east of our valley in Nevada, the brass acquiring a turquoise-blue patina over time. Wherever we walked we would find a line of blue dashes spaced about twenty or thirty yards apart, a tracery of death drawn fifty years before.

On her ranch at the north end of the Black Rock Desert, Dale told me that her barn had been bombed once, killing their best milk cow. She said later she had picked up a fallen military parachute on their winter range. For years she had made silk cowboy shirts for all her kids, using Rit to dye that white silk every color of the rainbow. She chuckled then.

I learned that the ranchers might indeed be highly patriotic, but that many of them who had cows in Nevada had a highly jaundiced view of the military pilots. And their jets.

⤏

In August, Citizen Alert called Mary to request that she testify before the Nevada Legislative Committee on Public Lands concerning the impending federal takeover of yet another huge piece of the sky above Nevada. Mary asked if we wanted to go too, though we lived in California. She knew the ranchers in Surprise Valley depended on the range in Nevada for their summer feed and were in many ways more connected to Nevada's politics than to California's.

When we arrived at the capitol building in Carson City, we made a hurried detour to the ladies' room. We had driven the two hundred–mile trip without the benefit of air-conditioning, and the day was hot. We needed to tidy up, wash our sweaty faces, and run a comb through our windblown hair.

I listened to the speakers scheduled ahead of me: some people from Dixie Valley. Located near Fallon Naval Air Base, this remote valley was much like ours and had had a Military Operations Area created over it several years before. I heard them tell of sonic booms that imploded windows, of cows run through fences. The stories sounded fantastic, but I had my own experience from home to give them credence. Now, they told the committee their land was being condemned. The military was extending its operations from the sky to the Dixie Valley floor. They were being forced to leave the valley and the lives they loved. It was obvious from the questions asked by the committee that they had seen these people from Dixie Valley before.

I had never spoken into a microphone. When my turn came after Mary's to address the panel, the tremor in my voice surprised me. I raced through the telling: the threat to ranchers' summer range, the intent to locate the new airspace over the Sheldon Antelope Refuge, the current low-level flight violations, how helpless we felt in the face of those violations and this new MOA proposal. I sat down with relief when I had finished my nervous, rapid-fire delivery. The committee chairman banged his gavel at the buzz of conversation that started up at the news of the new airspace proposal. He called an immediate recess.

The chairman collared us in the hallway of the legislative building as we were preparing to leave. He told us we needed to get our California legislators and county supervisors involved in fighting this thing. He offered to fly to Cedarville to help.

We organized a town meeting about the proposed MOA. We served cookies and coffee and listened to guest speakers from Dixie Valley who were determined to thwart the military's efforts to ruin more rural lives. More people in our own community were involved now. Our efforts had gathered some momentum.

Finally we received an answer from the air force to our queries about how to comment on their "Categorical Exclusion." That answer was the clincher. There was to be no further environmental analysis. There was no comment period to the "Categorical Exclusion." It was final. There was no way to get the air force to recognize the issues we had raised. *Yes, we could comment,* they said, *on the Federal Aviation Administration's (FAA) final decision. There would be a forty-five-day comment period. The FAA would allow comments to be made on their decision. But only on aeronautical issues. Environmental issues would not be considered.* We read that the only hearing to be conducted by the air force and FAA would be in Reno, far from any of us who would be affected. We wrote and called and complained. Finally the air force agreed to hold a hearing in Lakeview, across the state line, in Oregon, only a little more than an hour away for us and a four-hour drive for the folks in the Black Rock area or from the north around Denio. I called Mary. She called Carolyn. The telephone alert extended out across the desert.

When we arrived at the hearing, I was surprised to see the solid chain of cars parked around the block at the Lakeview Federal Building. So many had driven so far, all the way from the far-flung edges of the perimeter defining the huge airspace the military planned to take over: ranchers from California, from Nevada, and from Oregon, the whole vast area under the skies that the military wanted.

We asked the young air force captain who conducted the meeting why they needed to put the operations area over us. He answered that they had chosen it because nobody lived there. The moment he uttered it, he realized his mistake. There was a low, angry growl from all the people who had driven so far to come there to sit on the stiff metal folding chairs, filling that room, standing to overflow out into the entrance hall. We understood him to mean that nobody who *mattered* lived under the proposed MOA.

"Why not over the ocean?" we asked. He told us the F16 fighter jets did not have the fuel capacity to fly out over the ocean and conduct operations there. Yet, those of us who had read the proposal remembered that the air force would phase those very jets out of service even before the operations area was to be fully implemented. Newer jets with adequate distance capability would succeed them.

We asked why, when we reported illegal, low-flying jets to any of the military bases within flying distance of us, we were always told that those jets were not from that base, or that one, or that one? Somebody in the audience hollered out that maybe they were Russian MiGs.

Foolishly, we were elated at the end of the meeting. Our numbers and logic had won, we thought. We had shown up and shown them: people did live under the airspace the military wanted, people who mattered.

⟲

The second, larger hearing was held in Reno. Almost a hundred of us from Surprise Valley drove the four hours to be there. Lynn, Bettie, and I carpooled together.

As we drove around Pyramid Lake we watched the pelicans wheel. Hundreds of them in a flock spun and turned, flying high, unbelievably high in the sky, the sky as blue as the lake, the lake as blue as the sky. Every summer the huge wings flash all together in the sun, glinting pure white as the pelicans fly in formation, then seeming to disappear as if one being, wheeling all at the same instant, their wings angled away from the sun.

One pelican parent remains at the nest site with the pelican chick, all the babies together in a pod on Anahoe Island surrounded by the waters of the lake, safe from predators. The nesting bird squats, wings outspread to shelter the bald, ugly pelican chick from the hot summer Nevada sun. Every day the other parent flies, sometimes more than one hundred miles in a day, sometimes up to two hundred, to find food for their young, big wings pumping, mile after mile; the pelicans return, regurgitating the catch into the voracious chick gullet. The chick grows so fat that it will have to lose weight before it fledges.

We were on our way to Reno to a hearing that would determine the future of this blue sky filled with birds. It was then I remembered what Jason had said the summer before. He had been watching the pelicans, had seen the changing patterns made by the black-tipped white wings all turning in unison, and had said that he suddenly understood the inspiration behind the patterns of the petroglyphs that we find pecked on flat rock faces by the people who had lived here for more than ten thousand years before Europeans claimed this continent. I held on to Jason's vision, forcing back the image of a military jet slamming into the middle of the stately pelican waltz spinning silently above us.

⊖

The hearing was held at the Nugget in Sparks in a big conference room above the main casino. We looked around, recognizing many of the ranchers from the Lakeview meeting. Each person seated in the conference room rose in turn to speak, to ask, and to give reasons for their opposition to the proposed MOA.

As the night dragged on, cigarette smoke and the sounds of slot machines drifted up the stairs to the conference room from the endless party in the casino below. One by one we faced the microphone as supplicants before the officials seated above us all on their dais at the front of the large room. The air force representatives wore their dress blues. The FAA officials wore black or navy-blue suits. All of them looked bored.

We realized then that the meeting was simply an empty public-relations exercise. We realized then, though the hearing went on and on into the night, that the decision to proceed had already been made. We realized then, as we saw little children falling asleep in their mothers' laps, that we were being given the opportunity to vent, but that was all we were going to get.

Sure enough, the decision to implement the new MOA was announced soon afterward without even a gesture toward the citizens it would affect. A notice simply appeared in the *Federal Register* one day.

It is the way things are done in Nevada.

⊖

We could not just let go, roll over, play dead. Lynn and I took the truck out into Nevada, out and around and up the long dirt road to a remote valley on the Nevada-Oregon border just under the center of the new Military Operations Area. We were seeking the ranch of a young woman who, we had heard, was active in the political arena. She had developed some national clout, but she had not been involved in the MOA protest.

The ranch dogs barked as we pulled into the yard. Tails wagging, they clustered around the truck. At the big front door, we introduced ourselves.

She invited us into the ranch office. We told her what was now a fait ac-compli. We told her what was planned for the skies directly over her ranch. She immediately called the Natural Resources Defense Council and Sierra Club Legal Defense on her office phone. We were amazed. She was talking directly to people we had heard about, but never imagined you could just call up. And she was talking in a very friendly way to a Sierra Club lawyer. Weren't they supposed to be bitter enemies, ranchers and Sierra Clubbers?

She handed the phone to me, and I explained at length about how the air force had managed to create a Military Operations Area, against all rea-soned arguments, over an area "where nobody lived." Shortly afterward that summer the lawyer from the Sierra Club Legal Defense came for a visit all the way to Surprise Valley from the Bay Area, all the way to our house.

We took him camping, out to the Sheldon and Hart Wildlife Refuges, di-rectly under the newly created MOA. I worried because we rode in the old sage-green truck with the broken door on the passenger side. But he didn't seem to mind the bungee cord that held the door shut. And he didn't seem to mind the long, bumpy drive on corduroy roads out onto the refuges to meet the biologists. They told him what they had observed when the jets frightened the antelope kids. Of a study that suggested the sage-hen eggs didn't develop when the jets came down low and fast. How often the jets had come, even before the airspace had been made official. Of their frustra-tion that their complaints about illegal flights were ignored, as ignored as the Fish and Wildlife's comments about the inadequacy of the "Categorical Exclusion."

The lawyer filed the appeal as per the air force and FAA regulations. But when he received the FAA response to the appeal, they argued that he should have filed his appeal in the Ninth Circuit Court of Appeals. When he tried to change the venue, he found the FAA response had been made just after the window of time for such an appeal had closed. He remarked how Kafkaesque the whole procedure seemed. But the jet flights over the MOA and elsewhere have been quiet and high and legal since then.

⊸

I learned a lesson then. If we ask, and read and call each other and talk and write, somehow we will be heard even if we are few, even if we do not get exactly what we want. I learned to trust myself a little more. I had worried that in this place dominated by conservatives and traditionalists that our protests against the American military would be scorned as raging radical heresy. I was surprised and then relieved to find that plenty of ranchers love this high-desert country as fiercely as I do and will speak out for it. Lines in the sand can be drawn, but lines can be made to shift.

But what of lines in air? I am not sure I have learned much about those. And I am still haunted by what I saw with Lynn that day on the knoll: the boy behind the flight controls of a jet, pretending to kill us.

⏀

Fifteen years later, the airspace issue surfaces again. A notice in the local weekly paper announces some changes to the Juniper and Goose MOAs. After translating the aeronauticalese into plain English and laying out the changes on Lynn's maps, we discover the air force wants to double the size of the MOA to the west of us. We call. Another "Categorical Exclusion" from environmental analysis, claimed because the jets will be three thousand feet above ground level.

Two of Jason's friends have moved to the valley, Leisyka and Blair. Lynn and I watch with great delight as they, too, learn to live without electricity and without running water on a ranch on the east side of the valley. They tell me they would like to get more actively involved in environmental issues. I call them a week later to ask if they would like to take on the American military with me. I hear a little catch in Leisyka's voice.

Two months writing letters, calling environmental groups and environmental lawyers, being interviewed by PBS stations on the coast also under the threat of a similar airspace increase. We work together on a letter of complaint to the FAA and air force citing procedural issues, and I love the addition of all this youthful energy and enthusiasm. But after all our work, we end up in exactly the same Kafkaesque vortex of catch-22 military logic as we did fifteen years ago. It seems there is nothing we can do.

Linda tells me she saw a stealth bomber flying low across the valley last week. "It was absolutely silent," she says.

⏀

Heading north for home, we top the rise at Sand Pass, the place where the whole length of the Smoke Creek Desert is suddenly visible. The pale-blue shadow of the Granite Range holds up the sky and keeps it from touching the north end of the huge playa. We like to take this road sometimes. The Smoke Creek playa can be treacherous. Compared to the white surface of the Black Rock playa, Smoke Creek is tan: it holds moisture in a different way. There is only one route across the playa that we know of. It is so seldom traveled that you have to look hard to see the faint track. It is easy to find yourself stranded here in the mud hidden under the dry salt crust, so we take the gravel road. It is poorly maintained, skirting the western edge of the dry lake.

There is usually no traffic up the gravel road. It is slower than the pavement along the Winnemucca Lake route, but here we can pull over anywhere to indulge our curiosity and wander on a whim.

As we drop down the rise at Sand Pass, we catch the glint of a windshield about four miles up the road. Another truck. We can see that it is stopped at the lowest place on the road, the place where the road meets the edge of the playa, a place that once tempted us to walk out on the flat surface, shimmering with mirages in the midday sun. But a few steps out onto the seemingly bone-dry cracks brought us back, our feet breaking through the crust, slipping, skidding, sinking into the hot, wet clay just below. This year the playa is even wetter. We can see the reflection of standing water.

We watch the truck pull away from where it had been parked at the edge of the playa. It heads in our direction and eventually passes us, a new silver-gray pickup driven by a couple of guys in their late twenties, early thirties. A loaded gun rack fills the rear window.

And when we reach the place where they had parked, there on the edge of the playa, we see the delicate bodies, the broken, shattered bodies of the avocets they had shot. Cinnamon, pearl, white, and black, the dead birds litter the damp playa. Red spatters glisten. Picked off, one by one, I suppose because they were there.

Imagine: in the desert how each life stands out, visible, so clearly outlined by what seems a blank, uninhabitable place. Life for the taking. Life to take for the sport of it. Life that couldn't possibly count. Mere targets. The wing of one lifeless avocet points skyward, into the empty, silent blue.

✎ Steam

I LAUGHED OUT LOUD THE FIRST TIME I SAW THE PARMANS' TWO-TON stock truck parked down in the weeds below their house. They had painted their brand in big letters way up on the top boards of the front stock panel, like the destination sign on a bus: OZ.

"We're off to see the wizard!" I sang to Lynn as we drove into the ranch yard. Later I asked Bettie what OZ stood for.

"Oh, it doesn't stand for anything," she answered. "We just wanted a shoulder iron that would leave a brand that showed up real good from a distance. We wanted the brand Rafter 7 but someone already had it, so OZ seemed like a good one." She shrugged, practical as usual, deflecting any fanciful powers that I might attempt to lay on her shoulders. And that is how it has been between us for years: me and my unabashed admiration, Bettie demurring the attention, dodging the praise.

Yet the day came when I stood in opposition to Bettie, when I put our friendship on the line.

Lynn uses the California Geologic Map sometimes for his archaeological surveys. On that map, the bottom fields of the Parman Ranch are labeled with plain block letters, MUD VOLCANOES, a name I find particularly whimsical when paired with the truck from Oz.

Like Lake City, the Parman Ranch lies on the fault dividing the mountains from Surprise Valley's floor. Hot springs dot that fracture zone where the earth's skin is thinner, the magma closer to the surface. Water passes easily down through these faults and is heated. Heat and pressure drive the water back up to the surface to emerge as hot springs.

The Parmans' hot springs field looks like any other marshy area in the valley. In the summer, sandhill cranes strut and dance and trumpet their calls. Yellow-headed blackbirds sing from the tules. Frogs provide a constant background drone. It is only in winter that you might notice the water saturating the ground is hot. In winter I can see the steam exhaled by those hot springs. When everything else in this country is frozen and white, a small area of the marsh surrounding each of those steaming mouths is summer green, plant growth sustained by the breath from the interior of our warm-blooded planet.

The Parmans never farm that ground below the house and barns that surrounds the Mud Volcanoes. The cows are fenced out of those areas. But sometimes one of the Parman cows breaks in, lured by the lush feed, and gets bogged down in the mire. Usually they discover the cow in time to pull it out. Sometimes they don't. There are places so saturated in those fields that if you bounce on the ground you can watch a wave of what seems like solid meadow ripple away from you.

Those hot springs whisper to me of the remote past. The hot water is older than the water in cold-water springs. Layers of human habitation surround those springs. The throats of the springs breathe steam heated by magma, that substance that remembers the earth's birth. Those springs make me think of the remote future, too. Cow bones will fossilize. A paleontologist in some far-distant future will puzzle over that cache of fossilized cow bones. The scientist will turn them over and over, examining them as Lynn does when he finds bones in an archaeological site. That future scientist will do DNA tests and link the cows to European ancestors. He will then invent a theory and proclaim some sort of migratory bovine route from the Old World to the New. Will he be able to separate those bones from the culture that made all the stone artifacts that litter the Parman Ranch? Will be able to connect the use of horses and pickup trucks to those bones? From them, will he be able to reconstruct enough of our culture to know the mythology and meaning of a white cowboy hat?

The Parmans have made several attempts to use the hot water over the years. The midwinter greenery around the hot springs inspired Bettie's visions of a geothermally heated greenhouse.

"The last time anyone drilled and tried to tap into the hot water, I got them to run a pipe to my hothouse," she said. "But that water was so full of minerals it corroded those metal pipes and plugged them up right away. Maybe, someday, they could run cold-water pipes down in a closed loop through the hot water. I sure could start a lot more plants a lot earlier if I had that heat."

One night in the early 1950s, one of those springs erupted, blowing rock and steam far into the air. By happenchance, one of the companies to lease the geothermal potential from the Parmans had a drill rig parked there, straddling that particular spring, ready to start boring a new hole. It, too, had been caught up in the explosion. Bettie opened the red photo album covering her lap. She showed us pictures of the rig, a big 1950s Chevy truck, lying on its side, suspended over the throat of the spring. "That tall rig was the only thing that had held that truck back from a long slide down deep into boiling water," she said.

She told us how Jim had called from his ranch half a mile away in the wee hours of that morning after the explosion from the deep had rocked the area.

"Are you all having a party?" Jim had drawled over the phone lines. In typical rancher style, using that ironic sense of understatement, Jim went on, "You all must be having a real good time. Kinda noisy though."

The next company to lease the geothermal rights drilled wells higher on the ranch, on more solid ground. Then, as development money was scarce in the early seventies, they capped those steam wells.

Curious after hearing Bettie and Joe talk about them, Lynn and I walked up the lane that followed the long, dry-stacked wall in the first field, the lane that wound from Joe and Bettie's house to the yellow house perched at the top by County Road 1. We stepped across the cattleguard, crossed the pavement, jumped down into the borrow pit and back up the side to clamber through the three-wire fence on the uphill side of the road. Joe had told us where to look in the cover of the big juniper trees, just on the edge of where Powley Creek fell steep out of the mountain canyon. There a large pipe emerged from the ground.

A pit pond had been dug to capture the water that would gush from the pipe if ever the giant valve were to be opened. Beside the dry pond was the big twelve-inch pipe. Lynn and I tilted our heads down to the valve, ears to the pipe, hearing the pings and gurgles and hisses echoing up through the heavy steel walls. Down below, far below, slept the dragon of hot water under all the alluvium at the head of the ranch.

A mile or so farther up, County Road 1 cuts through the red rock of the hill they call Hot Hill. There the snow melts soonest, not as a function of solar gain, but because the earth's bedrock skin is even thinner there. The rock itself warms the road. Its heat comes from the hot water that feeds the several-mile-wide complex of springs surrounding the Parmans' Mud Volcanoes.

⟿

One summer morning our own phone rang. I answered and the person on the other end identified himself. He was a geologist working for a geothermal exploration and development company. He asked to speak to Jason who was on summer vacation just prior to his last year in high school. After asking around, Jason had been recommended as the local kid who would be dependable for extra fieldwork help.

Jason was hired and came home each night, boots and jeans wet and muddy from traipsing all day through the marshy fields that surrounded the Parmans' hot springs. To measure the conductivity of the rock under the soil, they had reeled out long, thin strands of copper wire to lie in a grid, cobwebby over the thick grass in the fields. It was all done to predict the best places to drill for more hot water, and to indicate the size of the hot-water aquifer that lay under Bettie and Joe's ranch. Jason earned good money for a couple of weeks, and we were glad for him.

Several summers later, the geothermal company itself came to town. I saw the announcement in the weekly paper inviting the whole community to a meeting at Golden's, one of the restaurants in Cedarville. I marked it on my calendar. Bettie and I went together.

"They came by yesterday to show us the lease agreement," Bettie said as we walked into the restaurant. "We ought to get some pretty good royalties out of this."

We filed past the bar to the table set up at the entrance to the dining room. A man and woman were introducing themselves, filling out name tags for us to stick to our shirts, offering cookies from the bakery next door, handing out cups of coffee.

"Hi. My name is Helen. This is Phil." She named her company, then asked for our names so she could fill out the name tags.

Helen seemed to recognize my name when I spelled it out for her. I wondered what was the context where she first heard my name, and why she seemed to remark it so emphatically, turning toward Phil and making sure that he noticed. A look passed between them. They urged us to take a paper plate of cookies, a paper cup of coffee.

In the big dining room, I picked up one of the handouts on the long table beside an easel with a flip chart. Instead of the usual dim, dinner-house atmosphere, the lights were turned on bright. We took our seats at one of the tables scattered around the room, nodding and murmuring our greetings to the others gathered there. It is typical of dining out in Surprise Valley that you must acknowledge everyone in the dining room. It is almost disconcerting to go to a restaurant in a larger town and realize that you know none of the other patrons and can forego this ritual of greeting.

Waiting for the meeting to begin, I glanced through the handout, diagrams of an electrical-generation plant, obviously much simplified with attractive graphics perfectly presented. The room rustled, quieting as Phil and Helen took their places, standing at either end of the long table in front of us. Phil wore a suit. Helen had on a pair of rumpled sweats. I couldn't help wondering if their choice of clothing was a deliberate attempt to relate to all possible demographics.

They would build the geothermal electrical-generation plant somewhere in the thick stands of juniper, fir, and Jeffrey pine just above the Parman Ranch on the west side of County Road 1. I listened to how they talked about their plans. They didn't talk about plans the way Lynn and I do, tentative, with lots of room for error and change. Instead of saying, "We plan," they skipped the plan part and said, "We will." It seemed odd to me that they expressed no doubt, even though Bettie had told me the first part of the project would be to drill test wells to see whether the geothermal resource was big enough to sustain a plant.

I looked around at the forty of us seated there. A few teachers, the owners of several of the stores. A representative from the bank and some ranchers. I tried to fathom from facial expressions what the people in the audience were thinking. A few really wanted this thing. I could tell. They nodded enthusiastically at whatever Phil or Helen said. But most of them maintained their habitual poker faces, concealing anything they might have been thinking. In a way our community is like a small island far from the mainland. We are suspicious, particularly when people from "outside" are trying to sell us something. I wonder if the poker faces are a mechanism that serves the old cowboy ethic of being a "good horse trader." Don't reveal your hand. Watch. Wait. Keep your chin pulled back. Look at people from the bottoms of your eyes. To ask questions would reveal ignorance. I was a little embarrassed for Phil and Helen that people reacted so woodenly to what they were trying to sell. Just to be sociable, a few of us asked questions. Phil and Helen were working so hard to put this meeting on.

I got a warning in my gut. It had to do with something about the slick way Phil and Helen made their sales pitch to the group of us gathered there, sipping coffee and nibbling the cookies they had bought at the bakery next door. In glowing terms they extolled the environmental benefits of the clean geothermal generation of electricity. Back and forth Phil and Helen hard-pitched to us the jobs this project would bring to the valley. Something rang hollow to me in the well-oiled tone of their voices. And they slid right past the questions we asked.

The next day, I called the National Center for Appropriate Technology (NCAT) in Montana. I had learned about this center several years before when I had illustrated a children's book for them. I was interested in alternative energy, and the NCAT was supposed to have the most complete information available nationally for all sorts of energy-related technologies.

I talked to several of the engineers there. At that point I didn't know enough to have very many questions, and my questions certainly weren't technical.

Their answers surprised me. I had expected to hear them say that geothermal electrical generation was a wonderful, renewable way to satisfy our energy needs. I wanted to believe Phil and Helen. I had eaten their cookies. I wanted to let go of my fears, count them as stupid suspicions. I wanted to hear that I had nothing to worry about. Instead, each engineer I talked to warned me in turn that the all-benign answer to the problems of energy production as portrayed by the company reps the night before was not the whole story.

I asked for reading material. The engineers sent me a huge pile of publications and technical papers about the geothermal industry. I pored through the heap. More unfamiliar words. Technical drawings and photos of electrical-generation plants similar to the handouts I had brought home from the meeting. I tried matching the megawatts Phil and Helen had cited to the images spread out before me. I tried to imagine an industrial structure that big in the trees above the Parman Ranch. I couldn't make the image coalesce in the eye of my mind.

What I read showed that the technology was not as free of problems as the company had represented to us. The problems ranged from air-quality issues to extreme fire danger, from aquifer depletion to water-quality degradation.

↩

Several years before, at the height of our efforts to help people file protests with the Nevada state engineer over Washoe County's water grab, Linda,

Sara, Bettie, and I had worked at a fairly frenetic pace. We had laughed together about some of the dumb things we would do. We wore our Surprise Valley Gardening and Terrorist Society T-shirts as a joke, but only sort-of-a-joke. One morning Sara was so deep in thought about the issues facing us that she had carried her ironing board upstairs to vacuum. We hooted when she demonstrated how she had tried to plug it in. We pantomimed to each other the expressions on our husbands' faces when they opened the refrigerator, looking for something to eat, hungry after our three weeks of increasingly inattentive domesticity.

At other times we marveled. It seemed as if we had a guardian angel, a little angel demonstrating to us that we were indeed on the cosmic side of a battle between right and wrong. Taking a break from her search for material to use in the protests, Sara had managed to find a few minutes to tidy her house. In her haste to complete the chore she had bumped into their big bookshelf. The blow caused a little booklet to fall out of the shelf above her, right into her hands. She called Linda, both amazed and excited. It was exactly the ammunition we needed and had been searching for. The State Department of Water Resources had published the booklet, a study on Surprise Valley's water quality. It had come home with Sara's husband, Ben, a building contractor, for some clients when they wanted to know about drilling a well. The water-quality studies consisted of readings taken from a sampling of wells scattered throughout the valley.

The serendipitous discovery of that pamphlet had alerted us to something we had suspected but hadn't known how to articulate. The water quality of the valley's hot springs was not like that of the cold-water aquifers. Our hot water was full of such wonderful chemicals as arsenic and mercury. Our cold groundwater could be contaminated by the hot water. I found similar references to water quality in the heap of papers from the NCAT. Pumping hot water could pull the good water into the bad and vice versa. If contaminated, the groundwater that provides stock water, irrigates the fields, and supplies our drinking water would no longer be usable as the pure water that we know. Now we had the word of authority to quote on the issue of water quality.

This same issue applied to geothermal development. That spring, while the geothermal company was trying to sell its idea, the Surprise Valley Water Advisory Committee was still working on drafting a groundwater-management plan in deadly slow and dull bimonthly meetings. I knew that we still had no legal mechanism in place to regulate pumping. I asked the committee to consider geothermal pumping in the management plan. But no one wanted to impede the promises of royalty money to the well-respected ranch families north of Lake City.

⟞⟝

The pile of papers from Montana listed many possibilities in the type of design for possible geothermal electrical-generation plants. All had their dangers.

Even the safest, most expensive plant was safe only as long as nothing went wrong. Then the dangers looked monumental: the fluid used to transfer heat was stored in tall towers. In a fire those towers would act like huge Bic lighters. I thought of the fire danger in July in all those trees on the uphill side of County Road 1 where the reps told us they planned to build their plant. Correction: where they told us they WOULD build the plant.

⟞⟝

At the next town meeting, three or four of us asked a lot of questions. Somewhat difficult questions. Both Helen and Phil kept telling us repeatedly that they welcomed input from the community about the proposed plant. But when we pressed them for specifics, they sidled right by the questions we asked, leaving them hanging while they drummed on about the jobs they would bring to our valley.

By the end of the meeting, it appeared the only community participation they actually planned to allow would be to let us decide what color to paint the plant after it was built. Like a snotty brat I thought to myself, *Shiny chrome might look nice. You might as well make it stand out. After all, how could such a thing look like it belonged here? With camouflage paint?*

The geothermal generation process would shunt a lot of steam into the air. At that meeting I asked how all that steam would affect a pogonip. Phil and Helen looked blank. They asked me to spell the word: p-o-g-o-n-i-p.

I believe it is a Paiute word. It is a word widely used in Nevada if not the whole Great Basin. In the winter in this high-desert country we have long periods of high pressure. Far from the temperate effects of the Pacific, the air gets very cold. Trapped by the lid of high pressure held in place between the mountains, the air grows stagnant. In Reno it turns brown and foul, smog stuck in a chimney that cannot exhaust itself. Here in our valley it stays clear. Here the sun can warm the days, although the nights may fall far below zero.

Enter the pogonip.

Most of the time the winter air trapped in a Great Basin valley is dry as a bone. But sometimes, if a high-pressure system crowds the heels of a storm that has dropped enough moisture, a cloud condenses from the moisture and freezes. It gets trapped in the valley. A frozen cloud of crystals deposits white feather boas on every strand of barbed wire, on every tree branch, on every blade of grass. It glazes the sagebrush white.

A pogonip is beautiful but very, very cold. The frozen cloud blocks the sun out and can last for days. The low nighttime temperature never rises during the day. The horses and cows in the fields look aged, frosted gray, with ice whiskers and beards. Feathers weighty with the frost, the eagles and hawks don't fly. But after a time, under normal conditions, the desert prevails. The sun burns through to warm the valley days again.

But what would happen if the source for the moisture was produced on a daily basis and came from the valley itself? Every winter morning, I see steam clouds hover over the hot springs. What would happen if the steam source were suddenly increased? At the next meeting I hid my snort of disgust in a cough when Phil told us what they planned to do. He told us they would build a very, very tall smokestack to vent all the steam, presumably above the layer of winter-trapped air. A five-thousand-foot smokestack?

↤

We started calling people and officials in other communities where recent geothermal development had taken place. The stories we heard did not inspire confidence in the project or in this particular company. They promised jobs, but we learned from the other communities that the jobs would be available only during the construction phase of the plant, and would necessarily involve big industrial contractors with their own army of workers from outside. Then, once the plant was completed, the workforce would dwindle to less than a dozen operators. Their skills would be specialized. Most probably, they, too, would be hired from outside the area.

During this time, Clarence was named by the Tribal Council as the official tribal member to contact when the Forest Service and the BLM needed to communicate with the tribe about cultural and archaeological issues.

"The tribe hasn't received any notification about this project from this company," he told Lynn one morning, the two of them seated at our kitchen table. "I am worried. There was a village that surrounded those hot springs. Since it is private land, the state controls the archaeology, not the feds. California doesn't give the tribe much time to answer with our concerns. I need you to help me watch this."

We knew that the project would have to go through the hoops of California's state environmental-quality laws. "Cultural values" are protected on private property in California primarily only if the cultural material has been found and recorded prior to the inception of the project. The next day, Lynn checked the state office to see if there were any existing site reports for archaeology in the immediate area. There were none recorded.

A ring of mortars and stone tools circled the entrance to Bettie's yard at the ranch, all found in the four generations of farming and ranching the place. Bettie and I had talked about trying to find the big bedrock mortar that some hunters had told her about. But she and I never did take the time to climb that far up the mountain above the ranch.

Lynn and I knew there had been a named Paiute village here, recorded in the only ethnology ever written about the Northern Paiutes of Surprise Valley. It was a name certainly known by those of Clarence's generation but not visited by them as it was part of the Parman Ranch. Lynn and I were sure the village must have been close to those hot springs. But because it was private ground, no archaeological work had ever been done on the site. (Practically the only archaeological work in our region is accomplished on federal public lands, driven by federal laws.)

Lynn and I had talked to Joe and Bettie before about wanting to survey the area and map it, to see if we could figure out the exact location of the village. Here is where things began to get sticky.

We went to Bettie and Joe one day and asked permission to survey the archaeology on their property. All four of us knew that mapping the site created a future obstacle that could slow the geothermal project and the royalties and fees promised to the Parmans. They gave us their permission. None of us mentioned the obvious.

It was a cold day and windy. I wrapped a wool scarf around my head to protect my ears. We surveyed transects up and down the steep slope. Most of the material we found was concentrated in the lower fields around the lowest, capped well. We mapped the areas of concentration and filed an archaeological site report with the state.

I tried to pretend that everything was the same when I went to visit Bettie. Our conversations felt forced. We each had to work to keep them going. We skirted the subject of the geothermal project. Joe didn't join in as usual and tease the two of us. He just watched.

᳁

I made a nuisance of myself to the county planner in the next few months. The planning department was in the process of writing the geothermal component to the county general plan. I knew that Phil and Helen had offered their expertise to the county to help formulate the plan. I wondered if the foxes were telling the county how to guard the henhouse door.

Other communities that we contacted had warned us of the loopholes we should close in the regulations spelled out by the general plan, holes discovered in their own plans and in the contracts with the geothermal companies who had constructed plants. We were warned of the gaps in planning that these other communities regretted in hindsight, of the holes that they were finding impossible to plug after the fact.

I kept my hands pressed down flat on Bettie's kitchen table on either side of my coffee cup the day I asked Bettie if they had a good water lawyer to look over the contract the company wanted them to sign. I felt patronizing and stupid, butting into their private business with my questions and fears. But I had talked to ranchers outside our valley, ranchers who had signed contracts and now regretted it but no longer had recourse to change the events happening on their own lands.

⊘

That whole summer was long and awful for me. There was no work for Lynn that season with either the BLM or the Forest Service. Congress had cut federal spending. By June we knew that seasonal archaeology jobs here had dried up. We had to find work if we were to make it through another winter here.

We signed on with an archaeological consultant and were hired for the season for a dig in central Nevada. We were to be on a crew of "digros" for a clearance for a giant gold mine. As soon as we had finished the required cultural clearances for the project, the mine would eat up the eight-by-eight-square-mile area we surveyed.

Ironically, our field camp that summer was a few miles from a large geothermal plant, a plant approximately the size of the one that was being sold to our community at home. Pipes twice the circumference of a man and waist-high snaked for miles across the ground, linking the hot-water wells, some drilled far from the plant. The pipes were wrapped with buff insulation. I wondered if the color had been coordinated by community involvement. It was an exact color match to the buff of the central Nevada loess, but looked alien and ugly just the same. And the big plant itself was painted that same buff color, but it did nothing to soften the appearance of the industrial-looking giant.

All night we were awakened by hissing rumbles and then screeches and roars as the plant belched out extra steam. We tried to imagine that sound at home. Then we tried not to imagine it.

The old Beowawe Geyser had once been visible from Highway 80, several miles away. It had been sucked dry by this project. A major prehistoric village site still encircled the springs, but the old meadow was now stark and sere. No green welcomed. No water trickled in the old hot-spring streambed.

I tried to imagine the plant up the road from us in Surprise Valley, looming over the trees in the hollow of Powley Creek above the Parman Ranch. I tried to imagine the marshes below the house dried up, with no sandhill cranes stalking frogs. I tried to imagine the sound of no frogs in our summers. I tried not to imagine it.

Back home in July for our four days off, we attended another meeting put on by the company.

"I talked to the Lake City fire chief," Helen told us enthusiastically. "Our company plans to donate special training and equipment to the Lake City Volunteer Fire Department. Isn't that just great?" She dangled this information in front of us as if it were a prize carrot that we would snap at. It was the first time I realized that they really did intend to have our tiny volunteer department take care of any emergencies.

↬

Home on a break from our fieldwork a few weeks later, Lynn called me inside from the garden. *Come watch this!* The TV set pulsed orange in the corner of our living room. The Reno newscaster spoke excitedly, and we watched firefighters, trained urban and industrial firefighters. Silhouetted against the flames, the little black shapes of all those men made futile efforts to contain a huge fire that had broken out in a geothermal plant south of Reno, a plant similar to the safest and best design available. A design that the company was telling us was too expensive to build in Surprise Valley. The fire was contained only several days later when one of the firefighters risked all to run into the inferno and manually shut down a valve. Even there, in that urban scene, it looked to me as if things had been left entirely up to chance in the design of that plant. What on earth had the designers and company been thinking?

I tried again to picture Lynn and Timothy and Gary and Johnny fighting such a fire. I compared the big trucks on the TV news to Lake City's little storybook 1946 Ford engine. And I thought of Jason, for he was now of age to be a volunteer. My stomach went cold. Lynn videotaped the story so that we would have it later should we need it.

Each time I received new information, I wanted to tell Bettie what I was learning about geothermal technology and this particular company. I couldn't. Our conversations had shortened so. We each stumbled over the forbidden territory that widened between us and the time that grew between visits.

But I couldn't stop myself from questioning the company and the county planner. Each new bit of information, each new answer, led me to ask more questions. I knew that it was no secret to the Parmans that we were the ones asking all the questions, the questions that were putting obstacles in front of the project and the royalties that had been promised to them.

Before, when I'd visit, Joe would end his cup of coffee by standing and stretching to his full six-foot-five height. He'd shove his cup over next to the big percolator, always hot at the end of the table. "Well, I believe I'll go find me some of that stress," he'd rumble. Out the door he'd go to one of the chores waiting for him. Now, whenever I walked into the kitchen, he walked out, saying nothing.

I don't know how much of that stress Joe ever found there on the ranch, but I managed to find a bunch of it that summer. I got allergies. I had never had allergies before. I attribute it to the conflict between my heart and mind, my loyalty to my neighbors, and what I was finding out about this particular company.

Bettie's daughter Bonnie had given her some sweet-corn seed early that spring. Bettie had passed some of it on to me. The patch that I planted with that seed grew to gargantuan proportions. On one of our breaks from the dig in central Nevada, I noticed that my garden looked small to me. Then I realized it was because of the huge sweet-corn plants. They dwarfed the rest of my garden. I picked the long yellow ears, sweet and tender. Yet, each time I would approach that patch, my nose would plug up, my eyes would swell, and my ears itched, deep down inside my head.

I helped Bettie set up her spinning demonstration at the fair that Labor Day. Eyes puffy and throat scratchy, I made the excuse of allergies to not sit and spin with her for the three days of fair time. I felt the strain between us more than I felt my itchy eyes.

❧

I have a little whorl on the tip of my right index finger. Once, when I was a teenager in France, my friend Noelle and I guppied for one of the street gypsies' offers to read our palms. I stood before this woman, wild in her wide skirt of colors, her eyes cold as ice. I remember nothing of what she told me until, tightening her hold on my wrist, she slid her forefinger down my arm until the tip of it rested on the very end of my own.

"Vous voyez ce cercle, là?" she started. *That circle there; it is a closed circle. Not open as on your other fingers. That first finger is for pointing. That closed circle holds the power to notice. To notice what is wrong, what needs to be done, what needs to be changed. It is a gift, that finger, but like all gifts are, it is also your weakness. Sometimes that finger will hurt you very much. And the ones you love. You must always be careful to point it with love, not hate.*

Bettie did not call that fall to ask me to come look at the new quilt she had finished, or to come taste the tart flavor of the cantaloupe that she had dried as an experiment. I thought a lot about the old practice of shunning, the new meaning that word had for me in this contained world of the valley. I missed her. Was it worth it?

⌀

I continued to bother the county planner on the geothermal portion of the county general plan. I had learned to put all my concerns in writing and to ask that each letter I sent be placed in the permanent record of the plan proceedings. The Slossons had taught us to write so there would be legal evidence to appeal the plan later if we needed to. I know the county planner must have wanted to swat me. I imagined the grimaces he must have been making to the rest of his office staff when I was on the phone with yet another question or concern.

I took my knitting with me to the next few town meetings the company held in town. I knew that the soft, hand-spun wool sliding through my fingers would quiet me as my stitches pulled the yarn into the sweater that grew there on my lap. The knitting kept me from having to look around the room and meet the glares from the other ranchers who had been promised leases and royalties.

⌀

Very late one night, Helen called me. Her voice was honey sweet.

"I have a job for you," she said. "Phil and I think you would make an excellent community information coordinator for our next project. We want to send you to a small community up in Oregon," she told me. "We plan to sell our next project there. You will be away from home a lot. This job will give you a chance to travel. Won't that be nice?" her dulcet voice purred. "I imagine you would like that very much." She mentioned a pretty high figure for wages.

I told her no, I preferred to stay home. I told her I did not want to help them sell their projects to somebody else. I thanked her for thinking of me and hung up. I wondered why she had called and why she called so late. I guess she hoped that if my mouth were jammed full of carrot I wouldn't ask so many questions.

I made a couple of tentative visits to the Parmans. The men held their backs straight, stiff, and unyielding. Bettie no longer offered the gifts of her garden. That Timmie still greeted me by thrusting her cold nose into my palm was small consolation. The Mud Volcanoes breathed visibly in those late-fall mornings. Each time I saw them I felt I was breathing steam too, the lump in my throat too big to swallow any of Bettie's good pie. And anyway, she no longer offered either pie or coffee. I holed up at home then, wondering if I was wounded or if I had wounded them, or us all, with my convictions.

I missed the sound of our friendship, the phone calls we would make to each other early, before the sun rose. To ask Bettie how to store the tomato seeds. To listen to her tell me to pinch off a stem of my best tomato plant. To root it in a glass of water, to nip off the flowers all winter, and to take cuttings from that one tender green branch to root in the spring as the starts for my tomato plants the next year. To listen to her tell me she had once talked to an old woman who had a tomato plant that went back one hundred years. In her garden each spring a new clone of itself had blossomed from that fall-pinched branch and in the summer bore sweet, red fruit.

⯎

The turning point came later that fall. Jim and Nancy Slosson sent me an article from the Susanville paper about a rancher who had signed a contract with the same geothermal exploration and development company that was courting our valley. The article quoted the rancher.

I could imagine his callused hands hanging empty when he described to the reporter how his land had subsided. After just a few years with a smaller plant than was planned here the land had collapsed in on itself to a depth of more than ten feet, sinking down into the cavity left in the depleted aquifer. Hot water, laden with poisonous minerals, had contaminated the cold water used by the ranch. The contract the company had given the old man to sign did not provide the means for him to correct such eventualities. He was stuck with the problem, forever.

I held the article in my hand and listened to the sandhill cranes gathering. They wheeled and called above town in the annual air ballet that would take them away. The winter skies would empty of their calls. Then, in February, we would start to watch the skies, to be the first to phone each other that we had seen them, once again, for another year, flying into the valley greening with spring.

I called Linda and read her the article. She asked for it. I gave it to her. She sent it to Bettie the next day.

↔

That winter the board of supervisors adopted the geothermal component to the general plan. I felt good about it, knowing it had good protections.

Shortly afterward, the geothermal company drifted quietly out of their plans to build a plant here in the valley. Some say there was not enough hot water in the geothermal field to support their plans. Some say the county's rules to protect the valley made it too expensive to build. Some say it is my fault that we do not have a big geothermal plant just up the road from Lake City. Some say it is not. I have heard that other poorly planned projects have been warned to leave Surprise Valley alone. "You can't fight those women that live there," they say.

The big valve on the pipe above the Parmans remains closed, vibrating with the hissing from far below the ground.

In early February, when I heard the first sandhill cranes returning to the valley, Bettie called to ask what kind of tomatoes I wanted to start in the greenhouse with her. When I drove over to help her she was wearing her Surprise Valley Gardening and Terrorist Society T-shirt.

Joe took a little longer. But by June, when I was loading some flats of flowers into my truck for my own garden, he hollered out to me, "Why in the hell do you want to raise them damned things? All you can do is just look at them. They aren't any good to eat!" The teasing was back.

I laughed and looked down at the springs, breath rising invisible on this warm May afternoon. I heard cranes trumpet, the frogs droning on and on and on.

⟿ Flood Mud Pies

OUR STREET, SOUTH WATER STREET, TURNS TO DIRT AFTER IT CROSSES
Main Street and heads up into the mountains. The rough one-lane road
climbs parallel to Mill Creek for a while and then crosses the creek a quarter mile above town just below the cliffs where the valley and steep mountain merge.

Here, a culvert eight feet in diameter once channeled the creek under
the road. Rushing from the mouth of the pipe, the water pounded out a
swimming hole, digging and swirling, a hole just right for Jason and his
friends on a hot summer day.

The boys deepened the hole by damming up the downhill side. They salvaged an old slide from the dump and spent full, long days there, swimming in snowmelt from Bald Mountain. Goose-bumpy and shivering, they
would bolt up the Monkey Trail, the name they gave to the deer trail that
leads straight up from the creek to the first scarp overlooking the cemetery
and the fire hall. There the boys entered a different universe of juniper and
rocks, where the adult world disappeared from consciousness and the boys
dreamed themselves self-sufficient as wild creatures in the small shelter
caves in the cliffs that they claimed as forts. I imagine that before Europeans arrived here, the children of Clarence and Julia's ancestors must have
played there, too, and spied down on their swimming hole and the big camp
farther down along the creek that spread out in the sun, away from the
shadow of those narrow cliffs.

A large corrugated pipe stood upended at the edge of the swimming hole. Inside it, a roll of graph paper slowly unwound, receiving inscriptions from a delicate mechanical arm that traced the peaks of high water on hot afternoons and the valleys that showed how the snowmelt dwindled on cool nights.

Hired by the valley irrigation districts, the water master said he could always tell when the kids had been playing in the swimming hole. Sure enough, the undulating line of ink registered sharp spikes from the afternoon before. Jason and his friends had been there, leaping off the end of the culvert, making cannonballs of their taut, brown bodies, drenching themselves in boy-size splashes that temporarily sluiced water out of the swimming hole over their little rock dam. The water master pointed to where the tracing on the government's graph leveled out again by late afternoon when the boys had gone home to chores and to supper.

Our region receives the bulk of its annual precipitation in the winter, mostly in the form of snow. Rain rarely falls in the summer, and the creeks dwindle. The Surprise Valley Irrigation District hires the water master to keep an eye on the rates of discharge from our creeks and to regulate the irrigation ditches. After the last snow melts from the top of Bald Mountain, he is the one charged with portioning out the water rights to us. His job grows increasingly difficult in August when the real heat sets in and old neighbors talk with sidelong glances about who is taking more than their fair share from the ditches and the homemade pipes that snake through our town to the houses and gardens and the fields below.

A hundred yards below the swimming hole, a cement weir divides Mill Creek in two. The north fork flows through town in a deep channel; the south fork crosses under Main Street in another culvert, passes our house on South Water Street, and bisects the block-long depression we call the town park. Bettie tells me that the Lake City community once kept the park watered and mowed and held Fourth of July picnics there across the street from the church. An annual tug-of-war soaked the losers in the creek, shallow from midsummer drought. But after the last flood some thirty years ago, nobody in the community pulled together to clean up the debris and restore the park. The ground is bumpy with big rocks imbedded in the sandy soil. Fir, ponderosa and Jeffrey pine, wild rose, locust, and willow grow here in a tangle, crowned with the turkey-vulture roost in the old cottonwood snag on Main Street.

Lake City's seasons are tempered by the sound of Mill Creek flowing through town. If you follow the creek from town up into the narrow canyon, the sound of the rushing water is engulfing—you hear nothing else. Only if you climb up out of the canyon, maybe taking the boys' Monkey Trail to top out on the big bench above the valley rimmed with the rocks where the vultures nest, only then do you know the larger stillness that is the mountain. There you can clearly hear the world, the individual melodies of the birds, the crash of a startled deer plunging through the mahogany thickets, the wind in the long needles of the Jeffrey pine, and the faint murmur of the creek far below.

In early summer and spring it is the sound of high water that dominates the town. In August, drought lowers the water level in Mill Creek. Moss dries and whitens on exposed boulders. The creek quiets. Then we can hear our neighbors again, calling for their dogs, sprinklers clicking round and round.

The autumn rains bring the voice of the creek back, to murmur before it falls silent again in deep winter. Then thick ice forms and the snow covers that. If you ski up into the canyon, though, the sound of the creek still whispers from small open pockets, the green moss brilliant underneath the snow.

Our canyon is like most in the Warner Mountains to the west and in the Hays Range to the east: snow melted and rain fell; the creeks carved out dramatic canyons in the relatively young rock, depositing heavy sediments on the valley floor. Lake Surprise filled the valley several times during the Pleistocene, and its waters spread the sediments flat. One day when we were out walking on the playa, I told Lynn what Jim Slosson had said, that a person would never guess that they were walking on sediments more than a mile thick with every step they took in the valley.

We looked back at Lake City that day and saw how the town sits on top of all the alluvium carved from the canyon by Mill Creek, that deep soil for the orchards. How protected from the winter winds the town is, sitting so close to the mountains. All that water. The full force of Mill Creek ran the Lake City Flouring Mill, the first real business in the first real community in our valley.

The canyon perches above town, tilted like a steep bowl, a large watershed collecting the snow and rain from more than six thousand acres, funneling down to a tight bottleneck less than a hundred feet wide between the steep rock walls just above the swimming hole.

From time to time we may forget that water isn't the only thing that mountains shed, but the land has ways of reminding us.

At the bottom of my garden there is a patch of extremely stony ground. When I first tilled the soil there I tried to remove all the rocks. A futile gesture. After several summers I realized that I was attempting to excavate what had once been the creek bed when it was free to meander back and forth on the alluvial fan it had built over thousands of years before the land was all divided up into tidy, fenced squares. The rocks in my garden are rounded and worn smooth, unlike the jagged ones on the mountain above. I try to imagine how long it took for them to tumble and roll their edges down. And how far they traveled to get here to my garden. I try to imagine what it must have looked like here before the town was built. Sometimes my rototiller churns up an old arrowhead, one that Lynn did not make. I brush off the dirt and extend it to him, palm held flat. He raises his glasses and peers at it, tells me, *It is an Elko point, maybe four thousand years old.* I want him to tell me who made it and how it came to be buried so deep in my garden. I want to use the past to help understand our present. I know I need to observe the present to help understand the past. Maybe both views will help us see into the future. I wonder if living half my lifetime in the same spot will tell me what I want to understand.

The Parman Ranch, where Bettie lived for fifty years, was on Powley Creek, three miles north of us. Smaller than Mill Creek, Powley trickled down through the heavy growth of forest that hid it from view on the steep west side of County Road 1. Passing next to the big geothermal pipe that gurgled and hissed, it emerged from the culvert under the road to meander politely through the Parman Ranch and the traces of the old Paiute village.

Powley Creek flowed on by the yellow house at the top of the ranch where Bettie's youngest daughter, Bonnie, lived with her husband, Mickey. Every Wednesday afternoon the school bus dropped off a load of kids who followed Powley Creek down to the old cabin Bettie had converted to a ceramics studio. She volunteered supplies and a whole long afternoon every week for 4-H, teaching children how to paint the porcelain green-ware she pulled from her huge collection of molds. Then on Monday nights and Thursday afternoons the women in the community came to sit in the cabin next to Powley Creek, to brush glazes onto pitchers and vases and lamp bases, to talk, to shorten the long winter.

The cabin and the double-wide that belonged to Bettie's oldest daughter, Carol, and her husband, Nate, were linked to the rest of the ranch by a little wooden footbridge. Under it Powley Creek gurgled on, past Joe and Bettie's house, the chicken house, the milk barn, the corrals, the big, metal hay barn, the lathe house, the greenhouses, and the toolroom and tack shed. Spreading quietly through the fields, Powley Creek ended by making a wet patch on the playa below the ranch.

Taken together, the buildings on the ranch spoke as well as anything in our valley of permanence and determination and a commitment to staying put on their place next to the creek. For it is the water from the mountains that ties each of us to our particular spot in this dry land. Without it we could not live here. Usually there is just barely enough.

That winter of 1996, though, we had twice as much snow before Christmas than we normally get all year. The week after Christmas, it started to rain. It was a warm rain, a gray rain, rain that made the town smell of the ocean. It went on for four days.

Bettie and I called each other. "Have you ever seen it rain like this? In January?"

"I'm tired of cleaning up the mud getting tracked in."

"I'd rather shovel snow."

"When will it stop?" I asked.

"When it's ready to, I guess," Bettie said.

On Sunday, two nights before New Year's Eve, Jason had called us fairly late to tell us the road over the mountains had been closed because of the heavy rains. He said not to worry, that he would stay there in Alturas at Michelle's house. I was relieved to know he wouldn't be driving that night.

The phone rang again at midnight. Our next-door neighbor, Randy, was on the line, yelling.

A flood? Something about a flood?

We stumbled into our clothes and opened the front door.

The streetlight spread a garish pink glare on a sheet of water running down our street past our house and beyond. Pebbles and rocks clattered on the pavement. Water poured out of the holes in the rubble-rock foundation of the church across the street. Rising fast, it pushed through our gate, down our front steps, and into our yard, banking up against our foundation. Lynn and I pulled on our rubber irrigation boots, grabbed the fire shovels, and dug a diversion ditch around the house.

Meanwhile, on higher ground, Randy fired up his tractor and drove it through the water to the front of our house. Hunched on the tractor seat he gestured to Lynn, the sound of the raging creek almost too loud to carry a yell. Together they wrestled the scraper mounted behind the tractor, orienting it so that it would cut at an angle. Lynn banged the bolt home with a rock. The tractor was Randy's present to himself that Christmas. Not even a week old, dark green and shiny, streaked now with the rain painted pink by the big streetlight in front of the church, here was its first opportunity to serve. Proud to be able to offer it, Randy told Lynn to use it like our own. Lynn widened the trench we had started with our shovels. The rushing water helped speed the digging, carrying the loosened gravel and rock downhill into the dark.

I worked inside the yard, shoveling another trench to divert the water around our shop below the house. Then the power failed. The pink streetlamp blinked out, and I was standing in moving water, blind. I felt my way into the shop to find a flashlight. There was mud inside, sloshing against my boots. I yelled for Lynn, but he couldn't hear me, so I waded back to the street, shrieking at him to dig another ditch below, along the street beside the shop.

Lynn kept his movements slow, the way he always does in an emergency. I wanted him to move faster, to fix the breech I was trying to stop, but somehow I knew that slow, deliberate pace of his was the best answer to the panic in my voice. The tractor motor purred along, Lynn easing it into the different gears, never grinding them, never jerking Randy's new machine. He pulled the ditch open with the big rear blade, moving downhill and on past the shop, enlarging it to catch most of the water and funnel it around our place, back into the channel of Mill Creek.

Three hours had passed. Lynn stopped the tractor. The only noise now was the rain and the sound of the creek.

"We need to get inside and warm up," Lynn called to me as he stepped down off the tractor. "Let's gather up all the shovels and take them inside with us in case we need to find them again in a hurry."

I needed a hug. When we wrapped our arms around each other I felt how hard Lynn was shivering, how our wet clothes clung clammy and cold to our skin.

We didn't speak much. We changed clothes. We stoked the woodstove and hung our jeans, socks, and sweaters in front of it to dry in the living room. We went out to the shop, opened the big door on the street side, and started pushing the water and mud out with snow shovels and the oversized shop push broom. The slurry ran down the street with the overflow from the park. We spent the rest of the night in the shop mucking the wet tools and supplies off the floor and stacking them on the workbenches, chairs, tables, anywhere higher than ground level.

Monday's dawn. We could see that the water level had dropped some. Mill Creek was still flooding, but not raging, seeming to rest sullenly after its midnight tantrum. In the lull we began helping neighbors. Lynn dragged the moat he'd cut in front of our house with the tractor blade when it filled with debris, sticks, and rocks.

Jason called from Alturas late that morning. He was surprised to hear about our night. I was surprised to know that just thirty-five miles away, in Alturas, life was wet, but normal. Lynn told Jason he had dug another trench below us to shunt the water down and around the old rat house into the fields below. He told Jason not to worry. The rat house was safe. We were safe. Everything was under control.

I called Bettie. "We had a night of it," I told her. "How are you all doing?"

"Oh, we're all right. I am getting damned sick of mopping up, though. We're not using the footbridge between Carol's place and ours anymore. It looks too rickety to be safe in all that water. Carol and Nate are staying over here at our house with us." Then she laughed. "That water looks just like chocolate milk, doesn't it?"

It rained all Monday and on through the night without letting up. Under normal conditions the sound of it drumming on our new metal roof would have made me feel almost cozy. But I lost that illusion of security when I thought of the water swirling around our rubble-rock foundation. I realized earlier floods had tumbled each of those rocks down the canyon, rounding off all the sharp edges. Around midnight, the creek began rising again, roiling and rushing through the streets and yards. We pulled on our boots and began going through the same motions as the night before. Our bodies felt wooden from the lack of sleep. The gutter trench that Lynn had dug the night before was now three feet wide and a couple of feet deep, running full and fast. I wouldn't have been able to stand up in it.

Four in the morning. The water reached a kind of roaring crescendo. The whole park was now the creek bed. Brown water frothed from South Water Street to North Water Street. The asphalt road next to our house was slumping where water had undermined it. Across the park, the front end of Dale's pickup tilted forward at a weird angle, sliding into a large hole the water had sucked out from under the pavement in front of their house. Boulders scraped and rolled downhill, tangled with branches, sticks, and small logs that had been blasted apart.

Tuesday's dawn. New Year's Eve day. A wet, gray mess. Mill Creek subsided, seeming to rest again. In a stupor, I toed a line of sticks and stones into place across the pavement, making a long barrier a couple of inches high. I watched it catch the water and turn it back into the hollow of the park where it belonged. Somehow I felt brilliant that I could stem the tide that easily even as I watched the ebbing water recede. I wished its rhythms matched our own; we desperately needed sleep.

Still no power. The phone line over the mountain to Alturas was down. Lynn and Gary hooked up the radio in the fire hall to some car batteries and radioed the sheriff's office there: the highway had washed out over Cedar Pass between the valley and Alturas. Translation: emergency services consisted of whatever we could muster on our own.

Back in our kitchen, Lynn and I wolfed down some breakfast. "I'm worried," he said. "The water has slowed down. If there's a rubble dam above town and it breaks . . . Let's go see how it looks up the canyon."

We shrugged into our rain gear again and scrabbled up the slippery sidehill until we stood above the dirt road where it crossed Mill Creek—or used to.

The flood had ripped the eight-foot culvert under the road in two. One section of the giant cylinder was halfway to Main Street, hanging tangled in trees ten feet above the creek bed; the other was twisted crosswise across the creek. Huge sections of road and the canyon walls had been gouged out. The swimming hole was gone—nothing but a pocket of enormous boulders vomited there by the torrents of water. There was no sign of the boys' slide. We moved closer together as we discovered each new clue revealing the force of the flood the night before. Another half a mile and we saw no major damming, even though the creek was choked with debris brought down in the night. The rain soaked us to the skin again.

The phones worked for a few hours that afternoon inside the valley. Linda called. "I hear you guys have it really bad in Lake City. Have you heard anything about the Parmans?" she asked.

"Bettie is all right. Carol and Nate can't get back over the creek to their place, so they are staying with Bettie and Joe," I told her. "I wish we had some sandbags. The sheriff told us we're on our own up here. Cedar Pass is out. A nap would be good, too, but it's too scary to sleep."

"We have all those old empty feed sacks," Linda said.

By the time she and John drove in from their ranch with the sacks, Lynette and I had rounded up volunteers. We shoveled sand into those old grain bags with that loopy sort of humor and energy that comes from no sleep and too much adrenaline. We dumped one load of filled sacks at the fire hall, the other on our side of the creek. Don Steger brought up a hundred gallons of gas in the big tank on the back of his feed truck to keep our tractors and backhoes running. The rain fell all day long.

Late that afternoon I called Bettie again. Her daughter Carol answered the phone, out of breath.

"We're leaving right now! Powley Creek just took out the footbridge, and mom's washing machine tipped over on the back porch. It's floating! We're on our way up to Bonnie's house now!"

Was there anything I could do to help?

"Nope. We'll be fine. You all have your hands full there! I gotta go now," and Carol hung up.

At dusk the water started to rise around us again. After what we had seen in the canyon, Lynn decided it was time to get Diane, a recently widowed neighbor who was sick with the flu, out of harm's way. Her property stood at the mouth of Lake City Canyon, the creek's two channels wrapping around both sides of her house, almost hidden from view in a thick growth of young pines. She had pulled the curtains shut. It took us a long time to rouse her in the darkened house.

"I just want to stay here," she told us softly. "I don't want to leave my cats."

I knew Lynn's male voice was what she needed to hear, so I went to the pantry to feed her cats, listening to him talk low. "They'll be fine. They can go upstairs if the water gets inside. But you need to be at David's," Lynn said. "We may not be able to get to you later, and you're too sick to stay here alone."

The rain hammering at her roof and the mounting roar of the creek just outside seemed to convince her. I carried the cat dishes up the stairs to the landing. Diane let Lynn help her gather what she needed to take to her son's.

Back home again, we moved all of our furniture up to the second story. Could our old house carry the weight upstairs? We had bought the place thinking it had a foundation. But later the cement masque had started to crumble away, exposing the rubble rock piled under the old log beams. The upstairs floorboards seemed to tremble with the load.

As evening settled into night, neighbor telephoned neighbor. The lines to the outside were still out, but we could call one another. "Peggy is staying with friends in Cedarville." "Diane is at David's." "There are sandbags at the fire hall." "I stuck plywood in all the irrigation culverts to keep them from plugging up with mud and sticks." "Guess we're not going to go anywhere for New Year's Eve this year!" "See you next year!"

Everyone was all right, for now.

⤴

New Year's Eve was the worst. The creek roused itself again around eleven and breached its banks above town. Our house was the first in its path.

Lynn jammed the dump truck through the water rushing over the main road and slid to a stop at the fire hall. I jumped out and mashed the fire alarm button. The blaring siren brought people in fast. We heaved the sandbags we had made earlier onto three trucks and headed in a caravan back toward the mouth of the creek where it entered town, coursing through that bottleneck under the cliffs.

The windshield wipers could barely keep up with the rain as we jounced up the canyon road in the dark to the break in Mill Creek's banks. *Oh God! It's too late!* Lynn slammed the truck into reverse at the same moment I realized we were no longer driving up a road, but through frothing brown water, the truck rocking and skidding and shuddering over boulders in the dark. The only thing to do was try to get home.

Part of me knew Mill Creek was simply doing what it has done for thousands of years: punching through its banks, spreading, splitting apart, braiding back together, digging new channels, and replenishing the alluvium my neighbors and I were pleased to cultivate. Another larger part of me was quite certain the creek had a conscious intent: erase all of this and start over.

It should have terrified me. Maybe it was the lack of sleep; maybe we had somehow gained some sort of geologic sense of scope and detachment. We simply slogged on, doing what there was to do.

Now Randy was hollering outside our door. "We need you to help us get Martha!"

In her nineties, Martha McCoy lived next door to Randy and Carol. The buddy system thrives in our town. As a neighbor grows old and infirm, it becomes the custom for one of us to visit regularly, to offer trips to town, to shovel walks, and to bring those small gifts that say: *Look, you are still part of the living.* Randy and Carol had chosen Martha as the one they checked on.

Lynn steadied Randy from behind as he staggered out of Martha's house with her on his back. Together they carried her to a waiting car through the thigh-deep water. Holding onto the door, I reached out across the water to help pull Martha into the front seat. A lit flashlight floated by us, an apparition, twisting and rolling in the muddy water.

Who had been carrying that flashlight, I wondered, *and where are they now?*

All over town, north and south of the creek, there was darkness, and everywhere, the angry roar, the furious bellow of the creek. Our throats were raw, our voices hoarse from shouting it down.

The little gutter that Lynn had made two nights before was now wider than I am tall and almost that deep. Muddy water foamed up over the top. Our fence, clogged with debris, had been holding the water out of the yard. I watched it sag and, with a gesture like a formal stage bow, sweep aside and welcome a torrent of mud and water into our yard.

But our house would be safe for a while longer, we thought, so that was the only place it made sense to go.

"I can't believe it!" I heard Lynn shout. "I just heard a jet flying really low! How, in this weather?"

It would be a few hours yet before we would understand. We went inside. We carried a kerosene lamp upstairs to wait for dawn.

⊸

Wednesday. The first gray light of the New Year. We saw surging brown water, logs and boulders. Instead of the creek, a river completely covered the park from our house to our nearest neighbor's. Our yard was full and flowing, too. When I let our dog, Pete, out, he snapped giddily at the sticks floating by. I noticed a couple of redband trout belly up on the sand and gravel that had been deposited on my lawn: the water was receding. The trenches had saved our house and outbuildings, Jason's house, and Randy's, too.

The rain had stopped falling.

Lynn and I sat, warming our hands over coffee, eyes bloodshot, hands chapped. We were waiting to cross the subsiding street-creek to see how the rest of our town had fared. I was glad Jason was in Alturas, with Michelle. I knew it in my blood that he was safe.

The phone rang—startled us. It was Lynette telling us that Joe and Bettie had been rescued from the ranch. They were at the fire hall.

We ran to the yellow dump truck, the only vehicle we owned with enough clearance to cross the road. A murky, brown rooster tail stood up behind us as Lynn forced it across, bumping and lurching over the rock and debris.

The Parmans sat next to stove in the fire hall. Barely lit, it gave off little warmth under the bleak, fluorescent lights. Joe was on oxygen. The voices of the emergency medical technicians echoed in the cold room. The fire hall snapped with the static from the fire radio. They would take Joe by helicopter to the hospital in Cedarville; the rain had washed out County Road 1 in four places between Lake City and Cedarville. It was the first time I had ever seen Bettie look overwhelmed. She told us about their night, their New Year's Eve. For the first time I noticed the sag to her posture that whispered her ordeal.

"We all went up to Bonnie's on New Year's Eve when the water started coming into the porch," she began.

There they are in the yellow house, the only building on the ranch with enough elevation to escape Powley Creek. They wait. They listen to the rain. Joe and Bettie, Carol and Nate, and Bonnie and Mickey. Bettie and her two daughters fix supper together and wait. It is not the New Year's Eve feast they had planned—they had left Bettie's house too fast for that—but it is food and it is hot and they are safe. Bettie is actually enjoying this time, all of them together. The little dachshund, Minnie, naps on Bonnie's big couch.

"Did anyone see Timmie?" Bettie asks, thinking suddenly of the hard-working stock dog.

"Oh, she's all right," Joe says. "She's somewhere outside, probably curled up in one of the trucks, out of the rain."

"I wonder if the door to the back porch will hold?" Bettie wonders.

"It'll hold," Carol says. "I slammed it tight. Our place ought to be all right, too. It is on higher ground and all."

They grow tired of hearing one or the other say, "I wonder when this damned rain is going to stop."

"It's a good thing we moved the cows to Jim's yesterday. Got 'em out of all this slop!" Nate says. The feed truck could no longer negotiate either the creek crossing or the dirt road into the winter pasture. Bettie and Carol wonder when they'll be able to get back home to mop up the mess. When it gets dark they light some kerosene lamps and listen to the rain on the roof, to the thunder of Powley Creek.

Around midnight, everything goes quiet. There is no sound but the rain drumming the roof. The creek lies mute, suddenly muzzled. They wait in suspense, but for how long they can't say, before the roar starts, a grinding noise, an infernal noise like nothing they have ever heard before. It thunders toward them, surrounding them. Downhill, uphill, the sound engulfs them. It shrieks. It roars like a jet coming down the canyon. The house trembles, and they tremble inside of it.

Bettie reaches for Joe's hand. It is ice cold. His face is ashen, his breathing shallow and fast. He breaks out into a cold sweat and has to put his head down between his knees. Bonnie hollers at him. She is tall and sure in the midst of all the shaking and Joe's distress.

"You stop it now, Daddy. This is no time to go having a heart attack!"

They lay him down on the couch and cover him with a blanket. Bettie gives him Minnie to hold. He seems to calm with the dog sheltering under his big, rough hands, warming his belly. The roar goes on and on.

Then stops.

The silence is thick. The rain pounds on the roof, but after what they have just heard it seems more like a whisper. They wait, listening. It starts again, the lurching rumble, the grinding, the pounding.

Carol yells, "I smell gas!" They blow out the flames in the kerosene lanterns. They turn on the one flashlight they have between them, thinking, *Not for long*. Thinking, *We may need the light if we have to make a run for it*. They turn the flashlight off again right away. Seeing each other's fear is worse than waiting together, blind. In the dark they listen to the awful noise and hold on.

It is Nate who snaps first. "I'm getting out of here!" He forces his burly body out of a window. One by one they follow him out into the wet and the dark. They can't see. The roar thunders so around the house that they clamber back in. They have to pull Joe up through the small window. He is so weak. They wrestle him back inside.

Three or four more times, none of them can remember exactly, silence falls, and then the noise, noise you can't begin to imagine.

They try to call 911, but the lines are still down to the world outside the valley. They can't call south either.

They call a neighbor to the north. Eddie tells them the creek that flows beside his place is so flooded he can't get out to them. Not even with the tractor. Not even with the backhoe. They call him more than once.

"Eddie, there are six of us in here. Tell them there are six of us," they urge him each time they call.

When first light comes, they see why they couldn't open the front door in the night. A tree, an old-growth pine, three feet in diameter, is wedged up against it, peeled of bark, its roots ground down to a nubbin. Like a gargantuan guardian angel, that ponderosa has diverted water, logs, boulders, and death itself around the little yellow house. That tree wedged up against the door is what has kept the house from crumpling like a paper bag.

A wall of rubble across County Road 1 above the house is layered twenty feet high and spans the whole width of the alluvial fan. Below the house it smothers all but forty acres of the original two hundred–acre ranch. Surrounds all their vehicles. Even the biggest tractor. The smaller one is tipped over on its side.

No way in, no way out. Joe's color is bad. For what seems like hours, they hear a bulldozer ramming its way toward them. Behind the bulldozer is what passes for an ambulance under the circumstances: Hapgood's tractor and feed wagon. It took them to the fire hall.

⟿

Jason showed up that afternoon with Michelle, surprising us. He had driven around the road barriers to Cedar Pass in his little red Jeep. He told us how he had straddled the one remaining bank of earth along Cedar Creek where the pavement was gone. When they got to Surprise Valley, they learned about the four washouts between Cedarville and Lake City. County Road 1 was closed. So they took the long way here. All the way out the causeway, up and around the east side of the valley, fording Sand Creek, and then past the dump, hoping they wouldn't get stuck when they edged around the lake that filled the curve in the road at Patches Corner. Seeing their beautiful faces, knowing they were safe, having the family together made me forget how tired I was. We sandbagged the front of our house. The creek bed was so full of rubble it wouldn't take much rain or runoff to raise the water level high enough to jump the banks again. At dusk, we watched the patches of blue starting to show through the ragged clouds.

Thursday, Bettie called early. Joe, she said, was improving at the hospital. "Would you and Lynn go to the ranch with me?" she asked. "I want to see what happened. I want to see if anything is left. I want to have some people there with me."

We pulled over and parked a quarter mile from the ranch at the south edge of the debris flow where it became impassable. She looked exhausted when we met her there on the edge of County Road 1. We would have to walk in from here. I could hear the bulldozer below us working its way through the trees and boulders that covered the ranch. Bettie pointed up to Buck Mountain where cliffs formed a V like the tip of a dagger pointed at the heart of the Parman Ranch. The mountain below the V looked as though it had been clawed. Here was where the conglomerate rocks of welded tuff had started slipping away, gathering momentum and more debris in the funnel of Powley Creek, scraping away everything in its path.

Boulders the size of our dump truck littered the ranch. Hundreds of old-growth trees lay tangled among them, stripped of bark, shorn of branches and roots, splintered and bashed and still full of sap. The air smelled of mud and pine needles, like a Christmas-tree lot.

Later, when Lynn walked up Powley Creek to where it was too steep to climb anymore, he saw what had been a heavily forested canyon that now looked like an enormous bobsled run, slicked smooth down to the bedrock. Trees had been snapped or snatched from the ground; every boulder had been plucked away. The debris flow had swooped and banked a hundred feet up on one side of the canyon before turning and cresting up the other side in a tight curve. It had thundered up over a tree-covered hill where the creek divided. The hill was left standing bald and sere. Here is where rain and melted snow and slipped stone and trees and gravity had combined and given life to the creature that had galloped down Powley Creek Canyon and consumed the Parmans' ranch.

The bulldozer had pushed a rough approximation of a lane through some of the debris near the houses. Too choked with debris for a truck to negotiate, we walked in to the ranch. The mobile home that Carol and Nate had lived in was barely recognizable, twisted and torn like a discarded aluminum can. The cabin where Bettie had held ceramics classes was gone. Yet, a hundred yards away, down in the field, I recognized a wall, one of the cabin's mint-green walls lined with shelves still stacked with unglazed plates and bowls of thin and fragile china, none of them broken after sailing through that sea of boulders and broken trees.

We picked our way through the debris to the main house. The greenhouses! Where were the greenhouses? I started to cry.

"Hush now. We won't have any of that," Bettie murmured and took my arm. "I'm not gonna let some damn mountain get me down. We'll just have to be bigger than it is."

The metal porch roof jutted into the air at an angle, bellied out like a sail on a boat in a storm. Two huge fir trees, denuded and splintered, had crashed through Bettie's kitchen wall, skewered the sink, and punctured through a second wall into their bedroom. They lay like beached whales in three feet of forest junk on the linoleum floor she had been futilely mopping a few days before—the butter-colored floor she had laid one weekend while the rest of the family was out buckarooing at Board Corral. I knew she had wrestled each of the heavy pieces of particleboard into the kitchen, one by one, by herself, as an underlayment for the new linoleum squares she glued down.

The yellow flowered wallpaper rose up out of the muck, pictures and clocks and Bettie's "little pretties" still hanging in place but splattered with mud flung clear to the ceiling.

"Lynn, see if you can get back there to the office and find the flour-mill ledgers," Bettie said. Years before, she had salvaged them from the old Lake City Flouring Mill, knowing how much community history they contained. One day she had pulled them out and opened them on the kitchen table to show us these records of the valley's oldest business.

"See, here it shows that the Hanks ground their four hundred pounds of flour in the year 1884," she had explained. "When people call me to ask about their families, I can look in these ledgers. If I can find an entry, it is proof that their families were here then." She had drawn her finger down the yellowed page, tracing the column of names written in graceful, old-fashioned script in ink gone sepia-colored with age.

With a flashlight Lynn picked his way back into Bettie's dark office off the kitchen. I watched him swing the beam of light around the room. Mud and debris from the mountain filled the bottom half of the room, but the light found her bookshelves intact. The ledgers were safe and were the first things that Bettie recovered from the wreckage of her house. Next was her sewing machine. Then her computer, with all the ranch records and business, covered with mud in the little room off the kitchen that was lined floor to ceiling with the library that Bettie had collected in a lifetime of curiosity and learning how to do things by reading, by asking, and by trying. But none of those books could tell her how to rebuild a life.

The sky cleared the day after the Parmans lost their ranch. The creek was running high but almost clear. It sounded like normal high water again. We knew that it would freeze hard that night. And we knew that if we were going to salvage any of the Parmans' possessions from that house full of mud, we had better get to it the very next day or they would be frozen into place until spring.

Bettie asked me to call some of their close friends and family. Twenty of us gathered with our trucks at the ranch on Friday. We came with boxes and strapping tape and marker pens and newspaper. Lynn and I took up some big pieces of scrap plywood to use as a work surface outside the house.

It made me nervous to go into the house. One large corner section of ceiling and roof hung suspended over what had been the north living room window, walls shattered by the impact of the fallen forest that had slammed into it. That north window would be our entrance.

Some of us stayed outside, to wrap and label and box. Some went inside to pry and pull and scoop from the mud whatever we could find and bring out more or less whole. We passed each item from person to person to the crew in the yard filling cartons with gritty, mud-encrusted treasures. We ferried trucks through the slime and boulders, carrying the boxes away to be stored.

Bettie's spinning wheel came out, treadle smashed. Cliff would fix it for her, using my wheel and treadle as a model. Her mother's china cabinet, glass in the door broken, but the precious old china intact. A nephew would repair and refinish it.

Stuff from the houses and cabin and barns had been swept away three hundred yards down into the lower fields. Bettie picked her way down through the mess to see where the flow had taken the various pieces of her life; some of it had slid all the way downhill and was swallowed by the hot springs below.

In the debris she recognized one of her four freezers, and then another. The first had all the beef intact, still frozen. They had just butchered. Neighbors took the meat to store for her until she could make a home somewhere.

We saw her open the second freezer. We heard her laugh as she hollered up to us, "Anyone want a pie?"

There were nearly eighty pies, actually, stacked "neat as saltines in the wax-paper wrapper," as Linda put it, each pie bagged and labeled, a freezer full of pies. When Bettie makes a pie, she makes twenty and puts nineteen in the freezer: apricot, apple, raspberry, strawberry, pumpkin, peach— enough pies to last a winter, enough for the family and the friends who are always at her table, all from a garden that was unrecognizable now, covered over with the tons of smashed timber and boulders and the thin layer of mud that had greased the skids all the way down the mountain.

The pies were still frozen. Yet another empty freezer in town was found to house them. Gone, though, was Bettie's legendary "cool room," crammed floor to ceiling with her canned and dried food. At one time or another many in the valley had relied on Bettie, her cool room, and those four freezers to provide food in emergencies. Who would have thought that she would be the one to lose everything but a couple of freezers full of pies and beef? I looked around at the ruined property, the houses, the barns, the corrals—everything covered over with the thick layer of splintered and pulped timber and rocks as big as the chicken house that we never did find.

I was afraid to ask about Timmie, the smiling dog. It was a few days before Eddie found her. He had just shut down his bulldozer after clearing more space around the Parman house when he heard a faint whimpering. He managed to fish her out of the pocket of mud between two boulders down where the milk barn had been. He washed her off and she was fine—hungry, of course, and stiff and sore for a week afterward.

⟜

I remember the first time that I realized that the solid earth is actually a fluid suspended in time. Lynn and I were on a dig. We kneeled, bent over an excavation unit, a meter squared, scraping down layer by ten-centimeter layer with our sharp trowels, then screening the released dirt for artifacts, lithic flakes, faunal remains, and bits of charcoal. I think it was the imposition of that geometric empty space into the earth that made me understand. Suddenly the idea of the solidity of the ground unraveled. I could see the flow of dirt and boulders and pebbles and gravel. The roots of the old ponderosa that towered over us were the interlopers, the newcomers, the moment of interruption in this inexorable journey of the earth from itself to itself.

I told Linda about that cube of empty space in the ground. One of us had phoned the other as is our habit very early in the morning before full light. We talked about the Parman Ranch.

"Can you believe their insurance company is going to give them NOTH-ING?" Linda asked.

"Fifty years of paying premiums!" I told her. "Bettie said it was almost five thousand dollars every year for the whole ranch."

But that was the way it worked. Our righteous indignation notwithstanding, the insurance company stated a landslide had taken out the Parman Ranch. The company listed landslides as exclusions. The Parmans could litigate against the insurer, but if a settlement was ever offered, it would be months, maybe years, away.

"What on earth are they going to do? They are too old to start over."

The conversation naturally migrated toward the other things we couldn't comprehend.

"Wasn't it weird, that one shelf of Bettie's hand-painted china, just sitting there out in the field, not broken at all?" Linda asked.

"And the freezer full of pie," I answered.

It was Linda who had the idea. She hooted. "Pie! That's it! We'll sell Bettie's pies!"

Bettie's Flood Mud Pies is what Linda called them in her article for the local newspapers. I designed a poster: Bettie, decked out in cowgirl duds, juggling an arc of pies. We sent the posters and copies of Linda's article out to our friends. We asked that people order a pie for a hundred dollars each. Letters and checks came flooding in. The most generous donations were from people who told of their own losses, either from the rains that year or from other causes, other years. Most of them were elderly. Lynn had always said it is not a bad thing to have fed off the bottom of the food chain. He believed it was a menu that activated compassion.

Linda took some pies to the Cowboy Poetry Festival in Elko. One sold for almost a thousand dollars, after it had been auctioned and then cut into pieces to be reauctioned during a particularly rowdy session at Cowboy Joe's Saloon.

It was a couple of weeks before we thought about inventorying the actual number of pies we had on hand to fill the orders. Uh-oh! And we hadn't exactly figured out how to mail the pies. Tender crusts were Bettie's trademark. We imagined scrambled pies leaking from their boxes in the post office. So we sent letters out to all the people who had bought a pie, inviting them to come to a Valentine's Day pie social at the Cedarville Community Church. There, they could come to eat pie together and claim their own to take home.

It was time for some serious pie making. We asked Garth if we could use the BLM Fire Department kitchen. The big stainless-steel oven there holds twelve pies at a time. We started early in the morning, six of us, with Bettie as the pie boss. Carol came with the news that her husband, Cliff, had Bettie's spinning wheel all back together. Linda brought some of her frozen peaches. I brought raspberries. Lynette arrived with little Garrett. Six years old. He would be our official pie taster.

We cut up fruit. We rolled out dough. We pinched and fluted the edges of the crusts. We brushed on thick cream and sprinkled sugar on top. We made sure we had enough pies to more than go around.

Jason was back at his last quarter of school in Santa Cruz when I called to tell him that at the church on Valentine's Day, Linda had handed Bettie a check for almost twenty thousand dollars.

⟿

Bettie used the money to buy Eva Jacob's little house in Lake City. I helped Bettie paint the rooms: bright pink in the bedroom, mauve and soft sea green in the kitchen. That spring, flowers bloomed in Bettie's new yard instantly, but these were silk and plastic flowers that Bettie had salvaged from the cemetery over the years, to add a little color and to make the starting of her new garden less daunting.

Joe adjusted as well as he could, spending his days sitting in the big easy chair, hooked up to oxygen, trying to breathe in that small, white house in town. He watched through the window and commented on everyone who came to the post office next door. With little Minnie in his lap, he sat, rendered as useless as the land lying covered all over with the suffocating layer of debris.

"Do you know of a good California insurance lawyer who might be interested in this case?" I asked a lawyer friend of ours, Nicky.

"Send me a copy of the policy," Nicky said.

Nicky came to visit and I took her to meet Bettie. I watched the way those two pairs of deep-brown eyes locked onto each other, and I understood why: as much as you want to help a person like Bettie, you come to realize over time that whatever you do, she will still be the one in the lead. Now Nicky has taken the case, a work of the heart. I wonder if the Parmans will get some relief.

I watched Nicky and Bettie together and thought about that day after New Year's Day, how Bettie, Lynn, and I worked our way down to the wrecked house, how difficult the walk was through the slick mud and rocks and broken trees, how familiar it felt when Bettie took my arm: strong and sure and unafraid. You would have thought she were leading me to admire her garden.

AFTERWORDS

The Flying Heart Museum
Carolyn Dufurrena

It's Mother's Day, a day we are in the habit of spending in the desert, low-growing phlox and buckwheat under our feet, checking waters and putting out salt. It's as close as we get to picnicking.

Sam has brought his sweetheart home from college at the end of his sophomore year, and also a load of stuff from his dorm room. He's taken a hotshot crew job with the BLM in Elko: he won't be home this summer.

"Next year, Mom, it's the smoke jumpers," he says, grinning at me wickedly. I shake my head, wondering at how we create our children, how they create themselves.

"No fair baiting me on Mother's Day," I say, only halfway joking.

When they leave to go back to Idaho, Tim takes me out into the spring-time. One of the neighbors has seen four cows and a calf way out on the refuge, searching the desert for water. It's been a dry winter, and a drier spring. We go to look for them, driving up the grade that leads to Sophie and Linda's country, looking for tracks. At the top, we turn back. Tim scans the valley below with binoculars: slowly, we search the gray-green space, piece by piece, through the glasses. It is empty of motion, even from this high vantage. We drive back to the bottom of the grade, pull over. He takes one side of the road; I take the other. There they are, fresh hoofprints, one set smaller than the others, in the dry sand.

The breeze blows humid, thunderstorms building over east, counterpoint to the sun on my back. We stop at the refuge office: a short-haired woman with a sweet smile, the local manager, is the only one there on this Sunday afternoon. She tells us she's seen the cattle, and she'll call if she sees them again.

"How long's she been there?" I ask Tim, seeing perhaps a new friend in this space. "A year, I think," he says.

We climb back into the pickup, and it's only a few miles out across the flat that he spots the cattle, just barely visible, in a far-away swale of Thousand Creek. He relaxes.

"All right. Now we can come get 'em tomorrow," he says, the schedule for the next few days clicking into place in his head. We head back across the wide valley.

Sunflowers and lupine, the soft green of new cheat grass underneath, carpet the burn like a bandage as we pass the Dutchman.

"Did the trees up there die?" I ask him, nodding at tall, blackened silhouettes. He shakes his head.

"They're coming back from the roots. There are little cottonwoods all over up there."

We stop at the Harness Place to change the water on the meadow. The cherry tree has set fruit: a few white blossoms still cling. The earth's infinite capacity for renewal, after all this that has gone by. I catch myself starting to tear up.

It rains on the way back, a sweet spring shower leading us down the valley home.

> May 15, 2001
> Quinn River Ranch

SHARED FENCELINES
Linda Hussa

The neighbor died in late summer just before the eight-year drought broke. According to his wishes we leased the ranch until a split in the family made it impossible to continue. Now the meadows lay fallow. The unharvested grasses are ashen and, without purpose, they die. No one cares for his ranch now. No one makes plans for next year.

Walter is eighty-six this year. Every day, leaning on an old shovel handle for a cane, he takes walks down the lane, rests at the corner, and walks home.

The Alkali Cattle Company was dissolved when the grazing permits on the Sheldon Antelope Refuge were bought up by the Audubon Society and the Mule Deer Foundation in the late '80s. No cattle have grazed those vast acres since. The fences and corrals built by Miller and Lux Cattle Company at the turn of the century, the saddle shed, and the Badger Camp cabin were torn down or burned by the Fish and Wildlife Service. Driving across the refuge now is a surreal experience. You see virtually no wildlife. Antelope are officially designated "a herd at risk," fawn mortality reaching 95 percent. John remembers one fire of a few hundred acres in all their years on the refuge, yet in the postcattle years three major fires have swept across it.

Dr. Slosson's firm is actively consulting on projects that affect the California landscape and its taxpayers. His recent work provided Erin Brockovich with investigative advice and the chemical analysis she needed to settle the Hinkley case with PG&E. He continues to inform and advise us on ground-water issues that have potential to affect Surprise Valley.

Lavelle Dollarhide sold her Eagleville ranch. Ron and Ginger Hopkins may be leaving the valley. If they do, the valley will be losing good neighbors.

Katie lives in Mississippi with her husband and son, Nicholas. They visit often. Nicholas is learning to be a buckaroo. He has a little bunch of cattle branded with the Cross Bar, an iron originally registered to his great-great-grandfather W. H. Hussa, known to many as Old Man Hussy.

The upside-down triangle of snow on Bald Mountain above Eagleville broke this year in the first week of April. The valley creeks stopped running after May.

There is a palomino colt born just five days ago outside my door. He belongs to Katie. She will be coming to see him soon. Nicholas has named him Popcorn.

Hussa Ranch
May 1, 2001

FIRE HALL
Sophie Sheppard

April 2001: The geothermal-plant issue has resurfaced, and this time it's not about Helen and Phil wooing us with cookies. A window of opportunity has opened for geothermal development, motivated by California's deregulated power industry and the alleged energy shortage that has pushed electricity prices through the ceiling. The governor has relaxed the environmental regulation of new power-plant construction.

This time there is no attempt to dangle carrots in front of the local community. Money makes promises unnecessary. There are no public meetings. The proponent is one of the new agribusiness entrepreneurs—out of one business and into the next—leasing farming ground for five or six years from one end of the valley to the other. He has name recognition, the edge all politicians count on. The front man is a member of the community, not particularly trusted but familiar. He has quietly approached Bettie and Joe as well as the other ranchers along the hot-water aquifers.

Can I talk to Bettie about it?

⊖

A month ago, planting seeds together as we have every year in the new greenhouse in Lake City, Bettie told me she was ready to sell their cattle.

"I am going to have to do it without Joe's knowledge."

Inside the house, he lay flat on the couch, trailing the clear plastic tubing that connected him to the oxygen machine. Owning those cows meant to him that he was still a rancher, even though he'd never sit a saddle again. Keeping the cows, keeping the ranch together, meant complicated financial juggling: paying wages to hired hands, borrowing from the bank to pay the wages, and working deals with neighbors.

"Those cows are breaking us."

Bettie didn't need to explain to me that the insurance company had appealed the settlement Nicky had fought for. No settlement in sight.

"They are just waiting for us to die."

I left my portion of this manuscript on the table for Bettie to read, apprehensive about her reaction to the chapter on the geothermal development.

"I wasn't all that mad," she said when I picked it up a few days later. I asked her if I got any of the facts wrong. "No, you got the important things right." Then she asked me what I thought about the new geothermal development.

This morning when I help transplant the seedlings we had started a month before, I plan to ask Bettie what she and the family hoped for from the geothermal lease fees and what problems would be solved. I want a list in her own words to add to this manuscript.

I arrive just before nine. Bettie meets me at the back door.

"Joe fell this morning. His legs are so weak I couldn't get him back up on the couch. I had to call Bonnie and Mickey to come help lift him. I think he busted a rib. There's nothing they can do for it except wait for it to knit."

She goes to Joe and puts the little two-way radio in his hand.

"See, this button in the middle is the call button. Push it when you want to call me, and then push this one down here on the side when you want to talk."

"Where are you going?"

"Sophie and I are heading out to the greenhouse to get the transplanting started."

Panic darts across his eyes. He can hardly stand to have her leave the room. Bettie is Joe's touchstone to life, always has been. Ten years ago he would sit—dusty black cowboy hat, spurs, long legs wrapped around the legs of a metal folding chair in the middle of the garden—heckling her, teasing her, asking her why the hell she wanted to plant all those damned old flowers anyway. Even then he never took his eyes off her as she stepped, and stooped, and transplanted petunias down the entire length of the center garden walk.

He grasps the little radio. His thumb trembles as he searches for the right buttons. "This one? This is the call button?" His voice shakes, too.

"That's right. And push on the other one when you want to talk," she says.

We are in the greenhouse only a few minutes before Joe calls.

"What do you want, Joe?" Bettie answers.

"I just wanted to make sure this thing works," he says.

Every few minutes he calls to ask how much longer she is going to be. "Just a few minutes more," she answers patiently while we clear space for the seedling trays, enlarging the plastic enclosure to hold in the warmth, pinning the pieces together with nails. Finally he needs her to help him up. She puts the radio down, touches my shoulder, brushes past.

I grasp a clump of seedling tomatoes, lift them from the moist dirt; the pale roots dangle, needing water and space to grow. I watch her open the swinging yard gate, going in to Joe. I don't need that list.

Lake City

April 27, 2001

ACKNOWLEDGMENTS

FROM SURPRISE VALLEY

A book such as this can find its way only by passing through the hands and hearts of many people. Our thanks to: Dawn Marano, an editor with vision and faith; Dr. James and Nancy Jane Slosson; Bob Sorvaag; Barbara and Ray March; Scott Slovic; Roger Farschon; Grace Potorti; Bob Fulkerson; Marge Sill; Susan Lynn; Christine Kelly; Sara Gooch; Pat Farias; Paul Herman; Nancy Kelly; Linda Dufurrena; Monique Laxalt Urza; Mary Bogard, in memory; Annette Wenda; and many others who joined in the effort to keep Surprise Valley healthy and whole.

FROM QUINN RIVER

First, thanks to the families, immediate and extended, for allowing me to share their stories. Buster and John B. Dufurrena and Sandra Bengoa withstood questioning, discussion, and rewriting with fortitude and patience. Jenny Poole and Connie Kretschmer gave endless support and encouragement. My students, especially Jose Huerta, Arturo Magana, Ismael Mendoza, and Angel Espinoza, showed me another way to look at the world. Ron Wenker kept me sane on the RAC.

Thanks to Dawn Marano, for digging and digging; Ray and Barbara March; and Nancy Kelly, for thoughtful reading.

Carolyn Dufurrena

For my boys, Tim and Sam, the brightest stars in my sky.

Parts of "Desert River," "You Are Learning to Drive Cows, He Said," and "Cherry Pie" appeared in *Range*. The fire portion of "Cherry Pie" also appeared in *Wildland Firefighter*.

Sophie Sheppard

To Lynn

"This Mano, That Metate" previously appeared in *Ascent*.

Linda Hussa

To my mother and to the memory of my father, to Katie, to Nicholas, and to John, for calling one fall afternoon long ago to say, "It's time to go to the desert."

"The Antelope Kid" appeared in *Cowboy Poetry Matters: From Abilene to the Mainstream;* "Nesting" appeared in the *ISLE: Interdisciplinary Studies in Literature and Environment* (University of Nevada, Reno). Some of the poetry appeared in *Blood Sister, I Am to These Fields* (Black Rock Press).

AUTHORS

Carolyn Dufurrena

Carolyn Dufurrena came to Nevada from the East as a corporate geologist more than twenty years ago and never went home. She is the author of *Fifty Miles from Home: Riding the Long Circle on a Nevada Family Ranch* and is a contributor to *Woven on the Wind: Women Write about Friendship in the Sagebrush West.* She teaches grade school and works on the Quinn River Ranch, where she lives with her husband, Tim.

Linda Hussa

Linda Hussa was born in Redmond, Oregon. She is the author of the biography and memoir *Lige Langston: Sweet Iron* (University of Oklahoma Press) and three books of poetry: *Where the Wind Lives* (Gibbs Smith), *Ride the Silence* (Black Rock Press), and *Blood Sister, I Am to These Fields* (Black Rock Press). She and her husband, John, live and work in Surprise Valley, California.

Sophie Sheppard

The daughter of Nevada artists Yolande and Craig Sheppard, Sheppard's paintings have been widely exhibited in the western states from San Francisco to Montana, and her illustrations have been published by several western presses. She is a dedicated environmental activist who works on issues of local importance along the California-Nevada border. She lives in Surprise Valley, California, with her husband, Lynn Nardella, an archaeologist.